The Origins of the American Civil War

ORIGINS OF MODERN WARS
General editor: *Harry Hearder*

Titles already published:

THE ORIGINS OF THE
FRENCH REVOLUTIONARY
WARS
T.C.W. Blanning

THE ORIGINS OF THE
CRIMEAN WAR
David M. Goldfrank

THE ORIGINS OF THE
ITALIAN WARS OF
INDEPENDENCE
Frank J. Coppa

THE ORIGINS OF THE
AMERICAN CIVIL WAR
Brian Holden Reid

THE ORIGINS OF THE WARS
OF GERMAN UNIFICATION
William Carr

THE ORIGINS OF THE
SOUTH AFRICAN WAR,
1899–1902
Iain R. Smith

THE ORIGINS OF THE
RUSSO-JAPANESE WAR
Ian Nish

THE ORIGINS OF THE
FIRST WORLD WAR
(Second Edition)
James Joll

THE ORIGINS OF THE
RUSSIAN CIVIL WAR
Geoffrey Swain

THE ORIGINS OF THE
SECOND WORLD WAR IN
EUROPE
P. M. H. Bell

THE ORIGINS OF THE
SECOND WORLD WAR IN
ASIA AND THE PACIFIC
Akira Iriye

THE ORIGINS OF THE
GREEK CIVIL WAR
David H. Close

THE ORIGINS OF THE
KOREAN WAR
Peter Lowe

THE ORIGINS OF THE
VIETNAM WAR
Anthony Short

THE ORIGINS OF THE
ARAB-ISRAELI WARS
(Second Edition)
Ritchie Ovendale

The Origins of the American Civil War

BRIAN HOLDEN REID

LONGMAN
London and New York

Addison Wesley Longman Limited,
Edinburgh Gate,
Harlow, Essex CM20 2JE, United Kingdom
and Associated Companies throughout the world.

*Published in the United States of America
by Addison Wesley Longman, New York*

First published 1996

ISBN 0 582 49177 0 CSD
ISBN 0 582 49178 9 PPR

British Library Cataloguing-in-Publication Data

A catalogue record for this book is
available from the British Library

Library of Congress Cataloging-in-Publication Data

Reid, Brian Holden.
The origins of the American Civil War / Brian Holden Reid.
p.   cm. – (Origins of modern wars)
Includes bibliographical references and index.
ISBN 0-582-49177-0 (CSD) – ISBN 0-582-49178-9 (PPR)
1. United States–History–Civil War, 1861–1865–Causes.
I. Title. II. Series.
E459.R45   1996
973.7'11–dc20   96-12116
                                                                  CIP
Set by 7
Produced by Longman Singapore Publishers (Pte) Ltd
Printed in Singapore

To Charles Roskelly

Contents

List of Maps

Editor's Foreword

In this volume Dr Brian Holden Reid has given an account of the Origins of the American Civil War based on important original research and interpretation. It is thus a significant work of scholarship, besides being a valuable addition to the series. It is the fifteenth volume in the series, and the third to deal with a civil war.

Perhaps more terrible than any war in Europe between Waterloo and 1914, the American Civil War caused immense loss of life, human suffering and material destruction. Responsibility for this massive struggle cannot easily be traced. On the one hand, Dr Holden Reid makes the general statement that 'wars have frequently resulted from a series of well-intentioned acts, and such was the case in 1861', but he has earlier reminded us that 'whatever the strength of public opinion, and electoral shifts of opinion, it is the *action* – the decisions taken by politicians – which determine the chain of circumstances that result in war or peace'. The politicians themselves could not, of course, foresee the full consequences of their actions, nor did they always express their motives honestly or explicitly. There were unspoken assumptions. The role played by 'unspoken assumptions' in policy-making was first suggested by James Joll, whose *Origins of the First World War* was one of the first two volumes, with Ritchie Ovendale's *Origins of the Arab–Israeli Wars*, to be published in this series. Two fine historians who wrote early volumes in the series – James Joll, and William Carr, who wrote *The Origins of the Wars of German Unification* – are sadly no longer with us: their two books have been immensely important in giving weight and authority to the series.

Certain factors which seem to be common to most, if not all, wars are present in Dr Holden Reid's history. There was the belief that the war would be a short one. In one sense the belief lessens the responsibility of the makers of war, but in another sense it underlines their lack of imagination. The men of 1914 cannot be blamed for failing to foresee the horrors of the Somme, but they can be blamed for lightly assuming that they could win the war quickly. The men of 1861 had no precedent on which to assess the nature of a great civil war, but they perhaps assumed too lightly that war was the only path open to them. Jefferson Davis, Dr Holden Reid tells us, said that he 'would rather appeal to the God of Battles at once than to attempt to live longer in such a union'. The remark is reminiscent of the medieval concept of 'ordeal by fire'. It is nevertheless not so cold-blooded as Bismarck's comment that 'German dualism . . . has regularly adjusted relationships in a radical fashion by warfare and there is no other means in this present century by which the clock of development can be made to show the correct time'. That warfare is a necessary component of progress is an ugly doctrine, but it is certainly arguable that the victory of the North over the South in the American Civil War marked a triumph of a more advanced form of civilization over an inhuman one. Does this, however, mean that a terrible civil war was the only way of 'telling the time', to use Bismarck's metaphor? The question raises the argument over inevitability, which has often arisen in the volumes of this series. It is a question about which Dr Holden Reid has much that is interesting to say.

There is an intellectual excitement to be enjoyed in the reading of this book, with its exploration of the origins of a war which provided one of the most important chapters in modern history.

HARRY HEARDER

Preface

Sir Llewellyn Woodward, in a preface to his short *History of England* (1947), wrote that writing a short history of a country with much to record 'is like trying to pack the crown jewels into a hat-box'. Writing an account of a great subject like the origins of the American Civil War, which has inspired some of the most distinguished historical writing of the twentieth century, is likewise akin to trying to cover the Statue of Liberty with a tarpaulin. Consequently, this book is not a comprehensive history of the *ante-bellum* United States, but a study of the origins of its civil war. I have tried to combine the necessity of providing an accessible introduction to this enormous subject for the beginner with advancing my own views on the nature of the complex political, economic, social and military processes which brought this cataclysm about. This book is, therefore, a synthesis resting heavily on the wealth of recent writing on the subject produced by American and British historians. The American Civil War is a subject which has engaged the attention of many British historians, although United States history occasionally provokes ambivalence. It was extraordinary that during the Thatcher years, for example, the British government invoked a 'special relationship' in language of striking sentimentality, yet presided over an unprecedented disintegration of American Studies academic departments. Fortunately, some of this damage has been reversed in recent years. Thomas Carlyle once exclaimed that the United States was a country of 18 million bores. On the contrary, the history of the United States is an exciting and turbulent subject. If I have an excuse for taking so long to produce this book, it is that I have become too absorbed by my subject.

My indebtedness to this veritable scholarly cornucopia is made clear in my footnotes and bibliography. Although my sources have in the main been secondary works and primary printed material, in my concluding chapters I have made use of my own research among manuscript sources for a much more ambitious book on the Civil War. Nonetheless, I have relied very heavily on the writings of my many distinguished predecessors. Although comparisons are indeed odious they should still remain in the province of the historian; so if I am forced to single out one work on this subject which I would carry with me to the proverbial desert island (assuming, of course, that I could cram it into my carpet bag during moments of some anxiety as the ship went down), it would be Allan Nevins's *The Ordeal of the Union* (8 vols, 1947–71). Sir Harold Nicolson, when indicating the influence of the works of Sir Charles Webster on the composition of his book, *The Congress of Vienna* (1946), remarked that 'It is from this huge quarry that so many of us have gathered our little heap of stones'. Like many historians before me, I have often scurried to Nevins's volumes, trowel in hand, never without gain.

I am indebted to a number of friends who have either helped me on detailed points, or read and commented on the entire typescript. My debt over the years to Professor Peter J. Parish is enormous, and he has gone to great lengths to straighten out what would otherwise be a tangled skein of ideas. Dr John White commented on Chapter 2, and gave me much useful advice on the vexed issue of race relations. I have relied on his advice for over twenty years and never ceased to profit from it. To Dr Martin Crawford I am especially grateful because he found time, despite many responsibilities as head of department, to read and comment on the entire typescript, greatly to its benefit. I am also indebted, in many unobtrusive ways, to Professor Richard J. Carwardine, Professor Bruce Collins and Dr Robert Cook, who helped pilot my course through treacherous and unpredictable waters. The advice that I miss the most is that of the late Marcus Cunliffe. I have no doubt his comments on my typescript would have been voluminous, delivered in that soft, gentle, but surprisingly firm voice, combined with an engaging charm. American Studies has still to reckon its loss by his premature death; as for myself, I miss his wisdom sorely. The ideas in Chapter 8 were first tried out at the University of Hull, Department of History, Alumni Conference, 2 June 1990. I am deeply grateful to two old friends, John Major, for organizing it, and Keith Simpson, my fellow 'old boy', for steadying words of advice and his mischievous jokes, which were sorely needed when my morale flagged. But my greatest debt is to the general editor of the series, Professor Harry Hearder. This book would not have been completed without his friendship, guidance, good sense and inexhaustible patience. It has been a pleasure to work with him.

Visits to the United States have been rendered even more enjoyable by invitations to lecture. Parts of my final chapter were first tried out at a conference on strategy held at the US Army War College, Carlisle Barracks, Pennsylvania. My thanks are due to Professor Michael I. Handel for encouraging my work in this area and for inviting me. My final obligation is to my many friends in the British Army who have sustained my work over the last few years. The Staff College, Camberley, is perhaps the ideal place for study and reflection. The Staff College Library is without doubt the best I have ever used, and I am deeply grateful to its staff for managing my numerous queries with such efficiency and good humour, especially Mrs Pam Bendall, the College Librarian, and Mr Ken Franklyn. I am also exceedingly fortunate in my secretary, Mrs Penny Eldridge, for all her hard work in producing a final manuscript to such a high standard. Only I know the full extent of the privileges that I have enjoyed over recent years. My friend and colleague, Dr Richard Holmes, once observed that I had been working on this book for as long as he had known me. I hope with its publication not only that I have shown that I have put my time to good use, but also that I have answered the question that has been put to me so frequently as to what I do with it; and to my most vociferous interlocutor this book is dedicated.

King's College, London – Arwenack House, Falmouth – Staff College, Camberley – The George Washington University, Washington DC

Brian Holden Reid

Introduction

> She [Mrs Lightfoot Lee] had read philosophy in the original
> German, and the more she read, the more she was disheartened
> that so much culture should lead to nothing – nothing.
>
> HENRY ADAMS, *Democracy*[1]

The Civil War is the decisive event in American history. Not only
does it furnish a pantheon of heroes which enjoy enduring,
irresistible appeal (and whose support is summoned by all
presidents no matter what their party allegiance and policy), but
the Civil War forms a fundamental touchstone, a symbol of
wisdom and inspiration, which is invoked during any polemical
controversy or national crisis. During the Gulf War of 1990–91 a
television series on the Civil War struck a moving national chord
in the weeks before the launching of the ground offensive,
Operation 'Desert Storm'. Although Americans pride themselves
on being a peace-loving people, the United States was born in war
and grew to maturity nourished on the legends of war, mainly of
the Civil War. Indeed one can go further and suggest that
American nationalism was born in the disunity of the
revolutionary struggles and nurtured in the fratricidal strife of the
Civil War. It was the Civil War that determined the course of
American national development. After the North's victory, the
term 'the nation' began to be used rather than the earlier 'Union'
to describe the American polity ('the nation' or 'this nation' is
now perhaps used to irritating excess to non-American ears).

The Civil War provides a sense of identity, of resurrection
through disintegration, and a set of common reference points for

---

1. Henry Adams, *Democracy* (New York: New American Library, 1961), p. 13.

1

all Americans – including, of course, a recalcitrant and sulky South, which remained on the margins of national development until the 1960s. Yet while remaining stubbornly apart, southern pride in the martial achievements of 1861–65, gave southerners a common link in a broadly American experience. North and South had shared a common loss, a common tragedy, and by about 1900 there was agreement (especially among New South reconciliationists) that they had shared a common triumph. 'I believe there is today,' wrote James Longstreet in his memoirs, '*because of the war*, a broader and deeper patriotism in all Americans; that patriotism throbs the heart and pulses the being as ardently of the South Carolinian as of the Massachusetts Puritan.'[2] Indeed Senator Joseph E. Brown of Georgia, irritated by the accusation of Roscoe Conkling of New York that former Confederate senators held their seats by grace rather than right, replied that he had indeed been 'a secessionist, earnest and active' and had sent a hundred regiments to the front. 'We fought you honestly. We were as earnest, as honest, as bold, and as gallant as you were in the struggle. We believed we were right.' But the war was over and southern politicians were prepared to acquiesce in its result and share in American expansion. The consummation of vast American economic potential, and the emergence after the Spanish–American War in 1898 of the United States as a great power, possibly the greatest power, seemed to vindicate those, like Brown, who were prepared to forgive and forget. 'Let us move grandly and gloriously in united effort,' he declared, 'to restore to every section of the Union substantial, growing, material prosperity; and we will then bring to the whole country peace, happiness and fraternal relations. This seems to me to be a consummation devoutly to be wished by patriotic people of all parts of the Union.'[3]

Yet this consensus – that the war constituted a shared triumph – had been achieved at ferocious cost. When Colonel Silas Lapham observes in William Dean Howells' novel, *The Rise of Silas Lapham*, 'Gettysburg. That's my thermometre. If it wa'nt for that, I shouldn't know when to come in when it rains', he speaks for a generation whose powers of decision were tempered by the experience of war, and offered up thanks to a capricious fate: they

    2.   James Longstreet, *From Manassas to Appomattox* (New York, 1896: Da Capo, 1992), p. xvi.
    3.   Quoted in Joseph Parks, *Joseph E. Brown of Georgia* (Baton Rouge: Louisiana State UP, 1977), pp. 522–3.

Introducti

had survived while others had not. Lapham continued, 'The day of small things is past, and I don't suppose it will ever come again in this country'. Lapham was an ambitious businessman who was conscious of the price paid for his (temporary as it turned out) prosperity.[4] The Civil War was the costliest of American wars. More corpses were strewn over Civil War battlefields than in all other American wars combined. The price of victory was 620,000 dead (360,000 northerners and 260,000 southerners), though less than half of these were actually killed in battle.[5]

The question, therefore, had to be posed by historians. Could this price have been less, or could such heavy payment, a colossal mortgage on the lives and health of young men, have been avoided? Could the American experiment have proved equally as successful (and bountiful) without a civil war? And, indeed, given the universal agreement among most Americans by the turn of the century that blacks should remain in a strictly subordinate, dependent condition, deprived of the rights and privileges open to whites, was the abolition of slavery worth the cost? Many thought not.

Thus a dual tradition developed. The Civil War was *both* a triumph and tragedy. One could celebrate the moral grandeur of Lincoln's Gettysburg Address, the bravery of men charging up the slopes of Malvern Hill or plunging through the thickets of the Wilderness, marvel at the resource and finesse of Lee or Grant, yet still deplore that the war could (and should) have broken out. Locating the causes of this vast fratricidal conflict became a veritable industry among historians. What was the issue, was it really Negro slavery? 'The prejudice of race', writes Alexis de Tocqueville in *Democracy in America* in the 1830s, 'appears to be strongest in the states that have abolished slavery than in those where it still exists; and nowhere is it so intolerant as in those states where servitude has never been known'.[6] Half a century later, the venom of this racial prejudice had not subsided. The migratory movements of southern blacks to northern cities had spread the racial problem to the North and had not excited the sympathy of any but the most earnest and determined liberals. In

4.   William Dean Howells, *The Rise of Silas Lapham* (Harmondsworth: Penguin, 1986), p. 16.
5.   James M. McPherson, *The Battle Cry of Freedom: The Civil War Era* (New York: Oxford UP, 1988), p. 854.
6.   Quoted in C. Vann Woodward, *The Strange Career of Jim Crow*, 2nd rev. edn (New York: Oxford UP, 1966), p. 20.

1884 Booker T. Washington, the distinguished black leader and educationalist, declared: 'In spite of all the talk of exodus the Negroes' home is permanently in the South: for coming to the bread-and-meat side of the question, the white man needs the Negro, and the Negro needs the white man'. Yet the white man North and South wanted the Negro only if he was prepared to forgo civil rights and accept permanent subordinate status.[7]

The idealistic aspect that had prefaced the war in regard to race relations in certain circles in the Republican Party, and which was given such a boost by the war itself, was forgotten after 1877. During the war years what else could justify the expense of blood and wealth than the destruction of the southern slavocracy and the emancipation of the Negro? In January 1867 Thaddeus Stevens declared to the House of Representatives:

> Unless the rebel States, before admission [after seceding in 1860–61] should be made republican in spirit, and placed under the guardianship of loyal men, all our blood and treasure will have been spent in vain. Having these states, as we all agree, certainly in the power of Congress, it is our duty to take care that no injustice shall remain in their organic laws. There is more reason why colored voters should be admitted to the rebel States than in the Territories. Without it all are sure to be ruled by traitors; and loyal men, black and white, will be oppressed, exiled or murdered.[8]

A consensus in the 1890s had grown up that the men who had advocated 'Negro equality' were hypocritical, shabby schemers, who had attempted to manipulate ignorant, helpless blacks for their own venal and partisan ends. This perspective was adopted towards the study of both the outbreak of the war and reconstruction afterwards, with some variations. Whereas the corruption of Radical Republicans was stressed after 1865, the deplorable fanaticism of abolitionists was stressed before 1861. Only the sagacity of Abraham Lincoln held both of these lamentable forces in check during the war itself; on his passing in 1865 the twin evils of passion and corruption ran riot.

Thus whatever the vagaries of historiographical fashion,[9] by the

7.   Quoted in John White, *Black Leadership in America: From Booker T. Washington to Jesse Jackson*, 2nd edn (London: Longman, 1990), p. 29.
8.   Speech, 3 Jan. 1867, in *Congressional Globe*, Thirty-Ninth Congress, 2nd Session, pp. 251–3, document 8 in John White, *Reconstruction After the American Civil War* (London: Longman, 1977), p. 66.
9.   Traced with skill and objectivity in Thomas J. Pressly, *Americans Interpret their Civil War* (Princeton UP, 1950).

second decade of the twentieth century, this consensus had taken a firm shape, much influenced by the American entry into the First World War in 1917 and the subsequent disillusionment. The 'revisionists' considered the outbreak of war in 1861 to have been an avoidable disaster. They believed that 'reality' conformed to peaceful norms; as the northern and southern peoples were not separated by any marked enmity, then the causes of the war were 'artificial' and could have been avoided if 'appearance' had been rejected and statesmen had concentrated on hard, substantive fact. Instead, they succumbed to the hypnotic, misguided blandishments of 'extremists'. The war, therefore, was the shameful result of perverted, idealistic fanaticism. This was a war without an issue. Charles Ramsdell argued that the 'one issue', slavery, was more apparent than it was real. Slavery had a 'natural limit' to its expansion. Anxiety over the territorial expansion of this institution thus resembled chasing shadows. The most distinguished exponent of this interpretation was James G. Randall. Randall's colleagues and followers propounded a thesis of such coherence and persuasiveness that we are still confronting its implications today, even if it is to reject it without reservation. Without a 'blundering generation' of over-zealous idealists or petty, partisan politicians there would have been no war. The interpretation of Randall and others focused on the operation of the political process in relation to public protest, and reserved its most powerful denunciation for the abolitionists. A second influential interpretation grew up simultaneously, but like Randall revisionism, it was no less a product of Progressivism, that liberal ferment of reform that emphasized *conflict* and strife in the American social fabric. This was advanced most brilliantly by that academic maverick, Charles A. Beard. He, like Randall, exhibited little interest in the condition of blacks, either slave or free, but unlike Randall, he wrote off the abolitionists as people of the utmost insignificance. For Beard the Civil War was a Second American Revolution, a 'social cataclysm in which the capitalists, labourers and farmers of the North and West drove from power in the national government the planting aristocracy of the South'.[10]

This interpretation catered to the hearty appetite before 1939 for explanations which stressed economic factors. According to Beard, the political system resembled a puppet theatre whose

---

10. Charles A. Beard and Mary Beard, *The Rise of American Civilization* (1927), II pp. 38–42, 54, quoted in Richard Hofstadter, *The Progressive Historians: Turner, Beard, Parrington* (London: Jonathan Cape, 1969), pp. 302–3.

strings were pulled by economic muscles and financial sinews. Beard's books were widely read and sold in large numbers. His work, too, added further interest to a discussion of the significance of the failure of the American political system in bringing about the war. This appeared quite inadequate to bear the strains imposed on it. The presidents elected in the years before 1860 were uninspiring and uninspired. Allan Nevins took up this argument after the Second World War. In appraising James Buchanan, he offers a tepid endorsement which actually damns Buchanan with faint praise as a prelude to a devastating indictment of those who preceded him.

> In a line of mediocre Presidents not one of whom would be esteemed fit today to lead a large corporation, bank or university, he had more ability than Taylor or Fillmore, more steadiness than Pierce, and more civil experience than the three combined. Yet he was as ill-equipped for a supreme test as they.[11]

No less an authority than President Harry S. Truman, who knew something about taking decisions, was widely read in the historical works of this period and is testimony to their popular influence, characterized President James Buchanan as 'The . . . last of these weak Presidents that brought on the Civil War, that at the very least allowed it to happen. . . . He [Buchanan] couldn't make a decision to save his soul in hell'. He summed up the unedifying list of chief executives with the critical comment:

> But there you are, five men. Tyler, Polk, Fillmore, Pierce and Buchanan, not counting Harrison and Taylor, and the five of them coming one after the other made the Civil War inevitable. Not that I'm saying that it might not have happened if we'd had strong men in office, but there's a chance that it wouldn't.[12]

Mr Truman's casual remarks capped the efforts of historians, given point by a stimulating essay by the Dutch historian, Pieter Geyl. Was the Civil War *inevitable?* Were the forces unleashed by political fanatics and sordid financiers bent on the transformation of the economic landscape, ineptly resisted by presidents who floundered and blundered, unstoppable? Historians and non-historians alike seemed to think that the war *was* inevitable.

Whether events are inevitable or not is a question bound to

---

11.   Allan Nevins, *The Emergence of Lincoln* (New York: Scribner's, 1950), I, p. 64.
12.   Merle Miller, *Plain Speaking: Conversations with Harry S. Truman* (London: Gollancz, 1974), pp. 353–4.

stimulate the imagination of historians. It also depends on the perspective adopted. The *further* one stands back in time from a sequence of events the less inevitable they appear. The alternatives are more clear cut, and an alternative sequence of events seems to beckon. The *nearer* one gets to the eye of a combustible chain of events the more inevitable appears the result, as harassed, tired and fallible statesmen struggle against the odds, against accident and the unintended, to control their actions and the actions of others. The sharper the focus on a crisis, especially as day follows day, the more intractable human affairs appear. This whole equation of perspective and accident is complicated in the American case by the truncated time scale. Marcus Cunliffe has best pictured this in the years 1789–1837. He writes of the 'speed of change', the 'compression of the American time scale', and observes of the Founding Fathers who worked merely eighty years before the outbreak of the Civil War:

> In the American time scale, logarithmic in range at the formative stages, the Declaration of 1776 and the Constitution of 1787 tended to be represented as closer to, say, the Magna Carta of 1215 than to the actual events of the decade after 1787. The documents, being of eternal significance, were in a sense out of time altogether.[13]

Americans refer habitually to the 'Age' of Jackson – a mere eight years, two complete presidential terms. The 'Age' of Elizabeth I covered nearly half a century, that of Louis XIV almost three-quarters of a century. The hectic, frenetic pace of American political life, in a much reduced time scale than in Europe or East Asia, should not be forgotten when assessing the reasons for the outbreak of the Civil War.

The approach to resolving the conundrum of 'inevitability' adopted in this study (which reflects the confidence of the 1990s that the debate is already over) is best conveyed by the novelist Simon Raven. In his novel, *The Survivors* (1976, the tenth volume in the 'Alms to Oblivion' sequence), Leonard Percival, the shadowy, omniscient, 'cloak and dagger man' observes that 'things are as they are. One must accept everything ... as having come about in the natural and logical continuation of prior events – any one of which might have been different, given a split second here

---

13. Marcus Cunliffe, *The Nation Takes Shape, 1789–1837* (Chicago UP, 1959), pp. 5, 127; Brian Holden Reid and John White, 'Marcus Cunliffe: A Pastmaster', in Reid and White (eds) *American Studies: Essays in Honour of Marcus Cunliffe* (London: Macmillan, 1991), pp. 11–12.

or there, but wasn't'. It is pointless to speculate about whether another course of action would have ensued if events had been different, or been altered by another course of action. These events did not happen. Historians can take account of pivotal events which mark out a certain course rather than another; but we cannot explain that which did not happen. Events happen because they do; obviously great cataclysmic events alter our perspective on the mundane. Perhaps we give them too much prominence, but we can hardly ignore them. What we may be sure of is that if one event had happened differently, then all the successive events that followed would have turned out anew. Then the process of historical change analysed by historians would be quite different. They should devote their energies to explaining their significance and not frittering them away in a fruitless search after an alternative version of no significance.[14]

There was one slightly unexpected by-product of these various interpretations advanced by the Progressive historians. It produced a strong southern bias in American historical writing. If slavery was not worth a war, then the moral indictment of the South's 'peculiar institution' was rather less pressing. An alibi could be found exculpating southern behaviour by reference to her desire for political independence. Indeed, who could blame the South for wishing to break bonds of affection which had been so cruelly exploited and debased by a group of blood-thirsty fanatics, many of whom could be found in the ranks of the Republican Party? That fanaticism could be found of just as alarming and combustible a kind in the South was a fact given rather less emphasis in many accounts. Books continued to appear well into the 1950s purveying a strong southern bias, notably those of Avery O. Craven. Such works, moreover, continued to focus attention on the political and economic sources of civil war in the United States because they were keen to advance a special, sectional case as to who was primarily responsible for the outbreak of war – and it was not the South – within the existing framework of analysis. G. M. Trevelyan, in a most stimulating essay on bias in historical writing, warns of the dangers of 'perpetual aloofness' in historians. We should occasionally, he avers, 'go down among the men and women of the past' and treat them 'like human beings just like ourselves'. He develops this point by suggesting that

14.   Simon Raven, *The Survivors* (London: Blond & Briggs, 1976), pp. 281–2.

Clio should not always be cold, aloof, impartial. Sometimes the maid should come down yonder mountain height, the Judge descend from the judgment seat, and the historian share the passions of the past, provided they are the real passions of the past and not a false reflection of some modern dogma or prejudice.

The problem was that southern historians, or those overly influenced by southern views, were still preoccupied with the passions of the 1850s and 1860s, not that they were projecting backwards the preoccupations of the 1950s. Thus much discussion still revolved around old sectional controversies as their main point of departure.[15]

Thus by 1950 an immensely impressive synthesis on the outbreak of the Civil War was in place, reinforced by the publication of James G. Randall's biography of Abraham Lincoln, the first two volumes of which appeared in 1947. In its confidence in the destiny of the United States and awareness of tragedy resolved, so that she emerged renewed and even stronger from her trials, this synthesis resembles the 'Whig' interpretation of British history in the seventeenth century. Like this formula (under which the historical process moves inexorably towards the heights of prosperity and liberty represented by the present), the 'revisionist'/Beard interpretation has undergone formidable criticism since the mid–1950s, often led by former students of Randall, with David Donald very much in their van. That grand, imposing, elegant edifice lies in ruins, like the remains of a long-buried Sumerian city dug out of the earth. Indeed its assumptions and arguments appear equally ancient. Its implicit southern bias has been discredited. The issue of slavery and race has been placed at the heart of discussion where it belongs – it cannot be ignored or hidden. And out of this debris created by the pneumatic drills of 'cliometrics', the employment of computer data and methods to analyse economic trends, first brought to bear on the economics of slavery, have sprung, newly fertilized, green shoots of the historical plant: urban studies, mobility studies, women's history, and so on. Each new area of study fragmenting grand political processes so confidently handled by historians of Randall's generation.

Historians had indeed taken Trevelyan's advice and 'got down among the men and women of the past' with a vengeance. The

15. G. M. Trevelyan, 'Bias in History', in *Autobiography and Other Essays* (London: Longman, 1949), pp. 77, 78.

social factor gained prominence, and the immense outpouring of books on slavery is a testimony to the success of this endeavour. But no new synthesis, a replacement of the old view, has emerged. Ironically, historians' view of Reconstruction, which has experienced a more thorough-going demolition than the origins of the Civil War, is a good deal more coherent, and it must be said, ambitious and sweeping. One of the reasons for this is the increasing tendentiousness of American historical writing, which is apt to fall victim to fads; and the tiresome and remorseless repetition of certain tags and phrases, which, once they fall out of favour, are immediately replaced by a new set. All this has left the study of the origins of the American Civil War in a state of limbo. The literature is enormous, and of a high quality but variegated. Indeed as long ago as 1960 David Donald was of the view that the life had been stamped out of the subject as a serious area of study and debate. As Eric Foner has written more recently, 'Historians' methodologies and value judgments have changed considerably, but the questions historians have asked of their data have remained relatively static'. What is needed to rejuvenate the subject is a new approach. 'Historians of the Civil War era seem to be in greater need of new models of interpretation and new questions than an additional accumulation of data.'[16]

The standard interpretation of the Civil War and its outbreak is, in large measure, the reversal of the old view. Southern special pleading on the race issue is ruled out of court. Race relations was, and remains, the dominant issue of American history. Slavery was the root cause of the war because it more than any other factor – as the South's 'peculiar institution' (a most significant generic term) – shaped southern consciousness, governed southern economic development, and determined southern social attitudes and racial phobias *vis-à-vis* the North. The subject of slavery has been the subject of immense scholarly labour since the mid-1960s, and produced writing of the very highest quality. The old southern bias (which was still evident in Avery O. Craven, *Civil War in the Making, 1815–1860*)[17] has been dismantled. The study of the North's political attitudes and realignments has borne much stimulating comment and fresh perspectives on the

16.   Eric Foner, 'The Causes of the American Civil War: Recent Interpretations and New Directions', in *Politics and Ideology in the Age of the Civil War* (New York: Oxford UP, 1981), pp. 15–16.

17.   Avery O. Craven, *Civil War in the Making, 1815–1860* (Baton Rouge: Louisiana State UP, 1959).

changing appeal of political parties, not least of the Republican Party.

Even in this area, the renewed interest in party politics and the social sources of electoral behaviour has added to the fragmentation of the subject rather than detracted from it. Attempts to find new and different interpretations have led to an increased emphasis on local, rather than national, issues. Certainly, explaining why voters acted in a certain way, does not provide a convincing explanation of why, let alone how, war came when it did, and not before. There is a tremendous gap between casting a vote and taking a shot at a uniformed enemy. The historians of political parties and voter behaviour manipulate their tables and draw up their columns and charts with dizzying exactitude. Yet in terms of developing an all-embracing synthesis of the outbreak of *war*, as opposed to explaining the political culture and behaviour of *ante-bellum* America, so much of this tremendous, fertile, outpouring of scholarship has proved rather disappointing. Indeed some historians of voter behaviour, immersed in intricate detail of turn-out and swings of opinion, neatly tabulated, have attempted to write the coming of the Civil War out of the political history of this period. Of course, it is correct to stress the importance of local issues; if the magnifying glass is applied to regional matters, then patently local controversy will loom up powerfully and in vivid colours. Interdivisibility in political life – when small matters block out great questions – should never be underestimated in history as in physical geography. But this should not mean that the great, national issue is unimportant. Increasingly, therefore, the attention focused by historians since 1918 on political and social sources of civil war in the United States has not changed – although the perspective by which these are viewed has been altered dramatically. The main historiographical consequences of this change of approach has been fragmentation of the study of the Civil War.[18]

An opportunity has thus been offered to attempt a fresh overview of this welter of research and attempt to look at these much studied matters from a slightly different perspective. It is not the intention of this book to suggest that all previous works have been wrong or to challenge the value of so much able research (indeed its fruits have been utilized to the full in the pages that

18.   See Joel Silbey, 'The Civil War Synthesis in American Political History', in Silbey, *The Partisan Imperative: Dynamics of American Politics Before the Civil War* (New York: Oxford UP, 1985), pp. 3–12.

follow). Clearly to attempt a massive reinterpretation on a huge
scale is the task of a lifetime and beyond the scope of this book.
But it will suggest that our thoughts on the origins and outbreak
of the Civil War require some readjustment. Previous works have
been too preoccupied with political and social questions, and have
treated them in too narrow a fashion. Sections of a country do not
hurl themselves into a civil war just because the populace votes in
a certain way, or their respective politicians stop talking to one
another. The breakdown of a political system does not provide by
itself sufficient cause for the outbreak of war; though clearly the
unique investment that nineteenth-century Americans made in its
operation is a cause for reflection. These questions must be viewed
within the broader context of an American penchant for violence
and violent solutions to political disputes. As Marcus Cunliffe once
observed, for a supposedly peace-loving people, 'The problem was
that warfare was a basic ingredient of American patriotism'.[19]

The influence of violence and views about its use cannot be
written out of accounts of the origins of the American Civil War,
in the same way as the Negro was in the accounts of the 1930s.
The political, economic and social factors must be given due
prominence, but so too should geopolitics, the relationship
between the evolving American polity and other countries in the
Western hemisphere, and indeed with the geographical
environment in North America. The domination of the United
States of North America could not be taken for granted in 1861,
though it most certainly could by 1865. It is very striking that the
great majority of United States historians of this subject interpret
it within the parameters of exclusively American concerns. They
rarely bother to ask why the war did not spread in 1861–62? This
is almost as important a question to ask as finding a solution to
the query as to why civil war broke out in Charleston harbour in
April 1861. By attempting to answer this question, the account
offered here does not stop at the firing of the first shots at Fort
Sumter, as is customary.

Of course, the political, economic and social factors must be
given due prominence in any historical analysis. The study of the
causes of any war can never consist solely in the tracing of violent
events, with the politics, social controversies and economics left
out, though many previous accounts have detailed these in full

19. Marcus Cunliffe, *Soldiers and Civilians: The Martial Spirit in America,
1775–1865*, 3rd edn (London: Eyre & Spottiswoode, 1969; Gregg Revivals 1993,
with a new preface by Brian Holden Reid), p. 68.

and left the violence out. All of these features of *ante-bellum* society must be drawn into a close relationship and related moreover to the geopolitical, strategical questions raised by the necessity of enforcing a fiat or policy on one section by another. Military calculations, and the means available on either side to enforce their policy cannot be ignored – even though contemporaries were rarely able to express themselves in strategic language. Nevertheless these calculations were present in 1860–61. Consequently, we need to understand the significance of *escalation* in political and strategic discussion in any war, but especially in a civil war. The questions posed by historians must include *how* a political issue has come to assume the significance attached to it by decision-makers, as well as *why* it reached a level of importance. Without such an equation filling the gap between *intention* and *action* becomes inexplicable. The process of war causation, in other words, does not stop simply because shots have been fired. The question of what *kind* of conflict has been envisaged by contemporaries embarking on a war must be raised and thus discussions of war aims come to the fore. Such discussions reveal the readiness of politicians to resort to force and what they expected to attain by employing it. This is almost as important a question as why they chose to go to war in the first place; indeed these matters are interconnected to an extraordinary degree. Indeed, new synthetic ideas on the war's coming are slowly emerging, especially the notion of a *domestic* conflict.

Southerners had been threatening to secede from the Union for thirty years prior to 1860–61. Few in the North believed them and adjusted their reaction to such threats accordingly. Yet the South did take this grave step and prepared, with remarkable rapidity, to support its action with military preparations. Delineating the change in outlook which resulted in such a precipitate and ultimately catastrophic decision is just as important as explaining, with a wealth of political detail, *why* secession took place. But was the decision of a state, like South Carolina, *by itself* sufficient cause to explain the outbreak of organized violence between the sections? Or should we also seek to explain why it arrived at the decision to secede, and assess the manner in which South Carolina pursued its objectives? At any rate, this book will attempt to consider these questions. It will trace the increasing political antagonisms of the sections in narrative form and then pause on two occasions to take stock. This brace of thematic, analytical chapters will assess how contemporaries viewed themselves and their sections *vis-à-vis* one another: in 1858–60 during the tumult over the admission of Kansas as a slave state and John Brown's raid on Harper's Ferry; and again in 1861 during the Sumter crisis, the final confrontation which resulted in war.

It will become apparent in the chapters that follow that the author does not share the widely held view that the South was a distinct cultural entity, although it entertained a certain loose, self-conscious sense of geographical contiguity. Consequently, although terms like 'escalation' are employed as tools of analysis, the author does not believe that the Civil War was the outgrowth of a 'Cold War' between the sections, motivated by ideological and cultural hostility. Decision-makers will take decisions under pressure quite unaware that they are acting as the instrument of any great social forces. It may be, on both sides, that politicians took decisions in isolation from the real sentiment of their constituents. It is perhaps the tragedy of the modern world that the results of violence galvanize mass involvement and precipitate bloodshed and destruction that was wholly unexpected when the strife began. This was certainly the experience of the men, often highly educated and schooled in the law as well as in politics, who took the decisions which resulted in war in 1861; men who were unaware of the kind of conflict they were unleashing on the American people.

There is one final matter that should be made clear at the outset. Increasingly in recent years historians have come under pressure to embrace the charms of 'theory'. This has come from two main sources. The first – and much the most pernicious – are those who have studied the past as part of the recent penchant for multi-disciplinary approaches, especially 'cultural studies'. This has drawn from the so-called 'human sciences'.[20] Through these have percolated the preoccupations of literary criticism – deconstructionism, post-structuralism and post-modernism. The value of such insights is reduced by the convoluted and clotted style in which they are expressed. The sentences of many of the practitioners of 'cultural studies' are as long and complicated, as Gore Vidal once observed, as their ideas are simple. Such ideas have become so influential in the United States (and have had a major influence on the teaching of American Studies in Britain)

---

20. See Richard King, 'Present at the Creation: Marcus Cunliffe and American Studies', *Journal of American Studies* 26 (Aug. 1992), pp. 265–8, esp. p. 268.

because of an obsessive desire to seek out some kind of formula. Long years of observation of the United States have reinforced my view that formulae have become so pervading in American life that the search for one – in the absence of a strong left-wing political tradition – has begun to affect the 'structure' of the intellectual process itself; such an issue transcends mere discussion of so-called 'political correctness'.

The most alarming feature of these approaches is their increasing tendentiousness. To use the language of its practitioners, a 'sub-text' seems to lurk behind this new preoccupation with 'theory' and an especial favourite term, 'discourse'. This is transparent in some recent contributions, even though their authors do their best to conceal quite simple arguments with jargon and elaborate syntax. The result is a bewildering panorama, 'a preprogrammed circuit of objectified simulacra'.[21] This notwithstanding, the perspective on the American past adopted by such writers is not difficult to grasp: they seek to replace 'the tautologies of exceptionalism with the transnational categories of gender, class and race', to quote the literary historian, Sacvan Bercovitch.[22] Such a post-Marxist formulation offers a breath-takingly reductionist approach, and a simplistic stress on social factors as the central core of historical explanation, which I utterly and unhesitatingly reject.

The approach adopted in this book at least shares a scepticism about American exceptionalism and the rhetoric too often resorted to by United States historians. Yet the 'cultural studies' approach, and its naked and crude assumptions, is, in my view, in great danger of raising up a 'Whig interpretation of history' in reverse. The old Whig historians wrote history from the biased angle of 'practical judgements and purely personal appreciations', in Sir Herbert Butterfield's words, and how far the past contributed to the present state of 'progress' they had congratulated themselves on reaching. This process has now been inverted. There is a growing tendency to study history 'with direct and perpetual reference to the present'. Given the rigid, self-imposed categories these 'new' historians have imposed – gender, class and race – the past is raked over in a disillusioned, often bitter spirit, to explain a *lack* of progress in these areas.

---

21. See Paul Giles, 'Reconstructing American Studies: Transnational Paradoxes, Comparative Perspectives', *Journal of American Studies* 28 (Dec. 1994), p. 339.

22. Ibid., p. 342.

Some of these issues are, of course, no less worthy in their own right than the concerns of earlier historians, but like the Whigs, they come from 'the transference into the past of an enthusiasm for something in the present', and condemnation or praise of the past by reference to our current (and swiftly changing) anxieties, not only is crude, but also hardly advances the level of historical explanation; on the contrary, it is not only simplistic but also downright dangerous and actually corrosive of history as *history*. As for American history, it still lacks perspective because under the pressures of this approach the United States is transformed from a uniquely good and progressive society, to a uniquely bad one, and thus remains exceptional.[23]

The second source of pressure to adopt 'theory' is less modish than it once was, or compared with the enthusiasm for 'discourse', but still deserves some attention. This is the assumption that history will become more 'scientific' if it makes more effective use of statistics, mathematical techniques, computers, and rigorous quantitative methodology. This enshrines 'data' as the historical lexicon and disapproves of argument by analogy or worse, by impressions drawn from a handful of documents.[24] We can concede the importance of examining aggregate data to test various propositions. Of course, this concern with 'theory' and 'scientific' history is hardly new, it has a long and respectable pedigree in historiography, but such quests have never succeeded or endured.

This is mainly because these recent efforts neglect subjects which do not fit the framework they have laid down. In short, they offer nothing to the historian of the origins of war. Indeed, by contributing to the process of fragmentation, they have set up further obstacles to our understanding. Furthermore, they downgrade the importance of cataclysmic *events* in history, which are so vital to an understanding of war causation[25] – let alone the many other subject areas which are not conducive to the 'gender, class and race' categorization. In politics, as in war, it is the person who counts, and we can *never* ignore the role of the individual in

23. Herbert Butterfield, *The Whig Interpretation of History* (London: Bell, 1931, 1963), pp. v–vi, 1–2, 4–5, 8, 11, 64–5, 96. The swift rise of a 'post-revisionist' school of Reconstruction historians as a response to Nixon and Watergate in the 1970s is a striking, earlier example. See Eric Foner, *Reconstruction, 1863–1877* (New York: Oxford UP, 1988), pp. xxii–xxiv.

24. R. W. Fogel and G. R. Elton, *Which Road to the Past? Two Views of History* (New Haven, CT: Yale UP, 1983), pp. 50–1, 91–2.

25. Ibid., p. 77.

crises pregnant with war. Individuals express the grandeur, as well as the pettiness and evil, of which the human spirit is capable.

If the reader is committed to the need for 'theory' in history, and expects to find in the following pages a 'theory' of the origins of the American Civil War, then this book is not for him or her. It is dedicated to the belief that the past is too complex – and demanding – to be placed within a narrow theoretical constraint; the past cannot be neatly poured into a much burnished casket with a trowel. Indeed, if we are to understand fully the place of violence in American society in the nineteenth century, we must rid ourselves of the recent penchant, remarked on by Eric Hobsbawm, for studying social forces in an atmosphere shaped by the odours of the seminar room – as if the world is one huge university.[26] The United States in the nineteenth century was a world far removed from 'discourse', the scribble of ball-point pens and the sound of A4 leaves of paper being torn from their pads. 'This nation has a strange indifference to life', reported Carl Schurz, shortly after arriving in the United States in October 1852, 'which manifests itself in its sports, its races, its wars and also its daily life'.[27] It was a restless, competitive, callous if not brutal world, in which violence lay just beneath the surface. We should not underestimate the desire for danger, challenge and confronting the ultimate test of fulfilment – in war. William S. McFeely has reminded us that pacific societies do not always breed pacific citizens: 'I do think Americans should face the unattractive fact that whether it was fought to end slavery or to preserve the Union, that war was also an outlet for emotional – animal, if you will – energy, an outlet that the society otherwise failed to provide in sufficient measure'.[28] What is even more extraordinary, looking at the world in which we live, and the problems it is attempting to surmount on the eve of the twenty-first century, is that academics need reminding of this omnipresent, harsh reality of our existence.

26. Eric Hobsbawm, *The Age of Extremes* (London: Michael Joseph, 1994), p. 510.
27. *Speeches, Correspondence and Political Papers of Carl Schurz*, ed. Frederic Bancroft (New York: Putnam's, 1913), I, p. 4.
28. William S. McFeely, *Grant: A Biography* (New York: Norton, 1981), p. xiii.

CHAPTER ONE

An American Experiment in Democracy

He that will apply new remedies must expect new evils; for time is the greatest innovator.

FRANCIS BACON[1]

The rise of the United States to occupy a continental hegemony in North America is the greatest development of the nineteenth century. The immense development of resources, the construction of towns and cities in such a short period of time, and the setting in place of durable and workable political and judicial institutions were staggering achievements. The forging of a democracy over great distances, over widely varying terrain, and amid environmental contrast, was novel and unprecedented. And the longer the system was able to mature, the firmer and stronger it became. 'The gentle but powerful, influence of laws and manners had gradually cemented the union of the provinces. . . . The image of a free constitution was preserved with decent reverence', wrote the historian of the Roman Empire, and his words are equally apposite of the United States in the 1820s.[2]

This new nation-state had managed to exert a continental hegemony over the virgin territory of North America and had frustrated the efforts of European states to restrict its expansion to that of a coastal client hemmed in by the Appalachian Mountains.[3] Yet though the security of the United States was

1. Francis Bacon quoted in C. V. Wedgwood, *Seventeenth-Century English Literature* (London: Geoffrey Cumberlege. Oxford UP, 1950), p. 22.
2. Edward Gibbon, *The Decline and Fall of the Roman Empire*, ed. J. B. Bury (London: Methuen, 1897) I, p. 1.
3. On the resistance of Indian tribes, encouraged by the British, to American encroachments in what is now Ohio, see Reginald Horsman, 'American Indian Policy in the Old Northwest, 1783–1812', *William and Mary Quarterly* XVIII (1961), pp. 43–4, 47–53.

18

reasonably secure by 1796, with penetration into territories which became Ohio, Michigan and Indiana, and a northern frontier resting on the Great Lakes, that security encountered a formidable challenge, and American prestige was bruised by the war of 1812 with Great Britain (which the belated victory at New Orleans in 1815 only partly rectified). Yet her great distance from the focal point of the European balance of power virtually guaranteed American security. American preoccupations were invariably of marginal interest to the European great powers; in 1812–14 Great Britain gave a higher priority to her struggle with Napoleon. And the great space of the North American continent frustrated any predatory European invader rash enough to attack the United States. It was immensely difficult for any state, however powerful, to achieve a rapid and decisive victory in any war fought on American soil. 'All the armies of Europe, Asia and Africa combined', declared the young Abraham Lincoln in his first substantial public address in January 1838, 'with all the treasure of the earth (our own excepted) in their military chest; with a Buonaparte for a commander, could not by force take a drink from the Ohio, or make a track on the Blue Ridge, in a trial of a thousand years'.[4] Geographic and strategic isolation was not only a preferred American policy stance but also an ineluctable reality: 'since history and experience prove', George Washington reminded his listeners during the Farewell Address in 1796, 'that foreign influence is one of the most baneful foes of republican government'. He urged that the United States concentrate on internal development so that it would muster its own vast latent potential. The United States enjoyed such an advantageous position that foreign states 'will not lightly hazard the giving us provocation; when we may choose peace or war, as our interest guided by our justice shall counsel'. This policy was based on a sure-footed strategic calculation of the greater strength of the parts of the continental state *vis-à-vis* smaller states:

'While then every part of our country thus feels an immediate and particular interest in union', Washington continued:

> all the parts combined cannot fail to find in the united mass of means and efforts greater strength, greater resources, proportionately greater security from external danger, a less

4. Address before the Young Men's Lyceum of Springfield, Illinois, 27 Jan. 1838, *Abraham Lincoln: Speeches and Letters*, ed. Peter J. Parish (London: Dent, 1993), p. 10.

frequent interruption of their peace by foreign nations; and, what is
of inestimable value, they must derive from union an exemption
from those broils and wars between themselves, which so frequently
afflict neighbouring countries, not tied together by the same
government; while their own rivalships alone would be sufficient to
produce, but which opposite foreign alliances, attachments and
intrigues would stimulate and imbitter.[5]

A sense of the indivisibility and accumulation of power
compared with other polities is central to American identity and
the evolution of the Republic. So long as the American
experiment is nurtured and protected then ultimately the wealth
and power of the United States would surpass that of her enemies.
Nonetheless, many Americans were afflicted by short-term worries
as to whether they could resist external threats. Yet long-term
confidence is given explicit recognition in the Constitution of the
United States. The drafters in 1787 were prevailed upon to
substitute 'the United States' for 'national'. In unity arose security
and potential power; in disunity lurked the calamities of
vulnerability and European intervention in American affairs. The
experiment in North America thus rested not just on the
introduction of a novel form of republican government but on an
acute appreciation of the cumulative effects of power. They were
indivisible. This did not prevent substantial opposition to unifying
tendencies in large sections of the republic in 1787–88. But as this
was overcome, the realization developed in the early nineteenth
century that democracy demanded absolute security from the
threat of European intervention to prosper, and such security
demanded the absolute banishment of the European balance of
power from North America. A policy had to be found which would
reduce the danger of intervention – especially from Great Britain,
but after 1798 from France as well – from states which, even in the
western hemisphere, were infinitely more powerful than the
United States.[6] In unity, therefore, was invested not only the
prosperity of the present but also soaring hopes for the future. As
the opening declaration of the Constitution opines:

---

5.   George Washington, 'Farewell Address', *A Documentary History of the United
States*, rev. edn, ed. Richard D. Haffner (New York: New American Library, 1965),
pp. 64, 66, 68.
6.   Gordon Connell-Smith, *The United States and Latin America* (London:
Heinemann, 1974), pp. 4–6, 44–6; R. W. Van Alstyne, *The Rising American Empire*
(Oxford: Blackwell, 1960), pp. 82–3.

We the people of the United States, in Order to form a more perfect Union, establish justice, insure domestic Tranquillity, provide for the common defence, promote the general welfare, and secure the Blessings of Liberty to ourselves and our Posterity, do ordain and establish this Constitution for the United States of America.[7]

Growing Pains

But given the enormous extent of the United States – even on independence in 1783 – in practice the assumption of cultural and ethnic uniformity made by the Constitution would not work itself out without difficulty. The United States has escaped some of the intractable and enduring problems of the Latin American countries. Since their independence they have been crippled by tensions between the urban coastal centres and the more remote hinterland, the iron grip of reactionary oligarchies based on landed wealth, and the alienation of the bulk of the population because of rigid class (and sometimes racial) barriers, all accentuated by great geographical obstacles and poor communications, which foster provincialism, and the rise of local, private armies mustered by and loyal to the *caudillo*. The rule of law was not always self-evident in these countries.[8] In many Latin American countries urban and industrial development has been restricted to narrow coastal plains hemmed in by great mountain ranges. In the United States, penetration of the areas beyond the Appalachian Mountains was not difficult. Here could be found an immense fertile plain over which towns and cities spread, all nourished by a comparatively efficient communications network of waterways and railways. Along these travelled with the settlers a common set of values and ideals and a universally accepted legal system that enforced American mores. Nonetheless, though this developing society enjoyed a measure of homogeneity, clearly the spread of United States civilization was greatly influenced by the geographical contrasts which marked its great expanse. Geography, and an understanding of geography, is central to our understanding of any nation-state, however strong or weak. Social

7. 'The Constitution of the United States of America', in Richard H. Kohn (ed.) *The United States Military under the Constitution of the United States, 1789–1989* (New York UP, 1991), p. 19, from which all other quotations are taken.

8. George Pendle, *A History of Latin America*, 2nd edn (Harmondsworth: Penguin, 1971), pp. 187–8.

organization determines political activity, and social organization is dependent on the resources available to be exploited by any community; in turn, these are the product of geological deposits and physiographic elements, including the weather, which influence the demographic spread. And in the United States, a grand historical vision of American development based on exploiting and opening up the frontier was linked to the spread of democracy across the heartland to the Pacific. It fired the imagination of politicians and animated their speeches. This nationalistic, ideological, republican vision has been termed correctly a 'secular religion'.

'The influence of geographical conditions upon human activities', wrote Sir Halford Mackinder, 'has depended, however, not merely on the realities as we now know them to be and to have been, but in even greater degree on what men imagined in regard to them'.[9] The expansion of American power and ideals, based on an exuberant confidence in their Constitution, a cult worshipping at the shrine of George Washington and other of the founding fathers, and an efficient judicial organization which seemed to set the need for military power at naught – this confidence in a superior political structure and phenomenal economic dynamism – what would later be termed the 'Manifest Destiny' of the United States – in the short term made unprecedented progress. But it contained within itself severe contradictions and tensions, and these, in large part, sprang from geography. The United States was less of a prisoner of her colonial heritage than the Latin American republics (though her republican heritage was divided, or confused, as to whether centralization or decentralization would prevail), but once she had escaped from the shackles of her colonial master, she declined to make a completely fresh start and abolish all colonial institutions. The spectre which would return to haunt her, like Banquo's ghost, was involuntary servitude.

One way in which regionalism was expressed was in the kind of labour force that was employed in a specific environment. The nature of the work-force determined not just the crops that were grown, and therefore the local economy, but the relations between the labourers and their masters. In colonial America much labour was unfree, and the relations between white indentured servants

9. Sir Halford Mackinder, *Democratic Ideals and Reality*, 2nd edn (New York: Henry Holt, 1942), p. 28.

and black slaves were close to a degree that would have surprised their nineteenth-century descendants. Much of the prosperity of the American colonies before the 1760s was due to the importation of indentured servants. These were Englishmen or women who, for whatever reason, paid for their passage across the Atlantic by contracting for a period of bondage terminated by a certain date, usually seven years; this act was not always voluntary. Perhaps 50 per cent of all colonists in the eighteenth century consisted of indentured servants, redemptioneers or convicts. Involuntary servitude was therefore an important feature of American life before Negro slavery became a pressing issue. 'The planters' fortunes here', a governor of Maryland happily observed in 1755 'consist in the number of their servants (who are purchased at high rates) much as the estates of an English farmer do in the multitudes of cattle'.[10] The tropical conditions prevailing in the southern states, the swamps, diseases and humidity increasing in both number and effect as the settlers advanced southward, favoured the spread of plantation agriculture. This required the clearing of inhospitable areas and required labour in which the involuntary aspect had to be increased, mainly because of the reluctance and general unsuitability of white labourers for this kind of work and the withering of the indentured labour system – although it did not finally die until the nineteenth century.

An alternative source of labour well suited (according to the conventional wisdom of the day) for working under the sweltering southern sun and clouds of mosquitos was slaves transported from Africa. The booming markets for southern plantation crops, rice, tobacco and later cotton, led to a considerable expansion of the Negro population; not just to work on the existing plantations, but because of wasteful methods and the rapid exhaustion of the soil, to open up new, virgin lands for exploitation. This process occurred remarkably quickly. In 1700 the Negro population in America has been estimated at 28,000; that is to say, something in the order of 11 per cent of the entire population. In 1770 this proportion had increased to 21.8 per cent. In the course of almost three-quarters of a century the percentage of the slaves

10. Quoted in Richard Hofstadter, *America at 1750: A Social Portrait* (London: Jonathan Cape, 1972), p. 34; Bernard Bailyn, *Voyagers to the West: Emigration from Britain on the Eve of the Revolution* (London: I. B. Tauris, 1987), pp. 313–14, the servant swore in an addendum to his contract that he had not been 'kidnapped or inticed, but [was] desirous to serve the above-named . . . or his assigns'.

transported from Africa had doubled, and their total number can be estimated at 459,000.[11]

Resistance among blacks sometimes occurred. These were desperate and forlorn insurrections. In New York City in 1712, for instance, some two dozen slaves deluded themselves into thinking that they would be rendered invulnerable by magic spells, and they set fire to a building and attacked those who sought to extinguish it. They were suppressed with extreme brutality. 'Some were burnt,' the Governor assured his masters in London, 'others were hanged, one broken on the wheel, and one hung alive in chains in the town, so that there has been the most exemplary punishment inflicted that could possibly be thought of'. In the same city in 1741 there occurred a number of unaccountable fires which excited anxiety that they presaged a massive slave revolt. In 1793 Albany experienced another bout of arson, which resulted in the execution of three slaves. Such action was usually covert – it was aimed against oppressive owners or overseers – and organized by small bands ranging from three or four slaves to groups of up to a dozen. Whites feared 'Horrid Murder' committed by poisoning. In Virginia in the years 1783–1814 owners of 434 executed slaves received compensation after their execution by the state authorities for such offences – a rate of about 14 per annum. Consequently, the spread of slavery can be associated with the spread of coercive, para-military force to enforce the peace (although perhaps it should be added that American democratic display has a military character, with a penchant for honorific military titles; fire brigades, police forces, and even sports teams all delighted in para-military overtones). These measures were the more severe where slaves were most numerous. There can be little doubt that the protection of slavery in the United States rested on force, or the threat of force. Increasingly, in her zeal to use police methods to intimidate the resident slave population, the South would be demarcated from the other regions. Such a fear of Negroes existed elsewhere, but their comparatively small numbers did not provoke the same ferocious response; it was a question of degree admittedly, but the degree was not insignificant.

The use of militia forces in activities that were not primarily military in character began early in the history of the South. Police duties, such as the Negro Patrol, were an urgent matter. This

---

11. Hofstadter, *America at 1750*, pp. 66–7; Peter Kolchin, *American Slavery* (Harmondsworth: Penguin, 1993, 1995), p. 16.

included the scouring of neighbourhoods from 8 p.m. onwards, to prevent crime and arson, and arrest any loitering Negroes. In South Carolina, provisions for the Patrol had been inserted into the militia laws as early as 1690. Great agitation was caused in the years 1739–40 by attempts by slaves to fight their way out to the Spanish colonies in the Floridas, urged on by the Spanish governor's proclamation which promised freedom for any slave who escaped to his territories. In New York a provision for a Negro Patrol was hurriedly added to the militia laws after the insurrection of 1712. A Virginian law of 1723 prohibited Negroes from serving in the militia, save as 'drummers and trumpeteers in servile labour but not to bear arms'. Indeed, the increase in the use of the Negro Patrol was welcomed by most militiamen because it ensured that they remained within their own neighbourhoods.[12]

Even before the drafting of the Constitution was completed in 1787, chattel slavery was already a vital ingredient of southern prosperity. Yet a fear of the dangers of slave revolts was becoming a pervasive anxiety that permeated southern life, and a less pressing worry in other parts of the country. The debates over the Constitution marked the first major confrontation between states from the northern and southern sections, though of a very mild kind. Since about 1760, aided by the pressure of urbanization, the roots of slavery were withering in the North. Indeed, at the very moment the Constitutional Convention was sitting and reviewing its procedures in Philadelphia in May 1787, Congress, then resident in New York, passed the North West Ordinance, which prohibited slavery north and west of the Ohio River.[13] This, like many other measures that followed it over the next three-quarters of a century, judged the existence of slavery in the regions below this line the business of the various state legislatures. At Philadelphia, discussion focused around the tax powers of Congress, calculated by the number of free persons, plus 'three fifths of all other persons including Indians not taxed'. This would have the effect of counting slaves in a poll count as though they were represented in Congress, when as chattels they were disenfranchised. The wording implied a constitutional sanction,

12. Hofstadter, *America at 1750*, pp. 128–9; Winthrop D. Jordan, *White over Black: American Attitudes to the Negro, 1550–1812* (Baltimore, MD: Pelican, 1969), pp. 392–3; Brian Holden Reid, 'A Survey of the Militia in 18th Century America', *Army Quarterly* CX (Jan. 1980), pp. 52–3.

13. See below, pp. 112–14, 116–18, 122–3.

which later defenders (and some critics) of slavery extension demanded should be enshrined in a constitutional amendment.

The other contentious matter concerned congressional powers to regulate trade with foreign countries, among the states themselves and 'with the Indian tribes'. Southerners argued that this favoured the North, and especially the New England shipowners, who could monopolize the southern export trade in staple crops. James Madison, a Virginian and later fourth president, secured a compromise and southern objections were dropped. But it serves to illustrate at this early date a revealing characteristic of American constitutional development: that so much of the tension between the northern and southern sections revolved around economic issues; but given the rapid economic development of the United States this is not very surprising. But it is characteristic, too, that the whole slavery question, a legacy of the colonial regime and of the harsher moral climate of the eighteenth century, begat fragile compromises that continually had to be patched up in the century of more disturbed emotions and tender consciences that followed it.

Even in 1787 such emotions could be engaged. Southerners proposed that Congress should be denied the power of levying a tax on the slave trade and prohibiting its exercise. George Mason of Virginia shocked some but impressed others with his declaration: 'I hold it essential to every point of view that the General Government should have power to prevent the increase of slavery'. This would be the dominant issue, at least among politicians, intermittently yet consistently for the next forty years after 1820. Needless to say, southern delegates from South Carolina and Georgia decreed they could not enter into any union in which their capacity to import slaves was endangered. Even at this stage spokesmen from the Deep South expressed themselves more vehemently than those from the Upper South against any restrictions on slavery. The pragmatic appeal of compromise now asserted itself for the first time. Reaching an accommodation on the slavery issue had an instant charm for harassed politicians, repelled by the thought of civil commotions and determined to make the Constitution work. Yet the placatory, smiling charm of compromise issued from a shallow and beguiling visage, rather like the picture of Dorian Gray, revealing hideous deformities and poisons beneath. Northern delegates were divided on the slavery issue. Some believed that a moral stand should be made to extirpate slavery; others did not consider the issue worth the trouble, certainly not on the Negro's account. Some 'middle ground' was preferable, and indeed the whole political system they were fashioning trained them to seek such an accommodation. All delegates eventually agreed that Congress should be prevented from legislating or prohibiting the slave trade before 1808. Southerners were pleased by a provision preventing the Federal government from levying duties on exports in return for which southerners dropped their opposition to import duties. This question, however, would be another matter of contention between the sections over the next three-quarters of a century. In these controversies, and in their seeming resolution, is offered to us a model of future disputation and the kind of solution favoured in the years ahead. Indeed, in these agreements, plus the important concession which permitted the return to their masters of 'persons held to service or labour who crossed state lines' (Article IV, Section 2) and thus upheld a duty to return escaped slaves, they cemented the disparate parts of the early Union together; but the masonry was fissile, and dammed up forces which could be released only by war.[14]

Such a compromise was important in validating the southern system of racial chattel slavery. The northern delegates, as so often in this saga, were unaware of its full significance at the time, which became clear only later. Plantation agriculture based on slavery received a fillip in October 1803 with the greatest territorial addition gained by the American republic resulting from the sudden, and for the Jefferson Administration, quite unexpected, cession of the entire French colony of Louisiana in return for $15million. The Jefferson Administration was fearful lest this territory's resources be mobilized by Napoleon against the United States. By acquiring this territory, Jefferson ensured the safety of the American experiment from perhaps the only potential foreign menace which truly imperilled its existence. Should Napoleonic monarchies be created in North American territories contiguous to the United States (like Napoleon III's short-lived adventure in Mexico in 1862–66), then republican democracy would be in grave danger. 'We have lived long', Robert R. Livingston exulted to James Madison, 'but this [the Louisiana Purchase] is the noblest work of our lives'.[15] But the most important result of this

14. Richard B. Morris, 'The Origin and Framing of the American Constitution', in Kohn (ed.) *The United States Military under the Constitution of the United States*, pp. 46–8.

15. Morton Borden, *Parties and Politics in the Early Republic, 1789–1815* (London: Routledge, 1968), pp. 68–9.

territorial expansion by purchase would be an immense extension, if not revival of plantation agriculture based on chattel slavery beyond the Mississippi River. Again geography would restrict such expansion, but nonetheless, by the 1830s the Louisiana Purchase raised the fundamental question of what *form* the American experiment would take? Would it be part of western civilization, then dominated by the liberal (if monarchical) values of Great Britain, or would it increasingly resemble the conservative, hierarchical and authoritarian empires of Latin America, like Mexico and especially Brazil (where chattel slavery thrived)?

A footnote to the Jefferson Administration concerns the conspiracy of Aaron Burr. Burr was Jefferson's first vice president. He was a man of considerable ability and eloquence; but he was also an intriguer with soaring ambitions. From about 1804 Burr cherished a treasonous design to detach the western states of the Union, and with British support, create a personal empire in this region. Such an effort would have invited intervention from outside the western hemisphere and reintroduced the balance of power to North America. Burr's plot was foiled easily, but incidents such as this are a reminder that we cannot take the inevitability of United States' domination of a continental republic in North America for granted. The true significance of Burr's conspiracy lies in the danger to the infant United States of convulsions unleashed by adventurers whose ambitions outweighed their common sense. Aaron Burr was the first 'filibuster'. The point is worth reiterating. For the United States to garner and protect the full benefits of the experiment she was pursuing – in developing her constitutional democracy and federal system as an alternative to European 'tyranny' – she needed to dominate without challenge the temperate zones of North America and fashion an economy suitable to that region. This required *unity*: only the *United* States could maintain sufficient power to protect herself against European intervention. Only continental expansion could defend republican democracy unsullied by the corruption of European monarchies and their attendant systems of balances of power, military aristocracies and standing armies. Philip Schuyler expressed in 1808 with exemplary clarity a fear that would surface half a century later. 'I dread a dissolution of all union. Immediate quarrels between the states will ensue. These quarrels will beget armies, these armies a conqueror, and this conqueror may give as much government as prevails at Constantinople'. Thus continental expansion marched hand in hand with the spread of democracy towards the Pacific Ocean; in the American experiment the two were inseparable. Yet with this spread arose the divisive issue of the future character of the republic as it expanded to the Mississippi and beyond. This lurked only half-recognized initially. In an optimistic mood in 1844, John A. McClernand of Illinois believed an advance north-westwards was but a matter 'of border safety, of territorial limits, and of relative political . . . influence, wealth and power'. The matter would not be quite so simple.[16]

However, the first evidence we have of the influence of centrifugal forces in the early Republic occurs not in the South, or South West, but in the North. Disaffection in New England was especially acute, and had festered within a decade of independence in Shay's Rebellion (1786). New England had also been disproportionately hit by the indeterminate embargo announced by Jefferson on trade with Britain and France in 1807 as a way of striking back at their naval depredations – especially Great Britain's attempts to break the Napoleonic Continental System aimed at her commerce. This frequently involved the seizure of neutral vessels, including many flying the American flag. When war itself spread to North America in 1812, the anxieties of New England were further agitated by the British occupation of Maine. By 1813–14 New England began to fear that it would be marginalized within the Union (as did the South during the 1850s). In October 1814 calls were heard for the meeting of a constitutional convention of the New England states at Hartford, Connecticut. At first these did not mention the possibility of secession but were concerned with specific constitutional grievances which might involve 'a radical reform in the national compact'. Consequently, the agenda for the meeting was preoccupied with parochial issues rather than with strategic, coordinated action on the part of the New England states against the policies of the Federal government. Perhaps the delegates to the Hartford Convention were intimidated by calls in Washington for the raising of a substantial force which could drive the British out of Maine and deal with them *en route*. At any rate, two

16. Dumas Malone, *Jefferson the President: Second Term, 1805–1809* (Boston, MA: Little, Brown, 1974), pp. 215–16; Richard Kohn, 'The Constitution and National Security: The Intent of the Framers', in Kohn (ed.) *The United States Military under the Constitution of the United States*, pp. 64–5, 89n17; note esp. on p. 79 the fears of a monarchy being set up in distant parts of the Union; Norman A. Graebner, *Empire on the Pacific: A Study in American Continental Expansion*, 2nd edn (Santa Barbara, CA: ABC Clio, 1983), p. 36.

regiments (of New Englanders) were billeted in Connecticut for the winter in case urgent action against the Convention had to be taken.

When the Hartford Convention met in December 1814 its tone was equivocal rather than defiant. It was too timorous for 'open rebellion', and attempted rather to give 'tone, confidence and *system* to an opposition which shall *continue* its *equivocal* course, possessing *all* the moral qualities of treason and rebellion and at the same time avoiding a liability to their penalties', as the military commander in Hartford sardonically described their proceedings. Although only fragmentary evidence of the discussion survives, it is clear that the Convention not only lacked the confidence or appetite for drastic action, but also lacked unanimity among the disaffected states as to their future course. Indeed delegates from Vermont and New Hampshire did not attend. Even delegates from Connecticut recoiled against the evils of secession. Thus the Convention lacked dynamic leadership, a burning issue around which to focus its energies, and most important of all, a network of sympathetic states which could be wielded into an effective coalition. These were the three essential factors in any successful secessionist move against the Federal government. The report of the Hartford Convention merely reiterated New England's grievances (for instance, calling for constitutional changes such as restricting the president to a single term and prohibiting the natives of one state holding the office for more than one consecutive term). Far from advocating secession, it seemed to be calling for a truce in sectional hostility. Indeed it would perhaps teach ardent secessionists of the future what not to do.[17]

Nevertheless, this incident is significant. It does indicate the path to be taken by disaffected states in dispute with Washington. The Madison Administration could not be complacent in its dealings with the Hartford Convention. Secession of the New England states was not a possibility to be ignored in the midst of a foreign war, and the possible involvement of Great Britain in supporting a secessionist movement was a spectre to be feared. If the New England states had been granted time to organize themselves, then their combination of wealth, population, maritime power and sizeable militias was a formidable one should they have attempted to create an independent state. European

17. Malone, *Jefferson the President: Second Term*, pp. 483–5; J. C. A. Stagg, *Mr Madison's War: Politics, Diplomacy and the Early American Republic, 1783–1830* (Princeton UP, 1983), pp. 471–2, 474, 477–83; Charles M. Wiltse, *The New Nation, 1800–1845* (New York: Macmillan, 1965), p. 50.

intervention was crucial in ensuring the success of any secessionist movement in North America. Yet in 1814 the New England separatists lost their appetite for a confrontation with the central government. Timely action by the Madison Administration (and the news of the belated American victory at the Battle of New Orleans) prevented any momentum for secession developing among discontented citizens. This was an aspect of the crisis which should not be neglected. The outcome of the Hartford Convention does resemble the proverbial dog who not only fails to bark but merely whimpers in its kennel at night. It was a timorous gathering, yet we are apt to overlook its significance in the later sectional crises. The Hartford Convention indicates the potential of centrifugal forces within thirty years of independence and only forty-five years before the outbreak of the Civil War. In historical terms these are trifling periods of time. The Hartford Convention marks out the later path to be taken towards secession for particularists from a different region, with different grievances, and of a more audacious timbre.

The struggle for stability

All political systems require precedent and longevity to guarantee their continuance. The longer they continue the more substantial their achievements appear, and the more such institutions are admired. In peace, as in war, nothing succeeds like success. The object of the administrations following the signing of the Treaty of Ghent, ending the war of 1812–15, was to control centrifugal forces by wielding the United States together by economic development, internal improvements and the growth of infant political mechanisms laid down in the Constitution. This was not achieved easily, and historians now recognize that a period once characterized by the Whig cachet, the 'Era of Good Feelings', was a period of intense stress, political transition and reorganization. In short, the administrations of James Monroe and John Quincy Adams sought to enshrine, cherish and nurture *political stability* but they encountered much opposition. 'Political stability', Sir John Plumb has pointed out, 'is a comparatively rare phenomenon in the history of human society. When achieved it has seldom lasted'.[18] Americans in the 1820s thought that their combination

18. J. H. Plumb, *The Growth of the Political Stability in England, 1675–1715* (London: Macmillan, 1967), p. xiv.

of universal manhood suffrage, the election of officials and representatives at stipulated intervals, and independent judicial regulation, gave them a unique and unprecedented instrument for civilizing the North American continent. This view looks persuasive when one compares the record of the United States with its neighbour Mexico, or indeed with Argentina, during this period riddled with anarchy and the rule of the *caudillo*. Professor Plumb defines political stability as 'the acceptance by a society of its political institutions, and of those classes of men or officials who control them'. He adds that conspiracies, plots, revolutions of various kinds and civil war – which have been a continual feature of the history of the United States before 1865 – 'in modern times, are obviously the expression of political instability'.[19] The paradox of American efforts in securing political stability was that earnest, enthusiastic efforts obsessed with observing the form and spirit of the Constitution, although initially unanimous, resulted only in disillusion, and a rejection of those institutions and the men who operated them. One reason for this extraordinary and petulant rejection of the Federal system, and resultant political instability and civil strife, can be found in the rapid economic development of the United States after 1820.

The United States during the nineteenth century enjoyed the fruits of one of the world's most dynamic economies. The conversion of a primitive subsistence economy and production of primary raw materials to the creation of a market economy in both agricultural and manufactured goods is tantamount to the 'market revolution' proclaimed in some recent accounts. This process was accelerated by the spread of communication networks, railways, roads and canals. In 1825 the Erie Canal connected the Hudson River with the Great Lakes; in 1852 easy travel between New York City and Chicago was made possible by the construction of a railroad. The railway line and the steam locomotive made possible the forging of some measure of social and cultural homogeneity in this new, massive country and facilitated social and economic movement and interchange. For it is not only people and goods that travel by train but also news, social comment and ideas. The railway was both a symptom of and a stimulus to economic expansion. Its expansion was most notable in the decade before

19. Ibid; in Samuel P. Huntington's opinion, 'Conspiracy theories were the midwife at the birth of the American republic', *American Politics: The Promise of Disharmony* (Cambridge, MA: Belknap, 1981), pp. 80, 96, quoted in Henry Astier, 'Americans and Conspiracy Theories', *Contemporary Review* 261 (Oct. 1992), p. 169.

the Civil War: in 1850 8,500 miles had been built, by 1860 this had increased to more than 30,000 miles.

The years between 1830 and 1860 witnessed a veritable explosion of agricultural production. In Milwaukee, for instance, 317,000 bushels of wheat were exported in 1851; a decade later this total had expanded to 13 million. The annual traffic along the Mississippi-Ohio had a value in commerce of $140 million in the 1850s. Industrial production broke out of the constraints imposed by the local, domestic system. The north eastern states, Massachusetts, Connecticut, New York, Delaware, Pennsylvania, and along the Erie Canal were the main sources of this industrial plenty, based on coal and iron, shoes and other leather goods, textiles, agricultural equipment, shipbuilding, industrial equipment, and a host of machine tools and consumer goods. The capitalist financial structure was set in place and along with it came the excitement, the reckless gambles, and exaggerated anticipations of the 'boom' years, and the abject despair and financial sluggishness bordering on collapse characteristic of the 'bust' years.

This expansion was accompanied (as elsewhere in those countries of the western world which experienced the agricultural and industrial revolutions) with a staggering growth of both population and urban construction. The population of Minnesota grew by no less than 2,760 per cent in the decade 1850–60. This reflects the significant westward movement of the population, so that by 1860 more than half of the citizens of the United States lived on the plains west of the Allegheny Mountains. In 1830 Chicago consisted of a few shacks amid green fields; by 1860 it was a thriving, wealthy city of 100,000 people.[20] This westward move would have significant political consequences.[21] The other noteworthy feature of demographic change was the great influx of immigrants in all parts of the United States, mostly from the British Isles, Germany and Scandinavia. New York state, for example, included 469,000 people born in Ireland and 218,000 born in Germany. Protest against waves of immigration became one of the most significant political issues of the *ante-bellum* years and was to provoke the formation of the American Party.

20. Of course, this process of urbanization affected other parts of the western world. What differentiates the United States is the scale of development. For example, in 1821 Middlesbrough was a village of 40 people; in 1901 it had 91,000 inhabitants. See Chris Cook and Brendan Keith, *British Historical Facts* (London: Macmillan, 1975), pp. 234–5.

21. On this, see below, pp. 121–5, 156–7.

The overall population growth in the 1850s was as follows: nationally 35 per cent every decade; in the country 30 per cent; in the cities 75 per cent. New York had the biggest population with 515,000 (612,000 if Brooklyn was included), Philadelphia with 340,000,[22] Baltimore 169,000 and Boston 136,000. This fecundity and dramatic urbanization would generate major social problems in a country, to use Richard Hofstadter's phrase, which 'was born in the country and has moved to the city'. And which was simultaneously wedded to an idealized Jeffersonian vision of a rural idyll as the prime source of vitality for its fledgling democracy, and to the advantages offered by boundless 'progress' in human affairs. Novel ideas and challenges arising from a dynamic economic system, and the prosperous educated bourgeois it bred, were to pose dilemmas which no quarter of the Union could avoid. Nonetheless, despite this rapid industrialization and the growth of towns and cities, it is important not to forget that the United States before 1861 was a predominantly rural society.[23]

The American political system in the first half of the nineteenth century was, more than anything else, the creation of an agricultural society. Paradoxically, however, the dynamic centres of American political culture since the seventeenth century have invariably been urban. In his book, *People of Paradox*, Michael Kammen observes of Stuart England that it was characterized by an 'unremitting ideological tension, and always the forces of mobility and growth were pulling against the strength of inertia, the forces of enterprise against those of custom'. Applying this insight to the early history of the United States, which inherited a good deal from Great Britain (more than is often acknowledged), Kammen comments, 'At several stages of our history, population growth has outstripped institutional change. The result in many cases has been violence, vigilante movements, or economic unrest, all with the special coloration of unstable pluralism'. Kammen

22.   In 1800 New York had a population of 60,000 and Philadelphia just under 70,000. Wiltse, *New Nation*, p. 6.

23.   These paragraphs are based on Peter J. Parish, *The American Civil War* (London: Eyre Methuen, 1975), pp. 20–3; J. G. Randall and David Donald, *Civil War and Reconstruction* 2nd edn (Lexington, MA: D. C. Heath, 1969), pp. 1–12; Wiltse, *New Nation*, pp. 75–6; Richard Hofstadter, *The Age of Reform: From Bryan to FDR* (London: Jonathan Cape, 1962), p. 23. This 'intimate American quarrel with history', between a rural idyll and faith in progress, is a central theme of Hofstadter's writing. See also *The Progressive Historians: Turner, Beard, Parrington* (London: Jonathan Cape, 1969), p. 7.

does not consider unstable pluralism – that is to say, a number of agencies or interest groups competing within the body politic – a distinctly American development. 'But I do believe that unstable pluralism on a scale of unprecedented proportion is especially American'.[24]

Kammen's eye is on the twentieth-century results of these tendencies. But one in particular of his themes is germane to this analysis. 'Even the American conception of sovereignty is pluralistic', Kammen observes, 'for federalism is the institutional embodiment of political pluralism'.[25] The nature of the American political system, the environment in which politicians and bureaucrats operate, is a central consideration in any discussion of the forces that contributed to a political crisis that could be resolved only by war. It is a fairly common assumption in general surveys of American history that the process of Civil War causation is triggered off only after the ending of the Mexican War of 1848. Yet this approach conceals the fact that a period of turbulent political change had taken place over the comparatively short period of forty years. Therefore to compartmentalize it further, and restrict a general survey of the origins of the American Civil War to the twenty years or so prior to the war, is short-sighted and artificial. Far from accepting that the Federal Union emerged from the Jeffersonian 'Revolution' in pristine condition, complete and fully armed, like the goddess Athena from the head of Zeus, the argument advanced in this book will turn such an approach on its head.[26] In the first place, the United States was an artificial edifice, she constructed *herself* (the term nation, for instance, does not appear in the Declaration of Independence). Secondly, American nationalism was the fruit of war not its cause, and a real sense of national belonging with all its attendant myths had perforce to be nurtured (or manufactured) not only during the Revolutionary War itself but also in the quarter of a century or so that followed it.[27]

24. Michael Kammen, *People of Paradox: An Inquiry Concerning the Origins of American Civilization* (New York: Vintage, 1972, 1973), pp. 131, 295; on the British provenance of many American nineteenth-century attitudes, throughout this book I have drawn on the perspectives outlined in Marcus Cunliffe, 'New World, Old World: The Historical Antithesis', in Richard Rose (ed.) *Lessons from America: An Exploration* (London: Macmillan, 1974), pp. 27, 36, 45.

25. Kammen, *People of Paradox*, p. 294.

26. James M. McPherson, *Battle Cry of Freedom: The Civil War Era* (New York: Oxford UP, 1988), begins in 1847–48.

27. Peter J. Parish, 'American Nationalism and the Nineteenth-Century Constitution', in Joseph Smith (ed.) *The American Constitution: The First 200 Years* (University of Exeter Press, 1988), p. 64.

The presumptive authority based on historical legends bathed in the sanctity of antiquity and the Middle Ages – Vercingetorix, Caratacus, Boudicca, King Alfred and his cakes, Robert Bruce and his spider, Joan of Arc, to name but a few, which bound together Britain and France, could not be extended to the United States. An intense process of myth-making followed during and after the Revolutionary War. Mr Gore, in Henry Adam's novel, *Democracy*, observes of George Washington, 'we idolize him. To us he is Morality, Justice, Duty, Truth; half a dozen Roman gods with capital letters'.[28] American social, patriotic and cultural bonds had to be woven in an enormous country, which in Professor Parish's words 'lacked a fixed geographical definition. . . . The shape of the country on the map was constantly changing and growing'. Indeed, the idea of growth can be viewed as a substitute for the fixed, often unwritten customs of Europe.[29]

Given these circumstances, a general argument can be asserted, namely, that far from being the product of special circumstances that pertained after about 1840, *separatism was inherent in American history and political development after 1783*. The whole *ante-bellum* period, not just part of it, exhibits centrifugal features, which gradually increased in strength. This is not to suggest that civil war was inevitable, only that it was far more likely than either contemporaries or later historians have been prepared to admit. We must surely agree with Carlyle when he asks of another Constitutional Convention: will it not settle all issues? 'Alas, a whole tide of questions come rolling, boiling; growing ever wider, without end!'[30] For secession to present a serious threat to the Union, all that was required was, first, the establishment of an ideology with a sufficient following among the educated middle classes for a group of them to lead a separatist movement; secondly, a region or section of the United States that enjoyed sufficient unity to form a new, breakaway republic; and thirdly, a political event sufficiently provoking to spark off the secessionist process; and finally, the high probability of foreign intervention on the side of the secessionists. As has already been noted, Jefferson was convinced that the New England states would try to secede in 1814, and he worried lest he lacked the resources to

28. Henry Adams, *Democracy: An American Novel* (New York: New American Library, 1961), p. 77.

29. Parish, 'American Nationalism', p. 65.

30. Thomas Carlyle, *The French Revolution: A History* (Leipzig: Bernhard Tauchnitz, 1851), III, p. 97.

suppress them. He also thought that secession movements would spring up in the new states and territories; the old states of the eastern seaboard, therefore, should be protected and cherished as the bastion of Unionism. But this was only one incident. There is not a decade before the Civil War which lacks discussion somewhere at some time of the possibility of secession and the consequent commotion. In other words, a sense of *national* identity is very tenuous throughout the period before 1850. A further generalization can be hazarded: that the more vocal the exclamations of loyalty and esteem for the Union, the more shallow were its roots entrenched; whereas it was often sincere one suspects that many Americans protested their love of country too much.[31]

The national symbols above all others were the Constitution and the Declaration of Independence. The first enshrined a form of very limited government by European or East Asian standards, 'limited' not only in the sense of restricting the concentration of power in the hands of certain men of decision, but also in the duties 'government' was expected by its citizens to carry out. The division between the executive and legislature, a delicate system of checks and balances, negated either efficient or intrusive administration of government. The two-party system that operated, in various guises, from 1787 onwards 'had to be invented' despite the best intentions of the founding fathers (who continually inveighed against 'party spirit', notably in George Washington's 'Farewell Address') in order to make the loose, federal system of central government work at all. It was, however, easier for American politicians to agree on what they were against, than on what they were *for*. Immense ambitious programmes of reform, like the 'American System' of Henry Clay, and the equally ambitious schemes of John Quincy Adams, were all to founder on the electoral appeal that the best form of government was no government.[32] Thus the Constitution operated as an essentially negative but binding reference point that served a dual purpose: it allowed the cultivation of a concept of a perpetual Union, which

31. Kenneth M. Stampp, *The Imperiled Union: Essays on the Background of the Civil War* (New York: Oxford UP, 1980), pp. 20, 35–6.

32. Wiltse, *The New Nation*, pp. 55–9; see the conversation quoted by Mrs Trollope, in her *The Domestic Manners of the Americans* (London, 1832: Folio Society, 1974), p. 89: 'How should freemen spend their time, but looking after their government, and watching that them fellers as we give offices to, doos their duty, and gives themselves no airs?'

could be nourished only over time; and it permitted the growth of a legitimate political opposition without a recourse to arms (which was a constitutional development which was not common in Latin America). The only difficulty with such a system was that it assumed a certain mode of conduct and, moreover, that the issues it should settle were amenable to accommodation and agreement. When certain groups were gripped by radical fervour, and refused to accept that doing nothing was a better substitute than trying to do the impossible, then this system was ill-equipped to cope and failed to provide stable government. In short, it worked best when politicians behaved cautiously whatever the rhetorical sweep of their speeches; it worked poorly when spokesmen of certain interest groups had the audacity to demand a measure and refused to accept a compromise let alone a rejection. Under such circumstances, an obsessive focus on 'the Constitution' as a nationalistic symbol proved counter-productive. Political disagreements automatically became vexed constitutional controversies, which required judicial intervention. Furthermore, both defenders of congressional authority and states rights enthusiasts were able to encrust the arguments advanced during these crises with legal enactments and language which not only obfuscated the political and moral issues under consideration, but also carried the imposing implication that somehow adjudication by the courts, and especially the Supreme Court, would settle the question with a grand flourish of finality. It is, of course, arguable that this deflected conflict into legal channels, thus inhibiting wider disturbance, yet the limits of this view were revealed by the Dred Scott decision of 1857. Legal decisions, it seemed, were more binding than political action. This was a fatal illusion.[33]

The courts played a most significant role in the dramatic series of crises that were to culminate in the secession of the slave states in 1860–61. When discussing the legal basis for the secessionist case, historians are prone to mock the 'hair-splitting logic and its forced analogies' as 'remote to us'; this may be true of the states rights question in particular but hardly of American political intercourse generally.[34] The judicial temper of American political

33. Parish, 'American Nationalism'. p. 122; Stampp, *Imperiled Union*, pp. 3–4.
34. E.g. Wiltse, *New Nation*, p. 122. There must have been good political reason why the states' rights question flourished for forty years 'before a comparable case for a perpetual Union had been devised'. See Stampp, *Imperiled Union*, p. 35. He is referring to Andrew Jackson's Nullification Proclamation of 1833; see below, pp. 58–9.

life is central to its proper understanding. Alexis de Tocqueville, in his study of Jacksonian America, is at pains to point out that judges were not political functionaries. But as in 'the United States the Constitution governs the legislature as much as the private citizen' (whereas in Britain Parliament makes the laws and the constitution), the American political system invokes the right of judges to found decisions pregnant with political significance 'on the *Constitution* rather than on the *law*'. Thus they are empowered 'not to apply such laws as may appear to them to be unconstitutional'. Such a system which breeds a compulsively litigious and a tiresomely narrow and inflexibly legalistic approach to politics (and a profession dominated by lawyers), contributed decisively to Kammen's concept of unstable pluralism because it not only introduced another agency which intervened in *ante-bellum* politics, but itself provided a forum in which manoeuvre, argumentation and disillusion after defeat were all experienced. As Tocqueville observes, 'In truth, few laws can escape the searching analysis of the judicial power for any length of time, for there are few that are not prejudicial to some private interest or other, and none that may not be brought before a court of justice by the choice of parties or by the necessity of the case'. Tocqueville himself praises such a system as a bulwark against the legislative tyranny of elected assemblies. Yet it had one irredeemable weakness during the *ante-bellum* years. It was a delusion throughout this period that, in a country which increasingly lacked a consensus on the direction in which her democracy should turn, that the judicial mechanism could somehow produce a formulation acceptable to all parties. On the contrary, although the bewitching half-light emanating from its beacons of constitutional wisdom certainly attracted admirers, the Supreme Court also repelled those scornful of the degree of illumination it offered. Rather like the Delphic Oracle, if the right answer was expected, then attention had to be devoted to asking the right question. But no agreement could be reached on what was the right question to ask. Thus the Supreme Court especially furnished compromises around which the conflicting groups manoeuvred; after a rebuff each side would wait for a suitable moment to mount a counter-attack based on a different point of law.[35]

35. Alexis de Tocqueville, *Democracy in America*, ed. Phillips Bradley (New York: Vintage, 1954) I, pp. 102, 104–5, 106–7.

An excessive faith in judicial intervention in politics is characteristic of the United States. Although applauded as a bastion against tyranny, the courts can serve as a means of guaranteeing tyranny, or at any rate protecting forces and institutions that are ademocratic, or potentially anti-democratic. Judicial pronouncements, however grandiloquent, cannot be the guarantee of a stable society. They cannot serve as a substitute for consensus *if that consensus does not exist.* Indeed a legalistic approach to politics can be considered a cause of the Civil War to the extent that both sides were prone to accept legal verdicts as having the potency of force in establishing a case. This was a dangerous potion for politicians (the vast majority of whom were lawyers) to imbibe, because it overstimulated the South and persuaded it to dangerously overrate its strength, and recklessly put that power, expressed in a constitutional interpretation of states rights, to the test.[36] Thus legal interpretation cannot be considered a substitute for effective policy or a firm will; it cannot serve as a substitute for force; nor can it necessarily justify the use of force – as in attempting to justify secession by the reiteration of otiose legal niceties. In short, valuable as they are in a civilized and democratic society, the courts cannot serve as their own political justification. The limits of judicial power in a political crisis must be recognized – as they clearly were in 1860–61.

But how did this crisis arise, and why was the pluralism of the American political system inherently unstable? In the first place, the federal system was permeated by localism. Therefore, the state government had a greater impact on the lives of its citizens than the Olympian missives of the Federal government. The division of sovereignty between Federal and state government often left an impression of fumbling ineffectiveness coupled with obeisance to an impotent overlord reminiscent of the Holy Roman Empire. Certainly like this medieval relic, the Federal government exerted little authority in the traditional areas of a nation-state's power: in ensuring the run of legal writ at home and protecting its citizens from foreign invasion. The maintenance of law and order, for example, was the prime concern of the state governments, as was the furthering of economic development. Clearly, such a division would have severe repercussions should the Federal government

36. On the 'legality' of secession, see the various Confederate viewpoints discussed in Thomas J. Pressly, *Americans Interpret their Civil War* (Princeton UP, 1954), pp. 62, 71, 81–2, 84–5, 88.

feel the need to assert its authority *vis-à-vis* a state government. The Federal government raised no direct taxes, confined itself to promotional and distributional duties, and employed 36,000 staff (of whom 30,000 were district postmasters).[37]

Yet though the sinews of federal power were feeble and underdeveloped, by comparison, party political activity was vibrant and healthy. Throughout the years before 1865 party political machinery, and especially that organized and financed by the Republican Party, was more dynamic and efficient than the system of federal administration. This contributed to a paradox that could be resolved only by war, even though the ultimate result of the Civil War was to reinstate the kind of loose federal structure that had in part caused it. The slavery controversy was surely the kind of issue that the federal system was calculated to solve, or at least repress by making parties intersectional. Yet this did not happen. On the contrary, the very vitality of party political life ensured that the arguments relating to this problem not only were elaborated but also grew more dogmatic and impassioned. Furthermore, the structural rigidities of the federal system, because they were designed to promote inertia as an antidote to overmighty central government, provided a virtually impregnable *limes* behind which chattel slavery in the South – which most agreed was the exclusive business of the states concerned – could shelter. Thus an alternative interpretation of 'liberty' developed there – a freedom to own human beings as property. An aggressive, defensive ideology eventually grew up, which formed a perversion of nineteenth-century liberal ideals. In American abolitionist circles this led to a measure of frustration which was not shared by their British counterparts. In the United States the political obstacles that had to be surmounted before the emancipation of slavery could be achieved were a good deal more numerous and hazardous than they had been in Great Britain. Thus the combination of frenetic activity on the one hand, and stalled constitutional machinery on the other, ensured that an explosion of one kind or another would result. Professor Parish is surely right in suggesting that it was 'precisely because it had grown accustomed to that particular kind of highly decentralized federalism, the United States lacked the safeguards and stabilizers

37. Peter J. Parish, 'A Talent for Survival: Federalism in the Era of the Civil War', *Historical Research* 62 (June 1989), pp. 178–9, 181–2.

– the institutional safety net – to cope with the great sectional crisis when it came'.[38]

It has often been asked by historians why the Union secured any loyalty from its citizens at all? As Tocqueville says, 'The Federal government is far removed from its subjects, while the state governments are within the reach of them all and are ready to attend to the smallest appeal'. Yet such a system excited the approval and loyalty of huge numbers of Americans. The encomiums lavished on its genius were to a very large extent justified; it had been tremendously successful in steering American political and economic development deftly. This loyalty was tenacious and was to survive in some parts of the southern states throughout the Civil War. Indeed the greatest tribute that can be paid to the system was accorded in March 1861 when the Confederacy tried to replicate it, making minor modifications to accommodate the special interest of slavery.[39]

Yet one of the basic problems of the years before the Civil War was more complicated than a mere question of loyalty, important though this was. In a pessimistic passage (so characteristic of American historical writing in the 1970s), Michael Kammen observes that 'Throughout our history we find, all too often, ironic contrasts between noble purpose and sordid results'.[40] No greater irony can exist in any country's history than the contrast between the sentiments expressed in the Declaration of Independence (1776), namely, 'We hold these truths to be self-evident: that all men are created equal; that they are endowed by their creator with inalienable rights; that among these are life, liberty and the pursuit of happiness', and the spread in the southern states for eighty years after the issue of that Declaration of an economic system founded on chattel slavery, and, moreover, the denial of basic political or civil rights to free Negroes who resided in the northern states. Not only did this constitute a blatant contradiction of a dictum that had been granted an authority comparable with Holy Writ in the years before 1861, but also it led to a perverse distortion of the meaning of the word 'liberty'. To southern politicians, the greatest 'liberty' they could enjoy, protected by the Constitution, was the freedom to own human beings as property. Property rights had been accorded a sacred

38. Ibid., p. 185.
39. Tocqueville, *Democracy in America*, I, p. 401. See below, pp. 298–9.
40. Kammen, *People of Paradox*, p. 290.

status by liberal political theory. Yet it was a liberty that was increasingly difficult to enjoy in the nineteenth century, especially after the abolition of slavery in the British Empire in 1833. Although Tocqueville commented on a further irony, namely, 'America is the land of freedom where, if he is to avoid giving offence, the foreigner cannot speak freely',[41] the significance of this embarrassing contradiction is perhaps twofold. It surely accounts for the savagery of the denunciation (notably by southerners) of the comparatively mild criticisms offered by books, such as Charles Dickens's *American Notes* (1842) of the evils of slavery and the limitations of 'liberty'. Dickens did not like the United States, as his novel *Martin Chuzzlewit* makes clear; but the *American Notes*, unlike Frances Trollope's *The Domestic Manners of the Americans* (1832), is not a peevish or bad-tempered book, and much of Dickens's criticism is directed towards the system of slave labour. It also accounts for some of the strands in the backcloth of rabid anti-British feeling which dominated these years.[42]

Anti-British feeling was especially strong in the southern states who feared a British annexation, or at least penetration, of Texas, as offering an opportunity for introducing abolition to North America by the backdoor. Any expansion of the British Empire in the Caribbean basin would mean the extension of a political system to the region which had eradicated slavery. An examination of the rhetoric of the Monroe Doctrine in the years 1830–60 must emphasize the assumption that one of the 'freedoms' it was designed to protect against European interference, was the maintenance of chattel slavery. This is a supreme irony, given the Confederacy's later faith in the imminence of British intervention in the Civil War.[43]

41. Quoted in Hugh Brogan, *Tocqueville* (London: Fontana, 1973), p. 38.

42. Charles Dickens, *American Notes* (London, 1842: Granville, 1985), pp. 104, 122, 125, 210–16; Mrs Trollope comments on the 'unconquerable dislike' of the Americans for the English (*Domestic Manners of the Americans*, p. 123), but one suspects that her imperious and condescending presence did not diminish it. On Dickens and America, see Malcolm Bradbury, 'A Rogue among the Detectives: Transcendentalism, Irony and American Culture', in Brian Holden Reid and John White (eds) *American Studies: Essays in Honour of Marcus Cunliffe* (London: Macmillan, 1991), pp. 158–71.

43. This is particularly true of older books, such as Dexter Perkins, *A History of the Monroe Doctrine* (Boston, MA: Little, Brown, 1955). Lord Palmerston, the British Foreign Secretary, favoured gradual emancipation; but he adopted a robust anti-slavery stance (mainly directed against the Portuguese and Brazil) which was politically popular in Britain. Palmerston made an anti-slavery treaty a condition for recognizing Texas. See Kenneth Bourne, *Palmerston: The Early Years, 1784–1841* (London: Allen Lane, 1982), pp. 622, 623–4.

But the most enduring significance of this profound contradiction between aspiration and practice lies in the tension it introduced in the American internal debate over American national character and ideals, and the future direction to be taken by American democracy itself. Garry Wills has commented in a number of places on American exceptionalism. Americans 'think ourselves as a nation apart,' he avers, 'with a special destiny, the hope of all those outside America's shores'.[44] (Kammen's comment quoted above is no rejection of this exceptionalism, only a complaint that it has not worked out as expected.) The language adopted by American politicians and publicists in their numerous speeches was rooted in the Bible and has strong religious overtones. Understanding the *spoken* word, and its inspirational power, is fundamental to an assessment of American political culture before the Civil War.[45] So, too, was the power of popular written material, especially newspapers and pamphlets, for the United States enjoyed high levels of literacy. So, too, was the strength and vibrancy of American idealism and confidence that they were directing an audacious democratic experiment (which generated so much national pride) in the *right* direction. Yet interpretations over that direction became increasingly at variance. Frequently, the United States has experienced disillusion over the progress of the direction taken, especially among her intelligentsia. Such dejection is not a rejection of the notion that the United States is an exceptional country; exceptionalism may assume an inverted form (for instance, in the years 1968–75 it was a common assumption in liberal circles that the United States was exceptionally wicked).[46]

The religious undertow of American political life very quickly came to focus on the glaring contradiction of chattel slavery enshrined in a republic dedicated to the furtherance of liberty. As in Great Britain, the growth of radical political and social reformist movements in intellectual circles in the nineteenth century reflected the shift from a mainly rural to an urban and industrial society. Although these groups came under increasingly secular influence, their attitudes and tone were nonetheless

44. Garry Wills, *Inventing America: Jefferson's Declaration of Independence* (London: Athlone, 1980), pp. xvi–xix.
45. Anne Norton, *Alternative Americas: A Reading of Antebellum Political Culture* (Chicago UP, 1986), p. 19.
46. Thomas R. Hietala, *Manifest Design: Anxious Aggrandizement in Late Jacksonian America* (Ithaca, NY: Cornell UP, 1985), is a good more recent example.

dominated by an inspirational and millenarianistic if not apocalyptic appeal.[47] And even those of a conservative disposition who had little sympathy for the more extreme eruptions of idealistic fervour, like that evinced by the Abolitionists, came to agree that the basic character of American democracy had to be protected from the iniquitous spread of slavery with its attendant restrictions of freedom of expression and movement of labour. These were seen as inimical both to the spirit and the letter of both the Declaration of Independence and the Constitution. In 1861 Lincoln admitted, 'I have never had a feeling politically that did not spring from the sentiments embodied in the Declaration of Independence'.[48] If one idea, or sentiment, came to be associated with being 'American', it was subscribing to the sentiments of the Declaration of Independence; alas, the meaning of those aspirations was subject to increasingly divergent opinions.[49]

Ideas rarely take a clear-cut form in politics. Politicians, and especially American politicians, pride themselves on being practical people concerned first and foremost with practical problems. In the first three decades of the nineteenth century, the problem of accommodating slavery in an expanding body politic was considered mainly as a problem amenable to all the arts of compromise. Yet some of the features of the impassioned anti-slavery debate, that were to become so strident in the 1850s, were already apparent in the debates which resulted in the Missouri Compromise of 1820 (indeed even earlier). The struggle to secure stability in the American political system resulted paradoxically in further instability. By 1819 there were already one and a half million slaves in the southern states, worth more than $300 million; this capital could not be transferred into other investments.[50]

It is important to remember that the controversy over the admission of Missouri as a slave state took place only five years

---

47. See Edward Royle, *Radical Politics, 1790–1900: Religion and Unbelief* (London: Longman, 1971).

48. Quoted in Wills, *Inventing America*, p. xxi.

49. Jefferson's precise attitude to slavery has been the subject of controversy. In 1787 he wrote: 'This abomination must have an end, and there is a superior bench reserved in heaven for those who hasten it'. Yet he was a slaveholder. But the paradox can be resolved by observing that Jefferson expected slavery to die out slowly but surely. This is consistent with his language and actions. Such a view was not unusual in the South before 1840. Fawn M. Brodie, *Thomas Jefferson: An Intimate History* (London: Eyre Methuen, 1974), p. 220.

50. Wiltse, *New Nation*, p. 69.

after the calling of the Hartford Convention. However, the controversy assumed a quite different form and was concerned with different matters than those which agitated the minds of the good gentlemen of Connecticut. In 1819 Congress had signalled its willingness to admit Missouri as a state of the Union with a state constitution embracing slavery.[51] A prolonged period of turbulence followed. Congressman James Tallmadge added two amendments to the Missouri enabling legislation. The first prohibited the transference of any further slaves to the state; the second required that all children born to the existing slaves should be emancipated on reaching the age of 25. This constituted nothing less than emancipation by stealth and was furiously denounced by southern representatives.

It is very likely that Tallmadge's motives were a mixture of the elevated and the self-interested. He was personally repelled by slavery, certainly; but equally important was the resentment felt by Tallmadge and his allies for the 'three-fifths' clause of the Constitution, which they felt was responsible for the southern domination of Congress and the electoral college. Though northerners, like Tallmadge, believed that slavery abused the cherished ideals of the Declaration of Independence, they were also keenly aware that many of the new states which would follow Missouri into the Union would be located in the north and west; they wished to limit slavery to its southern boundaries and not allow it to penetrate into the northern hinterland.

Stronger in numbers in the House of Representatives (105 to 80), the northern group secured the passage of the Tallmadge Amendment in February 1819. The Senate refused to accept it and deadlock ensued. The kind of war of words that would become such a common feature of political discussion over the next forty years erupted. Southern representatives claimed that the Tallmadge Amendment struck directly at slavery in the states and their freedom to direct the labour of their property, their slaves. It also prevented any spread of their liberties westwards. This provoked Senator William Smith of South Carolina to declare a counter-argument. Slavery, he opined, was a positive contribution to American civilization. This was an auspicious event, because it signalled the first public statement of an alternative interpretation of the Declaration of Independence. Older spokesmen of the

51. For legislation prior to 1819, and a discussion of the economic factor, see above, pp. 25–8, 32–4.

South, especially those from Virginia, were always prepared to admit the evils of slavery. Smith's argument was significant in indicating that increasingly henceforth the 'southern' viewpoint would invariably bear the imprint of the opinions of the Deep South, and that mark would not be a very moderate one.

At any rate, 'outside' interference was deprecated by all southerners, no matter how little they were persuaded by the notion that slavery was a beneficent instrument of social control. The real change in attitude was felt in the North, increasingly responsive to the tender sensibilities of the reforming, liberal conscience. Public assaults on the peculiar institution (a popular euphemism by which southerners were wont to describe the distinctness of slavery without explicitly stating what this was) in the North were countered by a dogmatic and impassioned southern defence. The latter argued that state governments should be permitted to govern in defence of their institutions without fear of the imposition of special conditions, such as the Tallmadge Amendment. Hence 'states rights' now assumed its pro-slavery flavour. The compromise finally agreed upon by Congress in March 1820 laid down the parameters within which all subsequent discussion revolved. Missouri was admitted as a slave state, and Maine as a free state; a line was drawn through the great territories of the Louisiana Purchase, 36 degrees 30 minutes latitude demarcating the boundary between the free and slave states.

During the controversy it was noted that 'in the private circles the topic of disunion was frequently discussed and with as little emotion as an ordinary piece of legislation'. In 1819–20 it seemed that the South placed greater priority on securing a slave state than admission to the territories. It would also appear that at this date, southern spokesmen admitted the power of Congress to intervene and regulate slavery in the territories. Yet this was a compromise that satisfied few. The Missouri Compromise line indicated that slavery would be free to expand westward, so long as it remained south of 36°30′, which would not satisfy the northerners who wished to restrict slavery; and congressional regulation of slavery in the territories was not acceptable to southerners who wished to see the peculiar institution flourish well beyond the Mississippi River. Southerners had failed to notice how limited was the scope for the westward expansion of slavery after 1820. The rhetoric of secession, furthermore, had been used to intimidate wavering northern votes and ensure that they supported the southern view. Few northerners were happy with the vague and open-ended nature of the compromise, but without this ambiguity the issue could not have been settled. The southerners exulted that they had won: it had prevented the intrusion of an 'outside' agency, like the Federal government, into the regulation of slavery.

This compromise, like all the others that followed it, settled nothing – in the long term. It succeeded in deferring to a later date the differences of perspective and outlook that underlay the necessity for reaching the agreement in the first place. The only really durable legacy of the Missouri Compromise was wholly negative – southern unity of action in the halls of Congress. From unanimity of thought and deed in the legislature, to considering themselves as representatives of a self-conscious section with individual interests at loggerheads with central authority, was a short step. The only question remaining was whether individual states should protect those interests or whether the slave states should combine to do so? Within twelve years South Carolina's impulsive actions would provide the answer.[52]

South Carolina and the Nullification Crisis, 1831–33

The most thoroughgoing assault on the powers of the Federal government before the secession crisis occurred during the Nullification Crisis precipitated by South Carolina in 1832. This was an auspicious event. Charleston was widely regarded during the Civil War as the cradle of secession and the first shots were fired there less than thirty years later. The Nullification Crisis concerned the capacity of the South Carolina legislature to 'nullify' measures passed by Congress, should its members deem this legislation opposed to the interests of their state. The association of Charleston with secession is unfair in this earlier crisis because the majority of the unionist leaders were Charlestonians, and the city voted for opponents of the nullification convention. There was certainly not a straight line of progression of secessionist advance between 1833 and 1861, but we should nonetheless accentuate at this point an important feature

52. This account is based on William J. Cooper, *Liberty and Slavery: Southern Politics to 1860* (New York: Alfred A. Knopf, 1983), pp. 134–43. For the 'three-fifths' clause, see above, pp. 25–6.

of *ante-bellum* history: the very rapid hardening of attitudes opposed to the Union, which was achieved by a rationalization of attitudes towards *slavery*. Some of these attitudes received an ambivalent airing during this crisis. A respectable argument can be made that 'Nullification should be viewed not so much as a harbinger of future radicalism as the logical, though not inevitable, culmination of the continuing debate over how best to defend the republican principles inherited from the Founding Fathers against the centralizing and corrupting tendencies of the age'. According to this view, nullification was backward-looking and genuflected towards Jefferson rather than grimacing approvingly towards Yancey and the secessionist rhetoric of the 1850s. But of course, very few historical events have a one-way historical significance, especially when the time-lag between events – a mere thirty years – is so small. The secessionists of 1860–61 also looked back for vindication to the Founding Fathers; but the lessons drawn from the Nullification Crisis, especially those bearing on increased cooperation between the slave states, indicate a tempered and enduring link between it and the later secessionist movements.[53] In 1832–33 South Carolina advanced the case for slavery in a halting and incomplete manner, but there can be no doubting its importance in inflaming the crisis in the first place. The Nullification Crisis was, in more ways than one, a rehearsal for the secession crisis of 1860–61 and the outbreak of civil war.

In four years from 1803, South Carolina legalized the slave trade and purchased 40,000 slaves from Africa. This eased the shortage of labour in the dank and inhospitable coastal belt, but it also added to that morbid sense of insecurity which characterized South Carolinians when surrounded by Negro slaves. Such paranoia was just as strong a part of the idle if tense planter outlook as their 'aristocratic' refinements: residing in mansions adorned with decanters of port wine, crystal goblets, tinkling pianos, and well-stocked libraries. South Carolina prided herself in the elegance and refulgence of her society, though it was of a shallow, provincial kind.[54] Nonetheless, the spread of *nouveaux*

53. Lacy K. Ford, Jr. *Origins of Southern Radicalism: The South Carolina Upcountry, 1800–1860* (New York: Oxford UP, 1988), pp. 125, 134.

54. The ban on the slave trade was due to a glut of slave labour, its withdrawal due to a shortage, and was justified on the grounds of large-scale slave smuggling. Congress was forbidden to end the trade before 1808. See above, pp. 26–7. Wiltse, *The New Nation*, p. 4; Jordan, *White Over Black*, pp. 318–19.

riches pretensions ensured that South Carolina politics would be influenced by the changing fads and churlish moods associated with the employment of slave labour. But South Carolina was an extreme case, and her lead was not followed by the rest of the south. It has been well said that by the 1830s, 'No other state in the Deep South had achieved such complete unification by the years of the Nullification Controversy'. It should be emphasized that just as national identity was nurtured and elevated during these years, so too was state identity. The development of affection for and attachment to the Union and the state was a simultaneous process and frequently they were in competition for the loyalty of their citizens. In the South the state became more quickly the focus of more parochial and passionate loyalties which jostled out an initial enthusiasm for the Federal Union. It was the ability of either the state or the Federal government to protect slavery which was to decide who won that competition in the South. South Carolina's planters were divided into two groups, those in the upcountry, who deeply resented Congress's tariff policy, and the tidewater (or lowcountry) nabobs, who were more nervous about northern anti-slavery mumblings. Their different perspectives, however, combined into one shared cause; this vigorous coalescence 'lashed each other into an increasingly frenzied campaign'.[55]

There can be no doubting the significance of the fiscal powers in these conflicts between the Federal government and the states before 1861. The raising of taxes and tariffs and the collection of duties and imposts invariably brought to a head festering grievances and tensions. Without revenue, governments are like aircraft without fuel; they may have pretensions to soar but their operating parts remain locked and grounded. These conflicts, moreover, have shadowed some of the graver economic and social crises in American history. Almost all federal coercive measures have been undertaken as a response to complications arising out of the administration of slave labour.[56] By the late 1820s cotton was being grown on the tidewater plantations with the expectation that capital investment there would in the future reap splendid returns; but capital was in short supply and the upcountry planters

55. William W. Freehling, *Prelude to Civil War: The Nullification Controversy in South Carolina, 1816–1836* (New York: Oxford UP, 1965, 1992), pp. 23–4.

56. Jerry M. Cooper, 'Federal Military Intervention in Domestic Disorders', in Kohn (ed.) *United States Military under the Constitution of the United States*, pp. 121–3.

were over-extended and vulnerable to market fluctuations. In the years 1818–29 the price of upcountry cotton fell by 72 per cent, but the cost of living fell by only 49 per cent. Planters were frustrated by the protective tariff because it contributed to a rise in consumer prices but did not contribute to an increase in the price of cotton. Capital thus flowed out of South Carolina, especially to the virgin lands of the South West, and the new states of Mississippi and Alabama, who presented formidable competition. The customs officers collected over $500,000 more in customs revenues than were lavished on the state by the legislators in Washington. The tariff seemed to resemble a spider which sucked out capital from South Carolina's decaying corpse, while keeping prices high. It became a scapegoat for the state's ills. This frustration reached a fever pitch pushing the state towards violent measures which most southerners, whatever their view on the tariff question, deplored.[57]

The other source of rage was the quite extraordinarily explosive South Carolinian over-reaction to the slightest hint of abolitionist sympathies. Citizens of this state could not conceive of civilization surviving any form of emancipation, and they indulged in a bizarre series of fantasies worthy of H. G. Wells. The Nullification Crisis, therefore, serves as a snapshot not only of the relations between federal and state authorities and the intervention necessary to regulate those relations, but also of the mentality which provoked the crisis. In 1829 David Walker, a free Negro from North Carolina resident in Boston and holding belligerent opinions, issued his *Appeal*, calling upon slaves to rebel. Two years later, William Lloyd Garrison sent to the press the first number of his abolitionist newspaper, *The Liberator*. Here in print was a deadly and insidious danger. Walker had exhorted the slaves: 'will you wait until we shall, under God, obtain our liberty by the crushing arm of power?' South Carolinians decided to employ that 'crushing arm' themselves to prevent the appalling prospect of a slave rebellion. The state contained $80 million worth of slave property, all of which seemed imperilled by irresponsible abolitionist chattering. Indeed such provocation amounted to a far more formidable economic challenge than any protective tariff. Such worries were given a further nervous edge after two slave

---

57. Ford, *Origins of Southern Radicalism*, pp. 121–4; Freehling, *Prelude*, pp. 32–7, 42–3, 47–8. Annually South Carolina aristocrats spent, on average, $500,000 while on holiday outside the state.

conspiracies, Denmark Vesey's in Charleston in 1822, and Nat Turner's insurrection in Virginia in 1831. These seemed to reveal to slaveowners the unpalatable truth that those slaves who had received the most kindness and consideration were the most likely to kill and mutilate their owners. The result was a belligerent effort to justify slavery and to stamp out abolitionist propaganda – though it was half-hearted by comparison with twenty years later. Sometimes violence erupted. When Maynard Richardson, editor of the Sumterville *Southern Whig*, pleaded 'for a *liberal* and *guarded* discussion of slavery', his good intentions led to a brawl with a pro-slavery editor and his supporters, who included a judge. Such were the violent passions even such caution could arouse; yet others may have been less convinced of the moral virtues of slavery. As Freehling observes, 'one of the crucial appeals of crusading for nullification on the tariff issue was that a weapon could be won to check the abolitionists without discussing slavery'.[58]

South Carolinian planters had always been in the forefront of those calling for free international trade. Yet the first major step towards enforcing state authority *vis-à-vis* the Federal government was taken, not in the economic sphere, but in that of slavery, with the creation of the South Carolina Association. This body enforced state legislation to restrict the movement of Negroes both slave and free after the Vesey Conspiracy. The latter might include 'agitators' who would rouse the slaves to rebellion. A number of black seamen from British ships found themselves imprisoned by zealous members of the association. Such action violated a treaty between the United States and Great Britain permitting free access to their respective ports. One such Jamaican born victim, Harry Ellison, applied in 1823 to the Supreme Court for a writ of habeas corpus and an immediate hearing on the grounds that all treaties ratified by Congress 'shall be the Supreme law of the land'. Although the South Carolina Associations's action was illegal, its lawyers argued that the treaty was unconstitutional. The national government's power to make such agreements, they argued, was merely delegated; the states, preserving their sovereignty, retained the reserve powers. If the South could not preserve herself from insurrection, her sovereignty would

<hr>

58. John White and Ralph Willett, *Slavery in the American South* (London: Longman, 1970), pp. 31, 60, 146 (doc. 47); Freehling, *Prelude*, pp. 49–51, 60, 63, 85–6; Ford, *Origins of Southern Radicalism*, p. 123.

disappear. Consequently, any action that reduced South Carolina's sovereignty by impairing her police powers could not be constitutional. Acts to prevent sedition or violence within South Carolina were thus of a higher legal order than any treaty ratified by the powers in Washington DC.

This spurious argument, which sketches in the kind of thinking used to justify nullification, confirmed that local concerns took precedence over the national. The Supreme Court rejected the plea on the grounds that the Constitution plainly stated that laws and treaties enacted by Congress were 'the supreme law of the land'. Yet if they could be controverted at the whim of individual states, this supremacy would be worn away piecemeal. 'Where is this to lead us?' asked the presiding justice, William Johnson. 'Is it not asserting the right in each state to throw off the federal Constitution at its will and pleasure'. Indeed this *was* the inexorable logic of nullification and states rights. It was like a corrosive acid that fragments layer after layer of the brittle rock of sovereignty, leaving small and disjointed splinters.[59]

Yet this setback did not discourage the putative nullifiers. 'The duty of the state', the upper house of the South Carolina legislature reaffirmed, '... to guard against insubordination or insurrection ... is paramount to all *laws*, all *treaties*, all constitutions'. That is to say, the duty of each *individual state*. South Carolina was not legislating for, or indeed considering the problems of other Southern states. South Carolina was considered by them to be extreme and headstrong. In this parochialism lay her strength – a neurotic desire to protect her citizens from further brutal rebellions led by the likes of Vesey – and her weakness: because she was isolated, and lacked the resources unaided to withstand the might of the Federal government. But a legal decision taken in the Supreme or any other Court cannot be *by itself* a representation of the mobilized power of central government if it is divorced from a capacity to enforce it with *armed force*. Because of such a disinclination South Carolina defied the ruling for years. Senator Robert Y. Hayne, later governor during the Nullification Crisis, asserted that South Carolina had successfully nullified the treaty, and this encouraged the nullifiers to take more audacious steps.[60]

Some of these emboldened souls tended to be those most

---

59. Freehling, *Prelude*, pp. 94, 112–14.
60. Ibid., pp. 114–15.

anxious about the future security of slavery and the parasitical effects of northern tariffs on southern agriculture. They read *The Crisis*, a series of essays written by a lowcountry planter, Robert J. Turnbull, dubbed by some 'the first bugle call to the South to rally'. Turnbull argued that tariffs were an insatiable drain on the South's wealth. He contributed to an outlook that began to doubt the value of the Union to South Carolina: the slaves were dissatisfied and restive; the economy continued to falter; section, and certainly state, seemed more worthy of loyalty. Men distant from home could be viewed as enemies and parasites; what was important in life was near to home. The 'nationalism' which had promoted good feelings rapidly seemed to be threatening rather than enlightened. The unionists also nursed anxieties about slavery. South Carolina was shaping a pattern to which other southern states would conform over the next two decades. Tariffs were interpreted in sectional terms, as they always had been, which is not surprising given their differential effect. Because Congress was unquestionably empowered by the Constitution to collect duties, nullifiers were forced to construe the *intent* behind the resulting legislation. They concluded that the Founding Fathers had never intended such powers to be used to promote an expansion of manufacturing industry. Hence the denunciation which was hurled at the authors of the 'tariff of abominations', who increased tariff duties from 37 per cent in 1824 to 45 per cent in 1828. South Carolinian congressional representatives sought to put together a southern group to mount a concerted defence. Other southern representatives were not enthusiastic. In Congress, as outside, South Carolina willingly pursued political solitude.[61]

Some of her politicians were aware that nullification ran a grave risk of involving the state in civil war. Nullifier leaders, like George McDuffie, called for a state tariff to be levied on northern goods. In the campaign of 1828 the denunciation of 'tyranny' became more vitriolic. The nullifiers, like the secessionists, who were their spiritual progeny, placed fire to their lips. They gambled: they willed violent opposition and radical action in pursuit of a conservative cause. They risked national prominence, as did later southern leaders, for local suzerainty. The role in the crisis of South Carolina's favourite son, Vice President John C. Calhoun, was more ambiguous. He supported nullification but still nursed a

61. Ibid., pp. 132–3, 138–9, 142–3; Ford, *Origins of Southern Radicalism*, pp. 129–30; Wiltse, *New Nation*, p. 104.

lingering ambition to win the presidency. Openly siding with the nullifiers would scuttle the barque of his exalted ambitions. In *Exposition and Protest* (1828), he drew up an elaborate theory of the tyranny of the majority; other interests should be able to concur with legislation before it was passed, thus giving each state a crippling veto over central government. The result of such an absurd theory would be fragmented, crippled governance.[62] This is a harsh judgement and can perhaps be qualified, to the extent that Calhoun at least had the intellectual honesty and discernment to grasp that the outcome of any political defence of slavery would be conflict of some kind. If compromise served only to postpone the hour of reckoning – and here he was prescient – then the South had to strive to ensure *protected* guarantees for slavery *within* the Union, which would allow it to accept or reject legislation unilaterally; by then it would not be a Union at all. As he wrote to Francis W. Pickens in 1831, 'as much time should be afforded as . . . possible before the State & the Union . . . takes sides finally'. The only result of Calhoun's theory that could be guaranteed was anarchy – the prime cause of revolution and civil war – the twin horrors he strove to avoid.[63]

The anarchy inherent in nullification was not always obvious to many of the protagonists. Calhoun's own motives were a mixture of the self-interested and the abstract. Calhoun had given the somewhat ambiguous doctrine of nullification a cutting edge, an intellectual respectability. His argument did enjoy a certain logic, and the nullifiers could not be dismissed as a group of ranting fanatics with the (as yet) tacit support of the vice president. Yet they could not avoid the harsh reality that by formulating federal and state authority as a duality, their system was unworkable. First, the Federal government had just as much authority to 'nullify' state legislation as vice versa. Calhoun rejected the suggestion that the Supreme Court was empowered to adjudicate disputes, since control of this tribunal could be seized by the tyrannous majority. The state constitutional convention should remain supreme, even

---

62. See Peter Paret, *Understanding War: Essays on Clausewitz and the History of Military Power* (Princeton UP, 1992), p. 175: 'Because it guarantees the state's existence, power in relation to other states is the ultimate standard by which the internal affairs of the state must be measured'.

63. Richard Hofstadter, *The American Political Tradition* (London: Jonathan Cape, 1948), pp. 70–1; Merrill D. Peterson, *The Great Triumvirate: Webster, Clay and Calhoun* (New York: Oxford UP, 1987), pp. 189–94; Ford, *Origins of Southern Radicalism*, pp. 123–8; George Dangerfield, *The Awakening of American Nationalism* (New York: Harper & Row, 1965), pp. 284–7.

though such a power to block laws would inevitably transform the very character of the Constitution – and at the instigation of individual states, not by a majority of three-quarters of them. Later secessionists drew the obvious lesson that such a formulation could work against the South as well as for her. Secondly, despite all the references to justice and the judiciary, the nullifiers overlooked 'the fundamental political law', as Martin Wight terms it, 'that the first condition of justice is an enforced order'. He further explains: 'It is possible to conceive an unjust order; it is possible to conceive, and even slowly to create, a just order; it is impossible (except for the theoretical anarchist) to conceive a just disorder'. Yet this is what the nullifiers demanded. The chaos and instability warranted by a bid to build a just disorder into the workings of the United States Constitution would have spawned conflict between the individual states as they attempted, in various shifting groupings, to jostle and compete with one another. They would transform the United States into an elected but impotent polity like the Holy Roman Empire, in which the name 'United States' would be reduced to a geographical expression. Within this region groups of states would seek supremacy and invite outside, stronger powers, to assist them in this object. That is to say, the mechanisms of an *international* rather than a national society would develop. 'Anarchy is the characteristic', Wight reminds us, 'that distinguishes international politics from ordinary politics'. Under such pressure the twin goals of continental dominion and the spread of democracy would be thwarted. Finally, it was this anarchy that later secessionist writers deplored; the means must be sought to unify the South, otherwise disparate parts of a slaveowning republic might fight one another. Such a process could not be sustained on the basis of South Carolina's singular feud with the Federal government.[64]

The crisis spluttered into life only slowly. In 1830 although provoked to fury by a bill presented to the House of Representatives by Charles F. Mercer of Virginia, permitting federal subsidies for the colonization of free Negroes in Africa, the nullifiers made little progress. The other southern states ignored their calls for a convention. South Carolina was a unique southern entity in these years; secessionist radicalism flourished because the upcountry and lowcountry factions were reconciled and not in

64. Freehling, *Prelude*, pp. 160–6, 169–70, 173–2; Martin Wight, *Power Politics*, ed. Hedley Bull and Carsten Holbraad (Leicester UP, 1978), pp. 102, 212–13.

competition. This was not true of, say, Virginia and Alabama. Calhoun knew that any rupture could be resolved peaceably only 'if the government abstained from enforcing the laws', and that seemed unlikely given the tenor of the man in the White House. With a reputation for revolutionary fervour, the nullifiers were defeated in the legislative elections of October 1830. By a small majority (and not the two-thirds required) they succeeded in saving face by pushing through a vote for a convention. On 12 July 1831, ignoring the vague but pointed declarations of the president that he would enforce the laws, the nullifiers set up a States Rights and Free Trade Association in Charleston. Its leaders then travelled the state in a tumult of excitement, reviewing the militia and persuading the electorate of the justice and glory of their cause. Those who disagreed were called 'submissionists' – supine and timid and neglectful of the state's honour. The unionists' response was hardly dynamic and striking; and the nullifiers, by deprecating the likelihood of 'coercion', gained ground. Their case was given point, with a hint of further potential of spreading the conflict, when Georgia ignored a Supreme Court ruling, supporting the right of the Cherokee Indians to stay on their lands.

In the 1832 campaign the nullifiers won 76 per cent of the popular vote and secured control of the legislature with ample majorities in both houses. James Hamilton Jr declared that the battle was one 'at the outposts, by which, if we succeed in repulsing the enemy, *the citadel would be safe*'. The previous year Nat Turner had gone on the rampage in Virginia. Yet the nullifiers still sought to defend slavery only indirectly by continuing to attack the tariff. Perhaps they needed a visible target on which to direct their distant and somewhat intermittent fire; the abolitionist movement was as yet so tiny and fragmentary that it was difficult to keep it in their sights or treat it as an ominous danger. But the relationship between slavery and nullification was incontrovertible. The nullification campaign was a pre-emptive strike. It would simultaneously improve the economic standing of slavery and deliver a fatal blow to the pretensions of the abolitionist agitators before they grew too strong. These calculations were worth the small risk of provoking civil war.[65]

65. Ford, *Origins of Southern Radicalism*, pp. 130–41; Freehling, *Prelude*, pp. 196–204, 206, 224–30, 231–6, 241–4, 256–9; Robert V. Remini, *Andrew Jackson and the Course of American Freedom, 1822–32* (New York: Harper & Row, 1981), pp. 232–4, and pp. 277–8 for the reasons for his acquiescence in Georgia's defiance of the Supreme Court.

It may have spluttered into life but once it had ignited the momentum of crisis gathered pace rapidly. In the space of a month a Nullification Convention had organized itself and met in November 1832. 'A protective tariff shall no longer be enforced within the limits of South Carolina', it declared. Threats of immediate secession were uttered if Congress sought to intimidate South Carolina with threats of force. But these declarations were only so much bluster. South Carolina was isolated and nervous in case of a slave insurrection provoked by federal intervention. President Andrew Jackson acted quickly and decisively. General Winfield Scott was dispatched to Charleston to take command of all federal forces in the region and Forts Moultrie and Pinckney. Jackson also moved to persuade Congress to lower the tariff and reduce South Carolina's sense of grievance.[66] By lowering the tariff, Jackson hoped, so Silas Wright confided to Martin Van Buren that 'it may keep the other states south steady while he disciplines Messrs. Calhoun, Hamilton and Hayne'. There was a personal edge to Jackson's resolute desire to crush the nullifiers at the first opportunity. 'Altho I do not believe that the nullifiers will have the madness & folly to attempt to carry their mad schemes into execution', the president explained, '. . . I must be vigilant [*sic*], and not permit a surprise, and to do this effectually, I must be at my post, and scan with great care the signs of the times as they may arise'.[67]

On 10 December Jackson issued his Nullification Proclamation, claiming that any attempt at disunion by force amounted to treason. The Proclamation, rather like a papal bull, in its first sentence struck out in an affirmative tone, 'Our Federal Union, it must be preserved'.[68] The United States was a nation, he declared, not a league; the nation was supreme and could demand obedience to its laws. The nullifiers responded by trying to enforce a test oath to enforce obedience to the Convention's decrees. This move underlined, as the secession crisis was to do in 1860–61, that

66. Freehling, *Prelude*, pp. 262–6. The next six paragraphs are indebted to ch. 8 of this book.
67. Richard B. Latner, 'The Nullification Crisis and Republican Subversion', *Journal of Southern History* 43 (1977), pp. 22–31; Remini, *Jackson and the Course of American Freedom*, pp. 380–1, 388–9.
68. When Jackson received an honorary LLD at Harvard in 1833, the Latin translation of this sentence, and the question whether it was uttered at the degree ceremony, occasioned some controversy designed to ridicule Jackson's lack of education. This effort rebounded on its authors. See John William Ward, *Andrew Jackson: Symbol for an Age* (New York: Oxford UP, 1962), pp. 83–6.

any move to free the citizens of any state from the tyranny of federal legislation required a restriction of that freedom within the state. The commotion thus engendered threatened to stir up disaffection from South Carolina's vocal unionists. The nullifiers tried to overlook the violent ramifications of their acts by attempting to secure goods confiscated by the federal authorities through the South Carolina courts – hardly a rousing manifestation of the martial spirit. The Charleston mercantile class was substantially unionist and willing to pay any duties owed to the federal authorities.[69]

Neither were the nullifier military forces very imposing. Twenty-five thousand volunteers were raised, but an army is not made just by calling men to the colours. They lacked discipline, training or arms; the reservoir of state funds was sucked dry before half of them were properly equipped. Threats by the nullifiers to resort to guerrilla tactics were empty; such action would have ensured the self-destruction of plantation agriculture. 'If in each District only *one hundred* such men could be secured' – the mounted minute men – 'we would have the means of throwing 2,500 of the *élite* of the whole State upon a given point'. An effective armed force, with a responsive chain of command and levels of training, cannot be thrown together in this casual manner. The nullifiers were absurdly optimistic. Yet the illusion, that armed force could be mustered quickly and thrown into battle to solve intractable political dilemmas decisively, grew rather than diminished over the next thirty years.

Of course, federal units standing on the defensive prevented the nullifiers from pushing matters to the proof. In a sense this was an unfortunate by-product of the peaceful resolution of the Nullification Crisis. If the nullifier volunteers had been routed then the exaggerated expectations of what force could achieve for the South might have been dissipated before 1861. In any case, the nullifiers were caught on the horns of a dilemma and they showed more prudence than would be displayed under similar circumstances thirty years later. They were in a clear minority in the South as a whole. They had to act defensively, yet defensive measures could not attain the quick, clean success that their deteriorating financial position demanded. The unwonted caution that the isolation of the state required not only meant that

69. Latner, 'Nullification Crisis', pp. 32–3; Ford, *Origins of Southern Radicalism*, pp. 140–1.

nullification was reduced to a mere legal expedient reliant on local courts, but weakened the armed force that the state was trying to raise. The longer the crisis continued the better organized became the 'Washington Societies' of 8,000 unionist volunteers. Jackson sent them 5,000 stands of arms and called them his *posse comitatus* – the 'power of the community'. These expressed Jackson's preference for dealing with the nullifiers through the processes of civil rather than martial law. Though he had full authority under the 1807 Act to employ the regular army and the militia, these two forces would still constitute a *posse comitatus* so long as a civilian remained in charge to enforce the provisions of the civil law. Jackson had little military power at his disposal. He was too experienced a general not to realize that the confrontation with South Carolina would be won by tilting the delicate balance of weakness in his favour. Jackson was also able to apply pressure on the nullifiers by maintaining the tariff by what amounted to a blockade of Charleston harbour. The only way the nullifiers could break this would be by a flagrantly aggressive act on the federal forts housing the customs posts. South Carolina was isolated and vulnerable; she would have to strike the first blow and escalate the crisis should she seek to escape from Jackson's grip.[70]

The success of President Jackson's policy of isolating and strangling South Carolina was endangered by two rather impulsive acts. First, he contemplated the arrest of the leading nullifiers. Any attempt to round them up would be opposed by the unionists on the grounds that it would provoke stronger resistance. Secondly, at the end of December 1832, Jackson issued a message seeking special powers which were embodied in the 'Force Bill'. This provided him with no substantially greater powers than he already enjoyed, but he was empowered to use the army swiftly without giving prior warning. The general tone of the Force Bill was conciliatory, stressing the need to avoid a clash of arms; but if this should occur South Carolina must make the first aggressive move. Given the bellicosity and exaggeration that greeted the mildest move by Jackson to resist South Carolina's pretensions, the Force Bill was denounced fervently by the nullifiers. Martin Van Buren, the new vice president, agreed that military forces should be used only *after* South Carolina had violated federal law. The predicament that would confront Lincoln in 1861 had already

70.   Cooper, 'Federal Military Intervention in Domestic Disorders', pp. 133–4.

been rehearsed in this crisis.[71] Momentarily, it seemed that South Carolina's isolation would be broken. A convention met in Georgia, a state which had dabbled in nullification; but its sympathizers were routed and the majority of its delegates supported the Force Bill. South Carolina remained isolated and friendless.[72]

The crisis moved slowly towards a peaceful close. Two public gatherings, on 21 January and the 'Fatal First' on 1 February 1833, summed up the South Carolinian dilemma. Jackson was burnt in effigy at the latter, but this was an outburst of frustration at the state's powerlessness; at the former it was decreed that 'all occasions of conflict . . . should be sedulously avoided'. The virtual blockade of Charleston was complete; all foreign ships were permitted to enter the port only after they had paid tariff duties. Nullification had been nullified, at any rate neutered. There was much South Carolinian bluster that an ordinance of secession would follow the ordinance of nullification. Calhoun now urged prudence. As Freehling observes, the attempt to avoid war by threatening war is 'a decided gamble' and a colossal risk for the friendless, weaker party who could not possibly win. For the nullifiers to plunge South Carolina into a civil war would have been suicidal.[73] The Force Bill passed comfortably through both the House and the Senate. Simultaneously, Jackson supported a compromise tariff that reduced the duties over a period of a decade to 20 per cent. This reduced further the already remote possibility of assistance from other southern states; indeed Virginia moved to mediate. In March 1833 the Ordinance of Nullification was repealed; yet as an empty act of defiance the Force Bill was nullified. There was an element of schoolboyish mischief about this act. But it was surely another example of the exaggerated faith in legal enactment as a substitute for real military strength. Even McDuffie, an unreconstructed nullifier, observed sardonically that 'the army and navy of the United States required something more than an ordinance to nullify them'[74] So ended, in rather farcical

71.   Robert V. Remini, *The Life of Andrew Jackson* (New York: Harper & Row, 1988), pp. 245–8: (p. 246) 'With respect to possible military action, the President's message was relatively tame'. Latner, 'Nullification Crisis and Republican Subversion', pp. 35–6; for Lincoln's dilemma, see below, pp. 121, 255.

72.   Michael P. Johnson, *Towards a Patriarchal Republic: The Secession of Georgia* (Baton Rouge: Louisiana State UP, 1977), pp. 91–2.

73.   Freehling, *Prelude*, p. 291.

74.   Remini, *Life of Andrew Jackson*, pp. 247–51: Freehling, *Prelude*, p. 297.

fashion, the most serious threat to her existence that the United States had faced since the War of 1812.

What was the final significance of the Nullification Crisis? 'Without union,' Jackson had proclaimed, 'our independence and liberty, would never have been achieved, without union they can never be maintained. . . . The loss of liberty, of all good government, of peace, plenty and happiness must inevitably follow a dissolution of the Union'.[75] Jackson had successfully prevented an attempt to dissolve the coherence of the Constitution by the unilateral action of one state. But, of course, it was perfectly possible for the Federal government to continue overawing individual states in this way so long as they remained isolated and without allies. The Compromise Tariff and the Force Act were signed together by the president on the last day of his first term of office. 'These are but the forms in which the despotic nature of the Government is evinced', claimed R. B. Rhett at the March convention which had signalled South Carolina's defiant surrender, ' – but it is the despotism which constitutes the evil: and until the Government is made a Limited Government . . . there is no liberty – no security for the South'.[76] That security could be attained by drawing the southern states into closer cooperation to reduce the overweening power of the Federal government to intimidate slave states into doing its bidding. Langdon Cheves lamented that 'The metaphysics of *nullification* is the worst shape in which the principle of separate action can be embodied. . . . I deprecate and deplore that principle in toto, as unwise, rash, dangerous, and in its effects worse than ineffectual'. The idea of establishing a cohesive southern group, first mooted by the president of South Carolina College, Thomas Cooper, in 1827 was given greater credence. Unilateral action by 'one of the suffering States alone', commented Cheves, 'will be a measure of feebleness, subject to many hazards. Any union among the same States, will be a measure of strength, almost certain of success'.[77] From their initial rebuff in 1832–33 secessionists drew the crucial lesson that if they were to challenge the Federal government successfully, their strength lay, not in the power of their vocal denunciation of Washington's iniquities, but in their numbers.

75.   Latner, 'Nullification Crisis and Republican Subversion', p. 20.
76.   Wiltse, *The New Nation*, pp. 122–3; Freehling, *Prelude*, p. 297.
77.   Archie V. Huff, Jr, *Langdon Cheves of South Carolina* (Columbia: University of South Carolina Press, 1977; Tricentennial Studies no. 111). pp. 219–20.

The reasons why the crisis did not explode into civil war are threefold. First, the nullifiers were too weak *vis-à-vis* the Jackson Administration. Jackson maintained the pressure on them unremittingly and ensured that they received no succour from other slave states. In any case, this was not forthcoming: conditions were not right in other southern states to produce a radical, united front opposed to the Federal government. Secondly, Jackson could act decisively and swiftly to contain the crisis because it was so restricted; it did not present an overwhelming challenge to the federal authorities on the scale of the secession crisis of 1860–61, during which significant numbers of commissioned officers resigned and federal installations were overrun. Jackson had acted skilfully and promptly throughout, although there are grounds for concluding that on a number of occasions the president acted correctly but his reasoning was based on faulty calculations. He underestimated the extent to which the behaviour of the nullifiers was governed by anxieties about slavery; he was inclined to explain their motives by reference to the unscrupulous behaviour of a clique of frustrated, ambitious demagogues who had conspired to sabotage the Constitution. But his actions did much to extinguish the lurking danger of civil war. Thirdly, the nullifiers themselves, for all their bluster, behaved prudently before plunging over the broken precipice of civil war. Calhoun rather than Rhett was their role model. South Carolinian unionism remained vital and acted as a brake on the more extravagant designs of the nullifiers. As the later secessionists refined their case, gathered strength and became more insistent, the steadying influence of caution and persistent unionism gradually withered away.[78]

Conclusion

This chapter has advanced a number of arguments about American history in the first half of the nineteenth century. It has suggested that centrifugal and separatist forces were inherent in the establishment of a great, continental state. Although different in many other ways, the United States shared this basic structural problem with some of the large states of Latin America. Obviously,

---

78. Ford, *Origins of Southern Radicalism*, pp. 141–4; Latner, 'Nullification Crisis and Republican Subversion'. pp. 23–8.

the search for the origins of a great war cannot be allowed to dictate our entire perspective on this period. If it did, then the *ante-bellum* period would be conceived as nothing more than the prelude to the Civil War, and all other historical experience reduced to a determinist teleology. 'Causation, like the circulation of currency', David Thomson once reminded us, 'is multilateral and complex and cannot be traced in straight lines from A to B to C'.[79] We must resist all temptations to think in terms of 'inevitability' in history.

Political disruption in the United States, and the rise of some form of separatist movement, would take a democratic shape. A meeting of alienated states in some form of convention (much as the United States herself had confronted the oppressive measures of the colonial power, Great Britain, in 1774–75) was possible. This process would take time and the elements fermenting discontent would need space, both figuratively and geographically, in which to operate, conspire and organize in safety. It is striking how all early efforts at separatism within the United States had failed because of the speed with which the federal government had acted against them. There was also a lack of propulsion within the separatist movement which failed to persuade the doubters both within and without South Carolina. The degree of force applied to persuade the malcontents to abandon their disloyal course was remarkably small. Moreover, they were not offered the opportunity to rectify the balance of force weighed against them by inviting an outside great power to intervene and assist them, thus reintroducing the balance of power to North America.

Indeed, it was the efforts of the United States in eradicating the balance of power from North America by continental expansion to safeguard democracy, that actually brought about the conditions – disruption and disagreement – that the Founding Fathers had sought to avoid. And that expansion raised in its most stark form disagreement over the future complexion of the Union. Thus the expansion and development of the United States made it more difficult to control the centrifugal forces that were unleashed, giving greater space and more time in which they could operate. Sectionalism flourishes when it can pursue an issue that reinforces physical separation, such as slavery. As slavery became pervasive in the South, so that all other issues were coloured by contact with it,

79. David Thomson, *The Aims of History* (London: Thames & Hudson, 1969). p. 64.

so disillusion would grow. But the South did not reject the ideology of Union; it expropriated it, and perverted it for parochial ends.

Such an argument should not overemphasize instability. There were strong factors promoting Union: the machinery of government and election, the inculcation of common political and social values and the shared (indeed exaggerated) respect for the judiciary.[80] But the main concern of this chapter is to assert the paradox of American history. Thus: even though competitive diversity was the essence of American growth, *within stability lay instability; at the core of Union lay disunion.* To suggest that some form of separatist movement was probable in the United States in the mid-nineteenth century is not to suggest that the Civil War itself was inevitable and bound to occur when it did. Historians (especially those of the 'revisionist' school) were prepared to argue that it was 'avoidable'. This is a common assumption of those who either live through an unpleasant historical experience or live with its consequences.[81] But to have provided the circumstances which would have rendered the Civil War avoidable would have demanded the creation of a quite different kind of state; and this certainly would not have afforded a guarantee that some other kind of war would not have broken out with quite different imperatives and causes.

80. Parish, *American Civil War*, pp. 24–5.
81. As E. H. Carr, *What is History?* (Harmondsworth: Penguin, 1971), pp. 97–8, has pointed out.

CHAPTER TWO

The South and its Peculiar Institution

The climate renders excesses of all kinds very dangerous, particularly those of the table; and yet, insensible or fearless of danger, they live on and enjoy a short and a merry life. . . . Can he [the author] imagine himself in a country the establishment of which is so recent?

J. HECTOR ST JOHN DE CREVECOEUR, *Letters from an American Farmer*[1]

An exquisitely sharpened hatred for the White Man is of course an emotion not difficult for Negroes to harbour.

WILLIAM STYRON, *The Confessions of Nat Turner*[2]

During his second inaugural address in March 1865, President Abraham Lincoln reflected on the coming of the Civil War. Commenting that the southern slave population 'Constituted a peculiar and powerful interest', he continued, 'All knew that this interest was, somehow, the cause of the war. To strengthen, perpetuate, and extend this interest was the object for which the insurgents would rend the Union, even by war; while the government claimed no right to do more than to restrict the territorial enlargement of it.'[3] How the South became the source of a separatist insurgency, the focus of a regional desire for independence is the subject of this chapter. Its main theme will be to demonstrate that slavery underlay the increasingly particularist

1.   J. Hector St John de Crevecoeur, *Letters from an American Farmer*, ed. Albert E. Stone (Harmondsworth: Penguin American Library, 1981), p. 167.
2.   William Styron, *The Confessions of Nat Turner* (New York: Bantam, 1988), p. 208.
3.   Peter J. Parish (ed.) *Abraham Lincoln: Speeches and Letters* (London: Dent, 1993), p. 288.

attitude evinced in the South. This eventually transcended an interpretation of what constituted the southern political and economic interest; it assumed a social and cultural aspect as well. By 1860 most southerners agreed that they had, in an incredibly short period of time, developed a distinct civilization, and were culturally different from other Americans. It is a secondary argument of this chapter that the distinctiveness of the South has been exaggerated. But it was *what* southerners really believed that counted, and most southerners assumed that their quest for a separate national identity was justified by cultural fact. 'The South is an attitude of mind', as one historian once put it, 'and a way of behaviour just as much as it is a territory.'[4]

The rise of slavery

Clearly, in any assessment of how distinct a region the South was before 1861, slavery must be the pre-eminent factor. Chattel slavery in the American South has been one of the central preoccupations of United States historians since about 1950. This effort has produced some of the most fertile and distinguished historical writing since then; clearly, it is an enormous subject and only an outline of it can be given in this chapter. The focus will be on those elements in southern society which contributed to the growth of separatism. No effort has been made to cover the social aspect of slavery in detail, the vitality, or otherwise, of the slave family, the plantation household, the 'slave community' and culture in the plantations, and other aspects that are not relevant to the study of war origins. But those elements which contributed to the tensions latent in the *ante-bellum* South will be considered.[5]

The striking feature about the *ante-bellum* South is that the southern economy was dominated by slavery; the social life of those who owned slaves was dominated by slavery; and the major political preoccupation of those whites who did not own slaves was determined by an overwhelming desire to dominate race relations, and ensure that the Negro population remained in a subordinate

---

4.   Francis Butler Simkins, *A History of the South*, 2nd edn (New York: Alfred A. Knopf, 1961), p. ix.
5.   On earlier changes in interpretation, see John White, 'Whatever Happened to the Slave Family in the Old South?', *Journal of American Studies* 8 (1974), pp. 383–90; the central work is Peter J. Parish, *Slavery: History and Historians* (New York: HarperCollins, 1990), especially Chs 4 and 5.

position. The one startling feature of slavery in the modern world (that is, since 1700) is the demographic change that it brought about. Before 1861 it has been estimated that some 9,566,000 slaves were transported to the Americas; 427,000 made their way to North America, that is to say, 4.5 per cent of the total. (The slavery exports to Brazil alone were 8.5 times that number.) Yet the total slave population in North America in 1865, at the time of the passage of the Thirteenth Amendment, was over 4 million. Thus the increase of the slave population was entirely due to domestic factors, and not to any sudden importation or revival of the slave trade. If the Brazilian slave population had increased on this scale, then by 1850 the number of Negro slaves in Brazil would have numbered 127,645,000, or double the number of slaves of African descent to be found in the *entire* hemisphere. Thus conditions in North America were suitable for a substantial increase by 1861 of the slave population.[6] Of course, the spread of slavery in the nineteenth century was denounced as wicked and un-Christian by various groups, broadly described as 'Abolitionists', but it is as well to be aware at the outset that though by 1860, the South was moving beyond the pale of western liberal civilization (although this would not prevent many British liberals, such as W. E. Gladstone and Lord Acton, from sympathizing with her bid for independence), the South was more like many other societies in the western world than the North. These sympathized with the South's dislike of unfettered democracy, her desire to retain a large measure of her work-force in a form of peonage, and applauded her elevation of rural mores at the expense of cold-blooded exploitation of market, industrial capitalism. Some societies (especially in eastern Europe) had illiteracy rates that exceeded the South's; they too upheld family, kin and patriarchy in social structures not dissimilar to feudalism as the essence of social life.

The peculiar and singular characteristics of southern society were the product of the invention of the cotton gin in 1793, a technological development which promoted the harvesting of the cotton crop (especially the short-staple cotton plant), and the

---

6.   James M. McPherson, *Battle Cry of Freedom: The Civil War Era* (New York: Oxford UP, 1988), p. 860. By comparison, other forms such as kidnapping were trifling, see Eugene H. Berwanger, 'The Case of Stirrup and Edwards, 1861–1870: The Kidnapping and Georgia Enslavement of West Indian Blacks', *Georgia Historical Quarterly* LXXVI (spring 1992), pp. 1–18.

Harrison Frontier Land Act (1800). This limited the minimum price of government land to two dollars per acre, and payment could be made easily in four annual instalments. These two developments prompted the frantic exploitation of the land acquired by the Louisiana Purchase, which was suitable for plantation agriculture. In addition, growth was stimulated by European demand for cotton and the rapid dispossession of Indian lands. Occasional setbacks occurred, such as the Recession of 1819, but until 1837 there were 'flush times in Alabama and Mississippi'. In 1836 an observer reported that 'they do business in a kind of frenzy, largely on credit'. These states exhibited the kind of restlessness characteristic of the frontier. One settler's daughter informed her brother that their father was getting restless: 'I don't know why it is but none of them are satisfied here. . . . You have no idea how tired I am of hearing about moving; it is the subject of conversation every time pa and brother meet and that is very often'.

A drain of population occurred in a south westerly direction, as settlers moved to open up virgin lands. For example, whereas North Carolina had one of the highest birth rates in the Union in the years 1830–40, thereafter her population remained static. But the population of Alabama and Mississippi increased by 76 per cent and 154 per cent respectively; and the slave population increased by even larger numbers, 114 per cent and 197 per cent respectively. During the 1850s, the population of Texas tripled. In eastern Texas during the decade 1850–60 the production of cotton increased from 58,161 to 431,463 bales.[7] Two conclusions can be drawn from this brief survey. First, that southern 'civilization' was extremely new and unsettled: its roots were shallow and its tradition short. Secondly, that the image of the great plantation was not so pervasive in the social life of the southern states as later sentimental apologists were inclined to claim. In the total southern population of some 8 million, only 46,274 were categorized as 'planters', that is, property-holders who owned more than 20 slaves. Indeed, fewer than 3,000 planters owned more than 100 slaves; only 11 men held more than 500 slaves. Southern agrarian life was dominated by small farmers who owned a handful of slaves or none at all. The limited number of

---

7.   Clement Eaton, *The Growth of Southern Civilization, 1790–1860* (New York: Harper & Row, 1961), pp. 25, 32, 35, 38–9, 44–5.

planters, however, does not by any means vitiate the argument that they dominated southern agrarian society.[8]

It is this strong inequality of wealth and the social and political dominance of slaveowners that demarcated the South from the North during this period. It was *not* that the South enjoyed a unique, long-established culture that was at variance with the North; on the contrary it shared many features with the North, especially the entrepreneurial emphasis, the fevered speculation in land, and the frontier spirit. But even though the North obviously experienced a fair measure of social and economic inequality, the two sections can be distinguished clearly by the question of degree.

It was one of the services discharged by the controversial book by Robert W. Fogel and Stanley L. Engerman, *Time on the Cross* (2 vols, 1974), that it succeeded in emphasizing the entrepreneurial strength of the South, with an argument which moved away from the old stereotype of a soporific, idle and generally decadent southern planter class, which was indifferent to making money. The massive increase in the output of cotton is without doubt supporting evidence; the South did not voluntarily place itself outside the mainstream American tradition of elevating 'the market' and the entrepreneur to a place of near worship. In 1790 cotton production was tiny, a mere 3,000 bales; by 1810 it had increased to 178,000 bales, then jumped to 732,000 bales by 1830, and then more exponentially to 4,500,000 bales by 1860.[9]

But Fogel and Engerman greatly exaggerate the productivity of slavery. They were inclined to judge the institution by the standard of modern managerial techniques. Furthermore, they confuse the phenomenal strength of the cotton boom with the efficiency of slavery, and tended to conflate the two. The tremendous appetite of growing textile industries for cotton in the industrialized world led to the opening up of virgin lands, with high yields in the cotton lands of the South West. This was not the result of a well-ordered, extremely efficient system of labour. It also indicates another area of fragility in southern prosperity, because the market boom was temporary (indeed the demand was reduced after 1860). Southern spokesmen were prone to assume that an expansion of the order of 70 per cent between 1857 and 1860 could be sustained and would remain a stable and permanent feature of southern political economy. This may help to explain

    8.   Ibid., p. 98.
    9.   Robert W. Fogel and Stanley L. Engerman, *Time on the Cross* (Boston, MA: Little, Brown, 1974), I, p. 44.

the arrogant tone and truculent manner of some southern spokesmen by the late 1850s.[10]

Yet though we may discount some of the sweeping comparisons made between southern and northern agriculture – that southern plantation agriculture was more efficient, that the slave labour force was closely regulated, highly organized and specialized, and that the quality of Negro labour was discounted because of racial prejudices, and that, consequently, the slaveowners reaped economies of scale – one outstanding fact emerges for our purposes. There was nothing like plantation agriculture in the North.[11] Yet this contrast has had a distorting influence on the study of slavery and the *ante-bellum* South, because (as a number of commentators acknowledge) studies of slavery have largely been focused on the atypical great plantations. To recapitulate, at the time of the presidential election in 1860, 47 per cent of slaves were the property of farmers who owned fewer than 20. This percentage actually increased in the Upper South, in Virginia and Tennessee in particular, with 61.7 per cent, but decreased in the Lower South, where only 38 per cent of slaves were the property of small slaveholders.[12]

We tend to think of slavery as essentially a rural phenomenon but it had an important urban aspect; an analysis of this is crucial in determining whether slavery could be exported westwards. Certainly 90 per cent of slaves lived outside the city; but the urban slave population grew steadily in the years 1820–50 and then declined. One explanation for this might be that slaveowners in the town could find alternative sources of labour when required. The temptation to sell slaves when their prices were high could not always be resisted, and it is as well to remember that the biggest slave markets were in the cities, and thus it was easier to dispose of them than it would be for others living far distant from the urban centres. The fall in the slave population in towns and cities probably had much more connection with the increase in the numbers of 'poor whites', who entered the labour market prepared to undertake menial labour, than it had with any 'decline' either of the political power of slaveowners or in the

10. *Time on the Cross*, I, p. 251. See Parish, *Slavery*, pp. 45–9, and Donald Ratcliffe, 'The *Das Kapital* of American Negro Slavery? *Time on the Cross* after Two Years', *Durham University Journal* 100 (Dec. 1976), esp. pp. 110–11.

11. *Time on the Cross*, I, pp. 192–6, 201, 203, 215–18; Parish, *Slavery*, p. 49.

12. Eaton, *Growth of Southern Civilization*, p. 83.

utility of slavery. Still, worries over the security of urban slavery remained strong.

Certainly the institution of slavery adapted to the urban environment. In theory the regulation of each slave's life was just as rigid as on the plantation. They could not venture out at night without a pass, and similar documents were needed to allow them to sell or purchase goods in the market or shops. But in practice many slaveowners found that it took time and bother to keep filling out passes, and because the majority of slaves were law-abiding, slowly this law was enforced with less zeal than previously. A grocer informed the *Charleston Mercury* in 1835 that 'The public voice is against the law, because it is opposed by reason and justice'. Certainly slaves were capable of a variety of skills and occupations, and the 'hiring out' of slave labour was common. The urban demand grew faster than the available supply and prices thus rose; simultaneously the price of free labour fell, a development which restricted the growth of urban slavery. It is, as modern scholars point out, difficult to imagine urban slavery – despite its adaptability – surviving the strains imposed by modern transport systems, increased educational opportunities and the factory system which followed in the train of industrial growth. Southern towns and cities before 1861 were far from being modern, industrial metropolises. They certainly showed, however, that slavery could adapt and survive outside the system of plantation agriculture.[13] But the tensions resulting from this between whites and blacks (free and slave, because free blacks always lay under a pall of suspicion and the perpetual threat of re-enslavement) grew, with resultant segregation, and the realization that slavery became unmanageable if not uncontrollable, as slave numbers grew. Therefore moving slaves westward became a more attractive proposition.[14]

One-quarter of all southern free blacks lived in the towns and cities. Free blacks endured a considerable measure of discrimination in jobs throughout the United States. In southern cities, if anything, their lot was happier than in the North. In the cities of the Deep South, for instance, there were greater employment opportunities than either in the Upper South or the North, so that opportunities for free blacks in Charleston or New

13. Claudia Dale Goldin, *Urban Slavery in the American South, 1820–1860* (Chicago UP, 1976), pp. 1, 9–10, 25, 27, 49, 123–7.
14. The dispute between Goldin and earlier scholars is not relevant to this study. For a discussion see Parish, *Slavery*, pp. 100–1.

Orleans were greater than in New York. The widespread racial prejudice that we associate with the South did not prevent the creation of employment opportunities for free blacks, though this certainly does not mean that access to employment was anything like equal with whites. One of the reasons for this comparative tolerance was that in the South the free black population was the product of manumission and not emancipation, and that southerners were accustomed to seeing Negroes working in various trades in both the towns and country. But this did not prevent the free black population from being the object of dark suspicion during periods of crisis, because in the South they were not subject, as many whites saw it, to the controlling influence of slavery; and both in North and South free blacks were often involved in the hiding and spiriting away of runaway slaves. Some southern free blacks represented the most able and diligent members of the entire black population. Some of these succeeded in making their way in a white man's world, acquiring great wealth, some political influence, and in the case of William Ellison, a mulatto master-craftsman, who had made a fortune producing cotton gins, owning larger cotton plantations and more slaves than many prosperous whites. But such men were very much the exception rather than the rule.[15] The great majority of southern free blacks remained firmly embedded at the bottom of the rural social order as labourers and tenants. The condition of free blacks, and the anomalous position they enjoyed in the South whereby they were tolerated more than in the North yet distrusted, illustrates the profound ambivalence and marked tensions that underlay the 'peculiar institution'.

The attitudes of whites to the slaves are, needless to say, difficult to categorize precisely. But we must not let twentieth-century reactions influence unduly our consideration of a nineteenth-century institution. This is the problem with Stanley Elkins's much discussed comparison of Negro slavery with what he terms 'concentration camps'. Whatever its other merits, this analogy which seeks to explain the formation in adults of 'Sambo-like', childish, giggling behaviour among Negro slaves, lacks a certain

15. Leonard P. Curry, *The Free Black in Urban America, 1800–1850* (Chicago UP, 1981), pp. 33–6, 229; Michael P. Johnson and James L. Roark, *Black Masters: A Free Family of Color in the Old South* (New York: Norton, 1984), pp. xi–xii, 25, 47–8, 53–4, 63.

exactitude,[16] because Elkins adopted an inappropriate model of a 'closed' system – the concentration camp – which he wrongly conflated with the plantation regime. Elkins's analogy might have been more persuasive if he had compared American slavery with Soviet Gulags, or other systems that perpetuate long-term incarcerations. In any case, Elkins's brutal and extreme analogy seems quite inappropriate for the nineteenth-century southern states.[17] Eugene Genovese has made the convincing case that as slavery preceded racism and strict racial subordination (segregation was largely a product of the 1890s) that the American South developed 'a historically unique kind of paternalist society'. The paternal element, though exaggerated was not altogether imaginary. Those slaveholders who lived on farms with ten or fewer slaves did not bother with a division of labour, and therefore lived and worked under conditions of considerable intimacy with their slaves. Having to live together in a stable society certainly engendered a more paternal tone than was true of Brazil, for instance, and this tended to disguise the element of real power differentiating the master and slave relationship. The slaves could bring influence to bear on their owners. This was most notable in regard to their relationships with overseers, and slaves were very quick to exploit differences between masters and overseers.

Thus Genovese argues that the southern legal system was constructed to protect slaves from brutal exploitation, 'however many preposterous legal fictions it invented'. Thus the law protected them more assuredly than was the case in Latin America. Some slaveowners even intervened in the affairs of cruel neighbours who maltreated their slaves, though their motive was just as much self-interest as benevolence. 'Harmony among neighbours is very important in the successful management of slaves', argued one planter. Race relations regulated by law codified white supremacy, but the overall effect was the fusion of

16.   For an example, see Frances Kemble's description of her arrival in Suffolk, Virginia: 'the Negroes gathered in admiring crowds . . . full of idle merriment and unmeaning glee, and regard with an intensity of curiosity, perfectly ludicrous, the appearance and proceedings of such whites as they easily perceive are strangers'. See her *Journal of a Residence on a Georgian Plantation in 1838–1839*, ed. John A. Scott (London: Jonathan Cape, 1961), Kemble to Harriet St Leger, Jan. 1839, p. 17; also see p. 49.

17.   Stanley M. Elkins, *Slavery: A Problem in American Institutional and Intellectual Life*, 3rd edn (Chicago UP, 1976), pp. 104–15. Elkins is actually describing an extermination camp here.

Anglo- with African-America, and a less harsh form of slavery than that which prevailed elsewhere in the western hemisphere. As Genovese sums up: 'for complex reasons of self-interest, common humanity and Christian sensibility, they [slaveholders] could not help contributing to their slaves' creative survival; that many slaveholders ... imbibed much of their slaves' culture and sensibility while imparting to their slaves much of their own'.[18]

These less than damning comments should not be misconstrued as in any way supporting the turn-of-the-century apologists of slavery, such as Ulrich B. Phillips. Phillips's books stressed the paternal regard of slaveowners, and the happy simplicity of the slaves' affection for their kindly, paternal masters. This approach was *ipso facto* a justification for the cause of the Confederacy and southern secession (which after all, had only occurred forty years before Phillips was writing). If slavery could be presented as a benevolent institution, then Phillips could place a moral gloss on the southern *casus belli*. Thus if secession could be explained exclusively as a political cause – a struggle for Independence – rather than a war to defend slavery, then slavery could be downgraded as a cause of the war, and the South presented in an altogether more attractive light. The accusations of the critics of slavery could be dismissed as baseless and the South could be depicted as seeking self-determination for her 'unique' society.

But the majority of slaveowners should be depicted as neither monsters of brutality, nor paragons of humanity. James H. Hammond, planter, senator from South Carolina and secessionist spokesman, had at least two children by slave women. Yet these children remained in slavery. 'I cannot free these people and send them North. It would be cruelty to them'. He concluded confidently, 'slavery *in the family* will be their happiest earthly condition'.[19] Yet though some years earlier, in 1841, Hammond claimed that he was not 'a monster of inhumanity', there can be no doubting his equation of slaves with his other animals, as 'slaves *are property* and that we have a right to claim them as such'. And lamenting the rigours of the unhealthy climate, he complained that 'I have lost 89 negroes and at least 50 mules and

18.   Eugene D. Genovese, *Roll, Jordan, Roll: The World the Slaves Made* (London: André Deutsch, 1975), pp. xvi–xvii, 3, 5–6, 7–10, 14–16, 22–31, 33–40, 42.
19.   J. H. Hammond to H. Hammond, 19 Feb. 1856, *Secret and Sacred: The Diaries of James H. Hammond, a Southern Slaveholder*, ed. Carol Bleser (New York: Oxford UP, 1988), p. 19.

horses in 11 years'.[20] Nineteenth-century liberalism developed exalting property as the foundation of freedom; in the southern states, 'liberty' was upheld with equal fervour, but the property that supported that freedom was human. This perversion was a striking example of an important characteristic of the South, namely that liberal ideas could be transmogrified into very illiberal views.

This was equally true of liberal societies outside the South. Many of the most ardent southern sympathizers were to be found in that other bastion of nineteenth-century liberalism, Great Britain. Lord Acton, for instance, who laboured for much of his life on a projected *History of Freedom*, was both pro-southern and pro-slavery.[21] Many of the literary sources, were composed by British visitors to the southern states, however, as well as by itinerant northerners, like Frederick Law Olmsted. These are far from admiring. Such works are important, not only because they present a view that was at variance with the southern self-image, but because British visitors themselves were not uncomfortable in a hierarchical society, and thus their observations were frequently penetrating and shrewd. Although Charles Dickens's *American Notes* sometimes presents an unflattering picture of the United States in the 1840s, what really seems to have provoked the wrath of many of his American hosts (and reviewers), was his (largely second-hand) portrait of American slavery and its brutalizing influences. Much the most ferocious criticism of his book came from southern journals. This is indicative of how much comment by Americans on their institutions was influenced by views on slavery. 'Slavery is not a whit the more endurable', Dickens wrote, 'because some hearts are to be found which can partially resist its hardening influences; nor can the indignant tide of honest wrath stand still, because in its onward course it overwhelms a few who are comparatively innocent among a host of guilty'.[22] Of Virginia, Dickens recorded, 'there is an air of ruin and decay abroad, which is inseparable from the system'.[23] Frances Kemble, the British actress who married the heir of a Georgia plantation, observed slavery at first hand. She deplored slavery, loathed its effects on her children, and recounted in her *Journal* instances 'of the horrible injustice of this system of slavery' which condemned men

20. Ibid., pp. 88, 101 (entries for 21 Mar., 5 Aug. 1842).
21. Hugh Tulloch, *Acton* (London: Weidenfeld & Nicolson, 1988), p. 27.
22. Charles Dickens, *American Notes* (London: Glanville, 1982), pp. 210–16.
23. Ibid., p. 122.

'endowed with sufficient knowledge and capacity to be an engineer' to a life 'of utter physical destitution and degradation such as the most miserable dwelling of the poorest inhabitant of your free Northern villages never beheld the like of'.[24] Kemble published her *Journal* to counteract pro-Confederate sympathy in Britain. But this kind of literature is also significant because it reveals the *defence* of slavery mounted by southerners in moments of casual, if earnest conversation. That almost all of this literature was published with a polemical intent does not reduce its value in this regard. The main theme that emerges is the omnipresent *tension* in southern life which persisted despite numerous efforts on the part of slaveowners to reassure themselves and their families.

The desire to physically intimidate and psychologically dominate Negro slaves was, of course, paramount as slavery relied ultimately upon coercion. Even paternal masters aimed at a 'Design for absolute control' over the lives of their slaves. This involved interference in every aspect of their lives. It also involved, certainly by comparison with the Caribbean, a plentiful diet and attentive medical care. Slave housing, however, was primitive and uncomfortable. So was their clothing. 'The condition of domestic slaves . . . does not generally appear to be bad; but the ugly feature is', reflected Frances Trollope, ' . . . they have no power to change it'. Another British visitor, teaching in Virginia in 1860, recorded an otherwise 'kind-hearted, feeling man' explaining that 'some Negroes require to be broken in like dogs and horses, in order to establish a power over them, and keep them in subjection'.[25] This coercive power was justified on the grounds that slaves were habitual and addicted liars. As Frances Kemble explained, 'No Negro was to be believed on any occasion on any subject'. They were dissimulating shirkers who needed to be driven to be worked. Women were as bad as men, 'shamming themselves in the family way in order to obtain a diminution of their labour'.[26]

The institution of slavery also encountered an insoluble dilemma. However benevolent southerners may have deemed the institution to be, the more the humanity and individuality of slaves were acknowledged, the less tenable the institution became. As

24. Kemble, *Journal*, p. 188 (entry 14–17 Feb. 1839).

25. Peter Kolchin, *American Slavery* (Harmondsworth: Penguin, 1993, 1995), pp. 113–14, 120; Frances Trollope, *Domestic Manners of the Americans* (London: Folio Society, 1974), p. 183; Catherine Hopley, *Life in the South* (London: 1863; New York: Augustus M. Kelley, 1971), I, pp. 149, 150.

26. Kemble, *Journal*, pp. 155, 170 (entry for end Jan./beginning of Feb. 1839).

Frances Kemble emphasized, 'Every step they take towards intelligence and enlightenment lessens the probability of their acquiescing in their condition'.[27] Consequently, the institution relied on force and fear, not just more frequently, but more inconsistently. Frederick Douglass, a former slave, writer and abolitionist leader, supported this argument, when he explained that 'slaves, when inquired of as to their condition and character of their masters, almost universally say they are contented, and that their masters are kind'. Benevolence was relative. Douglass 'always measured the kindness of my master by the standard of kindness set up among slaveholders around us'.[28] The system was also very capricious. Fanny Kemble recounted with horror an example of a slave who was flogged for getting his wife baptized. Here was an example of the slow, dutiful, Christian improvement in the degraded and dirty condition of the slaves that abolitionist sympathizers approved of, and some slaveholders claimed they approved of, and saw as one of the benefits conferred by slavery. Yet the slave was punished for it.[29]

As her *Journal* concluded, Fanny Kemble observed that the standard defence of slavery usually took up 'the old ground as justifying the system, *where* it was administered with kindness and indulgence'. The argument made before 1861, and advanced by later apologists, like Ulrich B. Phillips, was therefore crucial to the southern case. But the consequences of its inconsistencies, and the divergence between elevated aims and reality could not be avoided. 'Truly slavery begets slavery', wrote Fanny Kemble, 'and the perpetual state of suspicion and apprehension of the slaveholders is a very handsome offset, to say the least of it, against the fetters and the lash of the slaves'. Kemble also comments on the fear of white women of their slaves; and the small islands of whites set in a sea of black slaves is a feature remarked on by many observers of the southern scene.

Slaves certainly found ways of kicking against a system which was so weighted against them. Certainly opportunities presented themselves (and discipline was less draconian among domestic slaves) for offering their masters, when the mood took them, all

27. Ibid., p. 165 (entry for Feb. 1834).
28. *Narrative of the Life of Frederick Douglass, An American Slave Written by Himself* (New York: Anchor, 1973), p. 20. On Douglass's efforts to increase the drive for literacy among slaves, see pp. 81–2.
29. Kemble, *Journal*, p. 207 (entry 15–27 Feb. 1839).

aid short of actual help. Miss Hopley's account is of interest here, because she wondered whether, as a foreigner 'my manner was less imperative' than southerners; she certainly believed 'that only those who understand the Negro can manage him'. Nevertheless, she observed how 'favourite' Negroes (especially children) were 'much indulged, and sometimes very troublesome'. She concludes:

> Sometimes one would be tempted to wonder how those young Negroes ever grow up with notions of obedience and respect towards their masters, as so great a want of discipline and good training is observable.

As comparisons with servants and workers in industrialized societies, (much to their detriment) were made by southern slaveowners by the 1850s, it is striking that Miss Hopley noticed among domestic slaves 'those little licenses which would be so resented as impertinences in our English servants'. These included the tiresome habit of piling 'up an immense heap of blazing logs in sunny weather'; or bringing in 'a great pile of firewood, and throwing it down on the carpet before the closet door, so as to effectually prevent it from opening'. Miss Hopley considered that this laxity was tolerated because of the colour line, and also because the slaves exploited their masters' desire to be accepted as kindly and tolerant. 'It was a long time before I became accustomed to this freedom of manner in the Negroes', she wrote. 'No white servant in England would ever dare to venture an approach to it'. But Miss Hopley did not note that her acquaintance was restricted exclusively to domestic slaves, as field hands could not take such liberties; in short, her own pro-southern sympathies led her to give slavery (reluctantly) the benefit of the doubt.[30]

She, too, remarks on the fears of Negro insurrection, which became more exacerbated after 1858–59 and the 'anxiety beneath the surface'.[31] The permanent, paranoid fear was of slave conspiracies. By comparison with the number of slaves involved, and the lives lost, such slave rebellions as were provoked in the *ante-bellum* southern states were very small beer indeed. There was much plotting and little action: here the record is inferior to Latin American slave societies. The reason for this lies in the comparatively open character of North American slavery, and the

---

30. Hopley, *Life in the South*, I pp. 68, 70, 92, 145, 167, 229, 319–20, 349–50; Kemble, *Journal* pp. 310–11.

31. Ibid., I, pp. 255–6.

brutal retribution that followed. Because southerners claimed that they were kind and paternal, their reaction to putative betrayal was indignant and ferocious; furthermore, the system worked in the sense that in North America slave conspiracies were invariably betrayed by a loyal domestic servant. The irony was that such a relatively benevolent system 'surpassed more closed slave regimes in reacting with panicky signs of terror when slave plots were suspected'. Yet the Vesey Conspiracy in Charleston, South Carolina (1822) and the rising of Nat Turner in Virginia (1831) were trifling affairs. Turner's rebellion was 'the most successful' in American history. It was immortalized in William Styron's novel, *The Confessions of Nat Turner*,[32] but involved no more than sixty slaves running amok, killing about seventy whites. Yet the seething horrors of the southern imagination cast even longer shadows as the system of slavery became more consolidated after 1850, and the ideology underpinning it became more self-confident and aggressive. But these conspiracies underlay and were to a great extent a violent expression of the fundamental dilemmas of slavery and its 'paternal' character. Both Vesey and Turner were literate; both had enjoyed many liberties denied to the majority of slaves; both were provoked by the inconsistent brutality of masters claiming to be paternal; indeed Vesey was a free black (mulatto actually) bigamously married to several slaves. Yet they both turned violently against a system that had supposedly done so much to favour them. Not only was the sense of betrayal among whites bitter, but also suspicion was thrown upon groups, such as free blacks, who lay on the margins of slavery. The pressures to turn slavery into a closed, all-dominant system, brooking no opposition, were latent and grew in intensity.[33]

The ways that slaves sought to reduce the suffocating embrace of slavery were usually by minor harassment and imitation of whites. There was one other way by which the slaves could ameliorate their harsh and unattractive lot – by religious devotion. During the eighteenth century it was feared that the spread of Christianity would provoke turbulence, or even rebelliousness, in

---

32. The publication of this novel provoked controversy. On this, see John White, 'Novelist as Historian: William Styron and American Negro Slavery', in David H. Burton (ed.) *American History – British Historians* (Chicago: Nelson Hall, 1978), pp. 148–68.

33. William Freehling, *The Road to Disunion* (New York: Oxford UP 1990), pp. 79, 178–80.

slaves. As the religious climate changed, so missionaries hoped that the acceptance of Christian mores would improve the slaves, not only their morals, but also their moral character. Christian teachings would render them more manageable, docile and better disciplined; by no means did it follow that if slaves accepted Christianity they would be more content in their lot as a form of 'providential mercy'. But it did involve a modification of the very cold and rigid planter–slave relationship and contributed substantially to the spread of the myth, from the 1830s onwards, that the slaveowners were benign patriarchs caring for their perpetual children.[34] This did not mean, of course, that religious slaveowners, who sometimes included clergymen, were incapable of cruel behaviour towards their slaves, because they could be self-righteous and brutal.[35] But a mutual sharing of religious feeling underlined certain persistent tensions that pervaded slavery. The slaves' rejection of conventional white Christianity resulted in the adoption of secret, covert forms of worship (severe penalties could be incurred if slaves were caught at unauthorized prayer meetings). Slaves thus created an avenue of escape from omnipresent white regulation and this bubbled up in the form of music, especially the spirituals, whose theme was that life was still worth living.[36]

Slave religion also played a contributory role in 'Puttin' on ol' Massa', by prevarication and dissimulation. It provided a weapon in indirect and covert rebelliousness – a source of moral values for the slave to help in judging the world and in taking decisions, like running away. A religious emphasis helped slaves to exploit the deep and uneasy feeling of guilt that many whites felt about slavery. This was indicated by efforts at begging death-bed forgiveness. A slave John Brown remembered of his master, Thomas Stevens:

> Ever so many times before his time was come [he became frightened]. But though he . . . recovered from his illnesses, in his frights he sent for us all and asked us to forgive him. . . . I remember him calling old Aunt Sally to him and begging and praying of her to get the devil away from behind the door, and such like.

34. Albert J. Raboteau, *Slave Religion* (New York: Oxford UP, 1978) pp. 45, 49–50.
35. Douglass, *Narrative*, pp. 55, 58, 79–80, thought that religious slaveholders were the worst.
36. Raboteau, *Slave Religion*, pp. 214–19, 225, 258, 264.

This was a profoundly ambivalent and uncomfortable society. Doubts could be assuaged by a display of untrammelled dominance. Some slaveholders refused to allow their slaves to attend any church, on the grounds that they had no souls to lose.[37]

The growth of southern sectionalism

So much for the institution itself; how did slavery influence southern society and culture? The first aspect that impresses any student of the South is that it is a variegated and diverse region, as one should expect from such an enormous geographical area. In short, 'the South' did not exist. There were and are 'many' Souths. Also, like the North, it mixed areas in which settlement had thrived for two hundred years with frontier outposts twenty or perhaps thirty years old. There was also an air of mystery about the South; this was not a region which northerners knew very much about. Consequently, polemical books like Hinton Rowan Helper's *The Impending Crisis of the South* (1857) had an added impact because of the dearth of learned comment, even from southerners themselves. The suggestion that somehow the South was not 'American' was a product of a cultural ambiguity inside the South and ignorance outside of it. Attempts to supply a more clearly defined sense of identity were the more forceful and overstated as a result. In 1861 Miss Hopley spoke with a nervous and surprised federal prisoner of war. He had expected to be tortured, or at least ill-treated. 'I believe from what the man said, he had expected to come to fight savages or wild Indians'.[38] But a more persuasive, and politically potent image (discussed below) gained sway in the North in the 1850s, which referred not to the South's western heritage, but to the slaveowning culture of the Deep South – 'the Slave Power'. This imperious, 'aristocratic', crafty and rapacious group of wealthy planters brought on the Civil War, it was claimed, because of their attempt to extend slavery and dominate the Federal government in its interest. Yet small cliques of wealthy men dominated political and social life in the North – this is not very peculiar. Furthermore, slavery enjoyed a large measure of support among all groups as a means of securing

37. Ibid., pp. 220, 292–9, 305–9, 314.
38. Hopley, *Life in the South*, I, p. 420.

southern, white supremacy in a region where blacks were not infrequently in the majority. *It was this consensus that created a regional, southern sense of separateness despite geographical diversity.* The desire to extend and increase the reach of this consensus grew in the 1850s. As Bruce Collins has suggested, a sense of southern sectional identity 'arose more from the problems created by slavery than from any special class structure that grew out of that institution'.[39]

The institution of slavery also changed over time, and its influence was lessened in some areas and became more important in others. The most striking feature of the first half of the nineteenth century was that slavery was diffused southwards and westwards. The most important political consequence of this movement was that those controversial issues most readily associated with 'the South' really agitated the 'Deep South', the tone of whose representatives was more strident and uncompromising. Thus the average numbers of slaves owned by slaveholders in 1850 were as follows: five in the Border South, eight in the Middle South, and twelve in the Lower South. Slaveholders who owned more than twenty slaves show the same statistical frequency: 6 per cent lived in the Border States, and 62 per cent in the Lower South. Of those who owned large plantations of over a hundred slaves, a mere 1 per cent lived in the Border States, but 85 per cent in the Deep South. These figures also relate to a further economic and geographical reality, namely, that cotton flourished in sub-tropical, not continental or near temperate conditions. Consequently, non-slaveholders outnumbered slaveholders 6:1 in Missouri (a state surrounded on two sides by free states) and 60:1 in Kansas.[40]

The 'diffusion' (really the deportation or export) of slaves southwards was expected to 'solve' the slavery problem in the most northerly slave states – even by slaveholders before 1840. This demographic movement was actually occurring. In 1790 northern Maryland's slave population comprised 18.5 per cent of the total, by 1860 it was down to 13.7 per cent, while the free black population grew from 12,760 to 27,867. The state total increase in the free black population rose from 2.5 per cent in 1790 to 13 per cent in 1850. In that year Maryland also witnessed the largest number of runaway slaves in all the slave states, 279. These figures

---

39. Bruce Collins, *White Society in the Antebellum South* (London: Longman, 1985), pp. 4–5.
40. Freehling, *Road to Disunion*, pp. 18–19.

certainly reveal the fragility of slavery when surrounded by areas where it had been removed, and where it was not buttressed by special legislation. Indeed, Maryland was acknowledged even by abolitionist critics, notwithstanding its great traffic in slaves (12 per cent of the entire population had been bought and sold, 1830–40), as having 'totally divested [itself] of those harsh and terrible peculiarities, which mark [it] in the Southern and South-Western states of the . . . Union'.[41]

But in states like Virginia and Maryland this acquiescence in 'diffusion' relied upon two assumptions. First, that the black population could be physically removed, either by colonizing other parts of Latin America, or second, returning them to Africa. This argument was discussed on two notable occasions: in the Virginia Slavery Debate of 1831–32, when the state legislature considered emancipating the slaves, and during discussion of Henry Clay's Distribution Plan, introduced into Congress in June 1832. Clay sought to transfer the federal budget surplus to the states by a calculation of population made on the basis of the three-fifths rule. He urged that southern states give 'special consideration' to devoting this money to either colonizing or emancipating their slaves. This process might be aided by increasing the number of slave states, and many favoured the annexation of Texas on these grounds; British influence, with its pernicious 'abolitionist' mentality, would also be eradicated from the Lone Star Republic. This was regarded as beneficial because the fabric of race relations in the neighbouring slave states would otherwise be weakened. Slaveowners were fearful lest British influence in Texas destabilized the whole structure and unleashed a servile war. Southerners who favoured 'diffusion' wished to avoid dramatic and immediate action, and preferred prudent and judicious amelioration of slavery as the highest priority. Those who advanced such opinions, furthermore, did not count on the rise of a pro-slavery ideology. The Deep South was to witness an increase in ever more aggressive pro-slavery rhetoric; the initiative fell into the hands of aggressive slaveholders who did not share the assumptions of those who welcomed 'diffusion'. (Indeed such views had already surfaced in the South Carolina Nullification

41. Ibid., pp. 156, 188–9, 195, 199; Barbara Jeanne Fields, *Slavery and Freedom on the Middle Ground: Maryland during the Nineteenth Century* (New Haven, CT: Yale UP, 1985), pp. 10, 16, 23–5 (the quotation is from Frederick Douglass).

Crisis and others criticized the annexation of Texas on the grounds that it would weaken slavery, even in the Lower South.)[42]

All parties feared the sudden and dramatic, cataclysmic ending of slavery in the southern states. Giving freedom to the slaves would release their savage and brutal energies, kept in check by the constraints, or manacles of slavery, which had succeeded in nurturing the childlike 'Sambo-like' aspects of the Negro's primitive character. Once these manacles were shattered the laughing child would be transformed into a monstrous blood-thirsty guttersnipe, who would loot, rape, murder and utterly destroy southern 'civilization' in a servile war. Slaveowners did their best to stir up fears among poor whites of the horrors of black servile rebellion. They were certainly fearful of the results of 'unsupervised' contact between poor whites, free and enslaved blacks (who cooperated more fully than is sometimes recognized). The horrific image of the successful slave revolt in Haiti (1804) was conjured up in the southern mind to ensure racial unity against the threat of black savagery; here the civilizing influences of white rule had been overturned in a successful slave rebellion, an event which led many southerners to project all kinds of hysterical, often sexual and sadistic fantasies. The Negro brain could not cope with freedom, it became overloaded and too indulged in sensation, and the result was insanity. In 1849, a secret committee chaired by John C. Calhoun, concluded that a successful servile revolt could result only in the enslavement of southern whites:

> a degradation greater than has ever yet fallen to the lot of a free and enlightened people, and one from which we could not escape, should emancipation take place . . . but by fleeing the homes of ourselves and ancestors, and by abandoning our country to our former slaves, to become the permanent abode of disorder, anarchy, poverty, misery and wretchedness.

The stronger the appeal of pro-slavery ideology, the more fixated this fear became, and the more persuasive the argument that the slightest weakening of the slave structure would result in it crashing down. A deep-seated feeling of insecurity led to an increasingly shrill demand that slavery be extended to eradicate any exposed flanks, Northern interests were to be compelled, moreover to accept without qualification, any legislation that the

42. Freehling, *Road to Disunion*, pp. 156, 188–90, 274–5, 392, 410.

South sought to protect slavery in the states and consolidate its extension in the territories.[43]

What form did this pro-slavery ideology take? It is in this area that the singular, sometimes perverse southern stance, which set its face against the intellectual breeze of the age, became intransigent. The intellectual oddities, not to say perversities, of the literature produced are also apparent. It is no coincidence either that the issue of southern backwardness – the reaction to the publication of Dickens's *American Notes* is of interest here – became a subject of controversy in the 1840s. In part, the pro-slavery literature is a response to accusations that the more advanced, diligent and populous North carried 'the South on its shoulders' by subsidizing the South through federal taxation. Slavery was also blamed in a general sense for impeding population and labour mobility and financial development. The states of Alabama and Mississippi, for example, could boast only one bank each in 1860. Apologists for slavery replied with a vigorous defence of the 'peculiar institution'. The best known was George Fitzhugh of Virginia, whose works included *Sociology for the South* (1854) and *Cannibals All!* (1857). He argued that slavery was not 'peculiar' to the South but a universal condition, and that the form of benevolent and benign plantation slavery that had developed in the southern states, was much more humane than the ghastly, cold, de-humanized 'slavery' of factory-organized labour to be found in the slums of New England or Great Britain. Slaveowners behaved more like stewards than entrepreneurs; their primitive and childlike labour force was contented and well looked after: their limited abilities were harnessed to adequate tasks, so that they were neither over-taxed nor allowed to fall into slothful idleness or debauchery. In short, the slaveowners were doing God's work.[44]

There was an important 'symbiotic' relationship between the justification of slavery and the revival of Evangelical Christianity in

43. Howard Temperley, 'Competing Scenarios: Antebellum Images of American Society After Emancipation', in Brian Holden Reid and John White (eds) *American Studies: Essays in Honour of Marcus Cunliffe* (London: Macmillan, 1991), pp. 73–5; Charles C. Bolton, *Poor Whites of the Antebellum South* (Durham, NC: Duke UP, 1994), pp. 43, 49–50, 65, 127, 130–1, 137.

44. Collins, *White Society in the Antebellum South*, pp. 59–64; Marcus Cunliffe, *Chattel Slavery and Wage Slavery* (Mercer University Lamar Memorial Lectures no. 22; Athens, GA: University of Georgia Press, 1979), pp. 1–7; for a flavour of Fitzhugh's writing, see John White and Ralph Willett, *Slavery in the American South* (London: Longman, 1970), doc. 22, pp. 114–15.

the South. 'We who own slaves', claimed James Furman, 'honor God's law in the exercise of our authority'.[45] In 1829 Methodist and Episcopal planters in South Carolina asked the South Carolina Conference of the Methodist Episcopal Church to send missionaries among their slaves. The aim was to ensure that blacks subscribed to the same values as their white masters; in this, at least, they failed.[46] Yet though the Mission was undoubtedly motivated by anxiety and fear of slaves, and was an effort to insure chattel slavery, it was also coupled with a characteristic nineteenth-century passion for improvement and spiritual uplift. 'Having reduced them to ignorance', complained Charles C. Jones, 'and by our neglect of duty confirmed them in vice, we now quarrel with their stupidity and obduracy'.[47]

Given that southerners, from a quite different perspective, shared a northern passion for moral improvement, it is easy to argue that there was no such thing as a 'distinct' southern pro-slavery ideology – a part of a broader assertion of southern 'distinctiveness'. Certainly, this has been exaggerated. For example, there is a similar anti-democratic tone in the ideas advanced by northern clergymen, like Nehemiah Adams of Boston, which is comparable with sentiments expressed more recklessly in the South. Evidence may also be found of such 'conservative republicanism' in the North, even in New England. Yet finding sectional parallels for almost all southern viewpoints broadens and simultaneously planes down divergences of opinion to such a degree that it explains everything and nothing.[48] A clearer distinction should be drawn between the positive act of *justifying slavery*, which became increasingly prevalent in the South after 1850, and the negative act of deploring the activities of the abolitionists, which was widespread in the North. Deploring the inflammatory language of Wendell Phillips was not the same as applauding the spread of slavery. If this distinction is not drawn then the reasons for sectional tension before 1861 become an enigmatic riddle defying explanation, as North and South agreed about so much. But we simply cannot ignore the fact that spokesmen for southern distinctiveness, such as James H.

45. Donald G. Mathews, *Religion in the Old South* (Chicago UP, 1977), pp. 136, 170, 174.

46. Ibid., p. 139; see Raboteau, *Slave Religion*, p. 45, on their failure.

47. Mathews, *Religion in the Old South*, pp. 140–1, 146.

48. For this argument, see Larry E. Tise, *Proslavery: A History of the Defense of Slavery in America, 1701–1860* (Athens, GA: University of Georgia Press, 1988).

Hammond, who believed as early as 1844 that 'A separation of the States at no remote period is inevitable. It might now be effected peaceably and properly', were either unaware of any northern sympathy with their basic view on slavery or ignored it. But more than this, they deliberately posited their justification of the slavery system as *superior* to the North in every way and the basis for a thriving, *competing* republic. Indeed, pro-slavery ideology is permeated by a desire to reform and *modernize* slavery, so that it was just as secure as free labour, and just as 'progressive'. As Hammond boasted, during the Recession of 1857, 'we have poured upon you 1,600,000 bales of cotton just at the crisis to save you from destruction'. This whole discussion of the merits of chattel slavery versus wage slavery simply indicates that southern 'distinctiveness' should be qualified. The views of Fitzhugh did find northern echoes – but this should not be misconstrued as consensus.[49]

How should we view, moreover, the assumption which characterizes so much northern criticism of the South, that it was pulled headlong into conflict and war by an evil, rapacious 'slave power'? The slave power, so the argument went, rested ultimately on two sources of strength: its economic strength and political influence. As to the first, the diffusion of slavery throughout the South has been noted. Something like one southern family in four owned a slave, though this frequency was higher in the Deep South. Such widespread connection with the 'peculiar institution' made difficult the formulation of a coherent, exclusive 'oligarchical' view. There were many strands to slaveowning opinion, and some were contradictory. For instance, as the pro-slavery ideology became more strident, so did the treatment of slaves improve, at any rate to the degree that southerners prided themselves on the sense of 'family' that guided their society. As George W. Mordecai wrote in December 1860 on the threat of a possible slave rebellion, 'I would much sooner trust myself alone on my plantation surrounded by my slaves, than in one of your large manufacturing towns when your labourers are discharged from employment and crying for bread for themselves and their

49. Hammond, *Diaries*, p. 127 (entry for 24 Nov. 1844); Allan Nevins, *Ordeal of the Union* (New York: Scribner's, 1947), I, p. 467; Cunliffe, *Chattel Slavery and Wage Slavery*, p. 102; Bertram Wyatt-Brown, 'Modernizing Southern Slavery: The Proslavery Argument Reinterpreted', in J. M. Kousser and J. M. McPherson (eds) *Region, Race and Reconstruction: Essays in Honour of C. Vann Woodward* (New York: Oxford UP, 1982).

little ones.' Though opportunities for manumission were reduced, slave ideologues were more inclined to accept the sanctity of slave marriages; some in North Carolina were even prepared to admit that a measure of literacy could be permitted. All such efforts, however, would have involved ultimately a recognition of the essential humanity of slaves that could have resulted in a drastic weakening of the institution.[50]

The owners of great plantations represented a group whose membership oscillated dramatically, especially in the Mississippi basin. It was comparatively easy to enter the circle of great planters and extremely easy to leave it. In a survey of the larger planters in the counties of south west Georgia and Alabama in the decade before 1860, only 30 per cent of those in Georgia, and one-half of the Alabamans, actually remained members of the planting elite within the various county samples in each state. In the Upper South and in the South East the elite was much more stable.

Of course, planters may have been acknowledged as prominent, even distinguished, members of the political elite, but 'prominence' and 'dominance' are not the same thing. The low opinion held throughout the Union of 'politicians' in general was shared just as much in the South as in the North. The various state capitals gave no opportunity for conspicuous display (indeed the limitations of Montgomery, Alabama, in this regard would become all too obvious in the first months of Confederate independence). There was, in short, no focus for the authority of the 'slave power' to be exercised as its influence was distributed evenly throughout the southern states, unless it be Washington DC. Most property qualifications for office-holding had been removed in the 1850s by the majority of southern states; there were no southern equivalents of British 'pocket boroughs', and appointments had to be gained through usefulness to a patron or political leader – though such patronage was allotted by the very rich. But this power was not untrammelled, and was restricted by the democratic mechanism. Certainly *local* political elites invariably dominated their localities and the legislative programmes put before the state legislature in all southern states. The

50. Collins, *White Society in the Antebellum South*, p. 16; Eaton, *Growth of Southern Civilization*, p. 96; Genovese, *Roll, Jordan Roll*, pp. 50–2, 74. Mrs Margaret Douglass, prosecuted in 1854 for teaching Negro children to read and write, offered in her defence the numbers of Negro children who were literate – mostly taught by the leading citizens of Norfolk, Virginia. See Clement Eaton, *The Freedom-of-Thought Struggle in the Old South*, 2nd edn (New York: Harper & Row, 1964), p. 137.

overwhelming number of members of the various southern legislatures were slaveowners; but these should not be confused with the great planters, the 'nabobs'. The only exception to this was South Carolina; in four of the seven Lower South states planters represented less than 30 per cent of the legislature, and in five out of seven Upper South states (less Delaware) planters made up less than 20 per cent of the membership of the legislature. Indeed a persuasive case has been made that it was the very absence of a cohesive, self-conscious, prudent middle class dominating southern politics, that permitted the grip of slaveowners on southern politics to be both so tenacious and so reckless. These various groups had one overriding political demand – the survival of slavery. This tended to be more ferociously expressed and dogmatically demanded when directed outside the South. Within the South it was enthusiastically accepted by non-slaveholders because it gave them the political muscle to ensure that blacks remained in a strictly confined and subordinate place.[51] Yet for all that, there is a paternalistic, vaguely oligarchic aspect to southern society and politics which is alien in the North – though it is far less important than has often been argued by previous (especially southern) historians. This resulted in a more anti-democratic tone to southern political culture. 'You call yourself a democrat', wrote William H. Trescot of South Carolina to a Virginian, with a certain measure of scorn. But 'that word democrat has betrayed the South. Southern slaveholders in their strange zeal to be good democrats have been untrue to themselves and their position.'[52]

A southern 'civilization'?

The South's bid for independence and the trauma of defeat in a civil war have led many historians (southerners foremost among them) to assume that the South was a 'distinct' region of the United States. There are strong reasons for doubting the validity of such a generalization. Much of the emphasis on southern distinctiveness, in terms of history, culture and mythology, is a post–1865 development, and was one way of explaining the secessionist stampede after December 1860. Recent writing on the

51.   Collins, *White Society in the Antebellum South*, pp. 16–24.
52.   Freehling, *Road to Disunion*, p. 515.

history of ideas has argued that the issues agitating southern intellectuals were broadly related to northern preoccupations. 'The concerns that separated them', in the words of one historian, 'were, until the secession crisis of 1860, of less moment than the concerns that bound them together'. Both groups 'yearned for a tidy, harmonious social order based on both individual and collective codes of discipline, under the tutelage of educated gentlemen'. But if we emphasize these similarities unduly, as Marcus Cunliffe recognizes, then the tensions preceding the secession crisis become inexplicable.[53] There must be some features unique to this region which made a bid for independence and a relish to fight a civil war more than probable, and the effort must now be made to try and delineate them.

The brilliant southern publicist, W. J. Cash, in his famous book, *The Mind of the South* (1941), agrees 'that it was the conflict with the Yankee which really created the concept of the South as something more than a matter of geography, as an object of patriotism, in the minds of southerners'.[54] We may also note in this regard the importance of non-southern literary sources in determining an image of the South that prevailed before 1861. But Cash makes an even more important observation. How was it remotely possible that a coherent, sustainable and individual culture could establish itself, with an identifiable political outlook, in the course of some seventy years (in some states in less than forty)? Cash emphasizes the importance of the time factor: 'Men, who as children, had heard the war whoop of the Cherokee in the Carolina backwoods lived to hear the guns at Vicksburg'. The South was first and foremost a frontier society, and the great burden of taming the frontier and extending its social order over the wilderness engaged its energies. But even if that social order was distinct from that of the North, it does not follow that it was the product of a completely different culture. The most persuasive conclusion that can be drawn is that the act of subjugating the frontier encouraged a style of thinking that was at once presumptuous and arrogant, and pre-eminently parochial. This combination resulted, among politicians, in a gradual increase in local patriotism, and regard for sectional interest (they were supported by their electorates in this view), that culminated in a

53. Cunliffe, *Chattel Slavery and Wage Slavery*, pp. 102, 123n38; Drew Gilpin Faust, *A Sacred Circle: The Dilemma of the Intellectual in the Old South, 1840–1860* (Baltimore, MD: Johns Hopkins UP, 1977).
54. W. J. Cash, *The Mind of the South* (Harmondsworth: Penguin, 1973), p. 85.

desire for political independence. This drive was justified (among other things) by a passionate belief that the South enjoyed a 'superior' civilization that would flourish once it had broken free of northern inhibitions and constraints. This view 'was perhaps the least well founded', Cash notes sardonically, 'of the many poorly founded claims which the southerners so earnestly asserted to the world and to themselves and in which they so warmly believed'.[55]

The differences between the sentimental vision enjoyed by southerners of their 'civilization' and the reality is stark. The notion gained currency that the progress of the South had been held back by its connection with the North. This theme predated the Nullification Crisis, but became more persistent thereafter. Conscious that the South Carolina cotton crop was dependent on the New England carrying trade, the *Southern Agriculturalist* wrote in May 1825: 'These "terrible Yankees", . . . are too deep for us, they "*undermine* us" as the cant term in Charleston is. Why will the Charleston people not "*countermine*"?' Once the South had broken free, the South would flourish. R. B. Rhett conjured up this beguiling vision in 1860. He depicted 'a civilisation that has never been equalled or surpassed – a civilisation teeming with actors, poets, philosophers, statesmen and historians equal to those of Greece and Rome, and presented to the world the glorious spectacle of a free, prosperous, and illustrious people'. This was typical of the heart-warming, exaggerated hyperbole in which southerners indulged; the reality was rather more prosaic.[56]

The South's cotton certainly dominated any estimate of American exports. In 1850 it amounted to $72 million out of a total of $144.4 million. A decade later these figures had risen in absolute terms to a cotton crop worth $191.8 million, with total export earnings of $333.6 million. Cotton exports accounted for approximately 5 per cent of the total US gross national product.[57] But these figures do not fully represent the vitality of the southern economy, nor its relative position *vis-à-vis* the North.

The great majority of southern farmers were not opulent, wealthy planters but small yeoman farmers; despite the importance of cotton as an export, it actually represented just 25 per cent of the total production of southern farms (with sugar, tobacco and

55. Ibid., pp. 32, 110.

56. William H. Pease and Jane H. Pease, *The Web of Progress: Private Values and Public Styles in Boston and Charleston* (New York: Oxford UP, 1985), p. 11; Allan Nevins, *The Emergence of Lincoln* (New York: Scribner's, 1950), II, p. 334.

57. Collins, *White Society in the Antebellum South*, p. 27.

rice accounting for a further 10 per cent). The largest southern crop was corn, which could be grown without too much difficulty in hurriedly prepared soil, could feed hogs and other livestock (the South had prodigious quantities of hogs: between 1845 and 1860 67,026,000 hogs were marketed by southern farmers), and provided an urgent measure of security for the small farmer.[58] The nostalgia summoned up by the image of the classical style, pristine white mansion, resting in the shade, with its contented and chuckling household, was far from typical. Where it did exist and dominate the surrounding countryside, as Clement Eaton observes, 'The serenity of the big mansion was in thousands of cases troubled by the infinite vexations of slavery'.[59]

The most striking feature of these 'infinite vexations' was the effort made by all those interests who, for different reasons, supported the maintenance and extension of slavery, to create a 'closed system' in the slave states. This refused to permit any entrance through its fortress gates of either persons or ideas which could subvert the peculiar institution from the inside, and erected barricades against attacks organized by pernicious, progressive forces that lurked outside waiting to exploit the slightest, narrowest fissure that could bring the whole structure crashing down, with catastrophic consequences. Although its absolute importance in the southern economy has been exaggerated, Professor Collins is surely right in suggesting that the wealth invested in cotton and the system of slave labour ($4 billion) represented a 'community of interest'. He continues, 'Cotton helped keep white society fluid, mobile, enterprising, as well as drawn together by mutual commercial interests and racial pride'. The various meetings of cotton planters' (and businessmen's) conventions throughout the 1850s gave an important impetus, not just to a sense of the importance of cotton to the American economy, but to a feeling of distinct, sectional economic interest which should not be subordinated to the North.[60] This interest, though it cannot be defined so precisely as a 'slave power' was inseparable from it. The character of its identity was intensely conservative, and defined itself not in terms of cultural coherence,

---

58. Parish, *Slavery*, pp. 47–8; Collins, *White Society in the Antebellum South*, pp. 38–9; Grady McWhiney, *Cracker Culture: Celtic Ways in the Old South* (Tuscaloosa: University of Alabama Press, 1988), p. 55.

59. Eaton, *Growth of Southern Civilization*, p. 124.

60. Collins, *White Society in the Antebellum South*, pp. 39–40; Eaton, *Growth of Southern Civilization*, p. 111.

language or unity but in opposition to 'the North', which was regarded as an unvariegated entity of uniform hostility. The inaccuracy of this view and the common sympathies shared by some northerners and southern planters has already been remarked on (especially in deploring the activities of abolitionists). It was a tendency to extend absolute control over the intellectual and social life of the slave states that alarmed some northerners. By the late 1850s it began to contribute concurrently to the belief that 'the North' had an identity of its own. Yet it is amazing how long northerners tolerated the increasingly truculent southern attitude and its increasingly belligerent tone.

That this sense of difference apropos the North was not entirely dependent on pro-secessionist sentiment is indicated by the views of the Tennessean Unionist, William G. ('Parson') Brownlow. He criticized northern ideas, calling for the setting up of a 'Missionary Society of the South, for the Conversion of the Freedom Shriekers, Spiritualists, Free-Lovers, Fourierites, and Infidel Reformers of the North'. But if a loyal unionist felt like this, it was a salutary warning of the full extent of the 'fire-eaters'' ferocious determination to ensure that the peculiar institution be protected from the dangers of radical ideas from outside.[61]

This represents a major change of emphasis in the southern outlook. In the eighteenth century the South (or Virginia, at any rate) was the home of liberalism, scepticism and deism. The simultaneous spread of Jacksonian democracy and slavery led to severe criticisms of those who attempted to question, however mildly, the efficacy of the slavery system; the significance of 1831, of Nat Turner's slave rebellion and the first issue of the abolitionist newspaper, *The Liberator*, again becomes apparent. By 1852 and the publication of Harriet Beecher Stowe's novel, *Uncle Tom's Cabin*, what Clement Eaton calls a 'counsel-for-the-defence attitude' prevailed, even among southern intellectuals. The editor of the *Southern Literary Messenger* looked for a reviewer whom he could guarantee would write a 'review as hot as hell-fire, blasting and scarring the reputation of the vile wretch in petticoats who could write such a volume.'[62] Such sensitivity to finite degrees of criticism hardly denoted a bottomless well of self-confidence; it was reinforced by a tendency towards 'romanticism' (though this

---

61. Eaton, *Freedom-of-Thought Struggle*, p. 336.
62. Ibid., pp. 27–8, 30, 36–7, 46–8, 62–3; Eaton, *Growth of Southern Civilization*, p. 115.

seems more like sentimentality). This presented an ideal image of chivalry, loosely based on medieval models. The Upper South, by comparison with states further South, stagnated. Those enjoying the 'first fruits' of slavery were most vocal in its defence. Secessionist spokesmen allowed zeal for the South to blind them and they gave vent increasingly to intolerant and fundamentally provincial sentiments.[63]

The decline of a sense of philosophic discrimination in the South was reinforced by blind passion compounded by ignorance. Touring the small settlements of the Deep South, secessionist spokesmen like William L. Yancey had the capacity, in Eaton's striking phrase, to act like 'an enchanter' who 'waved his magic wand and temporarily deprived the audience of their reason'. Illiteracy rates in the South were high, and seem to be getting worse in the 1850s. Of white males over 20 years old, illiteracy was 20–30 per cent (in some regional pockets it was much higher), in the Border States it was 3 per cent, and in New England 0.42 per cent. This is often put down to the individualism of the southern people, though this quality is no less widespread in New England. It has much more to do with the neglect of schooling for poor whites, though the southern record on academies for the wealthy is rather better. But this achievement was limited and involved small numbers of students. For instance, in 1843, the city of Boston funded 15 grammar and 104 primary schools, which served one-third of the entire juvenile population; Charleston, by comparison, financed only the orphan house school. And whereas the College of Charleston was the first municipally funded college in the United States, it had only 39 students in 1834 (Harvard had 217). Many southerners preferred to send their sons to Harvard and Yale.[64]

But a growing awareness of the dangers of sending young southerners to northern colleges, where they might be tainted by dangerous abolitionist influences, was a major factor in boosting higher education in the South. It also contributed after 1836 to a determined effort to limit freedom of speech and conscience on the slavery issue and restrict the movement of ideas. In the first place, state legislatures passed legislation (and many of the most severe measures were passed by states, such as Virginia, which were

63. Eaton, *Freedom-of-Thought Struggle*, pp. 51, 66–7, 73–80; Eaton, *Growth of Southern Civilization*, p. 115; also of interest here is Clement Eaton's *The Waning of Old South Civilization, 1860–1880* (New York: Pegasus, 1969), esp. pp. viii, 22–3, 50.

64. Pease and Pease, *Web of Progress*, p. 108.

feeling 'exposed', as they were contiguous to 'free' states) which dealt out hard punishments for anybody circulating publications arguing for the restriction of property rights in any form; agents or sympathizers of organizations subscribing to such views would also be punished; and postmasters and justices of the peace had inquisitorial powers to inspect the mails to ensure that publications from such bodies could be intercepted. The powers of 'citizen's arrest' were granted to any white man who suspected that these laws were being infringed. Control of the patronage which disposed of such appointments was therefore critical to the maintenance of the slave system.[65] The other means was by physical coercion and ostracism, mainly the former – mob violence, assaults on editors and lynching carried out in an atmosphere of fevered hysteria. It is perhaps no coincidence that where the laws were comparatively mild, as in Kentucky, outbreaks of mob violence were more frequent.[66] Although Clement Eaton's classic study of this subject is entitled *The Freedom-of-Thought Struggle in the Old South*, it is clear from his account that after 1836, apart from a handful of individuals, sometimes eccentric or perverse, who insisted on going their own way regardless of consequences, there was no 'struggle'. The slave states demanded from their citizens a conformity of thought (in which the great majority obligingly acquiesced) and then demanded that everybody else conform as well.[67]

'Let our schools and seminaries of learning be "scrutinized", wrote W. W. Holden, 'and if Black Republicans be found in them, let them be driven out'. Among southern editors, intellectuals, academics and students there is a remarkably consistent conservative consensus – a broad agreement on the need to defend slavery based on a worst case analysis that saw 'the North' in conspicuously stereotyped terms. As they all agreed, few could see that they were infringing any freedoms. Nor can there be any

65. Eaton, *Freedom-of-Thought Struggle*, pp. 126–7. Eaton points out that legislation of this kind was never brought before the Supreme Court and put to the test of constitutional validity. Clearly, if an Administration held power in Washington that was prepared to see this tested, the whole structure would be tested, too. 'The whole affair is a striking example of the nonassertion of Federal power', in his opinion.

66. Ibid., pp. 129–30, 163–5, 185–93.

67. McWhiney, *Cracker Culture*, pp. 201–5; examples of puny opposition can be found, see Eaton, *Freedom-of-Thought Struggle*, pp. 133–43, 162, 273–6, 283, 298–9, 313; Eaton notes the 'Surprising fact . . . that they [the laws] were invoked so rarely' (p. 143). There was no need.

doubt that it was the *defence of slavery* that provoked a sense of sectional identity *vis-à-vis* the North, and the desperate search for measures that would ensure a uniformity of thought and deed throughout the section. Although the *ante-bellum* South does not feature in Seymour Martin Lipset and Earl Raab's book, *The Politics of Unreason: Right-Wing Extremism in America, 1790–1970* (1971), there is a good case for accepting that the consistent efforts to reduce freedom of expression and thought by legislative and violent means, served as a major challenge to the American liberal, democratic tradition. On this narrow, shifting but firm headland, the South may be said to have carved out for itself a distinctive, if unenviable feature.[68]

A sense of social and cultural distinctiveness followed the political and economic imperative, not the other way round. Given their short history and the sense of perpetual crisis and ghastly unforeseen cataclysm that seemed to haunt every unturned corner, many southerners groped for some historical analogy to provide stability. They looked back nostalgically to the ideals of the American Revolution and became preoccupied with a supposed decline of moral values. These and many of the other attitudes attributed to southerners were not unique to them. These feelings could be found in the North also. But the anti-democratic tone of this disillusionment was characteristically southern, 'a conviction that the civic values and ideals of the Revolutionary generation', in the words of William R. Taylor, 'had been eroded away by a half century of democratic change and territorial expansion'.[69] The historical pattern the South preferred was a cosy, refined, chivalrous and very sentimental one. Daniel Huntly observed in 1860, 'In this Country every man considers himself a gentleman, no matter what may be his social status'. Every woman was a lady. This longing for a stable social order, mixed with a preference for the 'frontier spirit' found expression in 'the cavalier' – a frontier gentleman hostile to materialism, mechanization and social progress. There was a tendency also towards orthodoxy in southern religious attitudes which confirmed

68. Eaton, *Freedom-of-Thought Struggle* pp. 161, 223, 236; Bertram Wyatt-Brown, *Southern Honor: Ethics and Behavior in the Old South* (New York: Oxford UP, 1982), pp. 111–13; Seymour Martin Lipset and Earl Raab, *The Politics of Unreason: Right-Wing Extremism in America, 1790–1970* (London: Heinemann, 1971), ch. 2, which concentrates on 'Know Nothingism'.

69. William R. Taylor, *Cavalier and Yankee: The Old South and American National Character* (London: W. H. Allen, 1963), p. 146; also see Wyatt-Brown, *Southern Honor*, pp. 484–5.

the 'cavalier' stereotype.[70] The whole summoned up images of grand mansions, refulgent living, refined and gracious ladies, but above all, a life founded on *honour*. Southern historical writing itself exhibited two paradoxical features: despite the paramount importance attributed to it, and the immense labour invested in justifying it, virtually no southern historians actually mentioned slavery. Further, although southern historical writing was tinged with anti-British sentiment, the 'cavalier' exemplar and his 'honour', could be firmly linked to British (and especially English) aristocratic mores. All of this cast southern society, as it came increasingly under attack, in a romantic, and in many ways a heroic mould; but it is significant that this desperate search for some kind of cultural identity should be bolstered from values drawn from outside the South itself.[71]

Yet the literature is suffused with attempts to explain the southern character. Sometimes this has focused on a supposed appetite for war and a strong 'military tradition'.[72] But in the main this has taken three forms and, although written at different times with different motives and for different audiences, caters to the American penchant for explaining the characteristics of peoples by reference to 'ethnic' origins rather than geographical or environmental forces, or for even allowing such factors a part in the explanation. The first is the English or the 'cavalier' myth discussed above; the second is the Creole myth; and the third (and most recent effort) is to explain southern difference by reference to their so-called 'Celtic' forebears. All of these explanations are prone to special pleading, and a breathtakingly oversimplified treatment of the homelands of the various ethnic groups. They tend to latch on to certain features of southerners, their hospitality, casual easy-going manner, laziness, weakness for drink, sensual and debauched behaviour, and explain these by reference to the most crude stereotypes. As attempts at historical explanation, they can be dismissed, but they are significant as efforts in the continuing search for an explanation of southern 'identity'. The South might now have forged an individual identity

70. Eaton, *Freedom-of-Thought Struggle*, pp. 213–17; Mathews, *Religion in the Old South*, pp. 122–3; Taylor, *Cavalier and Yankee*, p. 334; Wyatt-Brown, *Southern Honor*, pp. 168–9, 363, 438.

71. Collins, *White Society in the Antebellum South*, pp. 68, 70, 82; Michael D. Clark, '"More English than the English": Cavalier and Democrat in Virginia Historical Writing', *Journal of American Studies* 27 (1993), pp. 186–204.

72. For a discussion of this, see below, pp. 191–6.

of its own, although it is less particular than is often assumed. But this was far less clear before 1861.[73]

In conclusion, it is clear that the South was not a 'distinctive' region of the United States, but it enjoyed various levels of contrast with other regions. How can these contrasting features be delineated, and what was their significance? The most obvious contrast was in demography. The black presence was something that marked out the South. The total white population in 1860 was 8,097,500, and this was balanced against a black population of 3,953,700 slaves and 262,000 free blacks. That this population might rise and overthrow the rule of whites was an omnipresent fear.[74] It accounted for the intense fear of action by 'agitators' from outside the region, and also the assumption that 'the North' was a good deal more united and hostile than it actually was. But although the South was increasingly regarded as 'under siege' and that its institutions were threatened, it is difficult to see, other than in relation to slavery and its ramifications, in what lay the uniqueness of these institutions. Certainly there were economic differences: small pockets of industrialization can be found in the South, but these were tiny compared with developments in Pennsylvania or New York state. There were cultural and social differences, with an emphasis in the South on educating a privileged upper middle class and neglecting the education of the great mass of poor whites. Urbanization was much more advanced in the North than in the South.[75]

Yet, if these features are examined closely the atypicality of the great majority of them disappear. They seem rather differences in style, or emphasis, than in substance. In 1860, the North, too, was predominantly rural, and the bulk of the white population consisted of small farmers. Yet the transport revolution and economies of scale were rapidly breaking down the old rural life in the North and were acting as a powerful stimulus to

73. On the 'life of sensation and careless enjoyment' of the Creoles, see Eaton, *Growth of Southern Civilization*, p. 130; for similar comments on the 'Celts' (a very ambiguously defined group), see McWhiney's *Cracker Culture* chs 4 and 5.

74. To this extent only is the notion of a *herrenvolk* relevant to the period before 1865, much of its significance (and that of other comparisons with societies such as South Africa) is surely post-war. See George M. Fredrickson, *The Black Image in the American Mind* (New York: Harper & Row, 1971), p. 61. See C. Vann Woodward, *The Strange Career of Jim Crow*, 2nd rev. edn (New York: Oxford UP, 1966), p. 13 for the view that segregation was absent with slavery, although it was present in dealings with free blacks. Woodward's interpretation has recently been challenged.

75. Collins, *White Society in the Antebellum South*, pp. 29–30.

urbanization. Northern cities, although larger, suffered from some of the same problems as those in the South, especially from lawlessness and fear of urban tumult.[76] The emphasis that some commentators have placed on the reluctance of southerners to read, and their readiness to talk, has also been overdone.[77] The North was also a fundamentally oral culture.[78] On this, and so many scores, we find in the South an accentuation, and sometimes an exaggeration, of social features that may be found in the North. Thus Miss Hopley expressed in 1861 foreboding concerning the 'loose and objectionable mode' of southern expression 'in violent and extravagant language, which often means no more than the mere words, though they draw upon themselves a vast amount of opprobrium by the practice'.[79]

The argument about southern 'distinctiveness', in other words, is essentially circular. Those who seek to explain the 'uniqueness' of this region, assume its uniqueness as a given and then seek to explain it by extolling characteristics that are far from unique, and are often associated with 'the West'. The South is distinctive, therefore, it is unique. And of course it appears so when its features are studied in obsessive isolation from other parts of the United States. But, a paradox is now confronted. If the differences between the North and South were not great, why did a great civil war break out between these sections? The resolution of the paradox resides not in cultural differences (although to southerners the myth of the cavalier and his ineffable code of honour, to which Northerners did not subscribe,[80] was very real) but in political interchange. The South was not a distinctive but a self-conscious section. That is to say, this self-consciousness was the product of political and social sources, differences arising mainly

76. See Pease and Pease, *Web of Progress,* pp. 82, 143, 154, 157–8; James M. McPherson, *Battle Cry of Freedom: The Civil War Era* (New York: Oxford UP, 1988), pp. 14–21.

77. Especially by McWhiney, *Cracker Culture,* pp. 190, 196, 206.

78. See Anne Norton, *Alternative Americas: A Reading of Antebellum Political Culture* (Chicago UP, 1986), pp. 19–20.

79. Hopley, *Life in the South,* I, p. 397.

80. Norton, *Alternative Americas,* pp. 99–103, 105, 258; Wyatt-Brown, *Southern Honor,* assumes that this preoccupation was a Southern monopoly. Although northern writers like Henry James in *The Bostonians* use southern figures, like Basil Ransome, as models of the gentlemanly code, to assume that 'honour' is irrelevant to northern gentlemen is absurd. In the South it is more pronounced. See Colonel Lapham's observation that 'gentlemaning as a profession has got to play out in a generation or two'. William Dean Howells, *The Rise of Silas Lapham* (Harmondsworth: Penguin, 1983), p. 34.

from the peculiar institution, rather than from any sense of cultural separateness. This came later to explain (or justify) the increasing divergence.

Civil strife is just as much a product of provincialism as profound cultural contrast. Here the South is an object lesson. The slave states were not subject to immigration from the 1830s onwards, and White-Anglo-Saxon-Protestant dominance emerged by 1860 unscathed. The southern transport system connected its towns with one another and not the North; it was not geared to the wider world.[81] This reinforced a parochial outlook, and an obsession with regional issues – especially those connected with race. It was feared that these race relations were under strain from outside the region. Such threats were greatly exaggerated in the short term, although over the long term they were not insignificant. Contact with free labour invariably weakened the structure of slavery. It was the attempt to retard and prevent this process occurring which clearly demarcates the South from the North. The attempt to create a 'closed system', to control written and spoken expression and the movement of ideas, while glorying in the limitations of democracy in the southern states, was exceptional. As the spread of democracy was intrinsic to the success of the Union and the creation of a continental republic of imperial dimensions, any section that attempted to limit democracy, limited the reach of the Union and the breadth of the entire experiment. Should the South rely on forcing the issue on slavery, the northern response would be a paramount factor in determining whether war would result. But as to supposed cultural differences between North and South, these were useful expedients in justifying political action. W. J. Cash should perhaps close this chapter with some wise words on the southern aspiration to separate nationality:

> Do I need to add that the politician universally succeeds in the measure in which he is able to embody, in deeds or in words, the essence, not of what his clients are strictly, but of their dream of themselves?[82]

81. Eaton, *Freedom-of-Thought Struggle*, pp. 325, 345; Carl Degler, 'The Two Cultures and the Civil War', in Stanley Coben and Lorman Ratner (eds) *The Development of an American Culture* (Englewood Cliffs, NJ: Prentice-Hall, 1970), pp. 92–119.
82. Cash, *Mind of the South*, p. 92.

CHAPTER THREE

Sectional Tensions Resolved, 1840–50

> I speak today out of a solicitous and anxious heart, for the restoration to the country of that quiet and that harmony, which makes the blessings of this Union so rich and so dear to us all.
>
> DANIEL WEBSTER

The pace of American development in the decade 1840–50 was so accelerated that it inevitably generated debate over the future direction of this experiment in nation-forming. The United States witnessed immense expansion and striking victory in war. It saw the extension and rationalization of the second two-party system. But the greater the extension and development of the United States system across the North American continent, the more fervent became the debate over its fundamental character, and the more likely became a fracturing of that system. By 1840 there were two contrasting views of the nature of 'liberty'. Although the American political system endured other tensions and focused on different concerns – anxieties over foreign immigration, for example, began to fester during these years – the prime issue underlying sectional disruption was slavery, because only this issue could frame a regional divergence that would result in a resort to force of arms. Before 1850 such tensions could be resolved, not by force (although this remained a possibility) but by an acceptance of slavery as a legitimate facet of American constitutional and judicial life in the Union 'as it was'. Disquiet would increase when it became clear that southerners expected this to expand commensurate with the expansion of the Union after 1850 and extend its tentacles into northern political life. How this *modus vivendi* was reached is the subject of this chapter. As Daniel Webster declared, 'I profess to love liberty as much as any man living, but I profess to love American liberty, that liberty which is secured to the country by the government under which we live; and I have no great opinion of that other and higher liberty which disregards the restraints of law and the Constitution'.[1] The result of attempting to secure this constitutional protection for slavery was one of the most celebrated feats in American history, but one of the least enduring.

The rise of anti-slavery politics

One of the most potent catalysts for conflict and instability within the American body politic, which two generations of American politicians struggled to resolve, was provided by the growing influence of anti-slavery politics in the North. The 'threat' posed by these movements provided southerners with an 'enemy' against which their own sense of reciprocal identity was fashioned. The main achievement of these diverse 'abolitionist' groups, all of whom were motivated by a commitment to the unqualified abolition of slavery (as opposed to the gradualist anti-slavery movement of the preceding era), was keeping the slavery issue at the forefront of those political matters set before the electorate of the United States – even though their nostrums were unreservedly rejected by the voters. This achievement was all the more impressive in the face of pressure to suppress discussion of slavery; and there can be no doubt that there were many other issues that bore upon the attention, and tolerance, of the voters.

The abolitionists and their allies were an outgrowth of liberal, reforming movements which grew up in other western societies during this period. American abolitionists received inspiration and support from like-minded men and women in Great Britain. The passage of the bill to abolish slavery in the British Empire through the House of Commons in 1833 had shown how effective lobbying, and winning the moral and intellectual case, could bring about a major legislative victory.[2] The various abolitionist factions were concerned with ameliorating other social evils as well as slavery. They had strong views on improving education, on women's rights, temperance, on the evils of urbanization, on the

1.   Quoted in Major L. Wilson, *Space, Time and Freedom: The Quest for Nationality and the Irrepressible Conflict, 1815–1861* (Westport, CT: Greenwood, 1974), p. 167.
2.   Howard Temperley, *British Anti-Slavery, 1833–1870* (Columbia, SC: University of South Carolina Press, 1972), p. 193.

reform of factories, and the need for a religious revival. Although they themselves were not particularly sympathetic to the spread of industrial, urban civilization, especially in New England, they took full advantage of the spread among the well-educated, urban middle class of sensibility, anxiety and idealism. These developments were related to the Second Great Awakening of Protestant, evangelical zeal that stemmed from the late 1820s, the spread of Sunday schools, the Young Men's Christian Association (YMCA), and the increasing influence of itinerant, evangelical preachers. Much of this revivalism was focused on doctors, lawyers and business people. The importation of Methodism from Britain added to this effervescent cocktail. Although revivalism and abolitionism were not synonymous, they were infused with similar impulses and characterized by the same apocalyptic and religious rhetoric. Certainly the notion that slavery abused and defiled Americans as God's 'chosen' people was central to explaining the passion and missionary zeal of many abolitionists.[3]

Their leaders were men of unrestrained dogmatism and eloquence, William Lloyd Garrison, the formidable Theodore Weld and Angelina Grimké, Wendell Phillips and Benjamin and Lewis Tappan. They were dedicated to the notion that duty and the cherished belief that what was *right* should always triumph over expediency. Tactics were not their strong point. Garrison preached a doctrine ambiguously described as 'immediatism', that is to say, immediate abolition, which amounted to a declaration of an ultimate goal rather than a realization of what was immediately practicable. It is not surprising that many abolitionists felt a sense of release or fulfilment by launching their campaigns. Wendell Phillips once remarked that all abolitionists had 'good cause to be grateful to the slave for the benefit we have received to *ourselves*, in working for *him*'. Their ranks included one former runaway slave, Frederick Douglass, a brilliant, self-taught man, tenacious and brave. He was a dazzling orator, accomplished mimic and fine writer. But he was sensitive to criticism and quick to take offence; his relations with his white colleagues were sometimes tense. Given

3.   David Donald, 'Toward a Reconsideration of Abolitionists', in Donald, *Lincoln Reconsidered*, 2nd enlarged edn (New York: Alfred A. Knopf, 1989), p. 28; Richard Carwardine, *Transatlantic Revivalism: Popular Evangelicalism in Britain and America, 1790–1865* (Westport, CT: Greenwood, 1978), pp. 19–29, 42–3; Louis Billington, ' "To America We Will Go": British Methodist Preachers in the United States, 1800–60', in Brian Holden Reid and John White (eds) *American Studies: Essays in Honour of Marcus Cunliffe* (London: Macmillan, 1991), pp. 44–63.

such levels of (often naked) emotional commitment, it is not surprising to discover that abolitionists often spent more time warring among themselves than campaigning against slaveowners. They were imbued by a romantic quest to benefit American society at large. They thought that their movement, by mitigating racial prejudice, would benefit whites as much, if not more, than blacks. One may applaud their courage, though sometimes deplore their tactics and self-indulgence. They were inveterate campaigners and protesters whose forte was not executive leadership of institutions. In their own day they earned reputations for being insidious, fanatical, unbalanced extremists. It must be said that, on occasions, they did little to counteract this impression.[4]

But their initial forays in this campaign dedicated solely to the extirpation of slavery started modestly enough. The South was bombarded by anti-slavery pamphlets and Congress with petitions demanding the abolition of slavery. Some South Carolina post offices had their mail disinfected against such poisonous germs. A number of South Carolinians demanded that the North police itself against this fanaticism. A supporter of John C. Calhoun, Duff Green, called for all anti-slavery talk to be declared illegal. Another South Carolinian claimed that 'if the Non-Slaveholding States . . . will come forward patriotically, generously, and fairly and unite with the South – *then and only then will the South be saved'*. In 1835–40 the view that slavery was a positive good had spread to states other than South Carolina. But in evaluating this view a conundrum is confronted. The various abolition societies peaked at about 200,000 members in 1840. A good number of these included disenfranchised women; in the presidential election of 1840 the Liberty Party, whose candidate for the presidency was James G. Birney, secured only 7,000 votes out of a total of 2.5 million. Contrary to the southern view, abolitionists encountered a comparable level of hostility in the North to that faced in the South: greeting abolitionist sympathizers with fusillades of rotten vegetables and abuse was a common (and very popular) sideshow at abolitionist meetings; although the lynching of Elijah P. Lovejoy in 1837 was a glaring, violent exception rather than a rule. If the North was so opposed to radical anti-slavery movements, and racial prejudice against Negroes seemed to increase in inverse proportion to a proximity to the peculiar institution, then

4.   Merton L. Dillon, *The Abolitionists: The Growth of a Dissenting Minority* (New York: Norton, 1974, 1979), pp. 30, 36–8, 43, 58–9, 71; William S. McFeely, *Frederick Douglass* (New York: Norton, 1991), pp. 97, 108.

why should the South feel so threatened? 'If the North was never committed to abolitionism', asks William Freehling, 'why should the South have felt compelled to secede?' This, Freehling affirms, is one of the enduring riddles of the secession crisis. Certainly, when looked at in this light the wild claims of fanaticism on both sides made by the 'revisionist' historians of the inter-war years, appear utterly misconceived.[5]

But this approach, viewing the secession crisis as some kind of enigma, is really turning into a mystery something that is essentially not mysterious. If southerners exaggerated the degree to which the South was a cohesive social and political unit, it is hardly surprising that they exaggerated the unity and outlook of a section of the country of which the great majority of southerners were wholly ignorant. Historians are apt to believe that those who take momentous decisions have a profound understanding of the forces that they seek to direct. But decision-makers are not men of the study and often display an astounding misapprehension of the realities of the situation which they really face. In short, great dilemmas or crises do not invariably inspire deep understanding. But to suggest this is not to assert that the politicians that led the United States were in some way a 'blundering' generation, or that they were somehow more prone to blundering than any other generation of political leaders in the west. If they had a weakness it was listening to those who talked wildly about the advantages conferred by war while lacking any experience of it themselves. James H. Hammond, for instance, felt in 1835 that 'Fanatics' could 'be silenced in but one way *Terror-death*'. Incendiaries and other trouble-makers should be returned to the South to face trial or 'we shall dissolve the Union, and *seek by war* the redress denied us'.[6]

Contrary to the impression given by this kind of alarmist talk, the early abolitionist essays in politics were fumbling and rather aimless. Their efforts were confined to the dispatch of anti-slavery publications, petitions to Congress and the publication in the newspapers of lists of those who were 'pledged' to support the unconditional and immediate abolition of slavery. These attitudes were marked by the conventional (though, in this case, passionate) rejection of party politics. Indeed many abolitionists

5.   William H. Freehling, *The Road to Disunion: Secessionists at Bay, 1776–1854* (New York: Oxford UP, 1990), pp. 290–4; Richard H. Sewell, *Ballots for Freedom: Anti-Slavery Politics in the United States, 1837–1860* (New York: Oxford UP, 1980), p. 78.

6.   Quoted in Freehling, *Road to Disunion*, p. 295.

were of the opinion that their efforts would 'purify' party politics. Garrison adamantly opposed any party involvement, and Lewis Tappan argued against the creation of a third party; many were content to wait upon the election of the Whig, William H. Harrison, in 1840. Garrison favoured spurning political activities of any kind, which rather overlooked the necessity for central organization and funding for any successful movement. Yet Hammond in 1836 reacted to these puny forays by introducing the 'gag rule' which sought to reduce congressional consideration of anti-slavery petitions; under the original rule such documents could be tabled, which allowed a measure of recognition; but in 1840 this outlet, too, was sealed off.[7]

Thus was laid down the fundamental approach of southern politicians towards Congress and slavery. It was marked by a staggering degree of hyperbole and exaggeration of the influence and representativeness of abolition spokesmen. John C. Calhoun had argued in his resolutions of 27 December 1837 that Congress was first the 'common agent' of all the sovereign states and thus should exercise the prime duty of 'strengthening and upholding' the domestic institutions of all the states represented in the Congress, which included slavery. This provided the thrust for the southern argument of the 1850s which enshrined a paradox: southern spokesmen argued that slavery was a local matter and not the business of Congress; yet simultaneously they demanded the full protection of congressional authority, including complete constitutional and legal sanction in the territories. Congressional 'non- intervention' demanded by southerners, in short, was a code word for 'intervention'. Their overall approach failed to distinguish clearly between abolitionism and anti-slavery; the two were crucially different; after all, abolitionism was only the most militant form of anti-slavery; the anti-slavery groups advocated political action which favoured opposition to the further extension of slavery. This effort at extending control over congressional opinion and freedom of debate in favour of slavery, rebounded on its authors. At a time when American expansion once more became a heated issue, the activities of the 'Slave Power' began to agitate anti-slavery minds. It acted as a major force behind the

7.   Sewell, *Ballots for Freedom*, pp. 8–9, 16, 24, 27, 31–4, 39, 45–51, 64–6, 77, 88; Don E. Fehrenbacher, *The Dred Scott Case* (New York: Oxford UP, 1978), pp. 120–4. The value of Freehling's detailed study of the gag rule is reduced by his clotted and convoluted style. See *Road to Disunion*, pp. 310–12. The combination of cloudy rhetoric and 'Cagney and Lacey' street slang is very irritating.

creation of the Liberty Party and the discrediting of those who had argued (like Garrison) that the abolition of slavery was far too serious a business to be entrusted to party politicians. In the 1844 presidential election, the Liberty ticket polled 65,608 votes. Lewis Tappan, who had previously abhorred the idea of forming a new party, showed all the zeal of a late convert. Professor Fehrenbacher is surely correct in suggesting that the root of the intermittent sectional crisis, which erupted in the southern move to secede from the Union in 1860–61 that led to war, lay in their insecure reaction to the ferocity of northern anti-slavery denunciation. Often its ferocity was in inverse proportion to the degree of support it excited among northern voters. This was the source of anxiety, not fears about the restriction of slavery in the territories or the return of escaped slaves – which were but symptoms of the essential problem. The South seemed to want to munch its pastries and store them in the larder at the same time. It seemed to be risking all to lose all. To describe the gag rule, in William Freehling's words, as the 'Pearl Harbor of the slave controversy' seems unduly melodramatic, and assumes a continuity of escalation in this crisis comparable to the escalation of violence leading up to the Second World War, which is inappropriate in this context. But the 'gag rule' is certainly a significant milestone in the road to the politicization of the anti-slavery movement.[8]

Such southern congressional manoeuvres contributed to a widespread fear that the South was dominating American politics; that 'The northern states are treated as provinces to the South. We have given in too much to their extreme notions and abstractions', in the words of Gideon Welles, an ally of former President Martin Van Buren, who was adopting an increasingly vociferous anti-slavery stance. Van Buren's position reflected a bitter schism in 1847–48 within the New York Democratic Party between the Radical Democrats (popularly known as 'Barnburners'), led by the former president, who sought to establish 'permanent perpetual barriers against the extension of slavery', and the conservatives (or 'Hunkers', led by Senator Daniel Dickinson, who opposed the restriction of slavery). The New York Democracy was the only state Democratic Party that erupted into civil war – the Democratic Party maintaining its national cohesion until 1860. There was very little concern

---

8.   Fehrenbacher, *Dred Scott*, pp. 122–3; Sewell, *Ballots for Freedom*, p. 110; Freehling, *Road to Disunion*, p. 308.

expressed for slaves or free blacks in these bitter disputes, which focused rather on the nature of white supremacy. 'The question is not, whether black men are to be made free, but whether we white men are to remain free', one declared. Senator John A. Dix, later a member of the Buchanan Administration, exclaimed that Americans must realize their 'sacred duty to consecrate these [Western] spaces to the multiplication of the white race'.[9]

Throughout the 1840s the second electoral system that had developed since President Andrew Jackson's triumph over John Quincy Adams in the presidential election of 1828, began to break down. A conservative party, which eventually assumed the name Whig, competed with a more egalitarian party which summoned up the genius of the 'common man', the Democrats. The former advocated centralized government expenditure, a national bank and 'internal improvements', of the western territories and states, coordinated by these agencies. The latter tended to oppose all federally sponsored internal improvements as infringing the freedom of individual states and citizens. Paradoxically, although Democrats argued that the least form of government was the best, they preferred a 'strong', activist president, like the masterful and abrasive Jackson, or the grim, surly, diligent, suspicious and resentful James K. Polk, also from Tennessee. Polk was a 'dark horse' candidate, who surprisingly seized the Democratic Party nomination in 1844 and defeated the perennial Whig presidential hopeful, Henry Clay, in the election that year.

During these interminable and never-ending electoral contests, politics was influenced by two powerful forces. Because the Whigs themselves had been forced to adopt some popularist slogans to oust Jackson's successor, Van Buren in 1840, all politicians of both parties had to pay obeisance to the 'common man', and attempt to demonstrate that political measures and electoral triumphs were 'a response to grass-roots pressure for change'. This led a conservative party, like the Whigs, into a fundamental paradox that could be resolved only by fielding elderly, military candidates, who could run against discredited Democratic 'politicians'. The art of government was so uncomplicated, the argument ran, that its simple, basic tasks could be discharged by many men who required no special training or knowledge.[10] The second influence was revivalism, the emotional torrents of which stimulated

9. Sewell, *Ballots for Freedom*, pp. 143–7, 172–3.
10. Richard Hofstadter, *Anti-Intellectualism in American Life* (London: Jonathan Cape, 1964), pp. 166–71.

propagandists on both sides to employ the devices of antithesis, polarization and anathematization that increased the political temperature. Richard Carwardine has also suggested that an increased stress on such techniques in the innumerable elections that occurred every year 'encouraged them [Whig and Democratic propagandists] to present the election campaign as the agency of political renewal and community redemption'.[11] This led to two features that were inherently unsettling for the American political system. The first is the widespread acceptance among politicians that the United States was born with a political system that embodied perfection; yet this should be subjected to constant change because of the American passion for 'progress'. Hence the omnipresent *unstable pluralism* of American politics in the first half of the nineteenth century.[12] Secondly, because it was born in a state of pristine perfection, the American Constitution, and the political system derived from it, was in constant need of redemption – of being saved from the unwelcome consequences of that very progress most Americans enthused about. This process was complicated by the failure to secure consensus on the nature of the ideals that underpinned this novel experiment in republican democracy. All Americans were convinced that this experiment represented an example for the edification of the rest of humankind, even a model for its imitation – but a model of what? Was it to be individual rights and free, mobile labour, or was it to be the liberty of property-holders to enslave their work-force as the basis for a prosperous civilization? These pressing issues, enwrapped by fears about the character of American destiny, were propounded ceaselessly in elections without placating the two amorphous groups – pro- and anti-slavery – that gradually took shape in the late 1840s. This occurred even while other important economic and cultural issues remained crucial in dividing parties. Popular slogans such as 'Manifest Destiny' concealed as much as they revealed about the forces underlying American expansionism. The result, which was hardly surprising given the legalistic and moralistic character of American democracy, was to seek refuge in constitutional formulae, which could not solve the underlying divergence; over time it would exacerbate it. Such forces underlay

11. Richard Carwardine, 'Religious Revival and Political Renewal in Antebellum America', in Colin Mathew and Jane Garett (eds) *Revival and Renewal Since 1700: Essays Presented to John Walsh* (London: Hambledon Press, 1993), pp. 128, 143.
12. See above, pp. 31–2, 35–6.

the political disputes that disrupted the second party system and saw the rise of a third force, the Free Soil Party, and the replacement of the Whig Party in the 1850s by the spiritual progeny of the Free Soil Party, the Republican Party.

Needless to say, any move that resulted in the expansion of the United States added much additional pressure to a political system already impacted under the weight of its own contradictions. Such an expansion, on a massive scale, occurred as a result of the Mexican War, 1846–48. This dashing, decisive and short war, fought far distant from American territory, became a model for Americans of the 1850s of how a war would (and should) be fought. On 14 September 1847, United States troops entered Mexico City signifying the utter rout of the Mexican forces and signalling that a punitive peace commensurate with that victory would be imposed on Mexico. By the most important of the twenty-three clauses of the Treaty of Guadalupe Hidalgo, 2 February 1848, Mexico ceded almost half her territory, including Upper California, New Mexico (not to be confused with the modern state of that name) and offered confirmation of the United States' right to Texas (which had been annexed in the last days of the Tyler Administration in 1845). In return Mexico received from the United States $15 million, and a further sum of $3,250,000 to pay outstanding American citizens' claims.[13] Despite some outlandish expansionist demands for the annexation of all Mexico, the United States was more interested in Mexican territory than in the Mexican populace. This treaty was ratified by the Senate thirty-eight to fourteen on 10 March 1848, and American troops left Mexico City on 12 June. Largely bereft of inhabitants, a huge area was made available for settlement by whites and incorporation into the United States. These territories, minus Texas, comprised more than half a million square miles, and form what is now the modern states of California, Nevada, Utah, most of New Mexico and Arizona, as well as parts of Wyoming and Colorado. But which social form would be used to settle this vast acquisition?[14]

13. 'As was its custom, the United States paid for its territorial acquisitions in order to legitimize their military conquest', Raymond Aron, *The Imperial Republic* (London: Weidenfeld & Nicolson, 1975), p. xxviii.

14. Otis A. Singletary, *The Mexican War* (Chicago UP, 1960), pp. 160–3; David Potter, *The Impending Crisis, 1848–61* (New York: Harper & Row, 1976), pp. 1–6; Gordon Connell-Smith, *The United States and Latin America* (London: Heinemann, 1974), pp. 79–80.

The Wilmot Proviso

It is no coincidence that a number of measures were laid down, as legalistic formulae, within a period of less than eighteen months after the signing of the Treaty of Guadalupe Hidalgo. Each bore upon the question of the extension of slavery into the western territories. Slavery had originally been prohibited north of the Ohio River by the North West Ordinance of 1787. This had effectively turned a blind eye to slavery in the South West, though Thomas Jefferson continued to give the impression that Congress in 1784–85 had come close to prohibiting it throughout the West. What really counted was the pattern, and bias, of local political power, for the Ordinance outlawed slavery in all areas that came under the sway of congressional authority. Hence the long-running dispute over the nature of congressional authority in the western territories, turning on the finer points of legal and congressional interpretation. Professor Fehrenbacher argues persuasively that the North West Ordinance offered a precedent for a congressional declaration akin to the Wilmot Proviso, for the 1787 document 'did plainly amount to a strong assertion of Congressional control over the West' before statehood and the sale of land. This abiding question, as to whether Congress enjoyed the power to prevent slavery spreading to the western territories, would underlie the whole dispute over the expansion of the so-called slave power.[15]

This issue had surfaced occasionally before 1840. For instance, during the debate over the admission of Missouri in 1819–20, the Tallmadge Amendment was added to the statehood bill. Its authors argued that it should be added automatically to all new statehood bills, thus abolishing slavery within their frontiers as they entered the Union (and all slave children born therein were to be emancipated once they had reached the age of 25). Nonetheless the Jackson-dominated coalition in the Democratic Party which prevailed until 1840 attempted successfully to suppress the slavery issue, mainly because its core lay in the South. Martin Van Buren's conversion to the slavery restriction cause was as much a response to local as to national pressures. The Mexican War had effectively brought this agreement to disagree to an end.[16]

15. Fehrenbacher, *Dred Scott*, pp. 77–80, 82.
16. Fehrenbacher, *Dred Scott*, pp. 103, 117; John Niven, *Martin Van Buren* (New York: Oxford UP, 1983), pp. 565, 568–70.

Senator Calhoun had, during the Mexican War, brought his resolutions of 1837 before Congress again on 19 February 1847. With his characteristic desire to enjoy the fruits of both sides of the argument, this move recapitulated the southern position that slavery was a local institution outside the jurisdiction of Congress, and yet simultaneously demanded the full protection of Congress in the territories.[17] The Wilmot Proviso of August 1846 had no patience with such casuistry. It referred to the territory gained from Mexico, and declared that 'neither slavery nor involuntary servitude shall ever exist in any part of said territory': Congress had the power to prohibit slavery and should effectively use it. Even though some of its supporters were motivated by racial prejudice and a desire to keep the territories free of slaves, the Wilmot Proviso was a strong and unambiguous statement of anti-slavery sentiment (for one could still be prejudiced against blacks yet believe that slavery was wicked). Such feelings would be shortly described as 'free soil' sympathy. Its author, Representative David Wilmot of Pennsylvania, led a coalition of northern Democrats aligned on a series of issues, some far removed from a dislike of slavery, that were distinctly anti-southern (especially opposition to southern domination of political patronage). Furthermore, unexpected events, such as the 1849 Gold Rush to California, served only to highlight the intractable problems surrounding the settlement of the West.[18]

The Wilmot Proviso (which was never passed) became gospel for all of those who believed that, if only strict limits could be placed on slavery, it would wither and die. As Wilmot claimed, 'Slavery has written itself the seeds of its own dissolution. Keep it within limits, let it remain where it now is, and in time it will wear itself out'. The only alternative for slaveholders would be emancipation.[19] Some observers felt that such a formula was too black and white and forced southern slaveholders into a corner. The Polk Administration supported a proposal advanced in July 1848 by John M. Clayton of Delaware that the Missouri Compromise line of 36°30′ be extended westwards. David Potter writes with considerable enthusiasm in favour of this compromise proposal, as one would expect from a historian who was convinced that the Civil War could have been avoided. It was, he claims, 'the

17. Fehrenbacher, *Dred Scott*, pp. 122–3; Potter, *Impending Crisis*, p. 60.
18. Fehrenbacher, *Dred Scott*, pp. 128–9; Sewell, *Ballots for Freedom*, pp. 171–5.
19. Sewell, *Ballots for Freedom*, p. 191.

forgotten alternative of the sectional controversy'. It was
unambiguous, 'it spelt out clearly what each side would gain and
lose'.[20] Quite so, this clarity explains why it failed: for increasingly
self-confident spokesmen in the North were quite unprepared to
sanction any further extension of slavery westwards, in whatever
form. And that resolve would strengthen and not weaken. Any
suggestion that the Missouri Compromise could have provided an
enduring solution to these passionate disagreements is fanciful.[21]

That all these vexed matters agitated politicians, if not the
voters, is underlined by the emergence of the Free Soil Party to
fight the 1848 presidential election with Martin Van Buren as its
nominee. Van Buren was a handsome man, but his comely
appearance and charming manner concealed a calculating mien.
Indeed, Van Buren enjoyed a Machiavellian reputation and was
renowned as a dazzling political manipulator. Occasionally, his
reputation could be self-defeating and he excited a good deal of
ambivalence. Yet Van Buren's conversion to the Free Soil creed
was sincere, and out of a noisy, excited convention in the railway
station at Herkimer, New York, in 1848, had come the roots of the
Free Soil Party: 'Free Trade, Free Labour, Free Soil, Free Speech,
Free Men'. Charles Francis Adams, a byword for fastidious
integrity, was the vice presidential nominee. Van Buren gave shape
to this new party and added political weight and national
experience to its rather light air of enthusiasm. His conversion
points up the important distinction that southern leaders failed to
make between abolitionism and anti-slavery. Whereas the former
failed to excite little popular enthusiasm, the latter was now
attracting political leaders of weight and reputation.[22]

The Free Soil Party in the 1848 presidential election improved
upon Birney and the Liberty Party's showing, but not by much.
Van Buren had failed to gain a single vote in the electoral college
but had managed to get about 10 per cent of the total vote –
though more than half of his total stemmed from just two states,
Massachusetts and New York. Yet a dozen Free Soil candidates
were elected to Congress. Van Buren considered the campaign a
'forlorn hope'. The voters may not have shared the preoccupation
of politicians with slavery and its restriction but slow progress was
being made. In a tightly fought contest, the Free Soil Party had

20. Potter, *Impending Crisis*, pp. 56–7.
21. Sewell, *Ballots for Freedom*, pp. 144, 150–1.
22. Niven, *Van Buren*, pp. 575–6.

denied the Democratic nominee, Lewis Cass, New York and General Zachary Taylor, the Whig candidate and eventual victor, Ohio. Whereas the Liberty Party had paved the way for the Free Soilers, by securing cooperation among anti-slavery Whigs, Democrats and independents, the Free Soil Party laid the foundation stones for the rise of the Republican Party.[23]

All these disparate groups kept the slavery issue at the forefront of politics. Calhoun had warned 'Abolition and the Union cannot co-exist', and one might add those that Calhoun *presumed* to be abolitionists. Such views indicated a fundamental cleavage but one that did not reflect much political reality let alone strength. The abolitionists were not a powerful force, although they lurked incorrigibly on the flanks of American politics. Their real strength lay not in the numbers of voters they rallied to their cause, but in their articulacy and capacity to project, and defend an argument.[24] Out of this resulting controversy rose fear of the so-called 'slave power', a malign, ceaselessly active, anti-democratic conspiracy to advance the influence and wealth of the slaveowning oligarchy. Because northern conservatives came to the conclusion that public order and stability demanded the restriction, if not outright stifling of the freedom of speech of those who denounced slavery, the maintenance of the liberties of northern whites became a paramount fear in the anti-slavery agitation.[25]

Yet within months of taking office, the Taylor Administration was confronted by a sectional crisis that threatened to engulf the Union in war. Whatever the strength of political opinions, and electoral shifts of opinion, it is the *action* – the decisions taken by politicians – which determine the chain of circumstances that result in war or peace.

The Compromise of 1850

The confrontation culminating in the Compromise of 1850 was the most dangerous crisis confronting the Union since the Nullification Crisis, seventeen years before. It has been correctly identified as a 'fruit' of manifest destiny. The extension of American civilization across the continental heartland could serve

---

23. Ibid., p. 590; Sewell, *Ballots for Freedom*, pp. 155, 161, 164–5, 167.
24. Fehrenbacher, *Dred Scott*, p. 122.
25. Sewell, *Ballots for Freedom*, pp. 199–201; Rush Welter, *The Mind of America, 1820–1860* (New York: Columbia UP, 1975), p. 343.

only to resuscitate sectional strife. At bottom, this perennial and unavoidable conflict was paradoxical. As one historian has observed, 'If the removal of sectional controversy opened the way to new expansion, expansion would, in its train, bring on a renewal of sectional controversy'. The issues under discussion, although they were expressed in drab and legalistic language, came to assume a graphic and ominous symbolic significance.[26] In the opinion of various historians, the Compromise eventually arrived at should be judged an 'Armistice' and the process by which it was agreed, a forerunner (though successful, on this occasion) of the final crisis that followed a decade later. In Bruce Collins's view 'The crisis of 1850 was a dress rehearsal for the show-down of 1860–1. Many of the arguments were the same. Many of the participants were the same'.[27] The focus of the discussion here should be, not how and why the political crisis developed in the way that it did, but rather, why the efforts at compromise were successful and, further, why civil war did not erupt ten years before the detonation of 1861?

This significant sectional crisis grew out of the attempts to bring statehood to the immense patrimony seized after the Mexican War. In California this issue was especially urgent after the Gold Rush of 1849; that territory desired early admission to the Union as a 'free' state and had already advanced very far in organizing its own government unaided by federal agencies. President Zachary Taylor was anxious that, if this wish was not speedily attended to, California would declare her independence. The South demanded a new 'slave' state to balance this increase in the non-slave states. The threat of anarchy in the South West was given further point by the claim aggressively advanced by Texas to all the territory held by New Mexico, east of the Rio Grande, which included Santa Fé. The federal government denied this claim and the possibility presented itself of a bloody clash between federal troops and Texas volunteer forces. The threat of civil war was indeed very real and took a more substantial and menacing form than just politicians uttering windy threats at one another in Washington.[28]

A compromise was eventually arrived at and was justified on pragmatic grounds. 'Ask yourself if it is right', A. G. Brown of

26. Wilson, *Space, Time and Freedom*, pp. 176–7.
27. Bruce Collins, *The Origins of America's Civil War* (London: Edward Arnold, 1981), p. 86.
28. Allan Nevins, *The Ordeal of the Union* (New York: Scribner's, 1947), I, pp. 327–34.

Mississippi was to ask, 'to exasperate eight millions of [southern] people upon an abstraction; a matter to us of substance and of life, but to you the merest shadow of an abstraction'.[29] But at every stage in the crisis those seeking to broker a compromise confronted the rigidities and inertia of the American system of government. A suspicion of 'strong' government and efficient centralized control were the keynote of the age.[30] Zachary Taylor himself had little experience of executive government or of political tactics (his military tactics had tended to be ragged); he was another example of the 'outsider' who entered American politics at the top.[31] But he was not without shrewdness, was amenable to advice and had a sound sense of his own objectives and priorities. Above all, like Jackson before him, he understood the paramount need to safeguard the integrity of the federal government. His determination to uphold this was reinforced by flinty resolve and a determination not to be brow-beaten. That Taylor had arrived at this position was itself little short of astonishing. He was a Louisiana slaveholder. He was that rarest of political figures before 1860, a southerner who enjoyed a sense of perspective on the 'peculiar institution' and could see the northern point of view. To the horror of southern Whigs, Senator William H. Seward of New York began to exert considerable influence in the Taylor Administration. Whereas northern 'doughfaces' supported the southern view, southern faces were very resistant to dough or any other substance that shaped a smile of compromise that was tolerant of northern worries. Perhaps Taylor arrived at this position because he was not a politician at all. Certainly his stance led to Whig anxiety over the future of their party in the South.[32]

In the Congress, although the Senate was inclined towards compromise, the House of Representatives had been reduced to a state of powerlessness. A southerner, Howell Cobb, had been elected Speaker of the House after a bruising struggle and virtually all business had come to a halt by January 1850 (including consideration of the president's State of the Union address). Cobb

29. Quoted in Fehrenbacher, *Dred Scott*, p. 164.
30. See above, pp. 37–8, 40–1; Nevins, *Ordeal of the Union*, I, pp. 158–9.
31. Before his election as president in 1848 he had not once voted in a presidential election. Elbert B. Smith, *The Presidencies of Zachary Taylor and Millard Fillmore* (Lawrence, KS: University Press of Kansas, 1988), pp. 20, 50.
32. Fehrenbacher, *Dred Scott*, p. 158; Mark J. Stagmaier, 'Zachary Taylor Versus the South', *Civil War History* 33 (1987), p. 219.

openly sanctioned southern obstructionism; he ensured that the dispute over the Texan frontier did not come to the vote, and the president's policy was continually denounced. This paralysis was accentuated by the time-consuming preference of the age for expansive oratory; rare was the senatorial speech that concluded after two hours; four or five was nearer the average. This resulted in a southern seizure of the initiative in Congress, and the president was stymied.[33]

The essence of Taylor's policy was to secure California and New Mexico as free states at the earliest opportunity *without compensation for the South*, and further, to resist Texan lawlessness and crush any secessionist resistance by force if such an extreme measure was required. He was also determined to call a halt to filibustering. He was not blind to southern interests; on the contrary, he sought to gain California and New Mexico's entry to the Union without reference to the Wilmot Proviso (and congressional intrusion into the legitimacy of slavery in the territories) which would have been humiliating for the South.[34] By 1850, the 'Wilmot Proviso', in William Brock's words 'had transformed abstract discussion of southern rights and hypothetical abolitionist designs into a genuine popular movement in defence of southern society'. Consequently, there is a marked contrast between the frantic behaviour of southern politicians and their calmer northern counterparts.[35] The frenetic over-reaction of southerners was given shape, and indeed cloaked in respectability, by John C. Calhoun's 'Address of the southern Delegates in Congress to their Constituents' delivered in a secret session in January 1849. As an authoritative statement of southern views it has all the piquancy and persuasiveness of a Soviet *Pravda* pronouncement blaming the United States for starting the Korean War. All actions since the North West Ordinance (including the Missouri Compromise of 1820) were the result of 'aggression' against the South. In the 'Address' and in his last great speech to the Senate in March 1850, Calhoun argued that this would inevitably result in a disruption of the Union because of the increasing economic, financial and demographic imbalance which the census of 1850 revealed was increasingly favouring the North.

33.   Fehrenbacher, *Dred Scott*, pp. 159–60; William R. Brock, *Parties and Political Conscience: American Dilemmas, 1840–1850* (Millwood, NY: KTO, 1979), pp. 281–2, 288–9.

34.   Smith, *Taylor and Fillmore*, pp. 100–1, 102, 120.

35.   Brock, *Parties and Political Conscience*, p. 278–80.

Calhoun estimated that if slavery were excluded from the territories seized after the Mexican War, the numbers of senators from the North would reach forty, with only twenty-four from the South.[36] But despite the alarm sounded among southern politicians, this had not yet spread to their electorate. Calhoun assumed that 'the North' would always act as a unit and frustrate the South, and underestimated the extent of the tolerance of slavery to be found in that section. He also underestimated the extent to which the presidency would be filled by those sympathetic to slavery and the most outrageous southern demands. Slaveholders would continue to exert a commanding influence over the executive branch until they over-reached themselves, split the Democratic Party, and ensured the election of Lincoln in 1860. Calhoun's most influential legacy was his refinement of this sense of a grotesquely exaggerated, disproportionate threat and sense of northern alienation. By comparison, Taylor's measured policy and careful, if obstinate, assessment of the courses open to him, seem refreshingly realistic.

Yet, Taylor was opposed bitterly by 'moderate' southerners in his own party, such as Alexander H. Stephens and Robert Toombs. This would be a recurring theme of increasing southern separation; 'moderates' would show little appreciation of the northern viewpoint, while stressing their Unionism, and would eventually side with the extremists in rejecting that view. Stephens and Toombs probably felt a sense of betrayal because they had both been among Taylor's earliest supporters for the Whig presidential nomination; watching the ascendancy of William H. Seward must have been a bitter and disillusioning experience for them. In a heated clash with the president, the date of which is disputed (perhaps it took place in February 1850, but more likely a few days before Taylor's sudden and unexpected death in July 1850) Stephens and Toombs uttered some unpleasant threats. These had been foreshadowed by an earlier meeting with representatives of the southern Whig congressional caucus. They were dismayed that Taylor was not only 'obstinately fixed', but also prepared to protect the northern Whig base (of almost ninety congressmen) while sacrificing if necessary his vociferous and

36. Smith, *Taylor and Fillmore*, pp. 107, 112, 113–15, 117. In 1850 they were evenly balanced at thirty senators each. See also Collins, *Origins of America's Civil War*, p. 87, who considers Calhoun's 'Address' as 'a brilliant propaganda ploy . . . the great debating point among Southern politicians in 1849', which is true enough.

disloyal southern colleagues, who amounted to only one-third
their number. This was an unusual, not to say freakish state of
affairs – a southern leader who was prepared to put his northern
political base before his southern. The Secretary of War, George
W. Crawford, had 'leaked' privileged information to Taylor's
southern critics. When the president instructed that firm orders
should be issued to the commander of federal forces at Santa Fé,
that any Texan incursions should be resisted by force, Crawford
refused to sign them. Taylor signed them himself.

Toombs threatened not only the hostility of the southern Whigs
(perhaps leading to efforts at impeachment) but also war, because
the southern states would aid Texas if it came to a fight. Taylor
was not a man to be threatened. He may not have used the precise
words later attributed to him by memoir writers on the exact
occasions later described vividly by those who lived through the
Civil War, but there can be no doubt that they conveyed the
essence of his policy. It was reported that Taylor (like Andrew
Jackson before him) was determined to see the laws executed and
Texan lawlessness suppressed, and if necessary would take
command of the Army himself. If secessionists 'were taken in
rebellion against the Union he would hang them with less
reluctance than he had hanged deserters and spies in Mexico'.
Southern demands were impertinent, 'intolerable and
revolutionary'. Toombs was left in no doubt about the president's
bellicose intentions. 'The worst of it is,' Toombs admitted, 'he will
do it'.[37]

An unseemly newspaper story later circulated that Toombs and
Stephens had harassed Taylor on his deathbed, indeed that their
importunate attentions had hastened his death. But nobody had
realized how serious Taylor's illness (typhoid) was, and nobody,
least of all he, thought he was going to die. But the critical nature
of this confrontation is sometimes overlooked, because of the
ameliorating effect of the sudden removal of Taylor's obstinate
and courageous presence from the scene. This effect was hastened
by the sustained praise lavished on the later compromisers
(especially Clay and Webster) and the simultaneous ridiculing of
Taylor's inexperienced and bumbling efforts as chief executive.
Taylor would not modify a policy he deemed correct; he would

---

37. Smith, *Taylor and Fillmore*, pp. 104, 107; although Seward did not need to
support the president in the Senate, see Brock, *Parties and Political Conscience*, pp.
287, 289. Stagmaier, 'Zachary Taylor Versus the South', pp. 224–7, 237–9, is a
convincing reconstruction.

not surrender in the face of bluster – and he probably calculated that this was exactly what southern calls to 'act promptly, boldly and decisively, with arms in their hand' amounted to. Taylor was the only president from Andrew Jackson to Abraham Lincoln with extensive military experience who faced down such threats. He calculated that the South, like South Carolina in 1833, could be overawed by the threat of a blockade of southern ports and a small-scale police action. But one thing is strikingly clear: there was no difference between what his opponents were saying in public and private. Taylor was adamant in defending his constitutional oath and the integrity of the Union 'at all hazards'. Zachary Taylor was a courageous and underrated chief executive, who showed a rare touch of fire in dealing with southern critics. Had he lived there can be no doubting his determination not to endure the preliminary scorches inflicted by the rising temperatures of the putative southern firebrands. The likelihood of some kind of military confrontation with the southern states was strong, but a discussion of whether this would have resulted in a civil war in 1850 should be deferred to the conclusion of the crisis.[38]

Even before Taylor's death the titular leader of the Whig Party, Henry Clay (who had been denied the White House on three occasions) was jostling forward to provide a compromise solution of his own. Clay abandoned Taylor's insistence that there should be no compensation for the South in the event of California's admission to the Union. There was an undoubted personal motive for Clay's intervention. Though his sincere wish to provide conciliatory measures – a soothing balm to calm ruffled nerves – should not be doubted, Clay was not without vanity. He was determined to assert his leadership of the Whig Party, and show beyond peradventure that its leader lay in Congress, and not in the White House, even though he had been unjustly deprived of this prize by unscrupulous 'politicians'. Doubtless his view would have changed had he resided at 1600 Pennsylvania Avenue; yet as a Whig, who tended to deplore the rise of a 'strong' presidency, Clay felt it right and proper that any solution to national ills should come from the legislature and not the executive branch.

In essence, his proposals included the following: (1) the entry of California into the Union as a free state at the earliest possible

---

38. Smith, *Taylor and Fillmore*, pp. 104–5, 121; Stagmaier, 'Zachary Taylor Versus the South', pp. 238–41.

date; (2) the organization of New Mexico and Utah for statehood, leaving their legislatures free to decide on the future of slavery; (3) Texas was to give up any parts of New Mexico she had unlawfully seized, yet was compensated by the agreement of the federal government to assume responsibility for the debts incurred by the Texan government before independence; (4) the Federal government was also to introduce legislation permitting the more rapid recovery of escaped slaves; and finally, the North was to be compensated on this point by, (5) the abolition of the slave trade in the District of Columbia, which many anti-slavery northerners felt to be a mocking, hypocritical commentary on the very workings of the Federal government itself, lubricated by so many fine declamations on the miracles worked by American freedom.[39]

A manoeuvre which did much to smooth the course of success was Clay's enlistment of Daniel Webster as an ally. In what became a celebrated oratorical tournament, on 7 March 1850 Webster, gaunt, gloomy and sepulchral in appearance, but a model of sunny, good health by comparison with Calhoun, delivered a reply to Calhoun's 4 March speech. In January 1850 Webster had taken the complaisant view that, 'All this agitation, I think, will subside, without serious result, but still it is mischievous and creates heart burnings. But the Union is not in danger'. Two months later he appeared to think that affairs had deteriorated, but not to the point of ultimate danger, although they had *the potential* to engender violence and fratricidal strife. At any rate, Webster thought his speech 'probably the most important effort of my life, and as likely as any other to be often referred to'. In his anthem sung in praise of the Union, Webster placed great faith in 'the law of nature, of physical geography' which would prevent slavery spreading westward. The Wilmot Proviso was therefore irrelevant and enshrining it in law, would serve no purpose other than as 'a taunt or a reproach'. Like other northern conservatives before and after him, Webster denounced anti-slavery dogmatists, and especially the abolitionists for stirring up passion. He agreed that the South had been responsible for this, too, but southern defenders of slavery did not excite the venom which he lavished on its northern critics. Webster's eloquent address, as polished and smooth as the white marble of which the Congress was built,

---

39. Brock, *Parties and Political Conscience*, pp. 290–1; Fehrenbacher, *Dred Scott*, pp. 159–60. The Texas debt amounted to $10 million. See Smith, *Taylor and Fillmore*, p. 110.

rested on the standard northern conservative defence of the peculiar institution. But he ridiculed the notion of peaceable secession that had been advanced by Calhoun. Any attempt at secession would result in war; 'the common property' of the Federal government could not be shared out equally among the states.[40]

These speeches were uttered while Taylor was still president, and he and Clay, whose relations were in any case tinged with antipathy and not a little jealousy on both sides, differed profoundly on the question of compensating the South. Although Clay had at first allied himself in the Senate with Thomas Hart Benton, this provoked southern hostility, because Henry J. Foote of Mississippi and others feared that the dismantling of any 'omnibus' bill (containing all the various elements of Clay's compromise package) at the hands of a select committee (a move favoured by Benton) chaired by Clay would lead to a manoeuvre by which California entered the Union without due compensation for the South. Clay and his supporters increasingly veered towards the southern viewpoint during the summer of 1850. The death of Taylor removed one complicating factor from the scene – the second time since 1841 that a Whig presidency had been crippled by the death through illness of an elderly, military incumbent; this looked increasingly like carelessness in choosing candidates for the nomination.

Taylor's successor was the vice president, Millard Fillmore, a handsome, immaculate, intelligent but rather driven and inflexible, self-made man. Some elements of continuity with the Taylor Administration, such as a determination to control Texan bellicosity, carried over into the new. But the major change came, of course, in relations with Clay and Webster and those who demanded an 'omnibus' bill which would assuage the South. A rival of his from New York state, Fillmore had little time for Senator William H. Seward, whose influence in the administration was abruptly curtailed. Webster entered the Cabinet as secretary of state and Clay virtually became the president's emissary to the Senate. Furthermore, Fillmore, having previously presided over the Senate as its president, listening to the florid and lengthy orations of Clay and Webster, became convinced that they were

---

40. Maurice G. Baxter, *One and Inseparable: Daniel Webster and the Union* (Cambridge, MA: Belknapp, 1984), pp. 409–10, 415–16; Nevins, *Ordeal of the Union*, I, pp. 286–96.

right and Taylor wrong, and that the Wilmot Proviso was provocative and unnecessary. This attitude, too, signalled the end of Seward's influence. Thus the opposition of the White House to an omnibus bill came to an end. Clay and Webster relied for the congressional passage of the omnibus bill on a group of moderate southerners. The position was complicated somewhat by the fact that no single party dominated the government: a caretaker Whig sat in the White House, the Democrats controlled the Senate, and no single party dominated the House. In the last week of July in a series of manoeuvres which has correctly been described as a 'kaleidoscopic' vortex, the omnibus was defeated.[41] Seward was convinced that 'the *extreme men* of the South will reject the Compromise'.

Out of the chaos, with Clay's leadership stymied, Stephen A. Douglas of Illinois emerged in the Senate as a political craftsman of inexhaustible enthusiasm and guile. The compromise package was broken up into its constituent parts and each offered for consideration on its relative merits. The moral aspect – especially in connection with the Fugitive Slave Law (which was to provoke so much fury) – was neglected in the technical and rather tedious debates. This might be attributed to the important part played by the Democratic Party in passing the legislation through the Senate and the House, and especially the northern Democrats, and the all-important ambiguity as to whether Democratic calls for 'non-intervention' in the affairs of the territories would allow slaveowners to transport their slaves with them should they move there. The bland but rather convenient – and ambiguous – formula inserted into the bills, 'consistent with the Constitution' glossed over this severe interpretative difficulty – a difficulty, alas, that could not be smoothed over by a mere concoction of words, blessed with legalistic mendacity though they might be. In this form, with wafer-thin minorities, the Compromise, in a 'little omnibus' package, which separated those bills concerned with slavery from those specifying state and territorial boundaries, passed the House of Representatives and was enshrined in law in September 1850.[42]

Space does not allow a detailed discussion of the legislative majorities, opinion and voting tallies, which have engaged the

41. Holman Hamilton, *Prologue to Conflict: The Crisis and Compromise of 1850* (University Press of Kentucky, 1964), pp. 109–11, 114.

42. Ibid., pp. 146, 156–61; Freehling, *Road to Disunion*, p. 506.

attention of political historians. Although Douglas, in a Senate speech paid customary obeisance to the Compromise's symbolic import as a shining beacon of patriotic unity, as 'no man and no party has acquired a triumph, except the party friendly to the Union triumphing over abolitionism and disunion',[43] the Compromise of 1850 lacked a dedicated, supportive constituency dedicated to its defence. It excited the loyalty of some people who supported some parts of it; but very few, who were politically active, at any rate, uncritically and unconditionally supported all of it, all of the time. Latent tensions and disagreeable realities were bound to percolate and spew their vicious bile on to the fragile sheen of its legalistic surface. Sir Walter Ralegh, in a bitter mood, once reflected that the superficial glitter of the Elizabethan Court shone 'like rotten wood'. For all the praise that was heaped on it during the 1850s – and by historians since – perhaps *because* of it – we should apply a similar judgement to the Compromise of 1850. It is significant also how much the dispute that was pursued in the Senate and the House was very much a *politicians'* disagreement, and the sense of crisis was largely confined to the visitors' gallery in those esteemed institutions. Although there was a measure of anxiety in the newspapers, the public was not worried to anything like the extent it was in January–March 1861. The hyperbole and exaggerated threats of southern politicians did not reflect the opinion of the great mass of southern citizens, who were persistently loyal to the Union. However, the extent of this crisis should not be underestimated. Serious pro-secession talk was being heard for the first time from sensible southerners of experience and reputation.

That the Compromise of 1850 reflected the patching up of a rupture between politicians, rather than between peoples, perhaps explains the moral relativism that so permeated it. Politicians who favoured compromise were primarily concerned with ensuring that the machinery of government should continue regardless. Both sides should, therefore, be offered a stake in the continuance of that machinery, which should not be endangered on the grounds of 'mere abstraction'. It was largely because of a preoccupation with expediency and practicalities that Webster was excoriated by Charles Sumner and others in Massachusetts as an 'archangel revised' and 'a traitor to a holy cause'.[44] Though one might recoil

43. Hamilton, *Prologue to Conflict*, p. 147.
44. David Donald, *Charles Sumner and the Coming of the Civil War* (New York: Alfred A. Knopf, 1965), pp. 184–5.

before the venom of such language, it was justified to the extent
that those who framed the Compromise deluded themselves into
believing that legalistic formulae granted the sanction of law had
'solved' the sectional crisis; they had not. This perhaps indicated
an understandable sigh of relief that the confrontation had been
defused. The settlement had merely glossed over a deep-seated
dispute over what was going to happen to the territories seized
from Mexico in 1846–48. As these had precipitated the crisis of
1850, the treatment of all the residual territories and the manner
in which these were nurtured to statehood would only provoke
further contests as to the character of these new states. Inevitably,
expansion fuelled controversy because expansion was an
ingredient of American nationalism, and two competing
interpretations existed of the ideals upon which that nationalism
rested.[45] William R. Brock is surely justified in his judgement –
that in the west, at any rate – 'No regime can long endure when
condemned by the intelligent, active and articulate. It was not
merely that some intellectuals condemned the system established
in 1850, but that so few could be found to defend it.' Increasingly
in the 1850s this system would be attacked from two, competing
sides: from northern sceptics who saw it as advancing the
unscrupulous, nefarious designs of the 'slave power'; southern
critics held that it was doing too little to prevent the inexorable
advance of 'abolitionism'.[46]

The issue thus shifted from demanding the preservation, or
salvation of the Union, to worry over the complexion of the Union
that was being saved. Some southerners appear to have been
persuaded that the interpretation of the Constitution that was
enshrined in the Compromise of 1850 was pro-slavery. Perhaps
this accounts for the quiescence that settled over political life,
especially in the South, between 1850 and 1853.[47] The simple
answer to the question why did war not break out in 1850, was that
there were not two sides to fight one. It is doubtful even whether
there was one. In 1861, although it was patchy, there was strong
support for secession; in 1850 no such issue as the election of
Lincoln presented itself to stir up popular passions and fear;

45. Wilson, *Space, Time and Freedom*, p. 176; Hamilton, *Prologue to Conflict*, pp.
177–8, notes the general confusion that the Compromise of 1850 promoted in most
western state boundaries that lasted for almost a century.

46. Brock, *Parties and Political Conscience*, p. 330.

47. Wilson, *Space, Time and Freedom*, pp. 160, 177; Hamilton, *Prologue to Conflict*,
pp. 184–5.

certainly the question of the New Mexico–Texas frontier was no substitute for such an issue, no matter how strongly Alexander Stephens might denounce the unconstitutional character of Fillmore's policy. This illustrates the degree to which the crisis of 1850 was a politicians' crisis, and lacked a popular dimension. Politicians from both sections were still sustained by the continuing strength of the two-party system; it had been weakened but had not yet started to crumble in the South. Consequently, there was no enthusiasm for secession. The limited impact of the dispute could also explain Taylor's belief that he could strangle any rebellion without much effort or effusion of blood. Although Fillmore was a northerner, and thus could serve as a southern target, strong passions like secessionary fervour could not be conjured out of the air. Zeal for revolutionary action had to be ignited and stoked up to a fever pitch because of the urgent necessity of breaking the bonds of affection and loyalty to the patriotic symbols of the Union that secessionist sympathisers would have to overcome. With a slaveowner resident in the Executive Mansion, it was all but impossible to begin that process before July 1850.[48]

Of course, evidence of some secessionist sympathy can be found – mostly in South Carolina, Mississippi and Alabama. A Unionist, Benjamin F. Perry, wrote that most citizens of the southern states appeared content to accept the Compromise. 'South Carolina alone is disposed to be dissatisfied and overturn the government. This she cannot do'. Secessionist supporters made gains in the 1850 state elections. But a general reluctance to cast aside the existing political structure constrained the state legislature from rash action. Nonetheless, South Carolinians reserved this right to pursue such action should they deem it in their state's interest. Isaac D. Witherspoon feared that 'the abolitionist movement cannot be stopped; it may be checked for a season . . . but it cannot be reined in'. South Carolina 'has the right to act alone'. But herein lay a problem. After Nullification, the leaders of South Carolina lacked the confidence to act without the cooperation of others. Witherspoon cautioned the state that it 'should not cut itself off from others' by an unilateral act 'to force cooperation by precipitate action'. Some Democrats, such as James L. Orr, still retained a measure of faith in the capacity of the Constitution to preserve and protect slavery.[49]

48. Smith, *Taylor and Fillmore*, pp. 105, 184.
49. Ibid., pp. 196–7.

But the other main reason for the lack of an armed confrontation in 1850 was that no mechanism for promoting any form of alliance, or confederation, of slave states existed. In so far as inter-slave state relations existed, they were motivated by economic matters, especially worries over the tariff. Before his death in 1850, John C. Calhoun had called for the meeting of a convention in Mississippi in the autumn of 1849 to discuss 'abolitionist' designs. This, in turn, called for a southern convention to meet at Nashville, Tennessee in June 1850. Some secessionist sympathizers in South Carolina had already deduced that simple (even simplistic) lines of argument were the key to any future success; they should offer the voters a choice between secession or submission. But a more representative voice at this stage was Benjamin F. Perry. He opined that 'We are anxious . . . for a southern Congress, which will secure the rights of the slaveholding States, redress our wrongs, and preserve the Union'. Indeed, nine states dispatched delegations totalling 177 nominees (although 100 of these were from Tennessee alone). But the overall impact of the Nashville Convention on the political landscape was comparable with the Hartford Convention of 1814. The expectations it aroused were in inverse proportion to its audacity. It issued calls for an extension of the Missouri Compromise line to the Pacific Ocean, bemoaned the deteriorating position of the slave *vis-à-vis* the free states, and agreed to meet again. James H. Hammond consoled himself that 'The great point is that the South *has met*, and acted with great harmony in a nine days' Convention, and above all *has agreed to meet again*'. But this harmony was the product of inertia, not action, and the Nashville Convention showed that the secessionist dream of a unified, coordinated southern policy, let alone an independence movement, was a chimera.[50]

Was war, therefore, even a remote possibility in 1850? No real issue was evident that could have promoted its outbreak. Armies, or navies, were not poised to strike. Various southern states were even less prepared than South Carolina was in 1832–33 to assert an individual policy in defiance of the Federal government. The convoluted passage of the various legislative measures constituting the Compromise of 1850 may have excited politicians and all

50. Ibid., pp. 158–200; A. V. Huff, Jr, *Langdon Cheves of South Carolina* (Columbia, SC: University of South Carolina Press, 1970), pp. 228–9. 232; see also J. H. Hammond, *Secret and Sacred* (New York: Oxford UP, 1988), p. 206 (entry for 30 Nov. 1850), on the need for 'appearing cautious'.

those who observed political activity, but they hardly roused mass fervour. It would be easy to dismiss all the talk of war as so much hyperbole. But nonetheless the crisis of 1850 provided all the conditions that might have led to the outbreak of civil war by 1852/53. Should we, then, accept the term which has frequently been employed by United States historians to describe the Compromise, namely that it constituted an 'armistice'?[51] An armistice is a 'ceasefire', a truce that is reached which terminates a war but precedes a peace agreement or treaty. Should the armistice be broken then the war is likely to be resumed. But this analogy is misleading because 'war' between the sections had not yet broken out. The two sides were not clearly demarcated, let alone drawn up to commence battle. At any rate, the significance of the crisis of 1850 as a prospective clash of arms has been somewhat exaggerated.

The Compromise of 1850 may more accurately be described as a truce between politicians. But its terms were hardly held in universal repute. Whatever the precise balance of political power which the Compromise weighed, there can be little doubt concerning the *conditional* nature of the compact as far as the South was concerned. It depended first and foremost on the behaviour of northern electorates and their politicians. The South implicitly expected the latter to control the former; by enshrining in law a mechanism for coercing blacks back into slavery and demanding that northern state legislatures and judiciaries enforce it with the same zeal as if they were slave states, the symbolic reach of the slave system was extended. It was in this soil, fertilized by the blood and sweat of returned slaves, that anxiety about the growth of the 'slave power' sprang up. In truth, the Compromise of 1850 did not 'settle', once and for all, the contentious issue of slavery. It was delusion to expect that legalistic formulae, whose elegance might please politicians, would convince certain voters with strong views and deeply held convictions about the immorality of slavery – especially in a political culture so marinated in idealism. And it was delusion to believe that once a compromise could be concocted – 'non-intervention' in the territories, or relying on the opinions of the voters therein – 'popular sovereignty' – such facile formulae could permit the opening up of the territories and nursing them to statehood. This was the root of the problem – the character of the destiny of the

51. Potter, *Impending Crisis*, ch. 5; Freehling, *Road to Disunion*, p. 509.

United States – would it be dominated by a free labour system or by chattel slavery? Fresh from his triumph during the Compromise debates Stephen A. Douglas contemplated the future buoyed up by energy and optimism. This misdirected vigour would result within a decade with the rupture of the Democratic Party – the one political grouping that kept suspicious, cantankerous and impulsive southern politicians tied to the American political system.[52]

52. Collins, *Origins of America's Civil War*, pp. 94–6; Potter, *Impending Crisis*, pp. 118–20.

CHAPTER FOUR

Sectional Tensions Unsolved, 1850–58

I judged she would be proud of me for helping these rapscallions, because rapscallions and dead beats is the kind the widows and good people take the most interest in.

MARK TWAIN, *The Adventures of Huckleberry Finn*[1]

The Compromise of 1850 initially appeared to work. For two years afterwards an uneasy accord prevailed and the South made no more demands on the political system. Indeed, southern radicals were defeated in state elections. This prudent, conservative trend in political life was symbolized by the election in 1852 of another 'dark horse' candidate, Franklin Pierce. He restored Democratic domination of the Executive Mansion, easily beating the decaying Whig Party led by the pompous, opinionated General Winfield Scott, who broke precedent and actually campaigned on his own behalf. Consumed with his own importance, Scott was ill-at-ease with multitudes of ordinary people, and was an awkward campaigner prone to say the wrong thing at the crucial moment. A Whig sympathizer observed that 'Scott's person and personal appearance is doing something for him, when he says nothing, but when he talks he is sure to be . . . a damn fool'. Pierce won 254 votes in the electoral college to Scott's 42.

Pierce was born in 1804 in New Hampshire. He was exceedingly handsome, charming, a good persuader and always keen to make friends and keep them, though on occasions he could steel himself for uncongenial tasks should party interest demand it. He had served two terms in the House of Representatives and was elected to the Senate in 1837. If his career had one unifying

---

1. Mark Twain, *The Adventures of Huckleberry Finn* (Harmondsworth: Penguin, 1884, 1985), p. 131.

theme it was party loyalty. A scion of the Democratic Party, his flamboyant antics in the Mexican War were transformed by party publicists into the inspiration of a brilliant tactician, and he was likened to Andrew Jackson as 'The Young Hickory from the Granite Hills'. But as a statesman and leader, Pierce was vacuous. He had few ideas of his own, except to forge the strongest possible alliance with southern Democrats. This required him to accede to all southern demands irrespective of their effects on the northern wing of his party. Pierce typified the kind of politician who reached the pinnacle of his profession in the 1850s. He was conservative on all issues, accepted wholeheartedly the settlement of 1850, and represented the triumph of style over substance. Because of his good looks, amiability and reassuring mien, he was a great favourite with women. This was a factor that was not insignificant in the choice of James Buchanan to succeed him. But ultimately, Pierce was a tragic figure. He was catapulted into a position beyond his talents, failed to learn from his experience, and left the White House the same politician as he entered it. His presidency was a thoroughly disillusioning experience for a pleasant and well-intentioned man. Excited by his triumph, he left office embittered, his bibulous habits having degenerated into alcoholism as a result of enthusiastically throwing himself into Washington society. He was cursed by the very qualities that brought him success. Even his close friendship with Jefferson Davis, which survived the Civil War, brought upon his head the suspicion of treason. In 1857 he returned to the obscurity from which many believed he should never have emerged.[2]

Franklin Pierce was mainly concerned with preserving the unity of the Democratic Party and keeping it in power both in the executive branch and in Congress. He was the embodiment of the strength and the weakness of the two-party system; its managers had calculated that his amiability and conciliatory gifts were best suited to guide the party system and keep in check those tensions that had threatened political stability in 1850.[3] However, Pierce's measures only aggravated those tensions. Matters were not helped by the universal disrespect with which he was held by the end of his term: for Pierce was denied his party's nomination in the

2.   Larry Gara, *The Presidency of Franklin Pierce* (Lawrence, KS: University Press of Kansas, 1991), pp. xii–xiii, 18, 20, 24–5, 29–31, 37–9, 44, 48; Allan Nevins, *Ordeal of the Union* (New York: Scribner's, 1947), II, pp. 16, 20, 22, 29, 30, 32–3, 35, 38.

3.   Gara, *Pierce*, p. 180.

presidential election of 1856.[4] In pursuit of party unity, Pierce, like his successor, Buchanan, made too many concessions to the South. He did not, and could not, grasp that he was attempting to placate the implacable, and this grave weakness was concealed by his friendship with Jefferson Davis, and other southern politicians.[5] In pursuit of further concessions from the federal government, southern Democrats managed, by their maladroit conduct and bellicose manner, to alienate northern opinion, which was by no means hostile either to the South or slavery; it was certainly hostile to northern abolitionists. Indeed the mood grew that the growth of slavery should be *restricted.* More than any other factor, southern demands and their intrusive strategy towards the institutions of the northern states, coupled with the impression that southerners were over-represented in those chambers where the levers of power were pulled and manipulated, led to a slow but sure hardening of northern opinion against southern demands. This was misinterpreted by rash and quarrelsome southern politicians as northern 'aggression', and stimulated further southern aggressive actions resulting in an increase in secessionist influence.

Other complex forces, unrelated to the slavery issue, operated on it indirectly. But the overall result of these developments and the effect of political tumult was the disintegration of the two party system. Its strength had permitted the passage of the Compromise of 1850; its demise led to the rise of a sectional party, the Republicans, and the splitting of the Democratic Party into two constituent sectional halves. Its disruption, furthermore, led to the rapid spread of secessionism, which had been resisted (even in South Carolina) until the late 1850s. It is this fateful event that led to the anarchic state of 1860–61 and the sudden and dramatic events that resulted in Civil War. This is why the presidential election of 1860 is such a pivotal event.[6] Perhaps a statesman of greater insight and weight than Pierce could have built on the Compromise of 1850 an enduring solution to these intractable dilemmas. But his efforts gravely weakened and disillusioned northern Democrats. 'The old Democratic party is now the party of slavery', lamented Hannibal Hamlin, soon to be a Republican

4.   Ibid., p. 167; Nevins, *Ordeal of the Union,* II, pp. 44–5, 47–8, 51.
5.   See e.g. Pierce to Davis, 6 Jan. 1860, in *Jefferson Davis: Private Letters, 1823–1889,* ed. Hudson Strode (New York: Harcourt Brace, 1966), pp. 113–14, when he attributed the secession crisis to 'the madness of northern abolitionism'.
6.   See below, pp. 244–5, 398.

and Lincoln's vice president. 'It has no other issue in fact and this is the standard on which [it] measures everything and every man'. The opinion gathered momentum that the Democratic Party had succumbed to the slave power.[7] It is now time to consider those forces that contributed to the advance of new political parties.

The rise of the Republican Party

Despite the high hopes that the Compromise of 1850 would usher in a period of stability, consolidation and contentment, the years after 1850 witnessed upheaval and tumult. One major party, the Whig Party, disappeared, to be replaced by another, the Republicans – a sectional party with a more consistent anti-slavery character. Such a major transformation does not happen frequently in American history, and it has not occurred since. Previous historians, mindful of the momentous events that followed, the end of the second party system, the disruption of the Democratic Party in the presidential election, southern secession 1860–61, and the consequent outbreak of the Civil War, tended to view all political developments in the *ante-bellum* United States through the distorting lens of the Civil War experience. They then looked backwards in a frantic search for an explanation of the origins of the war, which were interpreted in rather narrow, political terms.

In the late 1960s this approach came under increasing attack, as the study of political history itself broadened, became more demanding in its statistical rigour, and responded to demands that it be informed by the social sources of political action and ideology. Historians, studying politics intensely in individual states, came to see that, 'Interpreting the rise of the Republican party in the North solely in terms of hostility to slavery or economic issues is, therefore, too simplified'. Such historians emphasized ethnic disputes and competition, cultural developments (such as the rise of Anti-Masonry) and racial fears as key factors in the Republican rise. They argued that the desire to limit the westward expansion of slavery into the territories was motivated by a concern that they be settled exclusively by white men. Anti-slavery critics were not inspired by any altruistic wish to help black slaves. These

7.   Eric Foner, *Free Soil, Free Labor, Free Men: The Ideology of the Republican Party Before the Civil War* (New York: Oxford UP, 1970), pp. 162–3.

arguments are debatable, but they performed a signal service in revealing the full significance of the 'Nativist' movement which was adamantly opposed to Central European and Irish immigration, the high tide of which was reached after 1848. Nativism was also characterized by a rabid anti-Roman Catholic prejudice. None of these issues were directly concerned with anti-slavery, sectional tensions (although they became harnessed to them). As this interpretation gained favour, it became increasingly persuasive to attack 'the habit' by which all political movements were interpreted with the events of 1861 in mind. Furthermore, certain continuities were observed between the politics of the 1850s and the 1870s. In one local study, a distinguished historian perceived that 'Beneath the surface rhetoric about slavery and the South, politics in Pittsburgh developed along lines historians have generally ascribed to the Gilded Age'. Thus ended the 'Civil War Synthesis': 'our previous image of American politics in this period', Joel Silbey believed, 'must be reconsidered in the light of this fact and despite the emergence of a Civil War in 1861'.[8]

The historiographical ramifications of this debate lie outside the focus of this book. But one feature deserves some attention. Much of value and insight has emerged from this adjustment of historical focus. Yet an interpretation which ignores, or at best underplays, an historical event as momentous as the Civil War, with almost three-quarters of a million dead, must surely be as misguided as that which seeks to fit all political activity into a pattern which explains its outbreak. There may not be precise unanimity as to the extent of the Civil War's impact on social and economic life after 1865, but it cannot be ignored. Yet in pursuit of ever more accurate voting returns, the 'new' interpretations sought to ignore what Richard Hofstadter (echoed by Eric Foner) once called the 'massive and inconvenient reality of the Civil War'.[9] We may also detect here not just an absorption with ethnic issues which has transfixed so many American historians since the 1970s, but an abhorrence from the unpleasant frequency of war. Such a reaction was exacerbated by the experience of the Vietnam War. This has led to an attempt, most striking among recent social

8.   Michael F. Holt, *Forging a Majority: The Formation of the Republican Party in Pittsburgh* (New Haven, CT: Yale UP, 1969), pp. 6, 8, 123–5; Joel H. Silbey, *The Partisan Imperative: The Dynamics of American Politics Before the Civil War* (New York: Oxford UP, 1985), p. 7.

9.   Eric Foner, *Politics and Ideology in the Age of the Civil War* (New York: Oxford UP, 1980), pp. 10, 11, 19–20, 30.

historians, to conceal the true significance of the Civil War; indeed write it out of the historical record altogether.[10]

This 'ethnocultural' approach (which by no means includes all those political historians interested in quantitative techniques) has also underlined another feature of contemporary American social and intellectual life – a fissiparous tendency. Joel Silbey frankly acknowledges that the difference in interpretation is rooted 'in a particular style of research'. And in the mid-1980s, he could look forward to establishing some future 'coherent perspective' on agreed anatomical lines, 'but its connecting tissue and the exact configurations of the thousands of cells have not been fully examined'. The prospect was daunting: innumerable local studies, overwhelming detail, with more in train, but geared to what? The overall perspective was vague, and for the Civil War historian, seemed to answer the wrong questions. The South did not secede because of foreign immigration, indeed it was hardly affected by it. Yet immigration to northern cities accentuated the differences between the North and South, and emphasized the growing urban character of the former. The South might have seceded because of the cultural distance that grew up between her and a North transformed by foreign immigration. Yet great armies did not fight monstrous and bloody battles for Roman Catholic rights, even when commanded by Roman Catholic generals like William S. Rosecrans. Was there not a danger that such a one-sided interpretation could lead to severe distortion? Were not the 'ethnocultural' historians focusing on the symptoms affecting the body politic rather than on a deep-seated malady which was choking its tenuous life? This suspicion seemed confirmed when a number of its distinguished practitioners began to backtrack rapidly and began to produce more traditional, very northern-centred and narrow political history, reminiscent of the 'revisionists' of the 1930s.[11]

There can be no doubt that these interpretative insights contribute significantly to explaining the political background to the secession crisis even though their connection with the actual

10. It is not suggested that these general observations should be attributed to any of the individuals mentioned in the previous paragraphs.

11. Silbey, *Partisan Imperative*, p. xx: Holt, 'Introduction', in *Political Parties and American Political Development: From the Age of Jackson to the Age of Lincoln* (Baton Rouge: Louisiana State UP, 1992), esp. pp. 11–13 for some stimulating comments; but even shrewder is Donald Ratcliffe's review of Holt in *Journal of American Studies* 28 (April 1994), pp. 142–3.

outbreak of war is *indirect.* The first of these developments, the disappearance of the Whig Party, now needs to be explained. All political parties live to gain office, and if they fail to secure this they offer their members no reason for remaining loyal, whatever their degree of ideological contentment. In truth, American political parties were vehicles for acquiring office and patronage, and compared with their European counterparts were not significantly divided over ideology. This accounts for the savage personal denunciation in which American politicians indulged. Whether 'anti-slavery' views represented an 'ideology' as part of a free labour view is a moot point. On two occasions in 1840 and 1848 the Whigs were unfortunate in their choice of presidential candidate, because he did not live to see the end of his first term; the result was fractiousness within the Whig Party, and when it failed to win a second term under the banner of Winfield Scott in 1852, that fractiousness became more intense, exacerbated as it was by lack of spoils.

American parties were loose coalitions of local parties with divergent views. Scott's conduct of the 1852 presidential election had been inept. But one aspect had major consequences. Scott had gone out of his way to flatter the Irish and German voters. This greatly annoyed Nativist Whigs and strengthened a conviction that a new party would spring out of the ruins of the Whig defeat. Between 1846 and 1855 the United States accepted over 3 million immigrants fleeing from either the Irish Potato Famine or the upheavals following in the wake of the revolutions of 1848. This influx predated the 1852 presidential election. Dynamic social and economic change helped to precipitate the Whig collapse; it was not just a response to defeat at the polls. The anti-immigration lobby, or 'Know Nothings', began as secret societies with arcane and elaborate rituals, like the Masons; if members were challenged as to the character of these rituals, they were enjoined to reply: 'I Know Nothing', hence the name. As they grew in confidence and influence, Know Nothings produced publications denouncing immigrants for their impious and dirty habits; immigrants were at the root of crime, drunkenness, but above all, corruption. Know Nothings abominated the worst features of the spoils system, with repulsive professional politicians pandering to new immigrant constituencies. But they also attracted large numbers of Protestant voters agitated by a deep-seated fear of Roman Catholicism. A visit of the Papal Nuncio in 1854 provoked hysterical and violent scenes. 'This election', observed a New Yorker of the Democratic defeats, 'has demonstrated that, by a majority, Roman Catholicism is feared more than American slavery'.[12] Other causes close to the hearts of evangelical Protestants, such as the temperance movement, eroded old party loyalties and structures; a prohibition law in Maine was passed in 1851 and support for such a law gained ground in New York, Pennsylvania and Massachusetts. In Maine, Connecticut and Ohio, this movement was intimately associated with Nativism and anti-Catholicism.[13]

The advance of these causes filled a political vacuum because the Whig Party's traditional causes – the national bank and internal improvements – were either dead or had been appropriated by the Democrats. Furthermore, the Scott candidacy had also reduced this appeal on two other issues: anti-slavery and Nativism. The pace of the Whig decay varied in individual states; by 1853 internal strife had thrown it into chaos. In the 1854 elections the Know Nothings made significant gains. In Philadelphia their entire ticket was elected. There were some Whigs who approved of this progress, because they believed erroneously that Know Nothingism would revive the Whig Party. But often Whigs, such as Senator William H. Seward of New York, led counter-attacks against the movement. Seward eventually won re-election against a Know Nothing onslaught in 1854. Another faction existed which sought to achieve a 'fusion' between Whigs and Know Nothings, but it was unclear what such a realignment represented.[14]

The evidence is certainly convincing that a variety of anxieties promoted the decline of the Whig Party and the rise of Know Nothingism. These were no doubt exacerbated by the recession of 1848–55, which badly affected northern urban craftsmen, traders and some manual workers; they were native-born and resented their hardship while others prospered. Robert W. Fogel calls this a 'hidden depression'.[15] Rapid urban and economic growth seemed to be upsetting the equilibrium of American politics. Know Nothingism signified a dissatisfaction with the style and conduct of American political life as much as a consistent view of policy. But

12. Holt, 'The Anti-Masonic and Know Nothing Parties', in Holt, *Political Parties and American Political Development*, pp. 115–19.

13. William E. Gienapp, *The Origins of the Republican Party, 1852–1856* (New York: Oxford UP, 1987), pp. 44–6, 50–2, 59–60, 95, 98, 142.

14. Gienapp, *Origins of Republican Party*, pp. 35, 37, 42–3, 81–91, 95–100; Glyndon G. Van Deusen, *William Henry Seward* (New York: Oxford UP, 1967), pp. 160–1; Silbey, *Partisan Imperative*, pp. 137–40.

15. R. W. Fogel, *Without Consent or Contract: The Rise and Fall of American Slavery* (New York: Norton, 1989), pp. 354–62.

the question must be faced. Why did these developments contribute to what William Gienapp has called 'the first faltering steps towards the formation of the Republican Party',[16] rather than the giant strides towards the creation of a new political realignment based on a Nativist Party?

The year 1854 was a major turning point in American history. Had the Nativists come to the fore then it is unlikely that the Civil War would have detonated in the way it did in 1861, though this is not to suggest that it might not have come a decade or two later. Yet the Know Nothing advance was too rapid and dazzling for the movement's own good. The more it advanced, the more difficult became the task of finding adequate let alone able candidates. It also attracted opportunists who lacked commitment. In a desperate effort to retain sectional unity, the Know Nothings supported the Kansas-Nebraska Act of 1854. This alienated northern anti-slavery elements who shifted to the Republicans. They also faced skilful tacticians such as Salmon P. Chase in Ohio and Henry Wilson in Massachusetts, who out-flanked them with a Free Soil appeal. The peak of the Know Nothings' success corresponded with a decline in immigration and an improvement in the economic outlook. As with other 'one issue' political parties, Know Nothings lost momentum. Finally, attention was diverted from the supposed Popish subversion of the Constitution by the storm of protest following the Kansas-Nebraska Act, the hyperbole arising from the Kansas Confrontation, and the caning of Charles Sumner in 1856.[17]

The axle around which the anti-slavery, sectional controversy revolved was the Kansas-Nebraska Act of 1854. But there was little awareness that legislation of this kind would lead to civil ructions. Men and women in these years, as David Potter reminds us, did not get up each morning and remind themselves that they were one day nearer the outbreak of war.[18] The Kansas-Nebraska Act was the brain-child of Senator Stephen A. Douglas. Douglas believed that Democratic Party unity could be maintained only by dynamic and creative leadership. He argued that the building of a

16. Gienapp, *Origins of Republican Party*, p. 103.
17. Gienapp, *Origins of Republican Party*, pp. 72–3, 145, 176; Fogel, *Without Consent or Contract*, pp. 309–16; Peter J. Parish, 'Ethics and Economics: Slavery and Anti-Slavery Re-examined', *Georgia Historical Quarterly* LXXV (spring 1991), p. 668; Holt, 'Anti-Masonic and Know Nothing Parties', pp. 119–20.
18. David M. Potter, *The Impending Crisis, 1848–1861* (New York: Harper & Row, 1976), p. 145; his ch. 7 is an authoritative account of the Act's passing.

transcontinental railroad would benefit not just the state of Illinois, and the owners of Chicago railroad companies who supported him, but also the Democratic Party. The settlement of these territories would demand a railroad, but their settling was the first priority. Douglas was eventually cajoled into accepting nothing less than the repeal of the Missouri Compromise, as he confidently believed that slavery could not thrive in the western territories; any electorate would automatically vote for a free state constitution. The legislation that he introduced between 14 December and 23 January 1854, in his capacity as chairman of the Senate Territories Committee, sought to organize two new territories; when debated in the Senate these were opened to slavery north of 36°30′; but their constitutions would be decided by a ballot of their inhabitants as an expression of 'popular sovereignty'. This was a term first popularized by Lewis Cass, the Democratic candidate in the presidential election of 1848.[19] Douglas took this concept over, and though he intended to use it as a means of finally settling all the fuss over the future of the territories, he only succeeded in returning the slavery extension issue to the forefront of American politics and smashing the remnants of the second party system. This was misdirected energy, for in attempting to forge Democratic Party unity, Douglas threatened to split it with what many deemed to be a craven surrender to the slave power. At any rate, Douglas enjoyed the tepid support of Franklin Pierce, who, in the absence of any legislative initiatives of his own, shared his belief that all pro-Compromise Democrats should support the measure. Pierce would have preferred an amendment acknowledging the validity of the 1850 Compromise. In addition, he knew the South would approve of being able to take slaves north of 36°30′. He remained convinced that sectional animosity arose from northern 'aggression'. Instead, all parties rejected Douglas's formula.[20]

The most savage denunciation of the Act came from the North. Free Soilers, like Charles Sumner, denounced the bill bitterly in the Senate, and Sumner, with a verbal ferocity that would rebound upon him in the end, dubbed Douglas as 'that human anomaly – *a northern man with southern principles*'. He, Joshua Giddings, and Salmon P. Chase issued 'The Appeal of the Independent Democrats

19.   Don E. Fehrenbacher, *The Dred Scott Case* (New York: Oxford UP, 1978), pp. 136–7; Robert W. Johannsen, *Stephen A. Douglas* (New York: Oxford UP, 1973), pp. 239–40, 404–13.

20.   Gara, *Pierce*, pp. 80–1, 91–2; Foner, *Politics and Ideology*, pp. 45–6.

in Congress to the People of the United States' on 24 January, but this did not prevent the bill being passed by the Senate on 4 March 1854 with a majority of thirty-seven to fourteen. As a disgruntled Chase and Sumner left the Capitol in the early hours of the morning, they heard cannon celebrating Douglas's victory. Chase muttered: 'They celebrate a present victory but the echoes they awake will never rest till slavery itself shall die'.[21]

It is often argued, and the 'ethnoculturalists' have not denied this, that the passage of the Kansas-Nebraska Act detonated northern opinion with unexpected ferocity and heat. Many northerners believed that it showed that the South always got what it wanted whatever obstacles were put in its way. This was an ironical twist considering that the South did not want popular sovereignty. Northern men rallied to defend the system of free labour: opposition to slavery was dear to the heart of many northern Whigs. They, and other Free Soilers, feared that the repeal of the Missouri Compromise would lead to an acceptance of the nationalization of slavery. The Democratic Party suffered severely in the mid-term elections of 1854, losing control of the House of Representatives. James Shields reported of Democratic losses in Illinois, 'The Anti-Nebraska feeling is too deep – more than I thought it was'. Yet this upheaval of opinion did not immediately result in a new party alignment. It was clear that the Nativist controversies had destroyed the Whig Party but the Know Nothings had not taken their place.[22]

An important catalyst in arousing emotions against the South, and channelling opposition, was northern clergymen – though anti-Nebraska groups were more successful in the western than in the eastern states. The Protestant evangelical churches were another national institution that split along sectional lines in the 1850s. We cannot overlook the great influence on Republicanism (and the importance for *ante-bellum* northern politics generally) of post-millennialism, and the fusing in many intellectuals of religion and politics. This undoubtedly influenced the overall outlook, though it may not have been shared by the huge numbers that went to the polls (perhaps not many knew what post-millennialism meant). The evangelical Protestants were probably not the

21. David Donald, *Charles Sumner and the Coming of the Civil War* (New York: Alfred A. Knopf, 1961), pp. 251–9; Frederich J. Blue, *Salmon P. Chase: A Life in Politics* (Kent, OH: Kent State UP, 1987), pp. 94–5. It did not pass the House of Representatives until May, and then with a much narrower majority.

22. Gienapp, *Origins of Republican Party*, pp. 73, 76–8, 104–5, 106, 126, 201.

Republican Party at prayer, but political evangelicalism certainly permeated every level of that nascent political organization. Thus the 'ethnoculturalists', and other historians concerned with tracing voter opinion in minute detail, too easily overlook the importance of intellectuals to the political outlook of the age. The moral issue of slavery, and not just anxiety about the economic impact of the spread of the slave power, lay at the heart of the sectional conflict. A political system that attempts to ignore the views of the most intelligent and articulate of its citizens is foredoomed. Any historical interpretation that rests on a similar misconception will not ultimately convince because it is narrow and sterile.[23]

Nevertheless, the explanation that the Know Nothings constructed a 'bridge' over which converts to Republicanism crossed from both the Whig and Democratic Parties, is a convincing one. Many Know Nothings suffered from the delusion that they would dominate the Republican Party. This was not likely, mainly because they struggled to present a coherent view of the slavery issue. Some Know Nothings hoped for an agreement with the South on slavery; others passionately opposed slavery extension. At the Know Nothing Convention in Philadelphia in 1855 this party, too, split along sectional lines, thus strengthening the Republican Party. The organization of the Whig Party had now entered terminal decline. Yet the future of Republicanism was still not assured. Despite Chase's success in winning the Ohio governorship in 1854, the Know Nothings still remained ahead of the Republicans in Massachusetts and New York. It was *national*, rather than local political moves, that effected a transformation of this state of affairs. The first was the election of the Speaker of the House of Representatives. Although this was finally won by a Know Nothing, Nathaniel P. Banks, Congressional manoeuvres accentuated the sectional flaws in the Know Nothing movement. The Republicans aimed at dividing them by emphasizing sectional disputes. The second was the emergence of former President Millard Fillmore as the Know Nothing candidate in the 1856 election. His stress on the Union, rather than Nativism, reduced the party's prime appeal, and its novelty, in the North and in the South.[24]

23. Richard J. Carwardine, *Evangelicals and Politics in Antebellum America* (New Haven, CT: Yale UP, 1994), pp. 246–7, 277–8.

24. Gienapp, *Origins of Republican Party*, pp. 183, 190, 200, 203, 224, 240, 243, 247–8, 251, 260–2; Holt, 'The Politics of Impatience', in *Political Parties and American Political Development*, p. 177; W. E. Gienapp, 'Nativism and the Creation of a Republican Majority in the North before the Civil War', *Journal of American History* 72 (Dec. 1985), pp. 529–59.

The third event was the caning of Senator Charles Sumner. It is certainly true that the strength of Know Nothingism in 1852–54 prevented the creation of a new party to replace the Whigs. Know Nothingism could not be overcome easily and needed the added force provided by a series of dramatic sectional events. Kansas-Nebraska was one. The sudden and unexpected assault on Sumner while he sat working at his desk in the Senate Chamber was the other. This was the kind of event in American politics, the product of bravado and impetuosity, that could not have been predicted. After the attack, Sumner himself whispered, 'I could not believe that a thing like this was possible'. After the Kansas issue had forced its way to the forefront of northern politics in December 1855, Sumner had delivered two meticulously rehearsed speeches on 'The Crime Against Kansas' in which he had showered personal abuse, in a characteristically undiscriminating, intemperate and counter-productive fashion, on Senator Andrew P. Butler of South Carolina. His nephew, Representative Preston S. Brooks, waited a couple of hours as if acting out a ritual, and then calmly walked from the House of Representatives into the Senate Chamber, and replied to Sumner's criticisms by raining down on Sumner's large, handsome and noble head, innumerable blows with his gutta-percha cane.

There was dark murmuring that other northern anti-slavery spokesmen should receive similar treatment. The Richmond *Whig* suggested that perhaps Seward 'should catch it next'. The atmosphere of violence and intimidation perpetuated by the slave power seemed to have reached the halls of Congress itself; northern liberties were imperilled. The so-called 'sack' of Lawrence in Kansas occurred on the same day and presented the Republicans with the vivid, if repulsive, issues of 'Bleeding Kansas' and 'Bleeding Sumner'. Sumner did not resume his Senate seat for four years. Brooks was threatened with expulsion from the House, but was saved by southern votes. He, in any case, resigned and was triumphantly re-elected. He became a southern hero. 'Every southern man sustains me', Brooks bragged. 'The fragments of the stick are begged for as *sacred relicts* [*sic*]'. He was showered with new canes; one was engraved, 'Hit Him Again'.[25]

Northern outrage had a galvanizing effect on the anti-slavery movement. Many felt they had been personally defiled and

25. William E. Gienapp, 'The Crime Against Sumner: The Caning of Charles Sumner and the Rise of the Republican Party', *Civil War History* XXV (Oct. 1979), pp. 218–23; Donald, *Sumner*, pp. 292–303.

assaulted by Brooks' brutal act of reckless bravado. 'Never in my life' reported one northern activist, 'have I felt anything like the stirring excitement and earnest determination which has been roused up by the blows of that bludgeon'. Republicans not only successfully linked the attack with the Kansas issue but also presented it as a question of free speech, for the Senate had done nothing to protect its privileges and censor its attacker. In an exaggerated manner, an anti-southern image was conveyed of a violent, unpredictable, uneducated, 'genteel' savage. These attacks had two important strategic advantages for Republicans. In a sectional confrontation, the Know Nothings were divided and unclear. Secondly, the northern Democrats were closely identified as the hapless puppets of their southern slavemasters.[26]

The caning of Sumner galvanized the Republican Party in the states. Party organization in all states was vital for success in the 1856 presidential election; it now began to operate in key states like Illinois. Such was the prelude to the Republican Convention at the Musical Fund Hall, Philadelphia. The Republicans devoted much attention to slavery – more than in 1860. They referred to the 'rights' of citizens, not aliens, but hoped to seduce moderate Know Nothings away from their first allegiance. They also appealed to immigrant, especially German, voters by nominating John C. Frémont, who was not tainted by any previous connection with Nativism. Frémont has been severely criticized as a candidate of poor stature, but comparison with many of the men who sought the presidency shows this to be exaggerated. Frémont enjoyed a superficial glamour and celebrity as the 'Pathfinder of the West'. Some years before, he had participated in a number of intrepid exploratory journeys. But in truth he was a rather halting and hesitant figure, much dependent on his formidable wife, Jessie Benton Frémont. Yet he was consistent in his views and by no means a poor candidate – though a poor speaker. By comparison with, say, Chase, however, he was a lightweight politician, floating in deep, murky waters, for no matter how hard he struggled, his feet could not touch the bottom. The Republican platform over which Frémont presided endorsed the Declaration of Independence and argued that the Founding Fathers were profoundly anti-slavery; slavery was damned as a relic of 'barbarism'. There were to be no more slave states and expansion

26.   Gienapp, 'The Crime Against Sumner', pp. 224–36; Potter, *Impending Crisis*, pp. 218–24.

of slavery into the territories was to be prohibited. Nonetheless, despite this radical thrust, mention of the Fugitive Slave Law was conspicuous by its absence, for fear that it would antagonize conservative supporters of the Compromise of 1850, who had previously voted for the Know Nothings.[27]

In the event, Frémont failed to win over the conservative Whigs. Although Frémont was defeated by the Democrat nominee, James Buchanan, in the electoral college 174 to 114 in an election which witnessed an 83 per cent turnout (a 7 per cent increase on 1852), this electoral defeat turned out to be the greatest victory of Frémont's troubled and disappointing career (in 1861–62 he was to prove a poor general). Whereas Buchanan gained 45 per cent of the popular vote, Frémont gained 33 per cent – a more than satisfactory performance for a new party facing its first major test. The signs seemed auspicious for 1860. Recent accounts stress the fragmentary and fragile state of the Republican Party in 1856. Of course, this is true of all new parties; they depend above all on progress at election time, especially in national elections, because this provides the all-important bridgehead for further advances. If it is accepted that defections to the Republican Party did not begin in some states (like New York) until 1858, Frémont made these moves possible by generating much needed 'momentum', which, in turn, inspired more organizational improvement and growing numbers of enthusiastic party members. The Republicans suffered occasional setbacks, but by 1856 had overtaken the Know Nothings and had formed a viable, sectional party which had effectively replaced the Whigs as the opposition to the governing Democratic Party.[28]

It remains to assess why such a sectional party succeeded in the 1850s whereas previous efforts had failed so miserably over the previous two decades. By its nature, the Republican Party had avoided the fate of Fillmore in 1856, who enjoyed sympathy but could not excite fervour because many southern conservatives voted for Buchanan to ensure that Frémont would not win (Fillmore gained eight votes in the electoral college with 21 per

27. Foner, *Free Soil, Free Labor, Free Men*, pp. 128–31; Potter, *Impending Crisis*, pp. 256–9; Gienapp, *Origins of Republican Party*, pp. 336, 342–3, 370; Nevins, *Ordeal of the Union*, II, pp. 462–3.

28. Michael F. Holt, *The Political Crisis of the 1850s* (New York: Norton, 1983), p. 198; Gienapp, *Origins of Republican Party*, pp. 358–65, 413, 417; Silbey, *Partisan Imperative*, pp. 134, 143–9, 162–5; Parish, 'Ethics and Economics', pp. 72–3. Parish is critical of Fogel's 'grudging' comments on the Republican achievement in 1856. See *Without Consent or Contrast*, pp. 377–80, 381–7.

cent of the popular vote). The Republican Party escaped the fate of a third party struggling in a two-party system. How did it manage this feat and overtake the Know Nothings? First, because of the importance of the sectional issue, on which the Know Nothings did not impress. This again became of crucial importance after 1854. But we can agree that this process was more prolonged and complicated than has been previously admitted. The realignment of the 1850s was moving apace before the passage of the Kansas-Nebraska Act. In this process the Know Nothings were not in a never-ending competition with Republicans, because they shared certain aims, such as temperance, and in the North, opposition to the Kansas-Nebraska Act.

Secondly, the Know Nothings dissolved previous party loyalties. The Republicans depended for their success on attracting to their ranks, not just former Democrats and Whigs, but those who had previously not been attracted by politics, and had been lured into the polling booths by Nativism. It was this factor, the Know Nothing 'solvent', to use Gienapp's term, that quickly eroded previous loyalties, thus destroying the Whig Party, that made the rapid Republican advance possible and distinguished it from earlier failures. The Republicans replaced the Whigs but they were not the Whig Party in bright new clothes; they appealed to members of the northern electorate who were concerned about a variety of issues, and the intensity of these concerns varied at different times for different reasons. Yet though this realignment began as a rejection of conventional politics, and a loathing of party politicians, it became transformed by contact with the national scene. Voters may vote in a contradictory fashion at local and national levels and not see the inconsistency.

But there can be no doubt as to the increased intensity of sectional hostilities as a result of the growth of the Republican Party. Anti-southern and anti-northern caricatures became more widespread, and sectional animosity in Congress began to assume a sharper edge after the caning of Sumner. Brawling between Senators was not unusual. Gienapp rings echoes of James G. Randall in his criticism of irresponsible northern agitation and the 'more strident' Republican attacks on the South. He suggests that such propaganda 'magnified' the growing conflict between the North and South. Perhaps he is right. But political historians like Gienapp and Holt, among others, tend to interpret the rhetoric of political life too literally. People may feel passionately about their political beliefs, cheer their leaders and cast their votes accordingly in the poll booth. But the relationship between these peaceful acts and the coming of organized violence is not a self-evident one. There were many politicians who used inflammatory language. Benjamin F. Wade in 1854 claimed, 'I go for the death of slavery whether the Union survives it or not'. But he was the exceptional politician rather than a representative voter. Four years later William H. Seward spoke of an 'irrepressible conflict'. This does not denote a northern readiness to accept war; on the contrary, it was a warning of its dangers, and Seward himself was a natural reconciler who tried frantically to avoid war in 1861.[29]

We must, therefore, not assume a readiness, let alone a willingness, to wage civil war because of the frequency of the warlike images and ferocious language resorted to by politicians. Northern public opinion remained remarkably pacific, and reluctant to face up to war – as opposed to stand up to the South in the political arena. The two are not synonymous. We cannot just assume that a chronological treatment (as called for by Professor Holt) of all the party political developments before 1861, both sectional and ethnocultural, somehow explains the causes of the war, or that they 'account for the war'.[30] This is far too narrow an approach, especially if we believe, like Clausewitz, that war is an instrument of policy, and further, that 'War is nothing but a continuation of political intercourse, with a mixture of other means'. To assess some of these 'other means' we must now turn to consider the legal background, before assessing the southern reaction to political and economic developments in the 1850s.

The Dred Scott decision

To be denied his own party's nomination was the most humiliating blow that could be inflicted on the self-esteem of an incumbent president (only Chester A. Arthur would receive comparable dismissive treatment in 1884). What kind of man did the Democratic convention in Cincinnati in June 1856 choose to replace Pierce?[31] All contemporaries agreed that James Buchanan

29. Gienapp, *Origins of Republican Party*, pp. 115, 443–8; Carwardine, *Evangelicals and Politics*, p. 274; Hans L. Trefousse, *Benjamin Franklin Wade: Radical Republican from Ohio* (New York: Twayne, 1963), pp. 63, 87; Van Deusen, *Seward*, pp. 193–4; see below, pp. 346–50.

30. Holt, 'Introduction', in *Political Parties and American Political Development*, pp. 12–13.

31. For a detailed account, see Gara, *Pierce*, ch. 7.

was a considerable advance on Pierce. J. H. Plumb once observed that it was almost impossible for monarchs to be dull, no matter how foolish their statecraft. Few American presidents have been stupid though a number have been dull. Although there are some presidents who are more interesting than Buchanan, there are many who are more uninteresting. Before 1856 he was a man of considerable reputation, especially in foreign affairs. He was deemed a knowledgeable and experienced politician, with skills beyond the ken of the hapless Pierce. In short, the portrait of Buchanan painted by post-war historians, especially Roy F. Nichols and Allan Nevins, as a quivering, psychologically maladjusted, weakling, putty in the hands of his southern-dominated cabinet, is exaggerated.[32]

Nonetheless, Buchanan's tenure of the presidency ruined his reputation. He was far from being a dynamic leader. He was an elderly, fussy old bachelor, who could be petulant and petty. Like other determined men who are overshadowed by more charismatic figures, Buchanan could be steadfast in his hatreds. He was a sly man who dominated his cabinet by guile and retained its respect. But Buchanan had worked so hard for the presidential nomination that he was mentally drained and had lost all spark. Once installed in the Executive Mansion with the panoply of presidential power he lacked ideas, except one, a profound emotional attachment to the South and the southern wing of the Democratic Party. Only the impulsive or foolish crossed Buchanan. If his power was challenged, he could act with masterful decisiveness, as Stephen A. Douglas discovered in 1857–58. Adept political manoeuvring, however, should not be confused with creative statesmanship. Buchanan failed not because he was supine or indecisive but because the pro-southern policy he pursued so obstinately was wrong-headed. Buchanan made mistakes but it is misleading to claim that his errors alone caused the Civil War, though they certainly contributed to the environment which made it possible.[33]

Increasing political tensions resulting from the decline of the Whig Party were expressed, and given symbolic form, in the Dred Scott decision enunciated by the Chief Justice of the Supreme

32. Brian Holden Reid, 'James Buchanan, 1791–1868', in Peter J. Parish (ed.) *The Reader's Guide to American History* (London and Chicago: Fitzroy Dearborn, 1996).

33. Elbert B. Smith, *The Presidency of James Buchanan* (Lawrence, KS: University of Kansas Press, 1975), p. 16.

Court on 6 March 1857. In a country as litigious as the United States it is perhaps not surprising that legal forms should intrude into the political forum with such authority – not least because American politicians who were not lawyers were exceptions rather than the rule. Consequently, their natural instinct was to view politics as an extension of the legal process. Clearly, such an approach has advantages, and it is striking that United States historians themselves view the intermixture of legal process and political activity as wholly admirable and natural, and they take it for granted. In this admixture, the American Republic can be compared with the Roman Republic. Although there were many differences between them, the two republics attached considerable political significance to the courts, and sometimes to criminal trials. Among the characteristics they shared was the enormous publicity that was generated around cases of political significance, which highlighted the careers of those who prosecuted and defended them. *Sub judice* has never been a strong point of American federal or state law. The criminal courts were, of course, open to all who wished to attend, and therefore not only symbolized free speech in both the Roman and American republics, but in Lily Ross Taylor's words, the 'language of the law court has gone over into the theatre'. Histrionics has always been an important feature of American political life. Finally, in both Republican Rome and America, the courts have provided a forum in which ambitious young men could make a reputation for themselves, especially in public speaking, and advance their political prospects.[34]

Yet, it has many disadvantages. Americans have a tendency to confuse litigiousness with the 'rule of law', which they equate with republican democracy. However, it is grossly misleading to assume that the 'rule of law' is not significant under political systems quite different from the American experiment (including other kinds of democracy). Furthermore, it also overlooks the possibility that litigiousness can not only lead to a major abuse of the law, but also result in its subversion. Justice itself can be (and is) subordinated to other priorities, whether they be financial, economic or political. No judicial decision, however majestic and authoritative, can be an adequate substitute for a political consensus. As for the hapless Dred Scott himself, Professor Don Fehrenbacher, in his

34. Lily Ross Taylor, *Party Politics in the Age of Caesar* (Berkeley: University of California Press, 1945, 1971), pp. 98–100.

masterly treatment of the entire episode, observes that Dred Scott was 'a pawn in the political game'.[35]

The intermixture of political ends with legal means resulted in one disruptive feature. American parties, or factions of parties who viewed themselves as defending political minorities, invariably tried to turn political differences into constitutional questions of profound import. This was in part a reflection of the low esteem accorded to 'politics' and an attempt to find a 'higher' justification for a political argument. But it was also an expression of the extremist tendency latent in American political rhetoric that threatened to upset its stability. The hyperbole indulged in by American politicians (especially southerners) strained reality and indulged in ghoulish imagery beyond the ken of their experience. So Thomas W. Cobb declared during the Missouri Compromise in 1820, 'We have kindled a fire which . . . seas of blood can only extinguish'. Such cries, therefore, were not the product of the 1850s only; they were endemic in the *ante-bellum* system. Recourse to legal disputation was an attempt to circumvent verbal confrontation of this stark and blood-curdling kind. Had not Senator Henry A. Foote of Mississippi in 1850 invited John P. Hale of New Hampshire to visit his state, a sojourn that would end with Hale '[gracing] one of the tallest trees of the forest, with a rope around his neck, with the approbation of every virtuous and patriotic citizen'?[36]

Such tiresome rhetorical bravado was a far cry from the prosaic facts of the Dred Scott case. Scott himself was a middle-aged, diminutive, illiterate slave, characterized by a certain dogged courage and obstinacy; but his personality is obscure because he left no written record of any kind – an unlikely figure to have inspired so much written, legal scholarship and disputation. Some time after December 1833 Dr John Emerson, a citizen of St Louis, on gaining a commission in the United States Army as an assistant surgeon, purchased Dred Scott from his previous owner, Peter Blow, and reported for duty at Fort Armstrong, Illinois. Shortly afterwards Emerson applied for a period of sick leave because he needed to seek treatment for a 'syphiloid disease' he had contracted after a visit to Philadelphia which had involved him in adventures rather more exacting than the mere consultation of

35. A. R. Myers, *Parliaments and Estates in Europe to 1789* (London: Thames & Hudson, 1975), pp. 14, 19; Fehrenbacher, *Dred Scott*, p. 287; Potter, *Impending Crisis*, pp. 283–4.

36. Potter, *Impending Crisis*, pp. 104–5, 148–9.

medical textbooks. This resulted in a transfer to Fort Snelling, then part of Wisconsin territory, in 1836. Scott had thus lived as a slave for two years in a free state and was removed to a territory and continued in bondage for another three years where slavery was prohibited. Emerson was posted to Florida in 1840, but left the service in 1842, returning to St Louis. In 1843 he moved to Iowa and died suddenly in December of that year. Dred Scott began his legal odyssey in 1846.[37]

In his will Emerson left almost all his estate to his wife and then his daughter. Scott at this time attempted to purchase his freedom, but to no avail. In April of the year that witnessed the debate over the Wilmot Proviso, Scott successfully sued Mrs Emerson in the Circuit Court of St Louis County for his freedom on the grounds that prolonged residence in a free state and in territory where slavery was forbidden had conferred liberty on him. Who sponsored this audacious act is not clear, but the verdict was reversed after a retrial in 1850.[38] The legal proceedings that followed this decision often displayed the American judicial system at its worst. Not for nothing is the Dred Scott case known as 'the most frequently overturned decision in history'. And at each litigious stage the issues presented, expounded and distorted by learned counsel, became further and further detached from the fate of Dred Scott until it came to have an important influence on the presidential election of 1856.

Mrs Emerson returned to the attack with an appeal to the Missouri Supreme Court in the autumn of 1851. This concluded that Scott was indeed still in a state of bondage. 'No state', Judge William Scott averred, 'is bound to carry into effect enactments conceived in a spirit hostile to that which pervades her own laws'. His judgment was really a manifesto for southern pro-slavery Democrats and his statement formed a thinly disguised public protest on their behalf against increasingly strident anti-slavery criticism. Here was illustrated one of the great dangers of muddling up legal intercourse with political controversy, because although William Scott concluded to his satisfaction, 'I regard the question as conclusively settled by repeated adjudications of this court', the legal process had not finished with Dred Scott. Each judge who approved of the verdict claimed that his court had pronounced the final verdict. But each successive judgment

37. Fehrenbacher, *Dred Scott*, pp. 239–48.
38. Ibid., pp. 250–64; Potter, *Impending Crisis*, p. 268.

against Scott provoked opposition outside the courts that fatally impaired their reputation for impartiality and probity, until the Supreme Court itself became the focal point of political controversy.[39]

The case made its way back to a Missouri trial court so that a judgment could be made on implementing the Missouri Supreme Court decision. Further skirmishing occurred in the Missouri courts before Scott's lawyers appealed to the United States Supreme Court. It was at this skirmishing stage in 1853–54 that the case began to acquire its reputation for conspiratorial overtones. Did the defence deliberately allow itself to serve as a punch-bag to absorb and repel anti-slavery blows? There is no evidence that Mrs Emerson, and her brother, John F. A. Sandford, were interested in any other matter than winning. The same was true of Scott and his backers. They were motivated by what Fehrenbacher calls 'honesty of purpose'. Their greatest failure was not looking beyond their immediate 'goal to the possible consequences of submitting such an issue to a hostile Supreme Court'.[40] It was parties indirectly involved with, or interested in the results of this case that manoeuvred with matters perhaps less noble than justice in mind.

Scott was represented by Montgomery Blair, later Postmaster-General in Lincoln's cabinet. A Free Soiler, and opposed to slavery expansion, he was out-matched by his two pro-slavery opponents, former senator Reverdy Johnson and Senator Henry S. Geyner. That all three of these counsel were practising politicians of repute is an indication of how much the law and politics had become mixed up. Until the case came before the Supreme Court the press had only given it perfunctory coverage. It now received rather fuller treatment, stirred by Franklin Pierce's final annual message in which he had intemperately claimed that Congress lacked 'constitutional power to impose restrictions' on states and argued that the Supreme Court had.

In February 1856 the Supreme Court heard the case, and then ruled in May that the case be reheard; this hearing consisted of twelve hours of arguments which were carried over four days. The fundamental issue was, could a Negro, enjoying the rights of citizenship, sue in the federal courts? If this was confirmed then such a legal decision would be comparable to placing a stick of dynamite in a crack in the Hoover Dam. If blacks had a

39. Potter, *Impending Crisis*, pp. 262–5.
40. Ibid., p. 275.

constitutional right to sue in federal courts then the Fugitive Slave Law of 1850 would be in the words of Roswell M. Field, an attorney working for Blair, 'of little value', and this was clearly a judicial decision with great constitutional and political import for the South.

The actual decision adumbrated by the Supreme Court on 6 March 1857 was heavily influenced by political interpretation. The issues before it, however, whatever the legal quibbling and hair-splitting, were four-fold:

1 Did the Supreme Court have the power to overturn the decision of the Missouri Supreme Court?
2 Was Dred Scott a citizen of Missouri who could take legal action in the federal courts?
3 Was Scott a free man because of the time he had lived in Illinois?
4 Was Scott free because of the time spent in the northern territories above the Missouri Compromise line?

All of these questions had profound political, constitutional, and ultimately, sectional implications.[41]

It is likely that the Chief Justice, the elderly, desiccated, Roger B. Taney, added material to his judgment unilaterally without consulting the other justices.[42] Taney's activity in these years contradicts the widespread assumption that physical decrepitude and a decline in intellectual vigour go hand in hand. Taney's logic is selective and warped by modern standards, but there can be no denying the energy that he injected into the pro-slavery argument in a wrong-headed effort to settle the issue, with all the solemnity and force of a Supreme Court pronouncement. The essence of the judgment was that the Supreme Court could rule on earlier judgments in this matter. Taney decreed that Negroes did not enjoy citizenship of the United States and therefore could not pursue cases in the federal courts (or indeed anywhere else). Dred Scott remained a slave: he had not become a free man while in the northern territories because, the Court ruled, the Missouri Compromise was unconstitutional and, moreover, Congress had no power whatsoever to forbid slavery in the territories. That is to say, any congressional enactment which attempted to restrict

41. Fehrenbacher, *Dred Scott*, pp. 291–304.
42. Ibid., pp. 320–1. Up to 50 per cent may have been added. Taney's denial that he had done this, Fehrenbacher considers 'inaccurate'.

slavery in the territories was *ipso facto* unconstitutional. Finally, Scott had not been freed by virtue of his time in Illinois because his legal status was determined by Missouri law, and not by that of Illinois. Thus was granted by legal sanction the power to extend the institution of slavery, and move individual slaves about the country where it had previously been abolished. It was then but a short step to demand a federal slave code that would protect slavery in areas outside the South.[43]

As politics in the United States is often the pursuit of power by means of legalistic style and language, it is not surprising that the Dred Scott decision had such an explosive political impact – not least because of the timing of the decision. Taney's judgment was severely criticized throughout the North. Some Republican state conventions and legislatures passed resolutions affirming Negro citizenship, and the Supreme Court of Maine agreed that free blacks enjoyed the franchise. This dedication to the belief that free blacks were citizens and that their rights deserved legal protection remained part of the Republican credo before 1861, and was upheld during the Peace Convention held in Washington DC in February 1861.[44]

But the worst and most pregnant consequence of Taney's decision was the air of collusion, if not outright conspiracy, that it introduced into the somewhat fevered political atmosphere. Two days before the decision was due to be announced, Chief Justice Taney attended the inaugural address and administered the oath of office to the president-elect, James Buchanan. They exchanged some whispered words, and Buchanan then announced in his inaugural that he believed that the question of whether slavery was permitted in the territories was 'a judicial question which legitimately belongs to the Supreme Court' and that he would 'cheerfully submit, whatever this may be' and urge that Kansas enter the Union at the earliest opportunity. There was a strong measure of disingenuousness in Buchanan's declaration because he had been informed by Justice John Catron of Tennessee of the general direction of the decision. Catron had urged the president-elect to write to the pro-southern justice Robert Grier of Pennsylvania in an effort to prevent him from siding with other northern justices, who opposed Taney's views. So Buchanan was

---

43. Potter, *Impending Crisis*, pp. 270–86; Fehrenbacher, *Dred Scott*, pp. 322–7; Bruce Collins, *The Origins of America's Civil War* (London: Edward Arnold, 1981), pp. 125–6. Taney was undoubtedly in error in denying Negroes US citizenship.

44. See below pp. 281–92; Foner, *Free Soil, Free Labor, Free Men*, pp. 292–5.

offering to accept a decision 'whatever this may be' because he knew that he agreed with it. His dubious behaviour and duplicitous action did much to provoke suspicion over the probity of the Dred Scott decision, even though Republican reaction to it was initially restrained. But Buchanan's anxiety over the Dred Scott decision and its timing, which had led him into such impropriety, had been caused by his desire to lay down a policy on slavery extension in Kansas. He was determined to demonstrate that the Dred Scott case would show that a territorial legislature, before statehood had been conferred, could not prohibit slavery – which was not a matter that had been put before the Supreme Court. But this example only reveals further the manner by which an attempt to 'settle the matter' by judicial action, only served as a pretext by which the political controversy was actually widened beyond the legal purview. Buchanan's attempt to secure a complete victory over northern 'abolitionism' was ultimately self-defeating.

Given the nature of the Supreme Court's decision with its obvious Democrat bias, and the Democratic Party's dominance of the executive and the legislature, it was only to be expected that many Republicans would draw the conclusion that this was not a coincidence. A conspiracy existed to strengthen the hold of the Democratic Party on all levels of power by pandering to the whims of the 'slave power'. After all, had not the optimistic words of the president been endorsed by a whispered conversation with the Chief Justice? The whole case had been manipulated to provide the decision that the Democratic Party both wanted to hear and needed to fortify its electoral victory. William H. Seward denounced the whole business as 'the first among all the celebrations of that great national pageant that was to be desecrated by a coalition between the executive and judicial departments to undermine the national legislature and the liberties of the people'. Several opponents compared Buchanan with a Roman Emperor or King Charles I. These were not intended as compliments.[45]

Of course, Buchanan's election had relieved the anxieties of the out-going President Pierce, and there was a considerable measure of continuity between the two Administrations, not least in the assumption that the slavery problem could be settled only if it was

45. Potter, *Impending Crisis*, pp. 287–9; Kenneth M. Stampp, *America in 1857: A Nation on the Brink* (New York: Oxford UP, 1990), pp. 92–3, 106–7; Smith, *Buchanan*, pp. 24–6.

taken out of the hands of politicians and placed before some 'higher' tribunal. Of course, Buchanan expected that it could be 'settled' only in the Administration's favour, and not in that of its critics. These were dangerous illusions.

The notion that the legal process could provide a siphon which could take bellicose impulses, defuse them, and channel them into peaceful political intercourse must be seen as dangerously complacent. So was the assumption that the courts could provide a substitute for a non-existent political consensus. On the contrary, violence had erupted in Kansas during the Supreme Court's deliberations and would get worse. Furthermore, Republicans were more than ever determined to seize control of the patronage, including, of course, appointments to the Supreme Court. This aim was to cause much alarm in 1859–60, especially among southern Democrats. Both their reputations and that of the Democratic Party, not to mention the United States herself, were to suffer much from the lack of political common sense exhibited by Franklin Pierce and James Buchanan in the 1850s.[46]

Finally, the Dred Scott decision had the opposite effect intended by its architect and supporters. Far from settling the matter once and for all, the Dred Scott decision provoked fear about the scope of the 'slave power'. It was transformed from a Republican bogey into a northern spectre. Abraham Lincoln, whose eye was firmly on the local political scene in Illinois, uttered a resounding phase in a speech delivered in Springfield on 16 June 1858, and for the first time made an impact on the national scene.[47] A house divided against itself, he warned, could not stand for long. Although national dissolution could not be expected, Lincoln did not believe that the prevailing condition of a Union half-slave and half-free could survive: the Union would become completely free or slave. Lincoln now believed the latter more likely, especially if northerners passively permitted the slave power to exert insidious control over their own institutions and legal forms. The Kansas-Nebraska Act made this possible, and the Dred Scott decision gave it legal sanction. No state could now legally, in the opinion of the Supreme Court of the United States, prevent

46. Gara, *Pierce*, p. 178.
47. Hugh Brogan, 'Tocqueville and the Coming of the American Civil War', in Brian Holden Reid and John White (eds) *American Studies: Essays in Honour of Marcus Cunliffe* (London: Macmillan, 1991), pp. 91–2, points out that the phrase was in common usage (it was, after all, a biblical phrase), but transforming and ennobling the commonplace lay at the heart of Lincoln's rhetorical genius.

slavery from moving across its boundaries. 'We shall *lie down* pleasantly dreaming that the people of *Missouri* are on the verge of making their State *free,* and we shall *awake* to the *reality,* instead, that the *Supreme* Court has made *Illinois* a *slave* State.'[48]

It was perhaps the most unexpected result of the Dred Scott decision that it conferred public prominence, and gave that initial impetus to the rise, of the politician, Abraham Lincoln, who would enter the White House, gain control of the patronage for the Republicans, and carry out 'the most sweeping removal of political opponents in US history'. Historians have pointed out on a number of occasions, however, that the fears that Lincoln and others expressed were greatly exaggerated. But politicians are not academics who enjoy the advantage of having access to a body of accepted knowledge and fact; they give expression to fears and feelings which are based on a sense of how events are moving, and sometimes the intellectual foundations for these feelings are fragile. Speeches are also expressions of political manoeuvre, or direction, as Lincoln moved to ensure that his position on the slavery extension issue, and combating the 'slave power' could be unambiguously distinguished from that of Senator Douglas.[49]

The threat of the slave power

The combination of the Kansas-Nebraska Act and the Dred Scott decision succeeded in keeping sectional antagonisms at the forefront of American national politics in the 1850s. Continual, and somewhat fevered, discussion contributed to the widespread apprehension of a political 'crisis' which might end with some kind of explosion. An outgrowth of this fear was revulsion at the 'slave power': a fear that this insidious, creeping and powerful conspiracy would throttle the life out of the tenuous American experiment in democracy. Indeed, some regarded it by 1857–58 as a distinctly 'un-American' threat against which all loyal citizens should be on their guard. The essence of republicanism itself was

48. 'A House Divided: Speech at Springfield, Illinois', *The Collected Works of Abraham Lincoln*, ed. Roy P. Basler (New Brunswick, NJ: Rutgers UP, 1953), II, p. 467. Don E. Fehrenbacher, *Prelude to Greatness: Lincoln in the 1850s* (Stanford UP, 1962), ch. 4, but esp. pp. 82–95; Fehrenbacher, *Dred Scott*, pp. 485–8.

49. Waldo W. Braden, *Abraham Lincoln, Public Speaker* (Louisiana State UP, 1988, 1993), pp. 51–2; Mark E. Neely, *The Last Best Hope of Earth: Abraham Lincoln and the Promise of America* (Cambridge, MA: Harvard UP, 1993), p. 168.

endangered. The existing political parties could no longer protect
the system. One was enfeebled and the other was in thrall to the
slave power. It was a disillusionment with parties as previously
organized that gave a potency to sectional alarms; yet sectional
animosity did not decisively weaken the political system until the
presidential election of 1860.[50]

But was this agitation just a symptom of the political crisis or
was it a root malady? Surely it was a crisis of fundamental import.
Comment on the exaggerated extent of the slave power's grip on
northern politicians and voters has become a commonplace. Yet
fear of the slave power conspiracy was a product of *belief*. What
people believe in politics has little to do with established objective
fact (which is, in any case, a retrospective reconstruction) but what
they perceive as happening from their everyday experience.

All that many involved in the northern anti-slavery movement
(and many who were not) could see after 1854 was a remorseless
advance of the slave power. Northern Democrats were regarded
contemptuously as mere puppets of the slaveowners. It seemed
that the forces of republican democracy were engaged in a battle
with a brutal, authoritarian and subversive threat. The response of
northern liberals in the 1850s can be compared with left-wing
reactions to the threat of fascism in the 1930s. The martial activity
in Kansas in 1856–58 can be compared with the efforts of the
various international brigades in the Spanish Civil War, 1936–39.
Both these movements stemmed from a comparable measure of
exaggeration of the threat they confronted. But their political
impact arose from this exaggeration and should not be
discounted.

Developments in southern party politics seemed to confirm that
the North faced a united and homogeneous foe. The defeat of
Scott in 1852 had thrown the southern Whigs into turmoil. Here
the Whig Party slowly unravelled (it controlled only two southern
state houses after 1853, North Carolina and Tennessee). Southern
Whigs blamed the northern anti-slavery Whigs for their plight and
attacked the Democratic Party as a free-soil fastness. Their plight
allowed southern Democrats to force their northern colleagues to
acquiesce in a southern interpretation of the Compromise of 1850
and ensure that popular sovereignty was imposed on *all* the
territories. The repeal of the Missouri Compromise line of 36°30′
which had been a prime southern demand was realized in the

---

50. Michael F. Holt, *The Political Crisis of the 1850s*, pp. 151–2, 184, 190.

Kansas-Nebraska Act. Here was a hint that the old Southern Whig–Democrat rivalry, based on wild assertions that the one was more anti-slavery than the other, would be replaced by a consensus that was essentially anti-Republican and anti-northern.[51]

Southern Whigs, like their northern counterparts, flirted with the Know Nothing Party. Know Nothing leaders realized that dedication to a consistent line on the slavery question was central to its survival as a major political party. They thus rallied round three prime tenets that were central to the southern case: untrammelled execution of the provisions of the Fugitive Slave Act, the Kansas-Nebraska Act, and popular sovereignty in all territories. After the split of the Know Nothings in 1856, the southern wing of the party came under a fierce barrage of fire from southern Democrats. They were accused of colluding with free soil and abolitionist forces. In the Deep South (except for isolated outposts like New Orleans) the party was decimated and this part of the slave states was now dominated by one party. The Know Nothings survived in parts of the Upper South and the Border states (including Maryland) in alliance with Whig remnants. The persistence of some form of two-party system in these states would have a major influence on the pattern and outcome of the secession crisis.[52]

The prime significance of these events was a shattering of the national perspective on American politics by these sectional interests. There was also a tendency to downplay the value of any northern alliance. Southerners had always been prone to demand that the interests of their northern colleagues be sacrificed at their behest, as was evident during the crisis of 1850. Zachary Taylor had not been prepared to do this, but both Franklin Pierce and James Buchanan (both northerners) were. Thus fewer and fewer southerners were prepared to participate in a national party which aimed to present a southern view of the politics of slavery. Where the two-party system degenerated so, after the setbacks of the elections that confirmed the Compromise in 1852–54, did secessionist fervour revive. The opponents of the southern Democrats tended to focus on local issues, but they were poorly organized and ill-coordinated; they even lacked a name, and were

51. William J. Cooper, *Liberty and Slavery: Southern Politics to 1860* (New York: Alfred A. Knopf, 1983), pp. 239–41.
    52. Ibid., pp. 245–7.

often vaguely referred to as the 'Opposition Party' which hardly created a positive impression. Many other southern Whigs joined the Democratic Party. Even within Democratic ranks, however, there was by no means unanimity on the wisdom of separatism. There were still some prudent voices that called for a national perspective, and even others who were audacious enough to call for a rally around the standard of Stephen A. Douglas. If Douglas faced disaster so did the South. But the great majority of southern Democrats saw control of the entire party as essential to their cause.[53]

The increasing stridency of southern demands is reflected in increasing calls for measures sponsored by the Federal government to protect slavery in the territories. Such a policy became the essential bedrock of the southern demand for protection against the rising strength of the Republican Party. Southerners loathed the Republican Party because of the acid tongues of its spokesmen and its propagandists' assaults on southern integrity and institutions. Those who ladle out vitriol, as southern spokesmen were wont to do, often do not like the effect when it is returned in full measure. They believed, furthermore, that Republicanism posed a danger to local political control that was central to the southern notion of liberty. The Republicans posed a major threat to the vaulting ambitions of certain southern Democrats. They were increasingly convinced that the security of the South and its peculiar institution demanded not just the unrestricted freedom to move their property into the territories, but the creation of at least one new slave state. This attitude culminated in 1859 with Jefferson Davis's call to have slavery protected in the territories 'under the Federal Constitution'. This amounted to a slave code. If the judiciary could not enforce it, 'it will then become the duty of Congress to supply such a deficiency'.[54]

The two Administrations of Pierce and Buchanan appeared suffused with southern attitudes, indeed appeared extensions of the southern interest. The Fugitive Slave Act was stringently enforced. In May 1854, a former slave, Anthony Burns, was

53. Cooper, *Liberty and Slavery*, p. 259; Silbey, *Partisan Imperative*, pp. 120–3; Holt, 'The Democratic Party, 1828–1860', in *Political Parties and American Political Development*, pp. 71–86, 125–6.

54. Silbey, *Partisan Imperative*, p. 122; Cooper, *Liberty and Slavery*, pp. 256–7; Potter, *Impending Crisis*, pp. 403–4; William C. Davis, *Jefferson Davis: The Man and his Hour* (New York: HarperCollins, 1991), pp. 268–74.

arrested in Boston. The spectre of slavery being accepted as a national institution could no longer be ignored, for it would restrict northern liberties. Fifty thousand people hurriedly assembled to protest, and an army of marines, soldiers and police kept them at bay while Burns was returned to enslavement in Virginia. The cost of this venture was about $100,000. In 1856–58 there were a number of other celebrated cases, but the numbers of escaped slaves were small, with an average annual loss of 1:5,000 slaves; in 1859 only 803 slaves escaped, and 500 of these were from the Border states. The 3,000 brave men and women involved with the 'Underground Railroad' escape route hardly warranted the opprobrium hurled upon this infinitesimally small group. Yet, though northern opposition to the workings of the Act has been exaggerated (only three examples exist of forcible rescue of arrested former slaves by northern mobs before 1856), the folly of attempting to 'solve' agitation over slavery by this kind of legislation was manifest. The Fugitive Slave Act sought to return not only recent runaways to enslavement, but also those who had long since thrown off their manacles and had made new lives for themselves in the North. This imparted to the Fugitive Slave Act a brutality, an arbitrariness, and a malicious character, and a propensity for elementary injustice, which was bound to inflame moderate northern opinion. This was shocked by the implications of the Act, even if most northerners did not share abolitionist views, or wished to see any alteration of slavery in the southern states. It forced northerners to confront the inescapable dilemma that slavery was not a 'peculiar' southern institution, but a *national* problem. It was not far distant, it was increasingly sinister and was beginning to intrude into the workings of northern democracy, and threaten 'free speech'. Would the next step be the legal silencing of not just those who criticized the Fugitive Slave Act but slavery itself? Under such conditions Republican warnings of a 'slave power' threat gained credence. In the broadest sense, the objective reality of the figures involved, of the numbers of escaped slaves, those helping them, and those returned to enslavement by the sheriffs, are irrelevant. The moral indignation, and the latent guilt on all sides, contributed to that series of unspoken assumptions and stereotypes which increased the animosity that eventually resulted in war – though that animosity was felt most pointedly in the South. It was in this kind of atmosphere that sales of Harriet Beecher Stowe's sentimental but tense and driven novel, *Uncle Tom's Cabin* (1852), flourished and popularized such stereotypes.[55]

The southern influence seemed paramount in foreign affairs as well. Pierce had exploited his gift of patronage by appointing pro-slavery expansionists to overseas missions. In October 1854 three of these ministers from London, Paris and Madrid had issued the Ostend Manifesto. James Buchanan was its final author, but all three feared the results if Spain abolished slavery in Cuba. The Ostend Manifesto argued that the United States should either purchase the island or seize it by force.

This document was issued at a time when demands for an expansion of the South into the Caribbean, and the creation of a great slaveholding empire, were gaining in persuasiveness. 'Filibustering' expeditions grabbed the headlines in Nicaragua and elsewhere. Jefferson Davis argued for a transcontinental railroad built along a southern route. The Gadsden Purchase (1853) of southern parts of New Mexico and Arizona made this seem more feasible. *De Bow's Review*, the premier periodical advancing southern states rights views, saw tremendous potential for southern trade in the west. This expansionism caused considerable disquiet in the North. Should the South expand at the expense of her Latin American neighbours, then her political character would come to resemble more closely that of Brazil rather than the original federal Union. It was not expansionism itself that northern critics opposed (as is sometimes implied), for northern anti-slavery critics, like William H. Seward, had expansionist dreams which appeared to know no horizon; what they objected to was expansion that would transform the political and social character of the United States itself. The fundamental ideals on which this polity rested were being altered and abused by a small group of unrepresentative southern 'aristocrats', whose political power was out of all proportion to the resources and population of their region. The Ostend Manifesto especially, by revealing the slave power's naked, aggressive designs, provoked much bitter denunciation.[56]

55.   Potter, *Impending Crisis*, pp. 130–40; Foner, *Free Soil, Free Labor, Free Men*, pp. 209–10; Bruce Levine, *Half Slave and Half Free: The Roots of Civil War* (New York: Hill & Wang, 1992), pp. 187, 189–90.

56.   G. Connell-Smith, *The United States and Latin America* (London: Heinemann, 1975), pp. 80, 82; Smith, *Buchanan*, pp. 15–16; Potter, *Impending Crisis*, pp. 180–92; Ernest N. Paolino, *The Foundations of the American Empire: William H. Seward and U.S. Foreign Policy* (Ithaca, NY: Cornell UP, 1973), pp. 8–11.

But it was southern action in Kansas that provoked more fear of the slave power than anything else. There have been many previous detailed accounts of these events, which have usually been interpreted from the political angle.[57] Their significance is assessed in the next chapter. Kansas had been the source of violence for several years. The source of the dispute was the legalistic doctrine of popular sovereignty and blatant electoral fraud. In the elections to the territorial legislature of November 1854, March 1855 and October 1857, fraud and intimidation were rife. This had been perpetuated by a rabble of drunk, unruly, unkempt, pro-slavery Missourians, several hundred of whom crossed the Kansas border in the best traditions of a frontier range-war. A series of pro-slavery laws were then passed. In response, free soil settlers mainly from New England (who constituted the bulk of the population) in the summer of 1855 set up their own territorial government in Topeka. Civil war seemed to threaten in Kansas, though the violence was on a very small scale. It was written up in the newspapers – especially in the 'Wakarusa War' of December 1855, and the 'sack of Lawrence' of May 1856 – as if the territory was being subject to the attentions of Attila the Hun himself.[58]

In October 1857 a convention of these unseemly pro-slavery enthusiasts met at Lecompton and put together a constitution of breath-taking audacity. They were hardly a group of highly educated lawyers, but they knew what they wanted and were determined to impose their views on the residents of this territory. They paid lip-service to the requirement for electoral endorsement by offering the voters the chance to *accept* the constitution with slavery but not reject it; voters were also presented with a Hobson's choice of how many further slaves would be permitted to enter the territory, not whether they should enter at all. No slaves could be emancipated who were already in Kansas, and the Fugitive Slave Law should be rigorously enforced. This was known as the Lecompton 'juggle'. A calculated vagueness on suffrage computations, by which all white males present in the territory on

57.   A good starting-point is Potter, *Impending Crisis*, ch. 12, and Stampp, *1857*, ch. 6.

58.   Allan Nevins, *The Emergence of Lincoln* (New York: Scribner's, 1950), I, pp. 159–61; Stampp, *1857*, pp. 145–6, 150, 153–4; Richard H. Sewell, *Ballots for Freedom: Anti-Slavery Politics in the United States, 1831–1860* (New York: Norton, 1976, 1980), pp. 279–81, 290, 294–5.

election day were eligible to vote, would enable large numbers of their cronies from Missouri – '*an horde of imported voters*', as they were described by one observer – to repeat the incursions of 1854 and 1855.[59]

President Buchanan decided to support the pro-slavery Lecompton constitution; Senator Douglas decided to oppose it, and thus confronted directly the titular head of his party over a matter of policy. The question of motives on both sides is not easy to disentangle. Buchanan had not excited much enthusiasm among southern Democrats in 1856, and it was likely that he was trying to strengthen his hold on that important Democrat bastion.[60] As for divisions within his own party, Buchanan could (and did) exercise his formidable command of the patronage to purge most of Douglas's supporters, especially in Illinois. In this he acted with decisiveness and also with the vindictiveness of which he was capable when crossed. As for Douglas, he had his eye on succeeding Buchanan in 1860 and was manoeuvring to ensure that his base in the Old North West would not be outflanked by Republicans. He had antagonized northern opinion by sponsoring the Kansas-Nebraska Act and he was anxious to restore his popularity. But a point of principle was involved: Douglas loathed seeing popular sovereignty abused, with gerrymandering calculated to produce a result the opposite of which he had always expected from this device. Buchanan, by contrast, accepted the spurious legality of Lecompton as legitimate. There is some evidence that northern opinion was divided, and was not so anti-Lecompton (and therefore so anti-Buchanan) as some previous historians have suggested. Nonetheless, the Republican Party thrived on the kind of turmoil that this dispute produced among Democrats. Then conflicting results were produced in Kansas in 1857 by the elections sponsored by the pro- and anti-slavery parties. The Lecomptonites produced a victory for the pro-slavery constitution of 6,143 to 569 opposed (though at least 2,700 anti-slavery votes were dismissed as fraudulent). The anti-Lecomptonites, in January 1858, however, gained a victory of 10,336 who rejected the pro-slavery

59. Smith, *Buchanan*, pp. 38–9; David E. Meerse, 'Presidential Leadership, Suffrage Qualifications, and Kansas: 1857', *Civil War History* 24 (1978), pp. 295, 310–11.

60. B. W. Collins, 'The Democrats' Electoral Fortunes during the Lecompton Crisis', *Civil War History* 24 (1978), p. 315.

constitution, against 138 who supported it (with a further 24 who wanted it without slavery).[61]

The other prime consequence of this dispute was to sow excitement, confusion, and not a little irritation in Republican ranks. In Douglas's many speeches denouncing Lecompton, he sounded more and more like a Republican. Some eastern Republicans, especially Horace Greeley, began to conjure with visions of some kind of electoral alliance with the Douglas faction; perhaps even a coalition; could not Douglas himself be tempted to join the Republican Party? Such views were not welcome among Illinois's Republicans, to whom Douglas was their natural and bitter enemy. They were especially annoying to that former Whig, Abraham Lincoln, who had served one term as a member of the House of Representatives, 1847–49. He had re-entered politics in 1854, had denounced Douglas and the repeal of the Missouri Compromise in two striking speeches at Peoria and Springfield, Illinois in 1855. He had stood down in favour of the ex-Democrat, Lyman Trumbull, during the Senate race of that year on the understanding that he would be the uncontested candidate against Douglas. By the summer of 1856 Lincoln embraced Republicanism. Out of this sequence of events arose Lincoln's epic battle for Douglas's Senate seat, and the Lincoln–Douglas debates of 1858.[62]

In these celebrated debates with Douglas, Lincoln strode on to the national stage for the first time, and he would not subsequently leave it. His prime significance at this date was delineating very lucidly the differences between mainstream, conservative Republicanism and Democrats of the Douglas hue. Lincoln did this so effectively that he presented himself as an available Republican candidate for the 1860 presidential election that was to stoke up southern fears and provoke the secession crisis. This strange, moody, enigmatic, quirky but eminently lovable and humorous man was now given the opportunity to show something of his true mettle. After this experience of debating with Lincoln (which had been foreshadowed in 1855 or

61. Smith, *Buchanan*, pp. 40–2; Stampp, *1857*, pp. 307–10; Collins, 'Democrats' Electoral Fortunes', pp. 325–6; Nevins, *Emergence of Lincoln*, I, pp. 346–8; David Zarefsky, *Lincoln, Douglas and Slavery: In the Crucible of Public Debate* (Chicago UP, 1990), pp. 11–17.

62. Fehrenbacher, *Prelude to Greatness*, pp. 49–50, 57–7, 73, 109; Benjamin P. Thomas, *Abraham Lincoln* (London: Eyre & Spottiswoode, 1953), pp. 95–101. On the differences between Douglas and Lincoln, see Harry V. Jaffa, *Crisis of the House Divided: An Interpretation of the Lincoln–Douglas Debates* (Seattle: University of Washington Press, 1959, 1973), pp. 107–10.

even earlier as they had jousted in the winter of 1839–40),[63]
Douglas never made the error (committed by so many in 1860–62)
of underestimating him. Lincoln's law-partner, William H.
Herndon, may have been right in thinking that his ambition
resembled a 'little engine' which never stopped running, but if so
this thirst for advancement was not achieved at the expense of
others. Lincoln was highly ambitious, but good natured, kind, and
much liked – a rare combination. Although wily, he was neither
unpleasant nor unscrupulous. He was to demonstrate wisdom
without self-satisfaction, eloquence without bombast, and never
talked down to his listeners. He was to prove shrewd without being
over-confident, and an uncannily accurate judge of character.

Lincoln was self-educated, but not an intellectual. He was a
thoughtful, practical politician. He was not audacious (unlike
Douglas), and never advanced far beyond the consensual mean of
his party. He was certainly not a superman. By the late 1850s he
was middle-of-the-road without being mediocre: he was inexperienced in administration, provincial and prone to diffidence.
Yet, whatever his inner torments and self-doubt, Lincoln did not
share Hamlet's fear of responsibility. His attributes were hardened
and sharpened by the harsh fires of challenge and experience.
Perhaps the gift that more than any other transformed him from
being a mere notable frontier politician to the most revered of all
American presidents is that, in the words of Mark E. Neely Jr,
Lincoln enjoyed the 'deepest form of self-confidence: he knew no
fear of the talent of others'.[64]

The Lincoln–Douglas debates were staged against the
background of Buchanan's ruthless and single-minded attempt to
settle the Kansas issue once and for all, reduce the potency of the
Republicans' appeal in the North, and lance with one thrust the
festering boil that threatened the unity of the Democratic Party.
He did not hesitate to employ cash bribes to ensure votes in
Congress. Here was the slave power at its most arbitrary and
determined, with its corrupt but willing tool doing its bidding. It is
surely correct to suggest that the attacks on Free Soilers in Kansas
incensed northern opinion to an extent that an assault on black

63. Zarefsky, *Lincoln, Douglas and Slavery*, pp. 36–8.
64. J. G. Randall, *Lincoln the President: Springfield to Gettysburg* (London: Eyre &
Spottiswoode, 1947), I, includes a detailed study of his early life, marred by the
belief that Lincoln and Douglas were divided by 'red herrings' (pp. 121–6). Also
see M. L. Houser, *Lincoln's Education* (New York: Bookman, 1957), Charles B.
Strozier, *Lincoln's Quest for Union* (Urbana: University of Illinois Press, 1987), Mark
E. Neely, Jr, *The Last Best Hope of Earth* (Cambridge, MA: Harvard UP, 1993), p. 167.

slavery, or the cloudy, legalistic phrases of slavery extension, could never have done. Here were graphically presented the struggles of ordinary men and women with whom northern voters could readily identify. But this is far from suggesting that the morality of the slavery was an irrelevant consideration.[65]

Douglas accepted Lincoln's challenge to debate with him on 24 July 1858, as he had no real choice in the matter: for to refuse would have left him vulnerable to the charge of cowardice, which was unthinkable for a frontier politician. In pursuing the electoral contest (which should not be confused with the eight Lincoln–Douglas debates) Lincoln made sixty-three major speeches and Douglas fifty-nine (most of these would have been about three hours long), while Lincoln travelled 4,300 miles and Douglas 5,200. Lincoln, as the lesser known candidate, had much more to gain from the debates than Douglas, but also more to lose; if Douglas worsted him his reputation would have been irreparably shattered. Douglas was a most formidable opponent: dynamic, alert, perceptive. One of Douglas's biographers described his voice as 'Round, deep and sonorous, his words reached his remotest hearer'. He was a brilliant master of fence, and particularly adept at misrepresentation – knocking his opponent off-balance by distorting his true views. He would be keen to exploit mid-western racism and depict Lincoln as an abolitionist who advocated full social and political equality for blacks, in a state where free blacks were denied the franchise.[66]

Like most such debates, little that was new was ventured in the confrontations. The arguments had been heard before, and would be heard again. What was novel was the jousting between the candidates, their degree of preparation, and the quality of the exchanges, given point by the *threat* – the threat of the growing strangle-hold of the slave power as exemplified by the Kansas-Nebraska Act, Dred Scott, the outrages in Kansas and the craven conduct of the Buchanan Administration in pushing for the admission of Kansas as a slave state. There were four general patterns of argument: conspiracy, legal, historical and moral. The first was a reconsideration of the whole nature of the slave power. This was a very flexible and somewhat indefinable argument, but it

65. See Holt, *Political Crisis of the 1850s*, pp. 193–4, 196–7, 203–4; Smith, *Buchanan*, pp. 42–3.
66. Zarefsky, *Lincoln, Douglas and Slavery*, pp. 20, 28, 30, 34, 51–1. On Lincoln's distaste for abolitionism, see Jaffa, *Crisis of the House Divided*, pp. 199–201; on his preparation, Braden, *Lincoln, Public Speaker*, pp. 52–4.

should not be dismissed because contemporaries believed in it, and the events of political life seemed to confirm the danger. In this context Douglas strove to reveal Lincoln as an abolitionist who, therefore, could be also presented as a disunionist threat. There can be no denying either that both Lincoln and Douglas had much to gain from exploiting fears of a slave power, as both sought electoral office by reference to its supposed dangers. Yet it is a big jump to assume from this that both were unscrupulous opportunists who cynically exploited the fears they were inflaming. Both understood that the issue of slavery was potentially explosive, but they differed over the means by which the crisis could be resolved. If it is true that most voters are against something rather than for it, then many northern voters were opposed to the slave power.[67]

The legal cluster of arguments demonstrate the legalistic nature of American politics and the veneration of the Constitution. The style of argument adopted by the candidates reflected their political style – they were both skilful, practising lawyers. Obviously the import of the Dred Scott decision was explored at length. Lincoln scored a major point by showing that Douglas's basic 'Union' appeal rested on a very vague formulation: that the two sections would interpret the same documents differently, and then would agree to disagree. Douglas retorted by warning of the dangers posed by Lincoln's 'House Divided' speech. 'Our fathers intended that our institutions should differ. They knew that the North and South having different climates, productions and interests, required different institutions'. But the most significant development occurred at Freeport, when Douglas enunciated his so-called 'doctrine', as a response to the Dred Scott decision. This was not new, he had said it before: Democrats should interpret the decision negatively – the Supreme Court did not demand that the territories recognize slaves as property with ownership rights. If, therefore, they failed to create a legal code for the protection of slavery, slaveholders would not dare risk bringing their slaves into the territories. This approach was typical of Douglas's ingenuity and sleight of hand. It provoked anger among southern Democrats because he appeared to be denying them their true constitutional property rights.[68]

67. Zarefsky, *Lincoln, Douglas and Slavery*, pp. 78–83, 86–7, 90–6, 99, 103–10; Holt, *Political Crisis of the 1850s*, p. 180; Jaffa, *Crisis of the House Divided*, p. 81.

68. Zarefsky, *Lincoln, Douglas and Slavery*, pp. 132, 137–8, 143; Nevins, *Emergence of Lincoln*, I, pp. 380–2; Fehrenbacher, *Prelude to Greatness*, pp. 135–42; Smith, *Buchanan*, pp. 52–3; Jaffa, *Crisis of the House Divided*, pp. 350, 357.

Exploring the historical arguments gave Lincoln an opportunity to address some of his favourite themes. He rejected Douglas's notion that the Founding Fathers had created the United States half free and half slave. They *found* it in that state and struggled with their heritage. Lincoln believed the Constitution to be fundamentally anti-slavery. The redolent phrase 'all men are created equal' lay at the core of Lincoln's case. He did not accept Douglas's accusations that he was in favour of 'nigger equality'. But he scored heavily off Douglas when he declared of all blacks, 'in the right to eat the bread, without leave of anybody else, which his own hand earns, *he is my equal* and the equal of Judge Douglas, and the equal of every living man'.[69]

This permitted Lincoln to develop the core of his case *vis-à-vis* Douglas's advocacy of popular sovereignty and his assertion that no community of free men could require of other free communities that they order their domestic arrangements in a certain way. Lincoln's view of the morality of the issue was not particularly daring by the most radical standards, but it was a risky strategy that paid off. It revealed most markedly the differences between Douglas and himself. Lincoln believed that slavery was unutterably wicked, and he exploited Douglas's moral relativism on this score shrewdly. Douglas could not admit that slavery was evil because it would infuriate his nominal southern allies. There could be no sectional truce, Lincoln contended, until slavery stopped expanding. Once this ceased, the North would become more contented, and in its turn, the South would stop attacking the North. The containment of slavery must be a high priority. 'I believe if we could arrest the spread, and place it where Washington, and Jefferson, and Madison placed it, it *would be* in the course of ultimate extinction and, the public would, as for eighty years past, believe that it was in the course of ultimate extinction.[70]

The debates were not about making proud and grand statements but about winning votes. The Lincoln–Douglas debates were not, and could never be, a philosophical seminar on the slavery issue.[71] In the nineteenth century senators were not elected by the popular vote, but by a vote in the state legislature.

69. Zarefsky, *Lincoln, Douglas and Slavery*, pp. 147–8, 152; Smith, *Buchanan*, p. 51.

70. Jaffa, *Crisis of the House Divided*, p. 31; Smith, *Buchanan*, p. 50.

71. See Zarefsky's criticisms of failures to 'grapple with the opponent's conception', in *Lincoln, Douglas and Slavery*, p. 224.

The way in which the counties voted was crucial to the result. Buchanan turned the full power of the Democratic machine against Douglas, and thus aided Lincoln. Lincoln gained a majority of the popular vote, 125,000 to Douglas's 121,000 (with 5,000 going to Buchanan supporters), but the breakdown of the legislative districts guaranteed Douglas's re-election, forty-six Democrats to forty-one Republicans.[72] No prizes are awarded for coming second in politics, but in Lincoln's case, it was a noble failure – and a useful bridgehead for a future advance. He showed beyond doubt a capacity to win votes. If he had been trounced by Douglas, then it is likely that William H. Seward, and not Lincoln, would have been nominated in 1860 as the Republican presidential candidate. But a close scrutiny of the results reveals that the voters in the counties gave comparable attention to economic issues, and it is to a consideration of this essential backround to the sectional crisis that we must now turn.[73]

The slump of 1857

The economic development of the United States in the nineteenth century was handicapped by a series of economic recessions that followed one another at almost twenty year intervals: in 1819, 1837, 1857 and 1873–78.[74] This chapter will conclude with an assessment of the impact of economic misfortunes on political tensions. Geoffrey Blainey in his book, *The Causes of War*, points out that the Scottish economist, A. L. Macfie, had argued that wars are more likely to be fought when economies are recovering rather than stagnant.[75] This has less to do with any jejune Marxist argument that capitalists are prepared to fight to enlarge an already growing market, or to conquer areas into which they wish to export capital. The evidence of the American Civil War indicates that the businessmen (especially of New York City) were the least enthusiastic for the commencement of hostilities (though

72. Potter, *Impending Crisis*, pp. 354–5.
73. Bruce Collins, 'The Lincoln–Douglas Contest of 1858 and Illinois' Electorate', *Journal of American Studies* 20 (Dec. 1986), pp. 410–11, 420.
74. Eric Foner, *Reconstruction: America's Unfinished Revolution, 1863–1877* (New York: Harper, 1988), pp. 512–24. The last was in 1893.
75. Geoffrey Blainey, *The Causes of Wars*, 3rd edn (London: Macmillan, 1988), pp. 91–6. Macfie was concerned primarily with international rather than civil wars.

they rapidly switched to belligerency). It has much more to do with the elementary but often overlooked fact that expanding economies lighten the prevailing mood and contribute to an optimistic outlook. This grants politicians the means to fight wars (by raising loans) should they decide to do so, as the Treasury Secretary, Salmon P. Chase, assured President Lincoln in April 1861.[76] Otherwise, it is doubtful whether there exists a link between prosperity and enthusiasm for war, except that those who are living comfortably invariably assume that their voluntary martial servitude and discomfort would be of short duration.[77]

A study of the economic vicissitudes of the 1850s offers a different perspective on the political disputes of the day, not least that of slavery, labour and the tariff. It also helps integrate the working-class unrest discussed above, which tended to focus on local and state issues, with the national questions. All parties, of course, whatever their perspective and political bias, agreed that the Federal government should remain small and weak and that it should have little or no power over the workings of the economy. The expansion of the American economy in the mid-1850s had, in any case, been due to factors out of the government's control, such as the Crimean War (1854–56). The United States had begun to export foodstuffs previously supplied by a beleaguered Russia; the ending of that war brought uncertainty. Another area of vulnerability lay in the rapid creation of an urban working class who made their grievances felt, and sympathized with mid-western farmers; this combination contributed powerfully to the Republican congressional gains in the 1858 elections.[78]

Economic setbacks obviously had an important impact on the voters, though mainly of a negative sort. The Republicans, for example, criticized slavery's economic backwardness. In 1857, however, the efforts of politicians were rendered superfluous during the months August–October, when panic erupted on Wall Street. Investors withdrew their funds, so that within a month total deposits had been reduced from $94,500,000 to $78,800,000. Bank failures precipitated a run on the banks, which led to a decline in

---

76. Philip S. Foner, *Business and Slavery* (Chapel Hill, NC: University of North Carolina Press, 1941); Chase to Lincoln, 2 April 1861, Robert Todd Lincoln Collection of the Papers of Abraham Lincoln, Library of Congress, Washington DC.

77. Blainey, *Causes of War*, pp. 95–6.

78. James L. Huston, *The Panic of 1857 and the Coming of the Civil War* (Baton Rouge: Louisiana State UP, 1987), pp. xii–xiii, 4–8, 31–2, details the decline of European purchases of American foodstuffs and cereals; David M. Goldfrank, *The Origins of the Crimean War* (London: Longman, 1994), pp. 255–6, 295.

investment and credit confidence, and a sharp fall in the prices for cereals. Bankers (and this is not uncommon in recessions) were excoriated for their selfishness and incompetence. The whole structure of finance in the United States seemed on the brink of collapse. By November 1857, the bottom of the recession was plumbed, but contrary to expectations, recovery was sluggish, and the Pennsylvania iron and coal industries were serious casualties. Strikes and even food riots broke out in the ensuing months. North eastern financiers were reluctant to make loans, especially to western agriculture, which, in turn, had a deleterious effect on the railroad industry.[79]

All of this brought much satisfaction to southern spokesmen. The 'South pays up its bills well and promptly, while it is almost impossible to get a dollar from the West' they claimed. Southern staple crops, cotton and tobacco, continued to sell well, and attempts were made to attract investment to southern railroads by pointing out the contrast between the two sections. The United States was not thrown into deep depression by the panic of 1857, but it was sufficient to arrest economic growth in the northern states.[80] But the recession had also brought hard times to the South and renewed calls for free trade rather than a protective tariff and direct trade with Europe. It was in the South that protest against the panic was heard loudest; in the North the initial impact was muted. There were renewed southern calls for a reduction in tariffs and an impetus was given to the economic value of slavery. Southern polemicists rounded upon the northern bread riots. They seemed to symbolize all that was rotten, capricious and unjust about urban civilization. The slump of 1857 seemed to contrast in a piquant form the relative merits of slave labour versus free labour. The South lacked rioting workmen, but had contented slaves; preconceptions were emphatically reaffirmed.[81] Provoked by the debate over the Lecompton Constitution, southern spokesmen claimed that the North was drowned in cries of 'Blood or Bread!' In a speech delivered on 4 March 1858 in the Senate, James H. Hammond offered an interpretation of politics based on economic wealth. The peroration of his speech was as inaccurate as it was famous: if

79. Huston, *Panic of 1857*, pp. 10–11, 14–15, 17–29, 32, 40; Stampp, *1857*, pp. 220–1, 222–7.

80. B. W. Collins, 'Economic Issues in Ohio's Politics during the Recession of 1857–1858', *Ohio History* 89 (1980), p. 50; Stampp, *1857*, p. 230.

81. Huston, *Panic of 1857*, pp. 62–5, 79, 80–4.

cotton was ever embargoed, 'old England would topple headlong and carry the whole civilized world with her. No, sir, you dare not make war on cotton. No power on earth dares make war upon it. Cotton is king.'

Hammond believed that the wealth of a region was governed by the quantity of its exports, and southern staples had held up during the recession. Indeed the North had depended on them. He likened northern 'freedom' to chattel labour: 'your whole hireling class of manual labourers and operatives . . . are essentially slaves'. Hammond's 'cotton is king' speech – an outgrowth of pro-slavery thought of the late 1850s – added to southern overconfidence and swagger. It contributed to a fatal overestimation of southern resources and their importance in the world's affairs. Furthermore, the debate over the effects of the Panic of 1857 and the Lecompton Constitution shared the common characteristic of revolving around whether an economic system was better served by a chattel or free system of labour.[82]

The electoral impact of the recession affected the North more slowly but no less significantly. The effect on the Buchanan Administration was serious because it led to a severe reduction in the Federal government's revenues which were drawn from customs receipts. The most significant event was the Democrats' loss of Pennsylvania in the mid-term elections of 1858. This state had witnessed an increase in protectionist sentiment, and recent studies have emphasized that the Democratic Party's divisions on this urgent question were effectively exploited by Republicans (and Nativists who supported protectionism because it struck at foreigners and aided distressed American workers). 'The tariff question', as observers noted, 'is really paramount to all others in the minds of the masses of the people of this [Chester] and Delaware Counties'.[83] The ensuing serious loss had grave

82. Huston, *Panic of 1857*, pp. 122–7; Stampp, *1857*, pp. 325–6; J. H. Hammond, *Secret and Sacred*, ed. Carol Bleser (New York: Oxford UP, 1988), p. 273 (entry for 16 Apr. 1861). Like most other symbols of southern nationalism, 'King Cotton' is counterfeit (see Hammond, *Secret and Sacred*, p. 63). The phrase had been coined by David Christy of Cincinnati in 1853. Another precious southern symbol, the song/anthem 'Dixie' (1859), was probably composed by two northern blacks. See Howard L. Sacks and Judith Rose Sacks, *Way Up North in Dixie* (Washington, DC: Smithsonian Institution Press, 1993).

83. Huston, *Panic of 1857*, pp. 42–53; Collins, 'Economic Issues in Ohio's Politics', p. 62; Holt, *Forging a Majority*, pp. 239–55, tends to underplay the significance of protectionism; Collins, 'Democrats' Loss of Pennsylvania in 1858', *Pennsylvania Magazine of History and Biography* (Oct. 1985), pp. 512–20, 522–6; Huston, *Panic of 1857*, p. 120; Stampp, *1857*, pp. 233–4.

implications for the presidential election of 1860, for Pennsylvania was one of only five northern states carried by the Democrats in 1856. The most convincing explanation of the relationship between state and national elections is the way these multiple elections shaped and endorsed emerging *impressions* about political parties and their 'image' and ability to govern at all levels.

For instance, in Ohio in 1858, the Democratic vote held up strongly against Republican pressure, and a collapse on the scale of Pennsylvania was resisted. In short, the multiplicity of interests and issues in state and county politics balanced party competition; but only at national level could this be disrupted. For all the enthusiasm and vigour with which voters embraced local economic and social issues, the anti-southern stance of the Republican Party *was* popular with northern voters. But in Ohio the demands of campaigning in a recession allowed the Republicans to focus on the need for 'retrenchment' and fiscal prudence, and present a less radical, more prudent, responsible image. In short, these important state elections made an important contribution to the coalescence of voter opinion and mood that would focus on national issues.[84]

'Political crisis' or war?

The fundamental question to be addressed is the extent to which the 'political crisis of the 1850s' caused the Civil War. The Republican Party had gained many of its objectives by 1858, and was to secure many more by 1860. The extension of slavery would be prevented and the growing influence of the slave power over liberties of northerners resisted. But the drift to war cannot be charted adequately by merely considering the vicissitudes of party politics. The real reason why the United States was thrust into civil war lies in the southern decision not to accept the decisions made by a majority of voters in supporting the views of the Republican Party.

As the territorial extent of the United States grew by 73 per cent in the years 1848–53, it is hardly surprising that such a rapid expansion should promote fervent discussion about its future. This debate covered not only the kind of political structure these

---

84. Collins, 'Economic Issues in Ohio's Politics', pp. 48, 61; Collins, 'Democrats' Loss of Pennsylvania', pp. 502–3, 536.

territories would enjoy, but also the very nature of the Federal government itself. Its functions had been enlarged. Should such a federal union be centralized or diffuse? The answer to this question revealed significant differences in cultural perspective and belief. Stephen A. Douglas felt that the Union should be made safe for cultural diversity. In December 1857 he argued, 'You have no more right to force a Free-State Constitution on Kansas than a Slave-State Constitution. . . . It is none of my business which way the slavery clause is decided. I care not whether it is voted down or voted up.' Communities, in his view, should decide for themselves how they wished to order their affairs.

During the years 1850–58, however, an increased polarization occurred. Voters were not obsessed by the slavery issue; they were also agitated by other issues – social, economic, cultural – that impinged more directly on their daily lives. Nonetheless, the result of these elections at the national level was the growth of an exclusive, sectional party, prone to disseminating abusive, anti-southern propaganda which confirmed certain unflattering southern stereotypes and basic prejudices about the slave power. Republican influence grew also during a time of enormous expansion in northern industrial power, population, and communications. The check this received in 1857 caused considerable southern satisfaction. But despite efforts to conceal the increasing disparities between the sections, the South appeared as a beleaguered and backward section, much in the minority. Dynamism within the American economy and society stemmed from the North, not the South. Yet the latter appeared to exercise excessive power within the Federal government. The South's material interests were not just protected, they seemed to expand in the 1850s. As a reaction to this, northern cultural nationalism became more powerful, and was dedicated to interpreting the federal union, its rights and powers, on northern terms.

The southern response was to liken the federal union and the states to a fleet of separate ships. 'And as the ship may sail away from the fleet, when her own safety demands it, so, in a similar emergency, may the state or states, secede from the Union'. Growing awareness of the disparity of northern power *vis-à-vis* the South had agitated southerners for some years. Jefferson Davis had warned in 1849 that the South might 'sink . . . to the helpless condition' of Ireland in the British Empire. The southern response was to make greater and greater demands on the political system, while abdicating a national perspective on its problems, and this stimulated hostility and resistance. Southerners believed erroneously that this was inspired by sectional feeling stirred up by 'abolitionists'.[85]

It is thus worth reiterating that the issues underlying these disputes were profound and genuine, not superficial, or somehow artificial. They reflected sincere, as opposed to spurious, anxieties on both sides. Some political historians give the impression that it was the party 'game' that was really decisive in provoking the crisis. Slavery (or any other issue) was just a pretext to advance careers and secure office. In the words of Professor Holt, 'Politicians who pursued very traditional partisan strategies were largely responsible for the ultimate breakdown of the political process'. Elements of opportunism and self-interest can be found without difficulty. But this effort to eradicate ideas, ideals and belief from politics is itself strained and artificial, and mistakes the symptoms for the disease. Here there are loud echoes of much older schools of historiography – not just the 'revisionists', such as Randall and Avery Craven, but of the followers of Sir Lewis Namier and his influential work on British politics in the reign of George III. Thus Holt downgrades Lincoln's attempt to raise the moral issue in his debates with Douglas. He suggests that it was a mere tactical ploy designed to 'supplement' the 'House Divided' speech. Politics could not exist without tactics, but tactics are not the object of politics. As for Lincoln, even Douglas, they may have manoeuvred, and changed the emphasis on certain issues, as it suited them, but they had more in mind than just attaining 'credibility'. Their political position rested ultimately on a hard core of belief and real feelings which did not exist in a vacuum. Their beliefs determined their responses to the challenges of party politics, and the slavery question was central to their development.[86]

Finally, the breakdown of the second party system did not by itself cause the Civil War. It provided, however, the essential preconditions that made war possible. Where the two-party system broke down, secessionism gained ground and confidence. It is the

85. Bruce Collins, 'American Federalism and the Sectional Crisis, 1844–1860', in Andrea Bosco (ed.) *The Federal Idea*, I, *The History of Federalism from the Enlightenment to 1945* (London: Lothian Foundation Press, 1991), pp. 54–5, 57–60, 62–4.

86. Holt, *Political Crisis of the 1850s*, pp. 184, 210.

secession crisis that provides *the* issue for a confrontation between the secessionists and the Federal government, and the circumstances which forced men to pull their triggers and yank their lanyards. But *why* decision-makers were disposed to use force can be explained only by reference to the hearts and minds of men, not how they allot their votes. The sources of the martial spirit will be the subject of the next chapter.

CHAPTER FIVE

Anticipations of War, 1858–60

Since the campaigns of Austerlitz and of 1807 Rostov knew by experience that men always lie when describing military exploits, as he himself had done when recounting them; besides that, he had experience enough to know that nothing happens in war at all as we can imagine or relate it.

LEO TOLSTOY, *War and Peace*[1]

This chapter is the first of two analytical approaches attempting to answer the question why the American Civil War broke out when it did. The 'models' that the two chapters seek to develop will abandon the more traditional kind of political history. Previous historians have relied too heavily, and exclusively, on its insights in seeking an explanation of the origins of the war. The main theme of this chapter is an exploration of what James Joll once called the 'unspoken assumptions' that men of power rely on when deciding whether to go to war or not. These are the views, myths and thoughts, that compound of education, prejudice and opinion, that shapes a perspective on the rush of political events and determines the course of action, the decisions, which political crises demand.[2] Consequently, the chapter will be organized around the relationships arising from how men feel, how they think and how they act. It is not claimed that any direct teleological links exist between these impulses, but they do have the advantage of drawing out consistent themes about how and why decision-makers reacted to the *possibility* of war.

1.   Leo Tolstoy, *War and Peace* (London: Macmillan, 1943) p. 712.
2.   James Joll, *1914: The Unspoken Assumptions* (Inaugural Lecture, London School of Economics: Weidenfeld & Nicholson, 1968).

How men felt

To men of the 1840s the Union was not just a nation-state like any other, it was very special. It was 'the Palladium of our National happiness'; in the words of Richard Carwardine, it was the 'handiwork of God'.[3] It exemplified a mission – the spread of a republican democracy as *the* form of democratic practice – and a civilizing quest to conquer the wilderness. During the 1850s – especially after the Mexican War – political commentary was full of worries not only that the young republic was failing to live up to its early shining promise, but also that the generations of politicians who succeeded the Founding Fathers were not displaying levels of genius and probity comparable to theirs. It was to the need to guard against this danger that many men's thoughts returned again and again, shaping their sense of urgent 'crisis'. There are five important sub-themes to be considered that complement (and occasionally contradict) one another: revulsion against corruption, fear of partisanship, a desire to uphold 'honour', suspicion of conspiracy, and finally, a growing impatience.

REVULSION AGAINST CORRUPTION

A major element of American exceptionalism was the notion that the United States experiment in democracy was pure; indeed that it had thrown off the corrupting and decadent embraces of Great Britain. 'Corruption stalks abroad. Nobody is honest but ourselves,' explained a newspaper. 'We alone can save our fellow-citizens from forty thousand horrors'. But the huge creation of wealth in the thirty years before the Civil War greatly increased the temptations. Corruption was a lurking danger that threatened to enfeeble the new republic. 'Our foundations are crumbling', warned Reverend Henry Ward Beecher. Such anxieties were accentuated after Andrew Jackson's rise to the presidency and the introduction of the spoils system. Government clerks were replaced by party nominees at all levels of governments. This had the advantage of checking centralization, ridding government of the petty tyrannies of bureaucrats, and protecting the rights of states and the prerogatives of local political leaders. In short, it guarded against the 'insolence of office'. But the spoils system led

---

3.   Richard J. Carwardine, *Evangelicals and Politics in Antebellum America* (New Haven, CT: Yale UP, 1994), p. 181.

to a revitalization of party as the means of government, and the growth of a class of politicians who depended on securing 'spoils' won at elections. Such a system released all kinds of tensions within the political culture which it was designed to protect. Where did sensible compromise begin and plunder end? Or to quote Jane Austen, where does prudence end and avarice begin? Republican values were demoralized and sullied by the means relied upon to nurture them.[4]

Such tensions had a major effect on the reputation of the political system and the trust invested in it. Newspapers were dismissed as mere 'hirelings' and editors as corrupt. Increasingly, the very mechanics of the democratic process became suspect. Examples of ballot box corruption and the purchase of the people's will, a suspicion of partisanship, and the violence it provoked, led to much denunciation. As Martin Van Buren said, it was 'sickening', and it contributed signally to the feeling of political crisis in the 1850s. The people remained virtuous and high-minded, for the evil men could be removed. Thus each election offered the chance of restoring the old standards, but disillusionment increased as these opportunities were squandered.[5]

Thoughtful citizens feared that republics were delicate flowers which were vulnerable to parasites within as well as contamination from without. The American experiment was endangered by its very success. Wealth was discolouring the pristine white of republican purity. Gideon Welles wrote of his fellow countrymen that 'Ours, I fear, are beginning to value wealth more than freedom'. This idea was given additional point by the assumption that greedy northerners were more prone to corruption than southerners – a view with which southerners emphatically agreed. The slave power had lined the pockets of northern congressmen and extended its influence within the space of one generation. The South had her views and stood by them unreservedly and incorruptibly. The South, moreover, exploited this northern weakness ruthlessly. Such fears were given a new dimension when the Buchanan Administration employed bribery to get its pro-southern legislative programme through Congress. Congressmen were bought, it was claimed, for $5,000 apiece. The corrupt

4. Mark W. Summers, *The Plundering Generation: Corruption and the Crisis of the Union, 1849–1861* (New York: Oxford UP, 1987), pp. 3, 16–18, 32–5, to which this discussion owes much.
5. Ibid., pp. 49–50, 53–61, 80, 109.

activities of the Secretary of War, John B. Floyd, and the Secretary of the Navy, Isaac Toucey (who distributed shipbuilding contracts on the basis of which employer could increase its labour force and ensure it voted Democrat), gave the Buchanan Administration the unenviable stamp of unprecedented corruption. At least Franklin Pierce had been honest, whatever his other numerous deficiencies.[6]

By the end of Buchanan's term, many agreed that the country and its governing system were in crisis. It also added to the apocalyptic, melodramatic atmosphere that prevailed by 1860. Indeed, this assumption, namely, that the Federal government was sinking into a putrid sea of corruption, strengthened the secessionist argument that the South needed to start anew, and that it might persuade some Border and northern states to leave the Union and join a new republic. Hence the (ironic) southern dissatisfaction with the Democratic Party that had been tainted by Buchanan and his 'buccaneers'. Buchanan's corrupt activities (through he was probably personally honest) simultaneously revitalized northern opposition to the slave power and agitated fears that a sickness was being pumped through the body politic by personal greed and ambition. Hence fears about corruption blended with other anxieties to prompt George Templeton Strong to warn in his diary in December 1858 that 'Our civilization is decaying. We are in our decadence. An explosion and crash must be at hand'.[7]

FEAR OF PARTISANSHIP

This feeling is closely associated with a reaction against corruption. Joel Silbey may be right that politics in this period was governed by a 'partisan imperative'. This might account, too, for the power and intensity of political debate, whose practitioners 'were schooled in certain unyielding truths'. He argues also that 'Moral commitments were particularly strong in the 1850s. Spiritual values, religious metaphors, and ethnic awareness abounded in

6. Ibid., pp. 168–73, 216–217, 224–5, 243–6, 253–4, 256, 259; Larry Gara, *The Presidency of Franklin Pierce* (Lawrence, KS: University of Kansas Press, 1991), pp. 54, 60–1.

7. Quoted in Marcus Cunliffe, *Soldiers and Civilians: The Martial Spirit in America, 1775–1865*, 3rd edn, with a new preface by Brian Holden Reid (London: Gregg, 1993), p. 376.

everyday life'. The outward signs of political debate and division reflected these, so that 'Party rhetoric [was], therefore, structured around different perspectives which became the centre of bitter, sustained conflict'.[8] But Silbey overlooks the possibility that one important way in which these moral imperatives were expressed was essentially *anti-party*.

By 1860 the term 'party politician' had become a term of abuse used by party politicians themselves to describe those who were unscrupulous, selfish and unprincipled. The Democratic Party came badly out of any comparison because it was tainted by 'machines', such as New York City's Tammany Hall, that were associated with immigrant voters in the big cities and the corrupt antics of the Buchanan Administration. Indeed, 'parties' in the general sense were thought to be no longer purveyors of ideals and ideas. An intense dislike of the so-called 'practical man' of the spoils system was often manifested. Parties were often assumed to be temporary arrangements that came and went on the political landscape. The reputation of party politicians was low. In March 1855 the New York *Tribune* wrote of the Thirty-Fourth Congress, that 'a Congress so prodigal and unfaithful – never before assembled in this country'. The Republican Party, of course, strongly benefited from its novelty and lack of association with political corruption and the besmirching of earlier party politicians. Lincoln's initial popularity arose from his image of honesty and simplicity; he would return the government of the country to a less partisan, less selfish system like that 'purity of practice and principle which characterize its early days under the administration of the Revolutionary patriots'.[9]

A consensus developed by 1859–60 that standards of public life were so low, its motives so base and the quality of appointments so inadequate, that the crisis of the Union was *caused* by party politicians. They had betrayed the principles of the American Revolution and Founding Fathers. Abraham Lincoln came to accept this view. The coming to power of the Republican Party was therefore represented as a veritable cleansing of the Augean stables. Room for manoeuvre was therefore limited because of the

8.   Joel H. Silbey, *The Partisan Imperative* (New York: Oxford UP, 1985), pp. 61, 171, 174, 175.

9.   Summers, *Plundering Generation*, pp. 175–9, 184, 202, 299. Seward's association with the corrupt 'wizard of the lobbies', Thurlow Weed, was a major disadvantage in his hopes for the 1860 nomination. See ibid., p. 270.

association of compromise not just with financial graft, but with the abandonment of political principle.[10]

These attitudes contributed later to a *determination* to stand up and be counted robustly. This was one of the reasons why Fort Sumter came to assume a symbolic importance in 1861 out of all proportion to its military value. It came to assume the embodiment, in the North, of selfless patriotism untainted by graft and party. Moreover, the most articulate came to look for an 'inner power' which would overcome the frustrations, tensions and littleness that they thought blighted their lives and ideals. The United States deserved purging and punishment for the iniquities into which it had sunk, and this coercive instrument could be provided only by violence. John Brown was described by the abolitionist, Wendell Phillips, as 'the impersonator of God's law, moulding a better future, and setting it for an example'. Under these circumstances, men who might (one would have thought) have been natural pacifists were those who actually looked forward to civil war. In the spring of 1861 Phillips wrote to Gerrit Smith, 'I trust *events*. The Adm[inistration] means war. . . . There must be *bloodshed*. Did you ever expect to see such a day – we truly are blessed to see the fruits of our toil'. This is an extreme opinion but one that would gain more support as crisis followed upon crisis.[11]

Such attitudes among intellectuals and abolitionists were a very strong reaction against the constraints imposed on American politics by the rigidities of the two-party system, an intense and formal legalism, and Constitution-worship. All three of these aspects were given expression in the 'partisan imperative'. Significantly, because American parties were weak and not ideologically riven as they were in Europe, the antagonisms over slavery intensified as divisions on other issues were dissipated.[12] William H. Seward had warned as long ago as 1850 that there was a 'higher law' than the Constitution. This was a prophetic warning that the most idealistic of political systems cannot be used indefinitely to give legal and constitutional protection to a perversion of those ideals, namely, an extension of the slave

10. Summers, *Plundering Generation*, pp. 213, 229, 291; William E. Gienapp, '"Politics Seem to Enter into Everything": Political Culture in the North, 1840–1860', in Stephen E. Maizlish (ed.) *Essays on American Antebellum Politics, 1840–1860* (College Station: Texas A&M UP, 1982), pp. 43–5.

11. James Brewer Stewart, *Wendell Phillips: Liberty's Hero* (Baton Rouge: Louisiana State UP, 1986), pp. 68, 202–6, 219.

12. Summers, *Plundering Generation*, p. 184.

system in the name of 'freedom'. A narrow, obstinate defence of constitutional forms relying on the letter rather than the spirit of the law stimulates violence, *not* respect for the Constitution. Where else but in the United States could Constitution-worship justify a revolutionary and secessionary movement? The southern states seceded in defence of their constitutional rights. Jefferson Davis wrote in his post-war apologia that 'It is a satisfaction to know that the calamities which have befallen the southern states were the result of their credulous reliance on the power of the Constitution, that if it failed to protect their rights, it would at least suffice to prevent an attempt at coercion, if, in the last resort, they peacefully withdrew from the Union'. What is so extraordinary about this passage is that an appeal to the Constitution seems to carry its own justification. Davis makes no appeal to great ideas, heroism, or the swell of public emotion or expectation, but to a narrow legalistic formula.[13]

A DESIRE TO UPHOLD 'HONOUR'

If one feature is associated with the southern planter class, it is honour. The courtly, impeccably attired, considerate and well-mannered southern gentleman has acquired almost legendary status. Though the cult of the gentleman is hardly unknown in the northern states, it has been most fully developed in the South. The original model is English.[14] In Henry James's novel, *The Bostonians*, the hero Basil Ransome, a southerner, persists in courtly politeness, even when it is shamelessly exploited by the ghastly Mrs Luna. There can be no doubt that the gentlemanly code can bring out the best, as well as the worst, in men. But in this chapter we need to consider the cumulative affect on *group* behaviour of those who subscribe to the code of honour, and that is rather less praiseworthy than its influence on the behaviour of individuals. Don E. Fehrenbacher, in an appropriate metaphor, likens the emotions demonstrated by southerners during the secession crisis to the sun's rays focused through a magnifying glass – they became scorching and intensely concentrated.[15] One

13. Jefferson Davis, *The Rise and Fall of the Confederate Government*, 2 vols (London: Longmans Green, 1881), I, pp. 228–9.
    14. See Philip Mason, *The English Gentleman: The Rise and Fall of an Ideal* (London: André Deutsch, 1982).
    15. Don E. Fehrenbacher, *The South and Three Sectional Crises* (Baton Rouge: Louisiana State UP, 1980), p. 63.

explanation for this acute emotion might be sought in the notion of honour.

Group sensation and activity tends to exaggerate and distort individual behaviour and attitudes. Bertram Wyatt-Brown characterizes the worst side of the code of honour as 'excessive touchiness, uncontrolled ambition, shameless servility to a fickle public, [and] self-destructive hospitality' – a pattern which accurately represents southern behaviour in 1860–61. It is, in short, a reflection of ancient localism, and it can be highly aggressive. Aggression is worked out through duelling rather than in any natural penchant for the military life. William Garrett Brown in 1903 offered a cogent explanation of the relationship between the cult of honour and parochialism. 'To the southerner', he wrote, 'liberty meant nothing less than the right of himself and his community to be free from all interference by the peculiar outside world'.[16]

Honour, as an expression of the social order, is intimately connected to community. It is designed to bring some sort of structure to life by emphasizing self-dependence. In a society based on slavery the virtues we associate with honour – especially in small, compact, cohesive and homogeneous slaveowning, patriarchal communities – could be transformed into vices. Loud boasting and haughtiness could be fashioned under pressure into condescension or blind arrogance. The resulting violence could be unjustified, flagrant, unpredictable, anarchic, and even self-defeating. It is a peculiar characteristic of southern honour that it placed great faith on judging the external features of behaviour – the spoken word and physical gesture, in particular.[17] Yet southerners knew little of the world – including the North – outside of their own communities and were absorbed in their own narrow concerns. Their judgements on the outside world and its behaviour towards them were uniformly disastrous. As the 1850s drew to a close, southern behaviour became increasingly erratic. The possibility of a Republican in the White House in 1860 summed up an apocalyptic threat and brought to the fore a provincial, paranoid surge of frustrated emotion and aggression. The qualities of inner serenity and reason seem to have deserted

16. Bertram Wyatt-Brown, *Southern Honor: Ethics and Behavior in the Old South* (New York: Oxford UP, 1982), pp. 22, 75, 111, 113, 168, 350–61, 438.

17. Ibid., pp. 9–10, 45–7, 59–60, 113, 138–40, 369–80; Richard E. Beringer, Herman Hattaway, Archer Jones and William N. Still, Jr, *Why the South Lost the Civil War* (Athens, GA: University of Georgia Press, 1986), p. 401.

that self-consciously honourable group of southern political leaders that precipitated the secession crisis.

SUSPICION OF CONSPIRACY

One of the most powerful emotions felt during the secession crisis was that southern secession was the result of a deep-seated, well-laid plot. Jefferson Davis specifically denied in his memoirs that any plan of secession existed.[18] In part, this fear was an extension of the slave power conspiracy. It was also an expression of long-running suspicion of other 'aristocratic' institutions, such as the United States Military Academy at West Point. In January 1863 Senator James H. Lane of Kansas claimed that if the North was defeated, its epitaph would be chiselled, 'Died of West Point pro-slaveryism'. Hinton Rowan Helper in his controversial book, *The Impending Crisis of the South* (1857), argued that the Federal government had been penetrated by the slave power and its sympathizers. In December 1860 secessionist cockades could be bought virtually on the steps of the Congress. Belief in the plot was given substance by John B. Floyd's corrupt activities and numerous resignations of southern officers from the US Army (though 275 out of a total of 1,033 does not appear excessive).

The only other evidence that credulous conspiracy theorists could find was Nathaniel Beverly Tucker's 1836 novel, *The Partisan Leader,* which predicted the coming of civil war; the rebels, commanded by a West Pointer, defeat the federal army. Seven thousand copies of this novel were circulated in New York in the month after Fort Sumter. But the paucity of this 'evidence' did not discourage the frantic search for agents of treason in all departments of state in the first year of the war.[19]

A GROWING IMPATIENCE

One of the most underestimated aspects of the final crisis that culminated in civil war is the understandable, human desire to see the crisis over and done with. The contemporary correspondence is frequently marked by the wearing effect of continual tension; better that civil war come than the tension continue indefinitely. This is, also, a characteristic of a political culture hardly noted for

18. Davis, *Rise and Fall,* pp. 207–9.
19. Cunliffe, *Soldiers and Civilians,* pp. 374–5; Michael C. C. Adams, *Our Masters the Rebels* (Cambridge, MA: Harvard UP, 1978), pp. 60–2.

its forbearance. Therefore, a desire to bring matters to a head underlined the whole crisis like a red thread. Yet, we should also recall, even when contemporaries were reminding themselves of the need for reason and prudence, that as Cyril Falls well said: 'Impatience affects the power of reason'.[20] It is now appropriate to turn to consider the ideas that mid-nineteenth-century Americans entertained about war.

Thinking about war

All of these feelings contributed to a universal expectation in April 1861 that war would be *short and abrupt.* American military experience in the nineteenth century led all to believe that wars were short – the War of 1812 (1812–15) and the Mexican War (1845–48), in particular. Of the former, Americans chose to remember the final, climactic Battle of New Orleans in January 1815, in which almost 2,000 casualties had been inflicted on the British at virtually no cost to themselves. The battle was, alas, fought after the Treaty of Ghent of December 1814 had been signed and thus had no strategic significance; the earlier indecisive and humiliating phase was overlooked.[21] The Mexican War, likewise, was seen as an outlet for excess energy in which rapid movement would inflict severe losses on the enemy, while sustaining few American casualties. 'Never since the days of Washington', a writer perceived of the Mexican War, 'has an excitement, so wild and universal, thrilled in the souls of free men'. These wars were also seen as validating, indeed forging anew, the triumphant heritage of George Washington and the Founding Fathers, and thus had a determined nationalist, later sectional, function.[22]

A sentimental, nostalgic coating was ladled over war, and this was personified in the figure of George Washington. The grandeur of Washington's memory, and all the ideals that it enshrined, concealed the realities of the war he had actually fought. War was conceived as essentially a contest of heroic generals. This is

20. Cyril Falls, *The Place of War in History: An Inaugural Lecture* (Oxford: Clarendon, 1947), p. 10. I am grateful to Major P. A. Fox, RA, for bringing this lecture to my attention. See below, pp. 196, 352.

21. Cunliffe, *Soldiers and Civilians*, p. 53; J. W. Ward, *Andrew Jackson: Symbol for an Age* (New York: Oxford UP, 1955), pp. 5–10, 101–3; J. C. A. Stagg, *Mr Madison's War* (Princeton UP, 1983), pp. 496–500.

22. Robert W. Johannsen, *To the Halls of the Montezumas: The Mexican War in the American Imagination* (New York: Oxford UP, 1985), p. 61.

confirmed by the rising cult of Napoleon that excited nineteenth-century America which has yet to be documented adequately. The figure of Andrew Jackson assumed such Napoleonic proportions that it was at times difficult to see when 'Old Hickory' began and the Emperor ended. In addition, the romance of war was injected into these conflicts by analogies drawn from antiquity, but especially the Middle Ages. Through the novels of Sir Walter Scott, mid-nineteenth-century Americans – the great majority of whom had not experienced its brutalities in 1812–15 or 1846–48 – came to envisage war as a chivalrous sport, an ideal counterpoint to the grubby, corrupt and materialistic ethos of the age.[23]

Occasionally in 1861 doubts surfaced about this essentially optimistic view of war. J. E. B. Stuart confided to George Cary Eggleston that, 'I regard it as a foregone conclusion . . . that we shall ultimately whip the Yankees. We are bound to believe that, anyhow; but the war is going to be a long and terrible one, first. We've only just begun it, and very few of us will see the end'. Benjamin F. Butler was also to argue in April 1861 that if his 25,000 men should 'die . . . a quarter of a million will take their place' until 'women with their broomsticks' would 'drive every enemy into the gulf'. One wonders whether 'long' here is not a relative term? If the war was expected to be over in a matter of weeks, then a year was a very 'long' time, and 'terrible'. This kind of rhetoric has a much closer relationship with 'blood-curdling' pre-war rhetoric than it does with any prescience over the harsh realities of 1861–65. It was habitual for the men of the 1850s to speak and write of war in terms of extreme hyperbole as they themselves had not experienced it, and Stuart and Butler's expectations fit this pattern.[24]

Groups who are confident in their cause usually expect success to come rapidly. The overwhelming force of received wisdom in 1861 was that a battle, and a campaign, let alone the war, were synonymous. Therefore, to win one great battle at the beginning would be sufficient to bring the war to an end. Here it might be pointed out with profit – in contradistinction to the customary generalization that Americans are excessively passionate in their

    23. Ibid., pp. 59–60, 70–1; Ward, *Jackson*, pp. 182–9; Cunliffe, *Soldiers and Civilians*, pp. 348–9; Gary Wills, *Cincinnatus: George Washington and the Enlightenment* (London: Robert Hale, 1984), pp. 122, 167, 171–2.
    24. Quoted in Emory M. Thomas, *Bold Dragoon: The Life of J. E. B. Stuart* (New York: Harper & Row, 1986), p. 97; Richard S. West, *Lincoln's Scapegoat General* (Boston, MA: Houghton-Mifflin, 1965), pp. 73–4.

warmaking, and too prone to transforming their wars into ventures with unlimited objectives – that most Americans have entered them – especially in the nineteenth century – thinking they would be short. Their expansion into brutal wars to the finish, as in 1861–65, was as much a product of disillusion with initial failures as from any inherent penchant for crusading.[25]

The second crucial element that underlines any thinking about war in these years is that it would be essentially *unorganized*, and fought with *volunteers*. That is to say, any war fought in the Americas would not be the exclusive province of standing, regular armies commanded by professional officers. The volunteer regiments were carved from the militia system that demanded universal military service, though such far-reaching demands were theoretical rather than practical. The volunteers could indeed be militia regiments but they were more frequently spontaneous gatherings of men eager to serve, to regulate their own affairs and dress, and participate in a military adventure that was called for by some urgent crisis. They were often excited by a feeling of *corps d'élite* and extravagant uniforms. They were more common in the North than in the South, and were increasingly associated with immigrant groups – often as expressions of urban ethnic identity.[26]

These regiments (who chose their own officers) were a fine testimony to a sense of 'community' and a passion for picturesque adventure that was so prevalent in *ante-bellum* America. Most significantly, these units contributed to a growing sense of state patriotism and also to an expansive restlessness.[27] The contrast between the boasting of the volunteers and their egregious appearance was often the object of scorn among regulars, as during the Mexican War.[28] Volunteers indeed may not have assumed any recognizable 'military' form at all. Here the experience of unorganized and vigilante action in Kansas is most significant. The Missourian 'ruffians' that swaggered into Kansas in 1854–55 were mobilized by the Platte County Self-Defensive

25. Marcus Cunliffe, 'The Formative Events from Columbus to World War I', in Michael P. Hamilton (ed.) *American Character and Foreign Policy* (Grand Rapids, MI: Eerdmans, 1986), pp. 10–11.

26. Cunliffe, *Soldiers and Civilians*, pp. 216–18, 220–6; Brian Holden Reid, 'A Survey of the Militia in 18th Century America', *Army Quarterly* (Jan. 1980), pp. 49, 53–4.

27. Johannsen, *To the Halls of the Montezumas*, pp. 26, 29, 63; Anne C. Rose, *Victorian America and the Civil War* (Cambridge UP, 1992), pp. 86, 99, 110.

28. See *The Mexican War Diary of General George B. McClellan*, ed. William S. Myers (Princeton UP, 1917), pp. 28, 38, 43.

Association. 'Self-defence' in this case required driving Free Soil settlers from their farms and burning their towns. Both sides in this dispute believed that the other benefited from a secret military organization, which did not exist, but the pattern of the violence was hardly 'military'. It was sporadic and on a tiny scale. The killing of one young man was sufficient to spark the 'Wakarusa War'. Twelve hundred Missourians gathered to attack Lawrence, though they held off. In May 1856 Lawrence was indeed 'sacked' – one man was killed and a pro-slavery raider was killed when a brick fell off the roof of the Free State Hotel. The much denounced, brutal murder of five pro-slavery supporters committed by John Brown's gang at Pottawatomie Creek was small beer, even by comparison with the twentieth century's more notorious 'serial killers'.[29]

The violence in Kansas – which was a series of exaggerated descriptions of frontier brawls – contributed powerfully to a view after 1858 in both North and South that the war, if it came, would not be of significant intensity. We should not confuse the rhetoric employed to describe this militarily insignificant activity with the conclusions drawn as to its future importance.[30] Thus 'drenching the Union in blood', to cite a metaphor much favoured by southern spokesmen, actually meant 'violence as *described* in Kansas'. It should not be construed as meaning that southerners *expected* any sustained or prolonged form of civil war. In the North, a view prevailed that should war be necessary, and the majority hoped that it would not, then it would resemble an affray like Shay's Rebellion in Massachusetts in 1786. Then the militia dispersed effortlessly a body of discontented and truculent farmers who threatened to seize a federal arsenal at Springfield. Similarly, during the Whiskey Rebellion of 1794 in Pennsylvania a force of 13,000 men was mobilized to suppress a rebellion of farmers who refused to pay an excise on the products of their whisky distilleries. The 7,000 rebels lacked organization and clear aims; they were easily dispersed with trifling casualties. It was in this spirit that Lincoln moved to suppress the Confederacy in 1861.[31]

29.   James A. Rawley, *Race and Politics: 'Bleeding Kansas' and the Coming of the Civil War* (Lincoln: University of Nebraska Press, 1969, 1979), pp. 85, 96–8, 132, 134.

30.   Rawley, *Race and Politics*, p. 160, estimates the total casualties 1855–56 at 200 and property loss at about $2 million: this is a maximum rather than minimum estimate.

31.   Cunliffe, *Soldiers and Civilians*, pp. 42–3; Thomas P. Slaughter, *The Whiskey Rebellion* (New York: Oxford UP, 1986), pp. 181–2, 188–9.

In a society as idealistic as the United States, thoughts of war had to be geared to higher aspirations or rationalization. By 1860–61 both sides thought they had right on their side. One side felt it was defending the Union against the depredations of traitors – it was the duty of the North to defend the integrity of the democratic process and the precious indivisibility of the American experiment in democracy. The other felt that it was defending the true heritage of George Washington and asserting just (and constitutionally justified) southern rights – the constitutional right to extinguish the constitution should southern interests demand it.

These feelings were perhaps stronger in the North than in the South. The United States was considered a very special polity – one blessed by providence. Not only did that providential example – as a beacon of democracy – need to be protected, but it was also right that, as this special polity had not reached, let alone maintained, the standards required of it, the United States be purged and be subject to divine punishment – war. 'Our present civilization is characterized and tainted by a devouring greediness . . .', wrote William Ellery Channing. 'The passion for gain is everywhere sapping pure and generous feelings'. The northern economy was regaining strength after the recession of 1857, but many politicians, Lincoln and Seward among them, thought that this was being achieved at the expense of moral values. Similarly, in the South men (and women) were prepared to acquiesce in the coming of war in the mistaken view that it would resuscitate ideals and a sense of community and obligation. War, therefore, became a stern test through which society should pass – a 'fiery trial' in Lincoln's words. This attitude, in short, contributed to a frame of mind that believed that the coming of war would not be an unmitigated evil.[32]

How men acted

It should not be assumed, of course, that a rigid distinction can be drawn between how men think and how men act, as there is an intimate relationship between them. The most important feature of *ante-bellum* military attitudes that shaped conduct was the belief

32. Phillip S. Paludan, *The Presidency of Abraham Lincoln* (Lawrence; KS: University Press of Kansas, 1994), p. 11; Rose, *Victorian America*, pp. 19, 100–2, 106, 252.

that if there was a single region in the United States that enjoyed a coherent, impressive military tradition, it was the South. According to one historian, the southern character exhibited great belligerence: indeed 'almost universal acknowledgement of their remarkable spirit and will to fight'. Southerners congratulated themselves on their 'indomitable energy in battle, humanity and moderation after victory... and the storm of war which shook Mexico to her foundations [in 1846–48], roused not the slightest ripple upon the smooth waters of our internal repose'. Such martial confidence, a zeal for war, and record of success, helps explain why the South did little to prevent the coming of war in 1861, and why her armies were so successful in 1861–63.[33]

Or does it? The great majority of the literary efforts that try to define southern 'character' distinguish firmly between 'the South' and other sections. They are largely a post–1865 development – they often seek to justify (or damn) the nobility of the southern cause and explain its martial record in the Civil War. Does all this, therefore, constitute a southern '*military* tradition' before 1861? The answer must be that warnings of a southern military tradition have been greatly exaggerated, and that this must be consigned to the long list of southern myths designed to promote some sense of southern identity.

On close investigation, all the elements of this so-called tradition demonstrate that attitudes to soldiering were broadly comparable North and South. The existence of the tradition was believed in, and acted upon, by contemporaries – but this does not render it valid. Enthusiasm for the novels of Sir Walter Scott and their romantic air of martial adventure was shared equally by northerners; there was no great domination by the South of military academies, though those in the South have become more famous; there was little sophisticated military thought in the nineteenth century, but what did appear was written by northerners; in terms of proportionate numbers to varying sectional populations, the United States Military Academy did not graduate more cadets from the South than the North. In an eloquent speech attacking secession, Alexander H. Stephens, pleaded the case for remaining in the Union because of southern dominance of federal institutions, including 'a vast majority of the higher officers of both army and navy' in 1861. This was not due

---

33. John Hope Franklin, *The Militant South, 1800–1861* (Cambridge, MA: Harvard UP, 1956), pp. 2–3, 10.

to the innate excellence of southern generals, but because of promotion by strict seniority, so that after 1840 the highest positions in the army remained in the same hands for decades at a time when the population balance was changing drastically in favour of the North. Highly organized minority opinion in the United States can gain great power over federal patronage, particularly if it is conservative in tone; the South was highly successful in asserting and protecting its interests in this regard.[34]

What, therefore, remains of the tradition? All accounts stress the importance of casual violence, vigilantism and duels as important elements of the southern outlook; this has more to do with the pattern of frontier violence than anything inherently southern. The slave system certainly nurtured a strong vigilante tradition and stimulated militia activities closely related to police functions – the 'Slave Patrol', for instance. These grew up in the eighteenth century, but they were not 'military' in import. In the various Indian Wars and in the Mexican War, southern commentators stressed the highly individualistic, adaptable, unfettered, unaffected 'natural' genius of their soldiers. This is not uniquely southern and is typical of the rhetoric of the 1840s celebrating the great talents of American warriors. But again, does all this constitute a military tradition as opposed to a taste for casual violence? Certainly not. Those countries with the most impressive military traditions, Russia, Germany and Japan, have been highly deferential to the prestige of the army, have not approved of lawlessness and individualism, nor (until recent times) have they been very democratic.[35]

A penchant for violence is not, of course, irrelevant, but we should be very careful not to confuse violence with war, as so many Americans did in 1861 – and some historians do to this day. It is striking that critics of Marcus Cunliffe fault him on the grounds that he underestimates a southern taste for brawling, duelling and tarring and feathering, especially of strangers or those who threatened the southern way of life. An account of a tarring and feathering occurs in Mark Twain's *The Adventures of Huckleberry Finn* (1884), when the 'king' and the 'duke' are discovered at their swindling tricks, and suffer for them. But all these writers who seek to find something *exceptional* and distinct in

34. Cunliffe, *Soldiers and Civilians*, pp. 342–4, 347–55, 360–6, 368–70.
35. Bruce Collins, 'The Southern Military Tradition, 1812–61', in Brian Holden Reid and John White (eds) *American Studies: Essays in Honour of Marcus Cunliffe* (London: Macmillan, 1991), pp. 31, 135.

southern behaviour overlook an elementary but fundamental point, namely, in Bruce Collins's words, that 'habits of violence acquired in dealing with slaves and in maintaining personal codes of honour had no direct bearing on the disciplined mass behaviour demanded of Civil War armies'.[36]

Southern 'filibustering' can be fitted into this tradition of casual violence. The most famous filibuster was William Walker, the so-called 'gray-eyed man of destiny'. Walker was prone to gathering small groups of men, calling this band an 'army' and launching it on raids in Central America, such as that inflicted on Mexico in 1853 and Nicaragua in 1855. The ambitions of these ragged groups of free-booters and plunderers were completely out of kilter with their discipline and martial prowess. And though Walker, briefly, made himself dictator of Nicaragua in 1855, he was shot dead the following year. This pattern of casual ill-discipline is so pervasive that it was carried over into the Civil War itself. If there is a southern military tradition – which is doubtful – its true exemplar is Earl Van Dorn, a romantic, vainglorious, empty-headed adventurer, in the spirit of Walker, rather than the studied professionalism of Robert E. Lee or Joseph E. Johnston.[37]

Yet even if the notion of a southern military tradition is rejected we cannot brush aside this confusion of riot, widespread disorder and violence (and the southern attachment to the belief that they had a rare talent for it) because it had an important bearing on southern conduct in the final crisis that led to civil war. William Howard Russell was shocked during his visits to the South in the early months of 1861 by the casual assumption of martial superiority based on the most spurious grounds. He recorded a number of conversations with southerners who asserted 'that the white men in the slave states are physically superior to the men in the free states; and indulged in curious theories in morals and physics to which I was a stranger'. Moreover, the great majority of

36. Differences of interpretation may be traced in Collins, 'Southern Military Tradition', pp. 130–5; Wyatt-Brown, *Southern Honor*, pp. 192, 484–5, 533–5; G. McWhiney, *Cracker Culture* (University of Alabama Press, 1988), pp. 147–57, 159, 169–70; James M. McPherson, 'Antebellum Southern Exceptionalism', *Civil War History* 29 (1983), pp. 230–44. McPherson claims that more southerners entered West Point, but Cunliffe had never denied this: see *Soldiers and Civilians*, p. 361, also Brian Holden Reid, 'New Preface to the Gregg Revivals Edition' (1993), p. xiii; this edition also includes Cunliffe's own (1973) response to his critics, pp. xvii–xxiii.

37. Allan Nevins, *Ordeal of the Union* (New York: Scribner's, 1947), II, pp. 368–74, 405–8.

southerners seemed to maintain that warfare was simply a brawl, or a duel on a larger scale (this last was certainly an unintended paraphrase of Clausewitz). Moreover, moral superiority in war was proven by instances of personal confrontations with northern representatives in Congress. The caning of Sumner was an especially comforting example.

> The notion that the northern men are cowards is justified by instances in which Congressmen have been insulted by southern men without calling them out, and Mr Sumner's case was quoted as the type of affairs of the kind between the two sides.

Russell included a conversation with a somewhat inebriated Senator (then also Colonel) Louis T. Wigfall of Texas, a noted duellist, who compared Sumner's caning 'as a type of the manner in which the southerners would deal with northerners generally . . . [and] in which they would bear their "whipping"'. Indeed Wigfall upheld his view that war represented some kind of sporting pageant, when during the bombardment of Fort Sumter, he had himself rowed out to the fort in a frantic attempt to persuade the garrison to surrender because they had proved their courage; his exhortations were ignored, yet it was typical of the shallow (and ignorant) southern view of war that he should make them.[38]

The whole notion of 'manliness' is thus wrapped up in the web of unspoken assumptions that men fell back on instinctively when teetering on the brink of war. It became an article of faith that southerners exhibited a high degree of manliness, and they also argued that the northerners lacked it. Some northerners agreed. They believed that an urban, industrialized society was at a disadvantage when set against a rural, outdoor one. George Templeton Strong was tired of hearing of the need for placating the South. What 'could stiffen up the spiritless, money-worshipping North? Strange the South can't kick us into manliness and a little moderate wrath. Southerners rule us through our slaves of Fifth Avenue and Wall Street'. Thus under the pressure of the secession crisis the myriad of unspoken assumptions came together in a complex and often contradictory matrix. The contempt for partisan attitudes, materialism and corruption, the fear of conspiracy and a dedication to honour, were compounded

38. W. H. Russell, *My Diary North and South*, ed. Eugene H. Berwanger (New York: Alfred A. Knopf, 1988), pp. 61–3, 89 (entries for 5 Apr., 17 Apr. 1861); W. A. Swanberg, *First Blood: The Story of Fort Sumter* (New York: Scribner's, 1957), pp. 318–20.

into a vision of short and bloodless wars. Many agreed that the South had a monopoly of martial virtues, and that northerners were only interested in making money; they were degenerate, and lacked patriotism and guts. This in turn persuaded numbers of northern politicians that they needed to 'stand up' to the South and be 'tested'. The impatience which these attitudes generated tended to result in a kind of fatalism. Let the matter be put to the ultimate test. As Jefferson Davis complained, he 'would rather appeal to the God of Battles at once than to attempt to live longer in such a Union'.[39]

Yet it was characteristic of the contradictions that can easily be found under the confident surface of southern attitudes that simultaneously with their denunciation of northerners as degenerate cowards, they were thrown into panic by the impetuous action of one northern man, John Brown, and a tiny group of his followers.

John Brown's raid, 1859

The famous but ill-starred attempt by John Brown to seize the federal arsenal at Harper's Ferry represents, in so many ways, all the themes that have been discussed in this chapter. To the South, it demonstrated the manner in which, should civil war come, northern fanatics and 'abolitionists' would attempt to destroy their society. It was imperative that the South act quickly and decisively, and if necessary brutally, to confront and stamp out this danger. Resolute, anti-slavery northerners expressed views that were often contradictory: as contradictory as Brown's raid was in representing them. Those who saw slavery as an unutterable evil that could be destroyed only by force, envisaged war in the form of a more ambitious Kansas incursion. Those who saw the possible use of force as a police exercise in returning seceded southern states to the Union envisaged military action as rapid, settling the matter before abolitionists of John Brown's temper could escalate the levels of violence and disrupt the existing pattern of race relations in the South. But in 1859–60 the great majority of northerners believed that a resort to force was unnecessary and that a further compromise agreement could be reached.

39. William C. Davis, *Jefferson Davis: The Man and his Hour* (New York: HarperCollins, 1991), p. 268.

So much of this contingency revolved around one extraordinary and eccentric man – John Brown. Brown was born in 1800, the son of a tanner. He was restless and continually on the move. He was not well educated; he was a semi-trained schoolmaster, who had dabbled in farming, failed at business and had fallen into bankruptcy. He exhibited all the certainties of the self-educated. He was arrogant, self-righteous, stern and unbending. Brown tended to be obsessive, and was consumed by religious feeling. He read the Bible with all the zeal of the late convert, and its imagery permeated and directed what passed for his thought. He did not know the meaning of self-doubt, and appeared to bookish abolitionists as the very embodiment of the warrior. Yet it was typical of these mid-nineteenth-century attitudes that this 'warrior' knew nothing about war – though he knew something about killing, having murdered pro-slavery settlers at Pottawatomie Creek in 1856. This was 'war' to mid-nineteenth-century America – the death of one man was 'one of the sure results of Civil War'.[40]

The most attractive side of Brown's personality was his complete absence of any racial prejudice. He treated blacks with unaffected simplicity – like he would anybody else; he did not patronize or condescend to them, and developed a close friendship with the black abolitionist, Frederick Douglass. He sought out his advice and attempted to involve him directly in his violent activities. Yet there is something chilling about the smooth, shining surface of Brown's moral certainties: only a man with no very clear understanding of means and the ends could launch an 'army' of twenty-two men to attack slavery in Virginia, as Douglass belatedly realized.[41]

Brown first believed that 'the great drama will open here [in Kansas], when will be presented the great struggle in arms, of Freedom and Despotism in America'. Then in 1858 he began to think in terms of founding a separate, black republic in the Appalachian Mountains, and beguiled Douglass with his plans. He spent time, too much time, drawing up a constitution for this chimera; he was not the first, nor the last, would-be American revolutionary, who thought that the first priority of setting up a new polity should be constitutional regularity.[42] Then he

---

40. Stephen B. Oates, *To Purge this Land with Blood: A Biography of John Brown*, 2nd edn (Amherst, MA: University of Massachusetts Press, 1970, 1984), pp. 108, 132–7.

41. William S. McFeely, *Frederick Douglass* (New York: Norton, 1991), pp. 186–7, 195–7.

42. See below, pp. 297–301.

considered setting up bases for escaped slaves in the mountains through which fugitives could be funnelled towards Canada. Brown seemed to think that just willing these grandiose schemes was enough; exactly how they were to be protected in the absence of armed strength never seems to have agitated his imagination. 'The Plan' which he finally settled on was equally grandiose, and egregious. He would take the federal armoury at Harper's Ferry, whereupon he expected the slaves to join him 'in a mighty black stampede'. The South would be paralysed with fear, the weapons would be handed out, and Brown and his joyous host would plunge southwards, liberating slaves, destroying plantations and securing more weapons from arsenals *en route*.

This escapade (which resembles many a plan concocted by ambitious generals North and South 1861–62 whose ambitions outran their military knowledge) was a vision in which the enemy had no place. Regrettably for him, Brown had chosen a part of Virginia with fewer than 5,000 slaves, though it had a white population of over 100,000. How, in any case, the slaves were to discover that their self-appointed liberator had arrived is quite unclear, as he had no means of communicating with them.[43] What was extraordinary, as Brown's raid was continually being discussed in nearby Chambersburg (and also in Philadelphia), was that he took the Virginian authorities completely by surprise. The details of the raid need not detain us. On 16 October 1859 Brown and his small band rode into Harper's Ferry as if intent on robbing a bank. On the contrary, Brown hoped (as he had explained to his northern admirers, known as the 'Secret Six') to provoke a sectional confrontation that would result in the destruction of civil war. Brown's 'raid' was therefore one of the defining moments of American nineteenth-century history. It symbolized the haphazard and careless thinking about war that characterized this society, which envisaged conflict as essentially unorganized and civilian in scope. To collect a group of men intent on violence, it was complacently assumed, was to raise an army. Furthermore, Brown's raid enshrined that faith which so many evinced (even if they were not yet in a majority), that cataclysmic violent acts were a positive instrument for good. This was a mode of thought that contributed to the *idée fixe* that any war would be short and decisive.

Frederick Douglass had predicted, should Brown attack Harper's Ferry, that he would throw himself 'into a perfect steel

---

43.   McFeely, *Douglass*, pp. 193–4; Oates, *Purge this Land with Blood*, pp. 278–9; Allan Nevins, *Emergence of Lincoln* (New York: Scribner's, 1950), II, pp. 74–8.

trap, and that once in he would not get out alive'. The whole escapade was idiotic, but it does illustrate a number of aspects of American violence that would recur in 1861–65. In the first instance, once Brown's attempted insurrection was discovered, popular, savage emotions were released. Stephen Oates has observed that 'By late afternoon the town [Harper's Ferry] was in chaos as half-drunken and uncontrolled crowds thronged Potomac and Shenandoah streets'. No slaves came to Harper's Ferry to be liberated, for confusion reigned and nobody knew what was going on. Brown had succeeded in getting into the armoury and was under siege in the engine house; with him were thirteen hostages. All around were militia and over-anxious half-armed farmers who shot at anything that moved – including themselves. Some regular units commanded by Colonel Robert E. Lee brought some restraint to the sea of confusion, and the engine house was stormed by a party led by Lieutenant J. E. B. Stuart; Brown was captured and the hostages released.[44]

As soon as things began to go wrong, Brown assumed a heroic pose. At his subsequent trial, he perfected this role of noble martyr. His conduct and demeanour throughout the case and execution perfectly suited his own histrionic skills and it transfixed both sections. But the significance of the raid transcends the political, sectional confrontation that is usually attributed to it. The raid served as a portent of the future rather than the climax of past rivalries. Historians have tended to emphasize the hysteria that gripped the South – as the frenzied emotions of the citizens of Harper's Ferry spread like a contagion throughout the slave states. This may account for the appeal of secession after 1859–60 and a desire to act quickly and put matters to the proof. But historians have been less successful in explaining why speed was so insisted upon.[45]

Once a raid like Brown's had happened, the realization dawned that it might happen again – the next time on a greater scale and perhaps with better leadership. This added a further fear to the litany that southerners were chanting of the dangers they faced should the Republicans win the 1860 presidential election. 'Cohorts of Federal office-holders, Abolitionists may be sent into [our] midst', one southern senator warned after the election; another southerner was even more explicit: 'Now that the black

44. Quoted in McFeely, *Douglass*, p. 196; Oates, *Purge this Land with Blood*, p. 296; Emory M. Thomas, *Bold Dragoon*.

45. David M. Potter, *The Impending Crisis, 1848–1861* completed and ed. by Don E. Fehrenbacher (New York: Harper, 1976), pp. 381–4.

radical Republicans have the power, I suppose they will [John] Brown us all'. A further deduction was made. The stronger the denunciation of Brown, and the more frantic the desire to bring Brown's northern admirers and backers to justice, too, the more powerful was revealed an underlying assumption that should civil war come, it would begin with raids, like Brown's, led by northern abolitionists, designed to provoke slave insurrections. As the secession crisis intensified there were more attempts to control the movement of free blacks, remove any anomalies in their position (so that 'nominal' slaves would lose their liberties), and if possible return them to slavery. The loyalty of free blacks could not be counted on, as their alliance with free white wage labour in southern cities might prove disastrous.[46]

The linkage in southern minds between slave insurrection and civil war may explain why so many sceptics who were not persuaded by secessionist arguments, hurriedly supported the Confederacy once the die was cast. The best evidence of this process occurred in Adams County, Mississippi in October 1861. A rebellion was planned by trusted slave drivers to coincide with General Winfield Scott's scheme to advance from New Orleans up the Mississippi River. The slaves planned to murder their owners, take up arms (mostly farm tools) and join Scott's forces. The 'whipping business would stop'. The plot was discovered, and the planters of Adams County acted with peremptory brutality. Few of these had been supporters of secession but now rallied loyally to the Confederate cause. The slaves were whipped until they confessed and then, without due process of law, twenty-four were hanged. The speed with which this conspiracy was crushed is evidence of a pre-existing urgency given further point by the crisis of civil war and the expectation that more John Browns would hurl themselves on the South. Certainly, his raid shattered any chance that a united opposition to secession would form in Virginia that was prepared to cooperate with the Republican Party. The fear of slave rebellion was never greater in southern history than after John Brown's raid of 1859.[47]

46. Bruce Levine, *Half Slave and Half Free: The Roots of Civil War* (New York: Hill & Wang, 1992), pp. 234–5; *No Chariot Let Down: Charleston's Free People of Color on the Eve of the Civil War*, ed. Michael P. Johnson and James L. Roark (Chapel Hill, NC: University of North Carolina Press, 1984), pp. 143–7.

47. Winthrop D. Jordan, *Tumult and Silence at Second Creek: An Inquiry into a Civil War Slave Conspiracy* (Baton Rouge: Louisiana State UP, 1993), pp. 90, 237, 257; Daniel W. Crofts, *Reluctant Confederates: Upper South Unionists in the Secession Crisis* (Chapel Hill, NC: University of North Carolina Press, 1989), pp. 70–2.

CHAPTER SIX

The Year of Decision: 1860

So even if he couldn't anticipate no war to save him, back in his mind somewhere he was still confident that Providence would furnish something.

WILLIAM FAULKNER, *The Mansion*[1]

In 1860 the United States submitted itself once more to what Nathaniel Hawthorne in his novel *The Scarlet Letter* called the 'periodic terrors of a Presidential Election'.[2] The intricate process of nominating and electing a presidential candidate was undertaken in the darkening atmosphere of increasingly hysterical threats of southern secession should a Republican candidate win a majority of votes in the electoral college. In previous years presidential elections had served to defer decisions; in 1860 something was actually decided. The electoral process offered up a decision despite itself, and the result was civil war. The campaign witnessed the disintegration of the Democratic Party. No fewer than four candidates energetically sought to gain entrance to the White House. Indeed, it was a measure of the perceived crisis facing the United States that one candidate even dispensed with tradition and energetically campaigned on his own behalf on the campaign trail. The destruction of the second party system, which had been dominated by the Democratic Party, provided the occasion for the process of disunion that followed the Republican victory at the polls in 1860. This is a complex process, and it is not sufficient to say that the disruption of the party mechanism inevitably led to civil war. Nonetheless, in a political structure as

1. William Faulkner, *The Mansion* (London: Chatto & Windus, 1961) p. 126.
2. Nathaniel Hawthorne, *The Scarlet Letter and Selected Tales* (Harmondsworth: Penguin, 1970), p. 44.

rigidly geared to the workings of the calendar as that laid down by
the United States Constitution, and whose parts are so
intermeshed with one another in a complicated series of
continuing elections at various levels, it was very likely that
disruption of one part would lead to ructions, violence and even
anarchy in all the others.

This chapter offers a case-study of a presidential election. It is
essential that the inchoate nature of American politics be
understood. It was characterized by ceaseless competition,
bargaining, manoeuvring and intriguing, and offered ample scope
for the pursuit of ambition. It is pointless to condemn the system
because it was the embodiment of an open, democratic society –
though it was hardly without its weaknesses and disadvantages. The
coming of civil war was a reflection of its flaws. The political
system was also so variegated that it made the imposition of any
compromise solution almost impossible; any attempt could be
effectively opposed by those so minded. This should not be
surprising because the American political system is designed to
breed tension, competition and conflict. If the South had been
protected by the conservatism of American political culture before
1850, then after 1860 it was threatened by a new consensus that
was less inclined to settle on southern terms.

Indications were not auspicious. The Republican Party was a
sectional party which self-consciously promoted northern interests;
the Democratic Party was the only surviving national party but
increasingly dominated by southern interests. Could this national
complexion survive further scrutiny, and heated debate? Given the
fear of a Republican victory prevailing in the South it seemed
doubtful. Victory at the polls in 1860 required above all that
parties remained unified. The grouping which maintained unified
effort would win, although this should not be interpreted as
suggesting that if the Democratic Party had not been split it would
have won. (On the tally of electoral votes it could not have done.)
Thus the object of the Republican Party was two-fold. It had to
retain the vote secured in 1856 (some of which may have been
shaky because of the personal appeal of Frémont's dashing and
romantic career which would not be transferred to a more
mundane candidate). Secondly, the party's appeal had to be
extended and broadened in the North. This in part required
allaying fears that Republicanism represented a radical, corroding
force that endangered the foundations of a fragile Union. There
were some leaders, notably Francis Preston Blair, who believed

that ultimately the Republican Party would spread its appeal to the Border states; yet this could be only a long-term goal.[3]

The first candidate to be nominated was that by the Constitutional Union Party, John Bell, who chose the orator, Edward Everett, as his running mate. Bell was an aloof, fastidious and austere man, with an elevated manner and opinion of himself. He was a traditional Whig in his education and superior attitude and in his faith in the power of negotiation to save the Union. He clearly filled a gap, especially for ex-Whigs in the Upper South where the two-party system survived. All the issues under discussion, in his opinion, were not especially important and all that was needed was a dose of common sense and patriotic virtue to achieve a solution that all right-thinking individuals would applaud. He was the spiritual heir of Henry Clay without his charm and guile. It is a testimony of how much events had moved on since 1850 that his views appeared anachronistic and he resembled a dinosaur; nevertheless he did not lack support and would prove an embarrassment to both Republican and Democratic Parties.[4]

The Democratic Convention

The choice of Charleston, South Carolina, as the meeting place for the next Democratic Party convention was cruelly ironic. It was chosen originally in 1856 because it was calculated foolishly that it would be conducive to affable feelings and a sense of party unity. It was certainly indicative of the increasing southern domination of the Democratic Party. In the fevered atmosphere following John Brown's ill-fated expedition to Harper's Ferry, northern delegates received a hostile reception from the arrogant and provincial citizens of Charleston. This was not an atmosphere in which a harmonious compromise could flourish. The soporific and putrid (the temperature was already approaching 100°F) atmosphere of the city was increased by a lack of hotel accommodation which forced many delegates from the North and West to camp in great dormitories, which promoted neither rest nor hygiene among

---

3. William E. Gienapp, 'Who Voted for Lincoln?', in *Abraham Lincoln and the American Political Tradition* (Amherst, MA: University of Massachusetts Press, 1986), p. 53.

4. David Potter, *The Impending Crisis, 1848–1861* completed and ed. by Don E. Fehrenbacher (New York: Harper, 1976), pp. 415–17.

their inmates. In short a less appropriate place for the convention at this date can hardly be imagined. Certainly the disagreeable conditions seemed to breed bad temper and a disinclination to accept a contrary point of view. What concerned northern delegates more than any other matter was their failure to convince their southern colleagues of the need to unite behind one candidate who could win *in the North*. This was where the election would be won or lost.

But the Democratic Party seemed unduly preoccupied with southern *not* northern interests. Some thought the solution to political strains within the Union was the election of a southern president; others looked in vain for the chalice of reconciliation which could be sipped by both North and South, if only both wings of the party would agree to find a compromise candidate in the hostile if graceful portals of Charleston, South Carolina. This city was also favoured by members of the out-going Buchanan Administration because it was the location least likely to smile on a Douglas nomination. The southern 'ultras' within the Democratic Party seemed to detest Douglas as much as any Republican nominee. They had had serious differences in the past over Kansas and the Freeport Doctrine.[5] Ever combative, the canny Douglas indicated that he would confront their attacks without hesitation. 'I do not intend to make peace with my enemies', he declared, 'nor to make a concession of one iota of principle, believing that I am right in the position I have taken, and that neither can the Union be preserved or [*sic*] the Democratic Party be maintained upon any other basis'. Throughout the nineteenth century, American politicians were criticized for their readiness to abandon principle and indulge in manoeuvres calculated to advance their own selfish interests and sordid ambitions. It is ironic that when they defended high principle to the uttermost the result was catastrophe, and they were still blamed for their adherence to partisan causes.[6]

5.   On the other hand, some of Douglas's more fervent supporters were vociferous in announcing that they would prefer to vote for a Republican candidate than any other Democrat save Douglas. See Robert W. Johannsen, *Stephen A. Douglas* (New York: Oxford UP, 1973), p. 746.

6.   Quoted in Damon Wells, *Stephen Douglas: The Last Years, 1857–1861* (Austin: University of Texas Press, 1971, 1990), pp. 203, 211–12. President James Buchanan may have hoped that if the nomination became hopelessly deadlocked his name would be advanced as a compromise candidate around whom the party could rally. But Dr Wells exaggerates Buchanan's desire for a second term, and if he was so keen on it, why should he have announced in his inaugural that he would not be a candidate for one?

The Democracy could guarantee 120 electoral votes from the southern states plus Oregon and perhaps California; but it needed 303 and the balance could be gained only by fielding a candidate acceptable in the Lower North. If another Democrat could be returned to the White House, then all the southern fears about 'Black Republicans' and their pernicious views and dangerous habits could be laid to rest. Northern Democrats had only one candidate in mind who could meet this requirement, and this was Stephen A. Douglas. To their intense frustration, their man was unacceptable to the southern Democracy. This divergence of opinion would result in heated and emotional charges stimulated by the overcharged atmosphere of Charleston. It was this kind of emotionally charged atmosphere that would set the scene for the secession crisis and the outbreak of war. We cannot ignore the contribution of hysteria and casual violence to the outbreak of civil war. This was symbolized by a rather untoward incident that occurred as senior members of the New York Democracy set sail from New York harbour. The New York delegation led by Dean Richmond, and including Peter Cagger and August Belmont, were loyal to Douglas. But they had recently been challenged by the renegade Fernando Wood, who swapped sides, began to favour Buchanan, and put together a rival delegation. Wood's supporters in boisterous mood threw oranges at the boat carrying Richmond's delegation to Charleston. August Belmont, portly and prominent, was an inviting target and was struck below the line of his capacious stomach; he was forced to retire below to a cabin in no little pain. This would be the first and most physical manifestation of many charges of hitting below the belt that would be made over the following weeks.[7]

The most important result of this increasing dominance of the Democracy by southern interests was a passionate advocacy of slavery expressed in dogmatic rhetoric. In part this reflected a sincere worry by slaveholders about the future of slavery; Democrats had acquired a sway over the Whigs by appearing more pro-slavery than the other party, and evidently this advantage would influence the kind of language employed. Nonetheless, the emotional, apocalyptic speeches made at this date denote heightened fears and a readiness to seek extreme solutions. The

---

7.　　Roy F. Nichols, *The Disruption of American Democracy* (New York: Macmillan, 1948), pp. 288–92, gives a brilliant, atmospheric account of the background to the convention; also see Nevins, *Emergence of Lincoln* (New York: Scribner's, 1950), II, pp. 203–4.

dominance of 'fire-eating' secessionist spokesmen, like Rhett and Hammond, is indicative of a marked change in political discourse after the John Brown raid. 'The South must go through a trying ordeal before she will ever achieve her deliverance', Rhett wrote in 1860, 'and men having both nerve and self-sacrificing patriotism must head the movement and shape its course, controlling and compelling their inferior contemporaries'. There was no doubt in Rhett's mind that he should be one such patriotic voice who would be persuaded to wield power in any future, inevitable crisis of relations with the northern states. The Democratic Convention at Charleston would witness a surging climax of millennial denunciations replete with religious imagery that would trigger the sectional schism. As Thomas R. R. Cobb exclaimed with reference to the 46th Psalm over a year later, the South defended the true faith against the 'hellish schemes of . . . a set of devils . . . out of Hell'; God would intervene against their diabolic machinations. 'God is our refuge a very present help in trouble,' he assured his wife. 'He has never yet deserted the righteous cause. He never will . . . I can go to the cannon's mouth with that psalm on my lips'.[8] It is striking how in the two years following Brown's raid, increasing numbers of southern moderates became imbued with this kind of imagery and came to accept the secessionist case; but by then it did not appear 'extreme'.

The Democratic Convention opened on Monday 23 April 1860. The proceedings were dominated, not by hubbub within the hall, but by the noise of traffic thundering over the cobblestones of adjacent streets. The first two days were monopolized by the setting up of procedural committees on which the views of the anti-Douglas forces predominated. Douglas himself, of course, stayed away from the Convention. He relied heavily in the days ahead on the skills of Congressman John A. Logan, John A. McClernand, Senators George Pugh of Ohio, George Sanders of New York, and William A. Richardson of Illinois, an old ally. Douglas was confident, perhaps too confident, and urged as many of his followers as possible to make the journey to Charleston to give him vocal support. He was the only Democrat who could unite the party and bring it victory. He was also buoyant because the two previous Democratic presidents had come from the North

---

8.   Michael F. Holt, *The Political Crisis of the 1850s* (New York: Norton, 1983), pp. 245–6; quotation taken from Avery Craven, *The Coming of the Civil War*, 2nd edn (Chicago UP, 1966), p. 414; William B. McCash, *Thomas R. R. Cobb: The Making of a Southern Nationalist* (Macon, GA: Mercer UP, 1983), p. 96.

and reconciled the South: he could claim that the Democratic Party was best led, and slavery better protected, by northern leaders. He had, moreover, the added bonus of representing the increasingly influential western voice in its counsels. A Douglas candidacy, in short, had much to commend it; but did it have enough?[9]

An initial blunder was made, and the Douglas forces played into southern hands, by accepting the suggestion that the platform be established first followed by the nomination of the candidate. August Belmont, Douglas's campaign manager, was impatient with these manoeuvres. He complained that an 'immense deal of time [was] lost by talking' in the enervating heat. Of a gathering of Douglas delegates, he complained: 'It was the most stupid of all stupid gatherings I have ever been at – there were about twelve ugly women with about sixty as ugly men'. This irritable attitude was to cost Douglas dear because it led to a certain carelessness. The Douglas men naturally assumed that they would muster the voting power to ensure that the platform would reflect their views. The South would dominate the platform committee but Belmont relied on Douglas voting power on the floor of the Convention. Douglas supporters troubled themselves no more than the secessionists over the possibility that there might be a split; if the secessionists departed the proportion of votes supporting Douglas would increase. This was to underestimate the secessionist and pro-Buchanan forces aligned to frustrate Douglas.[10] He perhaps tried too keenly to browbeat the southern delegates into accepting his candidacy. Douglas did not brush aside the possibility that such tactics might provoke a walk-out, but he persuaded himself that this would be a mere temporary interlude, during which tempers would cool and political antennae would become more acute. The interests of politicians would surely demand a compromise. This was a fatal miscalculation. Douglas could not win the nomination solely with northern backing even if every single northern delegate supported him, which was unlikely. He needed at least nineteen southern votes and these would have to be sedulously wooed.[11]

The error in permitting the drawing up a platform first lay in the scope it gave the southern, anti-Douglas forces to draw up a

9. Wells, *Douglas: The Last Years*, pp. 204–5; Johannsen, *Douglas*, pp. 746–51.

10. Irving Katz, *August Belmont: A Political Biography* (New York: Columbia UP, 1968) p. 69; Johannsen, *Douglas*, pp. 751–3.

11. Wells, *Douglas: The Last Years*, pp. 204, 206.

statement of policy that would effectively debar Douglas as candidate. The Byzantine manoeuvres that followed prevented the acceptance of a single platform and three alternatives were offered for inspection. All embraced the 1856 Cincinnati platform in some shape or form. This affirmed popular sovereignty, namely the right of people in the territories, when sufficiently numerous, to draw up a constitution and enter the Union whether they preferred slavery or not. The proposal advanced by vocal southerners on the platform committee added a rider which asserted in language that was heavily hedged with legalistic terms but the meaning of which was all too clear.

> That the Territorial Legislature has no power to abolish slavery in any Territory nor to prohibit the introduction of slaves therein, nor any power to exclude slavery therefrom, nor any power to destroy or impair the right of property in slaves by any legislation whatever. . . .That it is the duty of the Federal Government to protect when necessary, the rights of persons and property on the high seas, in the Territories, or wherever else its Constitutional authority extends.

Such a commitment to a slave code would be intolerable to Douglas and alienate voters in the North. The second alternative catered to Douglas's concerns and stressed that all questions pertaining to property in states or territories were a judicial matter. The 'Democratic party is pledged to abide by and faithfully carry out' Supreme Court decisions. Congressman Benjamin F. Butler drew up his own version which endorsed the Cincinnati platform. A New York delegate suggested a third alternative 'that any attempt by Congress or the Territorial Legislature to annul, abridge or discriminate against any equality of rights' among the states 'would be unwise in policy and repugnant to the Constitution' and that it was the 'duty of the Federal Government' to take steps to prevent any violations. Yet the southern 'ultras' refused to accept any platform which did not carry a ringing endorsement of slavery and the constitutional mechanisms required to protect its spread throughout the Union beyond its existing confines.[12]

The effect of words in politics is often an ephemeral one. Politicians may deliver sparkling, eloquent or exciting orations; they may inspire or even stir a desire to act. But frequently words have little effect once delivered – they are just sentiments drifting

12. Nichols, *Disruption of American Democracy*, pp. 296–9; Johannsen, *Douglas*, pp. 754–6.

on the ether; an arresting memory but nothing more. However, the United States in the nineteenth century was an oral culture – though also a highly literate one. The spoken word enjoyed a commanding sway in political life. Washington Irving went so far as to suggest that America was governed by words; 'the simple truth of the matter', he wrote, 'is that their government is a pure unadulterated logocracy or government of words'. This is the characteristic overstatement of an artist. One may have leave to doubt the capacity of American government to match sentiment to aspiration. Nonetheless in the highly unstable and emotional atmosphere of Charleston, circumstances promoted an orgy of rhetoric and, for once, this led to a chain of action and reaction sparked by men who held no responsibility for their behaviour. Referring to 'a great heaving volcano of passion and crime', Yancey, in the most influential address, implored the southern delegates to stand fast and not surrender their constitutional prerogatives. Significantly, he intoned that a defeat on principle was preferable to victory hedged with ambiguity. A leading Douglasite, George E. Pugh, rejected the call that northern Democrats legitimize slavery and accept that it was right. 'Gentlemen of the South you mistake us – you mistake us! We will not do it!' To have acceded to this demand would have been suicidal for northern Democrats – it would have destroyed their political base in the North West. By the following Monday, in a deteriorating atmosphere not aided by the refusal of President Buchanan to intervene (because it might help Douglas's nomination), rumours of schism grew louder.[13]

The southern delegates were in many ways the best organized and led at Charleston but they turned their talents towards disruption rather than finding a candidate who could carry both sections. They were dedicated to exposing and clarifying all the vagueness that had previously shrouded references to slavery in Democratic circles and in northern political speech-making generally. Their expostulations were increasingly imbued with a moral righteousness previously associated with the abolitionists. This reduced significantly any scope for manoeuvre or

13. Quoted in Anne Norton, *Alternative Americas: A Reading of Antebellum Political Culture* (Chicago UP, 1986), p. 19; Nevins, *The Emergence of Lincoln*, II, pp. 216–19; Johannsen, *Douglas*, p. 754; William E. Gienapp, 'Politics Seem to Enter Everything: Political Culture in the North, 1840–1860', Stephen E. Maizlish, *Essays on American Antebellum Politics, 1840–1860* (College Station: Texas A&M UP, 1982), p. 51.

compromise with their northern colleagues who preferred to play down the race issue rather than lavish so much extreme rhetoric on it. Secessionist leaders, such as Yancey, were pre-eminently concerned with maintaining southern dominance of the political institutions of the United States; or, should this be lost, with setting up a new party that would protect southern institutions from outside attack. The census of 1860 indicated a change in the balance of population growth that might warrant the loss of some seven southern seats in the House of Representatives. There was something in the loud and swaggering manner of many southerners which was excited by the possibility that a minority could continue to dominate the Union, or if this was impossible, that they could with impunity set up their own government. They presumed that the North would have neither the gumption nor courage to resist them. Their arrogant and turbulent behaviour was purely destructive; perhaps there was something in the abolitionist stereotype of the blustering slavemaster, so used to unconditional dominance, that when defied he would turn to violence to ensure that nothing would oppose his will. Although the 'ultras' by no means represented all southerners at Charleston or elsewhere, the very belligerence of their stance swept all who doubted along with them. 'They had nothing positive to offer at Charleston,' writes Damon Wells. 'They were united in their determination to block Douglas, but had no alternative candidate of their own, unless it was Lincoln or Seward, whose election would provide them with a convenient excuse for secession'.[14]

The weakening influence of southern moderation was represented by the waning fortunes of John C. Breckinridge at the Convention. In December 1859 Breckinridge had delivered an address at Frankfort, Kentucky, in which he had called for the congressional protection of slave property in the territories (involving a federal slave code); if this request was ignored, he warned of the incinerating effects of the flames of a border war. Only eight years before he had sympathized with those who had called for the eventual abolition of slavery. Although the possibility exists that he might have been tricked into making this speech by

14.   Craven, *Coming of the Civil War*, p. 425; Nevins, *The Emergence of Lincoln*, II, pp. 222–3; Wells, *Douglas: The Last Years*, pp. 208–10; but note Nichols's view (*The Disruption of American Democracy*, p. 308) that the bulk of the 'ultras' calculated that belligerent behaviour would make a compromise more likely. See Kenneth Greenberg, *Masters and Statesmen: The Political Culture of American Slavery* (Baltimore, MD: Johns Hopkins UP, 1988), pp. vii–ix, 3–22.

the Douglas camp (who tempted him by suggesting that they would support calls for such guarantees, and then once they were made, claimed that only their candidate was the true voice of moderation on the slavery extension issue) there can be little doubt of the change of emphasis on the slavery issue. This was given sharper point by Breckinridge's translation from Buchanan's vice president to the junior senator from Kentucky that month. But Breckinridge's chances for the nomination were reduced by a combination of his own tactics and the atmosphere of the convention itself. Breckinridge was an appealing candidate because he believed that congressional guarantees were the prime buffer against disunion. But he lacked organization and a strong factional base. 'I do not think I will be nominated', he wrote, 'for . . . I know of no organisation for me anywhere, and many of the friends of other gentlemen are actively whistling me down the wind'. Deprecating fanaticism in the North, he considered the plight of the American polity a 'mess'. But he could not maximize his appeal to reason and (as he saw it) sense, especially in the lower northern states like Pennsylvania and New Jersey. Breckinridge refused to place his name on the ballot. This reduced his flexibility of manoeuvre and reinforced doubts cast by the refusal of Buchanan to support him (seeming to prefer Howell Cobb).[15]

On the floor of the Convention, the Douglas forces initially carried all before them: they appeared well organized and drilled. But the numbers of Douglas supporters who provided valuable vocal support began to dwindle, worn down by the discomforts of Charleston and depressed by the endless wrangling. The Cincinnati platform of 1856 was reaffirmed, and so was the resolution that the Democratic Party would abide by the decisions of the Supreme Court pertaining to the territories. At this, southern delegates warned that if a slave code was not included in the platform, they would remove themselves forthwith from the Convention. Some Douglas managers began to worry that they had over-reached themselves (especially as seven southern delegations refused to vote on the platform). Douglas again exaggerated the degree of pro-Union feeling among the delegations representing the slave states at Charleston in 1860. In February he had written,

---

15. William C. Davis, *Breckinridge: Statesman, Soldier, Symbol* (Baton Rouge: Louisiana State UP, 1974), pp. 204–5, 206–9, 211–18; Breckinridge shared the commonplace disgust for 'politicians' and their works, see especially *ibid.*, p. 210; Holt, *The Political Crisis of the 1850s*, pp. 245–8.

'There will be no serious difficulty in the South. The last few weeks has [*sic*] worked a perfect revolution in that section'. Even southerners, like Andrew Johnson (who periodically contemplated joining the Douglas ticket as vice presidential nominee), whose loyalty was not in doubt, were inclined to distrust Douglas's consistency and reliability.[16] Instead of a resort to the time-honoured practice of politicians of glossing over their differences by some judiciously worded formula, southerners allowed their emotions to reach such a pitch that conciliation was impossible. Some southerners welcomed this contingency. Here the failure of Breckinridge to confront Douglas may have had some significance. He could never have seized the nomination but it is possible to speculate that he might have acted as a focal point for the anti-Douglas forces and demonstrated that Douglas could never unite the Democratic Party. Thus a repeat performance of 1856 might have been possible in which both Douglas and Breckinridge withdrew in favour of a compromise (possibly Border state) candidate with strong Union credentials. This might not have prevented ultimate disunion, though it might have postponed it; at any rate, the disastrous split in the Democratic Party might have been covered over by the thinnest wafer.

The dogmatism of the southern side was countered by increasing northern obduracy. Douglas could not risk alienating any of his northern allies, especially in the North West. Buchanan forces were not inactive here, and an attempt to insert a sympathetic pro-Buchanan delegation from Illinois was rebuffed. These manoeuvres merely served to provoke strong feelings among the loyal Douglas forces in the North West. They insisted on the condition that Douglas would not enter into any deals or agreements with the South that endangered the doctrine laid down in the Dorr Letter of 22 June 1859. During its composition Douglas had disclosed his adamant opposition to any revival of the African slave trade, the imposition of a congressional slave code, or the notion that the Constitution may establish or prohibit slavery regardless of the views of the voters. Should this stipulation be in any way threatened, the delegations of the North West made it clear that they would not remain loyal to Douglas; on this issue the New England delegations and those of the Middle Atlantic seaboard were much less dogmatic. But here was a warning that

---

16.   Wells, *Douglas: The Last Years*, p. 207; Hans L. Trefousse, *Andrew Johnson: A Biography* (New York: Norton, 1989), pp. 123–4.

Douglas could not ignore; here was a cleavage that would spread from within political parties to the body politic as a whole during the final crisis of 1861.[17]

In the absence of any such compromise, an unwonted determination took charge of the proceedings. L. P. Walker, chairman of the Alabama delegation, announced to the Convention that he was now obeying the instructions of the Alabama convention that if the Democratic Party failed to provide a slave code resolution, he should withdraw its delegation. The Alabamians were followed by all other cotton state delegations, except (temporarily), Georgia. The following day the rump of the Convention met in a depressed mood to nominate a presidential candidate. It was under these circumstances that the slavery moderates were inclined to sell the pass. Although Douglas had always been very popular along the Border states (indeed the only state he would win outright in 1860 was Missouri), during these anxious hours when it was vital for the Democratic Party to nominate a candidate of stature and avoid the fatal wrangling which had split the party, a delegate from Tennessee introduced an amendment which required the winning nominee to gain two-thirds of all the votes at the Convention – a massive task. This proposal was supported by the New York delegation, who hoped that a 'compromise' candidate would emerge around whom all the factions could unite, but this was a chimera. All of these moves, again, were to foreshadow similar designs in the secession crisis itself. Electoral politics were to form a microcosm of the moves which led to that catastrophe.

A dozen ballots followed and 45 more on the following day but all to no avail. To secure victory, 202 were needed but Douglas could not increase his tally beyond 152½ votes. He failed to persuade any of his rivals, not least James Guthrie of Kentucky, to follow his own noble example in 1856 of withdrawing once a rival had secured a majority, so that he could secure an outright victory. The Convention then adjourned. It was a rare example of politicians permitting their feelings and sense of principle to overcome their penchant for compromise. The dissolution of the Democratic Party foreshadowed the rupture of the Union. The pattern was all the more alarming in that its members shared an illusion that was

17. Johannsen, *Douglas*, pp. 704–5. The rush to put matters of principle 'on the record' alarmed some Douglas supporters. 'Your prospects for the Presidency brighten every day,' wrote one. 'But you must quit writing letters'. See also Wells, *Douglas: The Last Years*, pp. 176, 213.

widespread after secession, that unity could still be repaired long after the machinery needed to restore it was shattered.[18]

It was decided that the Convention would be suspended for six weeks. Efforts would be made to appeal to latent Unionism within the South and publicize fears about possibly disunion and secession. There was also justified comment on the 'suicidal' southern behaviour. 'What had happened', writes Allan Nevins, 'was that a minority of the gathering, who spoke for a minority of the party, had undertaken to dictate to the majority what they should put into the platform'. They sought increasingly to force the pace of national life. Would these tendencies cool after an interlude of a month and half? Not on the evidence of some testy exchanges in the Senate. But to the surprise of the Douglas faction, all but two of the bolting southern delegations agreed to assemble at Baltimore for the second stage of the proceedings on 18 June. By that date the Republican Party would already have chosen its nominee.[19]

The Republican Convention

The choice of Chicago as the venue for the Republican Convention in 1860 reflected the increased importance of the state of Illinois. The rise of Abraham Lincoln and the growth of the wealth and influence of Illinois coincided. Its population doubled in the decade 1850–60 from 851,470 to 1,711,951; most of this was concentrated in the northern counties which were less in thrall to pro-slavery arguments and which had backed Lincoln in the 1858 senatorial contest with Douglas. Illinois was a major producer of cereals. Corn growth had doubled and wheat trebled in the ten years before 1860; the Illinois Central Railroad bound the state together with a communications system which generated further economic and agricultural expansion. If the Republican Party was to win the presidential election in 1860 it had to win states like Illinois. Lincoln, who had not held any elected office since 1848, but had made a career out of opposing Senator Douglas at every turn, had secured the support of the Illinois Republican delegation at a state convention at Decatur in early

18. Davis, *Breckinridge*, pp. 217–20; Nichols, *Disruption of American Democracy*, pp. 300–5, 307–8; Nevins, *Emergence of Lincoln*, II, pp. 220–4.

19. Nichols, *Disruption of American Democracy*, pp. 310–14; Nevins, *Emergence of Lincoln*, II, pp. 223–4, 262–8.

May 1860. He had asked Norman B. Judd for the support of the *Chicago Tribune* in his ambitions to secure either the presidential or vice presidential nomination at Chicago. 'I am not in a position where it would hurt much for me to not be nominated on the national ticket,' he concluded realistically, 'but I am where it would hurt some for me to not get the Illinois delegates'. Lincoln was successful in steering a course through the various factions of the Illinois Republican Party, a skill that he would be required to exercise on the national stage. As evidence of his own rise and the prominence of Illinois in Republican calculations, he received discreet enquiries from the managers of Senator Simon Cameron of Pennsylvania as to his readiness to run as Cameron's vice presidential running mate. Lincoln's position was therefore strong, but not invulnerable within the state of Illinois, and he had to watch his flank against incursions from the camp of Lyman Trumbull who had denied Lincoln a senatorial seat in 1854. Lincoln obliquely warned Trumbull against issuing missives or statements that might be construed as critical of Lincoln or his nomination. 'The taste *is* in my mouth a little. There are men on the watch for such things [hints of disaffection] out of which to prejudice my peculiar friends against you'. Unity was the key to successful political action.[20]

Lincoln benefited not only from the location of the Convention in his home state but also from the very careful preparation that was undertaken by his campaign manager, Judge David Davis. All of Lincoln's close allies were closely organized and controlled from a headquarters. Davis placed himself behind a large table covered with paper, interrogated Lincoln's allies, issued his orders, and importuned delegates, urging them to vote for Lincoln. David Davis was a large, corpulent, prosperous-looking man, determined, forceful and equipped with a strong temper. In his indefatigable efforts, shrewd appraisals and powerful advocacy, he was the ideal complement to the languid, relaxed and somewhat detached Lincoln. Lincoln owed his nomination to Davis's hard work and explosive outbursts. 'Judge Davis is furious,' wrote a mutual friend of a not infrequent state of affairs. 'Never saw him work so hard and so quiet in all my life'. Before the Convention, 'Long John' Wentworth, Mayor of Chicago, former Democrat and engaged in a bitter feud with Norman Judd, advised Lincoln, 'Do like Seward

---

20. Don E. Fehrenbacher, *Prelude to Greatness: Lincoln in the 1850s* (Stanford UP, 1962), pp. 5–8; Willard L. King, *Lincoln's Manager: David Davis* (Cambridge, MA: Harvard UP, 1960), pp. 125–31, 133.

does, get some one to *run* you'. Lincoln was reluctant to acquire an alter ego like Seward's Thurlow Weed, preferring instead to wait on capricious fate and the hard reckoning of events; but in so far as Lincoln could be organized, he was 'run' by Judge Davis.[21]

The Convention was due to begin on 16 May. It was held in a new wooden building called the 'Wigwam'. A reporter, Murat Halstead of the *Cincinnati Commercial*, who was to make his reputation with graphic accounts of the Convention proceedings, described its improvised excellence for the occasion.

> The city of Chicago is attending to this convention in magnificent style. It is a great place for large hotels, and all have their capacity for accommodation tested. The great feature is the Wigwam erected within the past month expressly, for the use of the Convention, by the Republicans of Chicago, at a cost of seven thousand dollars. It is a small edition of the New York Crystal Palace, built of boards, and will hold ten thousand persons comfortably – and is admirable for its acoustic excellence. An ordinary voice can be heard through the whole structure with ease.

The Republicans at least escaped some of the discomforts inflicted on the Democrats at Charleston. The language, style and deportment of nominating conventions was already highly developed and is immediately recognizable to the modern reader. Cries taken up by journalists were ceaselessly discussed, debated, extended; their reiteration often led to as much misunderstanding as understanding. 'The favourite word of the convention is "solemn" ', wrote Halstead. 'In Charleston, the favourite was "crisis". Here there is something every ten minutes found to be solemn'. But there is one major difference between the nineteenth-century Convention and its twentieth-century counterpart; it actually chose nominees, it did not merely confirm their right to carry the nomination. Consequently, enormous effort was invested in exhorting the delegates to choose this or that candidate. Their ears were assaulted by a stream of loud, passionate advocacy. Their eyes were charmed by fancy decoration, portraits of revered political heroes and the unusual or just plain bizarre. 'The curiosity of the town', wrote Halstead, ' – next to the Wigwam – is a bowie knife seven feet long, weighing over forty pounds'. On one blade was inscribed '*Will always keep a "Pryor" engagement*' – a reference to Roger Pryor, a Virginia secessionist.

---

21. King, *Davis*, pp. 135–6; Don E. Fehrenbacher, 'Lincoln and the Mayor of Chicago', in *Lincoln in Text and Context: Collected Essays* (Stanford UP, 1987), p. 41.

The Convention was just as much theatre as political forum. Groups of men were enjoined to shout chants for their candidate; here Lincoln, a local figure, enjoyed an enormous advantage. Bargains were struck on the convention floor, gossip, the lifeblood of politics and the addiction of professional politicians, was exchanged, and agreement was reached. As Halstead made clear, 'the amount of idle talking that is done is amazing'.

> Men gather in little groups, and with their arms about each other, and chatter and whisper as if the fate of the country depended upon their immediate delivery of the mighty political secrets with which their imaginations are big. There are a thousand rumours afloat, and things of incalculable moment are communicated to you confidentially, at intervals of five minutes.

> . . . The current of the universal twaddle this morning is that 'Old Abe' will be the nominee.

Allan Nevins rightly described this gathering as 'bedlamite confusion'. Experts at political gatherings are often proved wrong in their predictions, and the most striking feature of conventions in the nineteenth century was their propensity for throwing aside famous and accomplished candidates in favour of the comparatively untried and inexperienced man. In 1852 the Democrats had chosen Franklin Pierce, a man overwhelmed by his responsibilities and unequal to the demands of his high office; in 1860 the Republican Party was rather more fortunate.[22]

The confusion and loquacity of the proceedings at Chicago at first sight appeared to be an obstacle to reaching a wise decision as to who should lead the party into the most important race since the unopposed election of George Washington in the first presidential election of 1792. On 16 May David Wilmot, now past his best, was appointed chairman. 'He is a dull, chuckel headed booby looking man', Browning thundered in his diary, 'and makes a very poor presiding officer'.[23]

At the beginning of the Convention a member of the Rhode Island delegation reminded the hall portentously that 'we are here on important business'. But despite the encomiums praising the 'Wigwam' there was so much bustle, confusion and noise that his

22. Quoted in *The Lincoln Reader*, ed. Paul M. Angle (New Brunswick, NJ: Rutgers UP, 1947), pp. 265–6; Nevins, *Emergence of Lincoln*, II, pp. 247–9; Fehrenbacher, *Prelude to Greatness*, pp. 154–6; Potter, *Impending Crisis*, p. 422.

23. *The Diary of Orville Hickman Browning*, 2 vols, ed. Theodore C. Pease and J. G. Randall (Springfield, IL: Illinois State Historical Library, 1925), I, p. 407 (entry for 16 May 1860).

voice could not be heard. The first two days were spent hammering out the party's platform, not an easy business at any time, but particularly muddled on this occasion. The platform was drawn up by a committee drawn largely from the West, though its chairman, Wilmot, came from Pennsylvania. One of its first actions was to remove a reference to 'those twin relics of barbarism, polygamy and slavery' which had adorned the 1856 platform. John Brown's raid was condemned as 'among the gravest of crimes', and the Republican Party pledged itself to introducing legislation to abolish slavery in the territories when it was 'necessary'. The 1856 platform had called for 'positive legislation'. The slight change of emphasis was more apparent than it was real. Although it seemed to hint at favouring Douglas's notion of popular sovereignty, actually the platform stated categorically that territorial legislatures had no power to 'give legal existence to slavery'; popular sovereignty itself was dismissed as 'a deception and fraud'. The implication of the document was that territories were offered by the Republicans the choice of either ridding themselves of slavery or having it done for them by congressional action. The illegal slave trade was denounced, calls were made to admit Kansas as a free state, and the Dred Scott decision was condemned though it was not directly referred to. The rising tide of southern secessionist rhetoric was denounced as 'an avowal of contemplated treason'; this could not be tolerated and it was 'the imperative duty of an indignant people sternly to rebuke and forever silence' murmurs of secession. Although there was much talk of moderating the Republican stance during the 1860 campaign by comparison with Frémont's campaign four years previously, the platform remained consistent with the main themes of Republicanism, simply expressing them in more guarded and less inflammatory language. It pledged to maintain 'the right of each state to order and control its own domestic institutions' and concluded with a flourish with a general reference to the Declaration of Independence, excoriating the 'new dogma' that the Constitution allowed the carrying of slavery into the territories, and instead declared it 'our duty' to uphold the constitutional guarantee against the deprivation of life, liberty and property.[24]

24. Earlier historians, David Potter, *Lincoln and his Party in the Secession Crisis* (New Haven, CT: Yale UP, 1942, 2nd edn, 1962; New York: AMS reprint, 1979), pp. 30–2; J. G. Randall, *Lincoln the President: From Springfield to Gettysburg*, I (London: Eyre & Spottiswoode, 1947), p. 172, rather exaggerate the extent to which the platform of 1860 was watered down by comparison with 1856.

Of course, politicians were not transfixed with sectional issues and the platform concerned itself with measures other than those dealing with congressional action and slavery. In 1856 more than half of the resolutions adopted by the Republican Party had been associated with the slavery problem; the only other matter it had addressed was government assistance to the construction of a Pacific railroad. An exclusive focus on this would have bored and dissatisfied the voters. A firm though not vituperative reference was made criticizing Nativism. Republicanism, as in 1856, would not side with those who demanded changes in the naturalization laws and the reduction in citizen rights and civil liberties 'hitherto accorded to immigrants from foreign lands'. This was an allusion to the Two Year Amendment introduced in Massachusetts which had laid down a two year period of residence before naturalized citizens were allowed to vote or hold office. Other planks concentrated on economic issues. River and harbour improvements, and a Pacific railroad were called for, as were a homestead law and a measure of tariff protection. The increased emphasis on economic issues is an important stage in the evolution of Republican identity, representing both its ideological and pragmatic facets. The homestead proposal may be interpreted as the northern vision for the territories and a counterweight to the extension of slavery. The stress on tariffs was mild and no doubt was focused on anxiety over this issue expressed by the delegations representing New Jersey and Pennsylvania, especially the latter, a key state in the election. The platform's authors did not trouble themselves with the likelihood that the leaders of the Republican Party would be required to cope with organized violence within the next six months; here was politics 'as usual'; peace would continue as it always had; war, for all the chilling rhetoric, was not only out of sight but also out of mind.

When submitted for the approval of the Convention, the platform raised the temperature a few degrees because the veteran anti-slavery campaigner, Joshua Giddings, attempted to restore the direct quotation from the Declaration that 'all men are created equal'. At first he was voted down. What ensued was not a profound clash between the radical anti-slavery group and those of a more conservative disposition, but as Fehrenbacher suggests, 'a debate over how much rhetorical padding should be included in a statement of party principles'. Freed momentarily from the need for judicious weighing of words and expediency, members of the Convention indulged themselves in soaring sentiments and elevated aspirations, and the quotation was restored. The platform then received a vote of unanimous approval and a cheer. In the early evening, at about 6 p.m., of this the second day of the Convention, the delegates decided to adjourn and reserve the selection of a presidential candidate to the following day's proceedings. This proved to be a crucial decision because it gave the various rivals of the front runner, William H. Seward, more time in which to prepare and complete their various bargains with one another.[25]

The candidates vying for the Republican nomination were a distinguished and ambitious group, perhaps as a group among the most able that ever presented itself for a presidential nomination in the history of the United States. Seward was former Governor of New York, Zachary Taylor's *eminence grise* in his short-lived Administration, the hammer of the Know Nothings, and senior Senator of New York. Seward believed that he had a just claim to the nomination, not only because of his distinguished record but also because he was widely viewed as the leader of the Republican Party and one of its most eloquent spokesmen. He was not frightened of using high-flown (if somewhat stilted) language. Seward began the convention with a formidable lead and a great measure of respect from the assembled delegates. Yet the question that they kept asking was quite simple, could Seward *win*? Winning the future contest was what counted – not displaying a distinguished past record. The Republicans were after all an opposition party and reassuring the electorate was an important objective. Here Seward's past expostulations concerning 'irrepressible conflict' seemed rather more radical than they actually were. He had also offended too many people. His enemy in the New York Republican Party, Horace Greeley, the editor of the New York *Tribune*, hypocritically posed as a Seward supporter while actually pointing out his weaknesses. Seward's alter ego, Thurlow Weed, dispensed from his broad coat a faint odour of corruption. The drunken and rowdy behaviour of the Seward supporters, moreover, did not win over any waverers, who were affronted rather than impressed with their beery denunciations of other candidates, braying voices delivering their verdicts in clouds

25. Randall, *Lincoln the President*, I, pp. 155–8, 172–3; on the platform Fehrenbacher, 'The Republican Decision at Chicago', in *Lincoln in Text and Context*, pp. 56–8, Potter, *Impending Crisis*, p. 423; Gienapp, 'Who Voted for Lincoln?', pp. 55–7; Nevins, *Emergence of Lincoln*, II, pp. 252–3; Fehrenbacher, *Prelude to Greatness*, p. 157.

of alcoholic fumes. But the central argument against Seward was that he could not carry the crucial states in the Lower North – Illinois, Pennsylvania, Indiana. So important was it for the Republicans to carry the major northern states that Governor John A. Andrew decreed that the Massachusetts delegation would be guided in its choice of candidate by whatever consensus these states arrived at. Being a front runner, the 'leader', as many candidates have found, is an unenviable place in American politics; possession of this title has often extracted a high price from the man widely expected to win. Henry S. Lane, the Republican candidate for Governor in Indiana claimed, so it was said, 'hundreds of times' that Seward could not take Indiana. Repeated a sufficient number of times, such warnings began to take their toll on the confidence of delegates committed to Seward. Yet with all his advantages, he was overconfident. Seward did not fail to gain the nomination, he succeeded in losing it.[26]

The other candidate with a real claim to the nomination in terms of past contributions and achievement was former Senator and now Governor Salmon P. Chase of Ohio (who was elected for a second term in 1857). Chase was a man of principle, a sincere champion of legal and voting rights for Negroes; his career had shown courage and real intellectual ability. Yet he had a chilling and elusive personality inclined to tiresome pomposity, and Chase did not trouble to hide his own high opinion of his inestimable worth. Because of his advanced views on granting Negroes the franchise, he was deemed unelectable, and in any case, whatever his other merits, here was not a man to charm the voters. Conceited to a fault, Chase lacked the political horse sense to organize his campaign, believing that the delegates would acknowledge the extent of his abilities as readily as he did himself. Chase was very quickly sidelined by those who took pains to organize themselves. On the conservative side, Edward Bates, from the important Border state of Missouri, was a strong candidate. He was deemed 'sound' on slavery, dour and rather dull, certainly not prone to outlandish statements, and had little to explain away. Bates initially enjoyed the support of Lincoln for these reasons. He would reassure the South. But Bates, although he found some favour in states, like Indiana, who had pro-southern counties, was tainted by cooperation with the Know Nothings in 1856. He would

26. Potter, *Impending Crisis*, pp. 424–6; Glyndon G. Van Deusen, *William Henry Seward* (New York: Oxford UP, 1969), pp. 221–7; Nevins, *Emergence of Lincoln*, II, p. 252.

antagonize German voters in the old North West and cancel out his advantages. Moreover, Bates lacked a solid base, unlike Chase or Lincoln, and there were even doubts as to whether he could carry his own state. But he enjoyed the support of powerful and vocal friends, like Horace Greeley (who saw him as a powerful weapon with which to hit Seward), and the Blair dynasty. Simon Cameron had a strong base in Pennsylvania but no constituency outside it. His wealth and influence were feared. (It was common knowledge but not proven that he had a corrupting effect.) Cameron was one of the most formidable political figures of his time and had to be treated with caution; he could not be written off.

Finally, there was Lincoln. Lincoln's greatest asset was that he was not a front runner and nobody expected him to win. Lincoln was hardly an unknown figure on the American political circuit. The Lincoln–Douglas debates had received much attention, his address to the Cooper Union in New York and a number of speeches in New England had been well received, and had brought him into the front rank of Republican figures. But his record of office-holding was limited (even Franklin Pierce had sat in the Senate). Consequently, he was the kind of politician who was respected by his peers and those who were politically active, but comparatively unknown to the general public. The gathering hordes of commentators had not bothered to include him on a list of twenty-one prominent candidates; when his name was included in their reports it was confused with Abram. Yet coming from behind and out of a shroud of obscurity was Lincoln's greatest strength. A Lincoln candidacy seemed to act as a lowest common denominator of support. Men who were not passionately for Lincoln, like Orville Hickman Browning, found him not sufficiently objectionable as an alternative when other candidates failed to attain the target of 233 votes necessary to gain the nomination.[27]

The Convention which chose the greatest of American presidents began its deliberations on the third day, 18 May. As this act culminated in the crisis which resulted in Civil War, it was

27.   Randall, *Lincoln the President*, I, pp. 161, 169, 171; Frederick J. Blue, *Salmon P. Chase: A Life in Politics* (Kent, OH: Kent State UP, 1987), pp. 126–32; Potter, *Impending Crisis*, pp. 426–8; Browning, *Diary*, I, pp. 395, 396 (entries for 8, 22 Feb. 1860); Kenneth M. Stampp, *Indiana Politics during the Civil War*, 2nd edn (Bloomington: Indiana UP, 1949, 1978), pp. 28–9, 36–8; James M. McPherson, *Battle Cry of Freedom* (New York: Oxford UP, 1988), pp. 218–19.

appropriate (as in much American democratic display) that the day should begin with strong military overtones. The convulsions of noise and turbulent confusion continued unabated. The Seward forces then committed a blunder. Halstead reported that

> The Sewardites marched as usual from their headquarters at the Richmond House after their magnificent band, which was brilliantly uniformed, epaulets shining on their shoulders, and white and scarlet feathers waving from their caps. . . . They were about a thousand strong, and, protracting their march a little too far, were not all able to get into the Wigwam. . . . They were not where they could scream with the best effect in responding to the mention of the name of William H. Seward.[28]

Judge Davis would not have committed this kind of foolish error: it reflected Seward's smug, overconfident approach. Davis and Lincoln's friends had spent the first two days of the Convention working painstakingly (often all through the night) on Lincoln's behalf. Davis was determined not to make unnecessary enemies. His strategy was guided by a shrewd piece of advice given by Wentworth to Lincoln. 'Look out for *prominence*. When it is ascertained that no one of the prominent candidates can be nominated then *ought* to be your time'. But Lincoln revealed an unexpected strength on the floor of the Convention, and as it moved forward the Lincoln dark horse revealed a lighter hue; keeping control of his forces was Davis's major problem, so that the horse was not blown before it reached the winning post. Davis had received a note from Lincoln, 'Make no contracts that will bind me'. Davis was reported to have exclaimed 'Lincoln ain't here and don't know what we have to meet!' Lincoln evidently did not wish to lose any freedom of manoeuvre. As the complexion of his cabinet would have a direct influence on the course of the secession crisis, the debate over the kind of commitments entered into by Davis at Chicago is an important question, and requires scrutiny. It has been mixed up by post-war mythology. There was a view that Lincoln 'emerged' at Chicago almost indicated by the hand of God. Alternatively, another view was propounded, the antithesis of this legend, that Lincoln's nomination was the product of a 'dirty' deal put together by corrupt politicians, though the Great Martyr himself rose above the sordid undergrowth. Both these versions reflect the moralizing that politicians themselves felt constrained to make about the practice

28. Quoted in *Lincoln Reader*, p. 268.

of politics under the spoils system. As Davis telegraphed Lincoln on 15 May, 'Nothing will beat us but old fogy politicians. The hearts of the delegates are with us'. The importance of this attitude in developing political action and the secession drama cannot be underrated.[29]

Davis's first step was to secure the allegiance of the Indiana delegation. A controversy has developed over whether this was achieved by the inducement of a cabinet place for Caleb B. Smith, the most prominent member of the delegation. Historians have been engaged by a desire either to extricate the great men of American politics from the sordid undergrowth of the political system, or to denigrate them by involving those of unsullied reputation in its mire. Much of this comment seems superfluous. Davis was not the candidate and therefore could hardly give cast iron commitments of cabinet places to ambitious men; Lincoln was not present at Chicago and, therefore, could justly claim later to Indiana politicians (including Schuyler Colfax, Smith's main Indiana rival for preferment), that he had made no such commitments; as indeed he had not. What Davis did do, and he was hardly alone in this, as Fehrenbacher points out (for the Seward forces not only had cabinet places to trade but also financial backing dispensed by Weed for a number of state elections), was to give *understandings*, the detail of which could be worked out at a later date. A former Whig, Smith had worked closely with Lincoln during Zachary Taylor's election campaign; he was not a stranger foisted on the unsuspecting Lincoln. Indeed he did render sterling service for the Lincoln campaign. 'I think him the finest speaker in the Union', Davis remarked. But though much of this debate revolves around a terminological quibble coated with moralizing, what really mattered was choosing a candidate who would *win*. All professional politicians are dedicated to winning elections; promises of any kind are superfluous unless the votes are piled up in their favour. The debate over promises to Smith is significant only because Lincoln *did* win. Therefore, what really counted with the Indiana delegation was the view that Seward could not take the western states, as a clean sweep of the North was vital if they were to win the presidency. Their switch to Lincoln began the process that transferred confidence from Seward to Lincoln. It was important for this change first and

29. King, *Davis*, pp. 134–8; Nevins, *Emergence of Lincoln*, II, p. 256; Potter, *Impending Crisis*, p. 428.

foremost; an offer of place, however informally proffered, was a bonus.[30]

David Potter has some wise words on this whole process. Do offers of office change votes? We cannot be sure of the mental gymnastics through which professional politicians exercise their minds, nor the exact order of their thoughts; 'shrewd politicians routinely try to get as much advantage as possible from agreeing to do what they already decided that they are going to do in any case. The fact that promises were demanded and given does not prove that votes were changed'. The Lincoln team's strategy was repeated with the Pennsylvania and New Jersey delegations. Of the former, Davis exclaimed to Joseph Medill, 'Damned if we haven't got them!' Cameron certainly formed the impression that he had been offered a cabinet place whatever the vague circumlocutions employed by Davis. On the afternoon of the first day of the Convention the four delegations moving towards Lincoln – Illinois, Indiana, New Jersey and Pennsylvania – all to some extent Border states, either with large pro-southern minorities among their voters or contiguous to slave states – met in David Wilmot's rooms in sub-convention. Davis chaired this meeting assisted by Caleb Smith. Greeley interrupted the meeting. He asked whether they had agreed on a candidate; when informed in the negative, Greeley at once reported to the New York *Tribune* that Seward would be nominated the following morning; this was not a contingency that Greeley viewed with much pleasure. But discretion at this stage was vital. If Davis had disclosed that this important group of delegations was coalescing around Lincoln then vital momentum would have been lost by attracting immense pro-Seward pressure on what was only a loose coalition. That it was beginning to form around Lincoln, and not the champion of the Border states, meant that in the forthcoming contest, Bates had no hope.[31]

But this meeting revealed unexpected Lincoln voting strength. This was reflected in the enormous din of well-orchestrated applause which greeted the announcement of Lincoln's name

30. On the 'promises', see Nevins, *Emergence of Lincoln*, II, pp. 256–7; on the view that no such promises were made, King, *Davis*, pp. 136–8. The nature of these 'promises' is all-important in this discussion. King is persuasive that nothing of a binding nature was offered; but none of his commentary seems inconsistent with my interpretation. Fehrenbacher, *Prelude to Greatness*, p. 159, is cogent and convincing. A short fair summary is McPherson, *Battle Cry of Freedom*, p. 219n35.

31. Potter, *Impending Crisis*, p. 428; Fehrenbacher, 'The Republican Decision at Chicago', p. 59; King, *Davis*, pp. 139–40; Nevins, *Emergence of Lincoln*, II, pp. 257–8.

being set down for nomination; his supporters, well drilled by
Davis, had been better organized than those of Seward, many of
whom waited impatiently outside the Wigwam. The balloting
began at noon. Lincoln himself was sure that he would not win.
Seward gained 175½, Lincoln 102, Cameron 50½, Chase 49, Bates
48. Lincoln had unexpectedly gained votes in New England states
– New Hampshire, Maine, Connecticut and Massachusetts. He also
had a majority in two slave states, Virginia and Kentucky. He had
acquired this total without the Pennsylvania delegation who had
voted for their 'favourite son', Cameron. Seward needed another
60 to win. His managers were not downcast, and felt that the
prestige of their candidate would draw additional votes. 'Call the
roll! Call the roll!' were the cries in a hot and excited atmosphere.
On the second ballot, 48 of the Pennsylvania delegation's votes
were switched, not to Seward, but to Lincoln along with the 10
votes of Vermont. More votes were gained by Lincoln in New
England, and also in Delaware, Ohio (Chase's home state) and
Iowa. A movement towards the dark horse was discernible. Lincoln
now had 181 votes, Seward 184½, Chase 42½, Bates 35, with 42
committed to an odd assortment of candidates. It was the third
ballot which proved to be the decisive turning point. There was a
mathematical possibility that at this point the Seward column
would turn to Chase, not to Lincoln. But to have done so would
have replaced a candidate who it was felt would just fail to win
with one who would definitely lose – hardly an inviting prospect.
The excitement and cheering for Lincoln reached a climax.

In a moment of high drama as the balloting began,
Massachusetts suddenly transferred 4 votes from Seward to
Lincoln, and as in 1852, an avalanche of votes fell into Lincoln's
column. The Blairs switched Maryland votes from Seward to
Lincoln, he received 52 votes from Pennsylvania, and more votes
from New Jersey, Ohio gave him 29 votes and only 19 to Chase
(Chase was gravely affronted by this splitting of the Ohio
delegation). The total indicated a triumphant victory was in the
offing, 231½ for Lincoln, 180 for Seward. Lincoln needed only
another 1½ votes for nomination. 'A profound stillness fell upon
the Wigwam; the men ceased to talk and the ladies to flutter their
fans; one could distinctly hear the scratching of pencils and the
ticking of telegraph instruments on the reporters' tables'. The
newspapers were unclear exactly as to the source of the handful of
votes required for victory, but it appears that an Ohio delegate
suddenly changed 4 votes from Chase to Lincoln. This was more

than enough: cheers erupted from Lincoln's supporters, tears filled the eyes of Seward's men. Later in the afternoon Hannibal Hamlin of Maine (a former Democrat who would balance Lincoln the former Whig) was selected as his vice presidential running mate. This cemented the alliance already hinted at by Governor Andrew between the prairie states and New England. Davis telegraphed Lincoln, 'Don't come here for God's sake. You will be telegraphed by others to come. It is the united advice of your friends not to come. This is important'.[32]

Davis was wary of precipitating an unpleasant scene, with Seward's supporters perhaps jeering Lincoln if he appeared at the Wigwam. This would hardly help the Republican Party at the beginning of the campaign. At any rate, it was not unusual for nominees to stay away from the Convention, a tradition which even Douglas had not broken at Charleston. Thus was nominated another in the long line of 'available' rather than qualified presidential candidates. Would Lincoln be another Franklin Pierce, who ended up being more despised by members of his own party than he was by his opponents? Lincoln had twice failed to gain entrance to the Senate; he had served only one term in the House; he had never sponsored any important legislation; never ran a state government or a department of the Federal government. Why should this man carry his party's banner in such an important election? The answer is simple. He was the *best* candidate, and could carry areas that would not have voted for Seward. His allies in Indiana and Pennsylvania were proved right. Time would reveal his staggering potential and elevation of spirit. He was inexperienced but sagacious. Experience does not always confer wise judgement, as the career of Buchanan – who was perhaps too experienced in the wrong things – or indeed Seward's behaviour in the secession crisis demonstrates. Immense strains would be imposed on the candidate, not least an exposure to which he was unaccustomed and not well suited to endure. But he was tougher than Pierce (though both suffered a tragic loss in the death of a son after their election as president), more determined and resilient. He was not only the available man, but the only man. At this date, such potential was not revealed to members of

32. I have based my account on the brilliant evocation in Nevins, *Emergence of Lincoln*, II, pp. 257–60; and the detailed discussion in King, *Davis*, pp. 140–1. Also see Benjamin P. Thomas, *Abraham Lincoln* (London: Eyre & Spottiswoode, 1953), p. 138; Stephen B. Oates, *With Malice Toward None: The Life of Abraham Lincoln* (New York: Harper & Row, 1977), p. 178.

his party; certainly not to Seward, who felt slighted by a nonentity; perhaps it was concealed even from Lincoln himself.

In the event, the Convention committee made the short journey to Springfield and visited the nominee in his modest though comfortable house. Carl Schurz wrote that 'Most of the Committee had never seen him before, and gaped at him with surprised curiosity. He . . . did not present the appearance of a statesman. . . . Then followed some informal talk . . . in which the hearty simplicity of his nature shone out, and . . . the Committee took its leave'. Neither Lincoln's appearance, which was more imposing and comely than many contemporaries would admit, nor his gait, which was unimpressive, nor his style and speech, fitted mid-nineteenth-century stereotypes of 'statesmanship'. Lincoln, a sensitive, brooding man, aware of the insoluble difficulties he would inherit should he be elected, 'looked much moved, and rather sad, . . . feeling the heavy responsibility thrown upon him'. His confidence could not have been boosted by the knowledge that so many were already concluding that he was unequal to these challenges. Those who met him that afternoon were not unimpressed. Judge W. D. Kelley of Pennsylvania said to Schurz on leaving, 'Well we might have done a more brilliant thing, but we could certainly not have done a better thing'. He was wrong on the first count, but as time would prove, absolutely right on the second.[33]

The presidential campaign

The campaign began with some unfinished Democratic business. In June the Democrats reassembled in the no less sweltering city of Baltimore, Maryland. Once more the choice of venue appeared calculated to increase the temperature of a highly agitated and febrile body politic. Moves were still afoot to replace Douglas with a compromise candidate; these failed utterly because of the determination of the north western bloc of delegates who refused to shift from the standpoint of the Dorr Letter. They were doubtless fortified in their resolve by knowledge of Lincoln's

33. Randall, *Lincoln the President*, I, p. 174; Fehrenbacher, 'The Republican Decision at Chicago', p. 61; Thomas, *Lincoln*, p. 139; Potter, *Impending Crisis*, pp. 429–30, concludes: 'there seems good reason to believe that the Chicago strategies were realistic in thinking that Lincoln was the only genuine Republican who could be elected'.

appeal in their section. Douglas himself moved decisively to ensure that he controlled the Convention and that the complacency of Charleston was swept away (he had boosted his chances by inserting his own supporters in the places vacated by 'ultras' who had resigned from the party). At last the majority report on the platform was accepted; the southern response was again to stage a walk-out; the convention adjourned. The following day balloting of the remaining 192½ votes of the original 303 began, and on the second ballot Douglas gained 181½; it was deemed that he had secured a two-thirds majority, and at last, after a struggle lasting more than ten years, Douglas was nominated for the presidency. The essence of his platform was that contentious issues, such as the relative power of the Congress to impose its views on 'domestic relations' in the territories, should be decided by the Supreme Court. It was an irony that at the moment of his triumph, Douglas should turn to the expedient adopted by his greatest enemy, President Buchanan, to solve the intractable problems facing him.[34]

In a short acceptance speech, Douglas warned of future hazards. He would fight on popular sovereignty and a need to avoid extremes of arguments. 'Secession is *disunion*. Secession from the Democratic Party means secession from the federal Union'. Several days later in a letter formally accepting the Democratic nomination, Douglas wrote, 'The Federal union must be preserved . . . [and] the constitution must be maintained inviolate in all its parts' – a theme which would be reiterated frequently in the early months of 1861. If the United States faced revolutionary ructions, he asked 'where shall we look for another Clay, another Webster, or another Cass to pilot the ship of State over the breakers into the haven of peace and safety'. But the time for pilots had passed; Douglas now embarked on a bout of frantic activity in which he would climb the mast of the ship of state and gaze over storm whipped seas and shout cries of warning. But could dramatic action now replace an earlier generation's skill at reconciliation? Douglas would soon be put to the test.[35]

It simply remained for the rupture of the Democratic Party into sectional groupings to be confirmed. Southern delegates trooped into the Maryland Institute of Baltimore and adopted the Charleston platform favouring explicit protection of slave property: 'it is the duty of the Federal Government in all its

34. Nichols, *Disruption of American Democracy*, pp. 314–19; Nevins, *Emergence of Lincoln*, II, pp. 268–72; Johannsen, *Douglas*, pp. 767–72; Davis, *Breckinridge*, p. 222.
35. Quoted in Johannsen, *Douglas*, pp. 772–3.

departments to protect, when necessary, the rights of persons and property in the Territories, and wherever else its constitutional authority extends'. The favoured candidate of the pro-slave rump of the Democratic Party, John C. Breckinridge, began to reveal that marked ambivalence towards secession so characteristic of southern moderates. Formerly Buchanan's vice president, Breckinridge was by his lights an honourable and decent, though ambitious man. He had originally indicated his loyalty to the Union and to an indivisible Democratic Party; he had given a pledge that in his view the election of Lincoln could not justify secession. At first he was inclined to reject the nomination proffered by the seceders. Then he was persuaded to accept it on the grounds that his strength (especially in the South) would be such that he would force Douglas to withdraw from the election and the Democratic Party would be reunited around a new candidate, either James Guthrie of Kentucky or Robert Hunter of Virginia. This was a nonsensical plan, which indicated just what miscalculations the southern slave moderates were capable of, and their dreadful judgement of character. Douglas would not be intimidated in this way. He retorted that if he stood down, his supporters would vote for Lincoln. But whatever its practicality, the main significance of Breckinridge's timorous and reluctant candidacy was that it continued to play into the hands of the secessionists. It confirmed the split in the Democratic ranks; it made the election of Lincoln more likely; and, finally, should a Republican occupy the White House, the secessionists would again force the moderates' hands by demanding that they take a position on secession; at every turn they lost the initiative.[36] At any rate, Breckinridge accepted (and chose as his vice presidential nominee, Joseph Lane), and his ambivalence was reflected in the anxiety that many delegates felt at Yancey's closing address which wreaked of 'the ultraism of Alabama' and might frighten voters. Yet such men as Rhett and Yancey forced the pace of the controversy whatever the fears of others, who eventually caught up with them, and then made more demands in the secessionist direction. Yancey, Rhett and Hammond truly began to exercise power without responsibility. The southern delegates 'sick of the

36. Wells, *Douglas: The Last Years*, pp. 245–6 casts doubt on the plan to force Douglas to withdraw in a 'fusion' scheme; Davis, *Breckinridge*, pp. 223–5, makes out a persuasive case for it.

very sound of the human voice' adjourned with relief and hurried off to the campaign.[37]

The significance of the campaign of 1860 is self-evident. In the words of one American historian, 'Certainly no election in our history precipitated such a serious national crisis or had such profound consequences'.[38] But despite the dangers that many agreed the United States was facing, what is striking about the election is a determination to continue with politics 'as usual'. Even the most rabid secessionists awaited the verdict of the election and took no action until after its verdict was delivered. All agreed that whatever happened afterwards, the election itself was one of the most orderly and least frenetic in recent years. This state of mind had one pernicious consequence. It contributed to a somewhat smug view that no matter how grave the crisis, the system would somehow cope with it and that actual violence could be avoided. Although there was much loose talk of war, men had grave difficulty actually visualizing organized violence on a grand scale. Perhaps this serious state of affairs was somehow the fault of the selfish and wicked manoeuvrings of the 'politicians'. Many politicians themselves accepted this view. The solution to the difficulty in their opinion lay in the replacement of the current group of blundering politicians with themselves, as they were not 'politicians' in a pejorative sense but men of principle. As for the South, this talk of secession had been heard so many times before and it had come to nothing. The secessionist threats were not believed, or if they were taken seriously, it was expected that some concessions would soon persuade southerners to embrace once more the bosom of the Union. The election of 1860 contributed to a dangerous complacency that aggravated the gathering sectional crisis. The usual alarm signals which prompted special care in deterring war were not sounded in politicians' minds with the urgency that was needed.

The irony of this development was that the 1860 presidential election cannot be described as a *national* election. Parties serving sectional interests operated within those sections and secured convincing victories within their boundaries. The Republican Party did not operate effectively within the slave states; the Deep South had for some years been a one party region. In the North, the voters were confined to a choice between Lincoln and Douglas; in the South, Breckinridge vied with Bell. Only in Missouri and on

37. Nichols, *Disruption*, pp. 319–20; Johannsen, *Douglas*, p. 772; Nevins, *Emergence of Lincoln*, II, pp. 268–72.

38. Randall, *Lincoln the President*, I, p. 174; Gienapp, 'Who Voted for Lincoln?', p. 51.

the Pacific coast was there anything remotely resembling a four-cornered race.[39] The most significant fact was the splitting of the Democratic Party, the last national party. Douglas calculated that, given his local strength in the free states, if he could hold on to the Democratic gains of 1856, he could still win. But this proved an illusion (probably not shared by the local bosses whose prime concern was preserving intact their local satrapies in order to be prepared to retake lost ground two years later and in the 1864 presidential election). Losing the entire South was a tremendous blow to Douglas from which he could not recover. To increase his appeal in the South, he wanted as his running mate Alexander H. Stephens, a former Whig. Douglas himself was not in the best of health, and as Stephens did not enjoy robust health either, Douglas was persuaded to pick former Governor Herschel V. Johnson, a Georgia Democrat.

Douglas was determined to make no concessions to those who favoured secession. In his abrasive way he attacked them head-on. On 6 September 1860, in a speech at Baltimore, Douglas suggested that secessionists wanted Lincoln's election because it would justify secession. 'I do not believe that every Breckinridge man is a disunionist', he declared, 'but I do believe that every disunionist in America is a Breckinridge man'. He believed, quite rightly, that he was the only Democrat who could carry the free states, and if he could persuade southerners that he posed no threat to slavery, they would turn to him. He made the fatal calculation that once they realized they faced the alternative of voting for him and assuring the safety of the Union, or Lincoln and secession, the voters would turn in overwhelming numbers to him. What Douglas overlooked was the sectional factor. The Republican strength undercut his regional base. Actually the polarization of voters around sectional issues resulted in Douglas falling through the middle. He could pile up popular votes in both sections without decisively winning votes in the electoral college in either. True, the opposition to the Democrats was also split, but it proved to be more powerful within individual sections. A candidate occupying the middle ground sometimes fails to persuade voters to support him in overwhelming numbers.[40] At

39. William R. Brock, *Conflict and Transformation: The United States, 1844–1877* (Harmondsworth: Penguin, 1973), p. 185.

40. But note Fehrenbacher's persuasive argument (*Prelude to Greatness*, p. 160), that Douglas, leading a Democratic splinter group, was a more formidable opponent for Lincoln, especially in the North West, shorn of his pro-slavery allies.

any rate, Douglas decided that such a strategy demanded his personal advocacy, and for the second time in American history a presidential candidate decided to abandon the pose of remaining above the sordid contest for votes. Douglas actively campaigned on his own behalf (General Scott having set the precedent in 1852). As for Stephens, he gloomily contemplated the worst. When asked after the Baltimore Convention what he thought of affairs, he replied. 'Why that men will be cutting one another's throats in a little while. In less than twelve months we shall be in a war, and that the bloodiest in history'. Here was striking evidence that whatever claims would be made later, and not least by Stephens himself in *A Constitutional View of the Late War Between the States* (1868), the argument that in 1860–61 secession could be viewed with equanimity as merely a constitutional expedient was not convincing. The act of secession by an individual state, or collection of states, could never be regarded as simply an exercise in constitutional rights – a legalistic, clinical execution of a constitutional mechanism divorced from the political and social environment. The decision to secede from the Union was a political decision pregnant with disruption and civil war from the outset.[41]

The hideous potential consequences of this election were belied by Lincoln's serene behaviour during the election campaign itself. He had a well-filled campaign treasury and could afford to put on a colourful display of marches and displays. Much attention was devoted to Lincoln's humble origins and his career as a 'rail splitter'. In this the campaign of 1860 resembled Harrison's twenty years earlier, except that claims that Lincoln was born in a log cabin were not bogus. There were stalls selling fence nails; Springfield resembled, it was said, 'a Hindoo bazaar'. The *Illinois State Journal* reported the existence of 'A Political Earthquake! THE PRAIRIES ON FIRE FOR LINCOLN'. In Springfield an elephant was observed with its trunk wrapped around a banner declaring, 'We are Coming!' – the first recorded use of the symbol of the Republican Party. A somewhat monotonous campaign jingle caught the ear:

41. Nichols, *The Disruption of American Democracy*, pp. 335–40; J. G. Randall and David Donald, *The Civil War and Reconstruction*, 2nd edn (Lexington, MA: D. C. Heath, 1969), p. 132; Nevins, *Emergence of Lincoln*, II, p. 262.

Ain't I glad I joined the Republicans
Joined the Republicans, joined the Republicans
Ain't I glad I joined the Republicans
Down in Illinois

The substance of the Republican campaign did not match the colour of its style. Lincoln made no speeches at all. He made no effort to reassure the South. He was determined not to become embroiled in local party feuds. His views, he averred, could easily be located in his many earlier speeches; '*bad* men . . . North and South' would only distort any further utterances for their own nefarious purposes. Thus the unfortunate, mythical figure which was painted in the South, reaching diabolic proportions, was not corrected. Lincoln was allegedly illegitimate, of Negro extraction, a cheap party hack with a traitorous Mexican War record, thrown up by the 'Black Republican, free love, free Nigger Party'. It was put about in the South that if Lincoln was elected, Negroes would be granted the federal patronage. An Atlanta newspaper referred in colourful terms, in language that was becoming increasingly common by the late 1850s, to 'drenching' the Union in blood. Such phrases were all too easy to coin, rather more difficult to imagine in hard reality: 'the South, the loyal South, the constitution South, would never submit to such humiliation and degradation as the inauguration of Abraham Lincoln'. Some historians have suggested that it was a pity that Lincoln made no statement of policy to reduce the impact of such hysteria. It was very doubtful whether Lincoln could have disposed of these falsehoods, for he could provide no reassurances without offending his core political support. He should have done more than make simple, pleasant effusions to parades and well wishers. He relied, too complacently, on the sentiment that 'The good people of the South have too much good sense and good temper to attempt the ruin of the government' – a somewhat exaggerated estimate of southern rationality when racial fears have been invoked. Secession he believed to be a hollow threat. Douglas refused to be intimidated and went South; he refused to be browbeaten and spelt out future prospects with a clarity and common sense which had deserted his Democratic rivals; he refused to indulge himself in hysterical fancies. Douglas ridiculed southern fears of the result of a Republican victory. 'The President', he proclaimed, 'can do nothing except what the law authorises. . . . Four years will soon pass away, when the ballot box will furnish a peaceful, legal and constitutional remedy for all the evils and grievances with which the country may be afflicted'. Douglas probably neglected his north western heartland by his wanderings. Ridiculed and abused, crafty and facile, in the presidential election of 1860 Douglas dedicated himself to principle and did not profit by it. 'I did not come here to ask your vote, nor your suffrages for office. I am not here on an electioneering tour. I am here to make a plea, an appeal for the invincibility of the Union'. Douglas was the moral victor of this campaign.[42]

Lincoln was already feeling the strength of pressure to make concessions to the South, notably from business interests from New England. Lincoln replied sternly in private that he would not bargain Republican principle for commercial prosperity. The twin pattern of the secession crisis – an unmollified and hysterical South raging at a somewhat complacent political class, combined with a strong urge to appease this section from the North East, pleas which fell on the deaf ears of a president whose firm resolve was underestimated by all – had fallen into place during the presidential election.[43]

The main themes of the Republican campaign were laid down by other speakers, often by men whom Lincoln had beaten for the nomination. This may have contributed to the later erroneous assumption that Lincoln's administration would not be his own. For example, Salmon P. Chase, having offered 'hearty and cordial support', spoke on Lincoln's behalf not only in Ohio but also in Kentucky and New York. His attacks on Douglas were stinging, but he made it abundantly clear in Kentucky that the election of a Lincoln Administration would *not* result in federal interference with slavery in the southern states but only in its restriction to the existing slave states and eviction from the territories. Even if Lincoln can be accused of ambiguity, his position was being defined for him. Chase affirmed that the Republican Party was antagonistic to 'hostile aggression upon the constitutional rights of any State'. This could be read two ways, of course. The Republicans opposed the constitutional infringements of the slave power on the rights of *northern* states. Southerners viewed this constitutional 'danger' exclusively in terms of the potential danger

---

42. Wells, *Douglas: The Last Years*, pp. 253–8: Douglas was 'a different man' in October 1860 from his first foray in August; Johannsen, *Douglas*, pp. 789–92.

43. Thomas, *Lincoln*, p. 142; Oates, *With Malice Toward None*, pp. 185–9.

that Republicanism posed for slavery in the *southern* states. 'The object of my wishes and labors for nineteen years', Chase wrote, 'is accomplished in the overthrow of the Slave Power' – by which he meant power over the northern states. An important thrust of the Republican campaign was a scathing attack on the corruption which had characterized the Buchanan Administration. Senator James W. Grimes of Iowa went so far as to conclude that 'our triumph was achieved more because of Lincoln's . . . honesty and the known corruption of the Democrats, than because of the negro question'. Lincoln's image as 'Honest Abe' was very persuasive. Speakers tried to associate the Douglas Democrats with the Administration; every session of Congress, they declared, between December 1857 and June 1860 had discovered (mainly through the agencies of the Covode Committee and Congressman John Sherman's investigation of the navy yards and Navy Department contracts) overwhelming evidence of Democratic corruption. The Republicans also suggested that the Constitutional Union Party had prostituted itself by forming an alliance with the anti-Lincoln forces. The Breckinridge Democrats were most sensitive to these allegations, and published a pamphlet detailing Republican abuses, for in truth, their record was hardly unblemished. Breckinridge's declaration of love for the Union also provoked scorn. Yet this evidence of sensitivity to charges of corruption is important in indicating that the presidential election of 1860, contrary to some accounts, lacked an exclusive, obsessive focus on slavery and secession.[44]

Buoyed up by the state election results in mid-October in Pennsylvania, Ohio and Indiana which saw the election of Republican state tickets, Lincoln was optimistic as to his chances. The anti-Republican opposition mounted a fearsome campaign as a result to try and hold New York, but on the whole attempts at 'fusion' only confused the voters. At 9 p.m. on the evening of 6 November, Lincoln and his friend (and co-manager) Jesse K. Dubois wandered over to the Springfield telegraph office to hear the early returns. They were joined by Senator Lyman Trumbull. It was soon clear that Lincoln had carried New England and the Old North West. Cameron wired to say that a Republican victory in Pennsylvania was a certainty. 'If we get New York that settles it',

---

44. Blue, *Chase*, pp. 127–8; David E. Meerse, 'Buchanan, Corruption and the Election of 1860', *Civil War History* 12 (1966), pp. 116–31, esp. pp. 118–19, 121–4, 127, 131.

Trumbull observed. As always, Lincoln remained calm and unagitated, as he had throughout the campaign. When news arrived that New York had indeed fallen into the Republican column, Dubois ran outside to inform the growing crowds, and the news was greeted with rumbustious enthusiasm: supporters went 'perfectly *wild*; the Republicans were ... *singing, yelling! shouting!!* Old men, young, middle aged, clergymen and all!' The settlers of the Old North West have never been celebrated for understatement. As the telegraph then began to record the southern results, Lincoln said, 'Now we shall get a few licks back', for he did not gain a single southern electoral vote. His victory was indeed a sectional triumph.[45]

In the South the mood had swung from noisy swagger to grim foreboding. Miss Hopley, walking the streets of Richmond, 'encountered crowds repeatedly'.

> Long and continued shouts and huzzahs assailed one's ears from time to time till towards midday. Success seemed to gleam around. By-and-by the shouts became less frequent. News from more distant regions must have changed the aspect of affairs and chilled their hopes. . . . By dusk a funeral cloud seemed to hang over the city . . . the silence of solitude had been sought by all.[46]

This gloomy foreboding was the prelude to drastic action in all the slave states, though the pace at which it progressed varied in individual states.

Who did Lincoln represent? Lincoln received less than 40 per cent of the total votes cast in the 1860 presidential election. The final tallies were: Lincoln 1,865,593, Douglas 1,382,713, Breckinridge 848,356, Bell 592,906; the scores in the electoral college were: Lincoln 180, Douglas 12, Breckinridge 72, Bell 39. It would appear at first sight that Lincoln was a minority president and that his victory had been distorted by the votes in the electoral college which did not represent opinion in the country. It was a commonplace on the Democratic side that they would have won without the party split at Charleston. 'Our break up there', a New York Democrat observed, 'elected Mr Lincoln'. Certainly individual elections within states accentuated the divisions within Lincoln's rivals; as under the British electoral

45. Gienapp, 'Who Voted for Lincoln?', p. 62; Johannsen, *Douglas*, pp. 792, 803–4.
46. Catherine C. Hopley, *Life in the South* (New York: Augustus M. Kelley, 1971 reprint), vol. I, pp. 134–5.

system, the winner in each state won the total electoral vote however small the majority. Lincoln had few wasted votes – all were made to count in his favour. Presented at its worst, he obtained hardly a vote in ten states; in three others, Kentucky, Virginia and Maryland, his poll was minute; in Missouri his wasted votes numbered 17,028 and in Delaware 3,815; in New Jersey he got a slight majority in the electoral college on a minority of the popular vote. Compare this with Douglas. His wasted vote was enormous: 1,255,000 did not secure a single presidential elector. J. G. Randall refers to a 'structural absurdity' in the American electoral system which granted Lincoln victory even though his opponents secured over 900,000 votes more than him. Passing over the objection that such an absurdity is not unique to the United States, it seems to overlook the reality that the Republicans were a sectional party. One reason why the Republican appeal remained sectional was that the party was denied opportunities to organize in the South – often by force and intimidation. Yet whatever the hard, political realities, the democratic argument is not irrelevant to the outbreak of the Civil War because an important issue was the refusal of the South to acknowledge the verdict of the electorate and to accept a continuance of the normal workings of constitutional machinery, irrespective of the southern opinion of the personality of the victorious candidate. Disputation arising from Lincoln's failure to win a majority of the popular vote seems academic. 'This issue embraces more than the fate of these United States,' Lincoln wrote later. 'It presents to the whole family of man, the question, whether a constitutional republic, or a democracy . . . can, or cannot, maintain its territorial integrity'. But the issue was not a clear-cut one because Lincoln's endorsement was sectional.[47]

Therefore what was significant was that Lincoln carried all the northern states except one; his victory in the popular vote here was overwhelming; the Democratic Party had lost its northern constituency. August Belmont reckoned that a switch of 28,000 votes in the New York state election out of a total of 700,000 would have kept it in the Democrat column. Belmont blamed this on Buchanan's corruption, as change was 'ardently desired by thousands of conservative men out of politics'. Half a million votes had been added to the Republican total gained in 1856. But what

47. Fehrenbacher, *Prelude to Greatness*, pp. 159–60; Gienapp, 'Who Voted for Lincoln?', pp. 63–4; Potter, *Impending Crisis*, p. 442; James M. McPherson, *Abraham Lincoln and the Second American Revolution* (New York: Oxford UP, 1990), p. 29.

is really significant was that Lincoln *would have won even if the opposition vote had been combined against him.* If examined critically, Lincoln's tally reveals that only in three states did he win because the opposition was split, in New Jersey (where he did not win all the electoral votes), Oregon and California. These provided him with only 18 electoral votes; if these had been lost, Lincoln still had a cushion of 9 electoral votes to guarantee his election. The main sources of his support were not the Germans, as stressed by earlier historians, but disillusioned previous supporters of the American Party, who feared their vote would be wasted. Only in Massachusetts and Maine did Bell secure a larger share of former Fillmore voters than Lincoln; Lincoln himself was an old Whig; his criticisms of Know Nothingism had been made in private correspondence. It is very unlikely that Seward, had he been the Republican nominee, would have scored so heavily among Know Nothing voters, especially in Illinois and Indiana, where Lincoln's margin of victory was not great. Lincoln's strength appeared to be concentrated in the countryside rather than in the towns. The strength of the Democratic Party outside the South was essentially urban. 'The strength of our opponents lies mainly in the populous cities', Carl Schurz explained, 'and consists largely of the Irish and uneducated mass of German immigrants'. The German vote remained divided, and was not noticeably pro-Republican in mid-western states (it tended to divide on religious lines with Roman Catholics remaining loyal to the Democrats, while Protestants turned to the anti-Catholic Republicans). It is also important to recall that sectional issues that concerned the politicians did not always agitate voters. Douglas complained at one point that 'the Republicans in their speeches, say nothing of the nigger question, but all is made to turn on the Tariff'. In the South, moreover, as the combined anti-Breckinridge vote amounted to 55 per cent of the votes cast, this contributed to the widespread feeling that southern unionism remained a thriving political force that would subdue secessionist feeling.[48]

It was reported that Lincoln said to a group of newsmen the day after the results had been declared that their problems were over, his about to begin. One initial problem that would haunt him for the next five months was the attention which he received from shameless office-seekers. Herndon wrote in disgust that 'men

48. Gienapp, 'Who Voted for Lincoln?', pp. 63, 65–7, 68–9, 71–3; Potter, *Impending Crisis*, p. 442; Meerse, 'Buchanan, Corruption and the Election of 1860', p. 131.

and women rushed around [Lincoln] – kissed his feet – rolled in the dust begging notice . . . begged for a hair from the tail of his old horse'. He was so importuned that Herndon found him refuge on the second floor of a warehouse where he could concentrate on making some initial drafts of his inaugural address. Herndon was dispatched to find reference works for the president-elect's use. Lincoln would not make concessions to the South, he predicted. Rather than compromise, Lincoln would choose that 'his soul might go back to God from the wings of the Capitol'. Herndon was not inaccurate in marking out Lincoln's course, although the latter would have preferred less high-flown language.[49] It was to the problem of naming a cabinet and actually putting together an administration under the extraordinary circumstances of the secession of southern states that now began to receive Lincoln's close attention.

The aftermath

The results of the presidential election were felt mainly in the South. In the North a tense calm and nervous expectation fell over the section. In the South the white population fell into a hysterical state. The problem with a press which conducts its daily business in vituperative language is that no scope is left for increasing the temperature in times of strife. All sense of proportion was lost. As before, the opinions of 'the South' were really expressed by the Lower or Deep South; in the Upper South Unionism still prevailed because, among other reasons, some semblance of the two-party system survived. In the Deep South politicians, like Joseph E. Brown of Georgia, were well aware that Lincoln would not carry any slave states. 'I am strongly influenced by the belief . . . that Lincoln will carry the Democratic free states', he wrote, 'under the plurality rule of voting and will be elected by the popular vote'. Therefore the South was confronted by a cohesive northern bloc and no accumulation of southern votes could possibly force the election into the House of Representatives. In this calculation, of course, Brown was absolutely right. He greatly regretted the splitting of the Democratic Party and, on the whole, had favoured the

49. David Donald, *Lincoln's Herndon* (New York: Alfred A. Knopf, 1948), pp. 143, 145; Thomas, *Lincoln*, p. 143; Oates, *With Malice Toward None*, p. 189.

Breckinridge–Lane ticket: 'as a southern man, I think it best to vote for him, while I condemn the action of the wire workers who produced the split more for the gratification of selfish motives and vindictive feelings than for patriotic emotions'. This judgement was typical of the condemnations of the manoeuvres accompanying the conventions, though it was inaccurate; politicians had become a universal scapegoat.

It was significant, however, that though Brown objected both to the disruption of the Democratic Party and to the behaviour of some secessionists, that he was prepared to follow their lead, rather than reject their shrill and discordant cries. Little room for manoeuvre or thought had been granted by the southern defence of slavery. The ultimate logic of its defence demanded secession, no matter how many doubts might be harboured about the wisdom of seceding or departing from beloved institutions and the protection these had afforded slavery in the recent past. That these doubts were expressed by experienced and respected politicians seemed to carry no weight. The doubters seem to have been swept along by the torrent of denunciation, from belligerent even hysterical speeches, to hurried and careless action, to secession, to war. Thomas R. R. Cobb wrote to his wife in October 1860, on hearing of the Republican success in Pennsylvania, 'I can see no earthly hope of defeating [the Republicans] in November, and success then, whether we will it or not, is *inevitable disunion. . . . Separation is desirable*, peaceable if we can, forcibly if we must'. He continued, expressing a measure of lamentation for the chosen course, the 'Union or the South one or the other is irretrievably gone, if Lincoln is elected. I confess I feel *very sad*. The forebodings of my mind are of the most depressing character'.[50]

But men like Brown would not give a positive lead in expressing their doubts and overcome the gloomy forebodings of those who thought like Cobb. They became hedged in by the ultimate logic of the defence of slavery, secession, and the passion with which it was enunciated. To doubt a little seemed to suggest a disloyal or supine thought. The secessionists therefore gained the moral initiative and made a heartfelt appeal; the doubters had little to offer and nothing exciting to say. Often in a crisis a small number of people can be persuaded to support an audacious act, a novel programme, a step into the unknown, and this small number

---

50. Joseph H. Parks, *Joseph E. Brown of Georgia* (Baton Rouge: Louisiana State UP, 1977), pp. 107–8; McCash, *Cobb*, p. 184.

grants the necessary power to act. Such were the conditions in 1860. Douglas had exaggerated: although all secessionists – especially in the Upper South – voted for Breckinridge, by no means all his voters were secessionists. Indeed the Georgia picture highlights the small margin of secessionist support and the local pigment colours the broader, southern background. Breckinridge received 51,893, Bell 42,855 and Douglas 11,580 votes. The anti-Breckinridge vote was therefore greater than his tally. True, Breckinridge had won 72 out of the 120 electoral college votes of the slave states, but the combined popular vote for Douglas and Bell in these states exceeded that of Breckinridge by 100,000. Indeed Douglas had failed to carry the city of Richmond, later the Confederate capital, by a mere 400 votes. Yet the drama and fervour of the secessionist case prevailed despite the small margin of support. That it did so had more to do with fear and anxiety than with popularity.[51]

What responsibility did Lincoln bear for this mental state in the South? He may be criticized for not giving the impression that he was in charge, but it must be agreed that his task of reassurance – except in his own party – was a most difficult one. Apart from virtually dissolving the Republican Party and declaring slavery a benefit for the Union – an inconceivable eventuality – how else could exaggerated southern fears have been set to rest? This is perhaps reflective of the general southern mood, which sought to win what modern commentators would describe as a 'zero-sum game': they demanded all for no concession, and simultaneously risked all by demanding it. Lincoln stood on much stronger ground when he enquired during the campaign, 'What is it I could say which would quiet alarm? Is it that no interference by the government, with slaves or slavery within the states is intended? I have said this so often already, that a repetition of it is but mockery, bearing an appearance of weakness'. This latter phrase was a clue to Lincoln's future policy, should matters be put to the proof. Any comment would lead only to further hysteria, which would not redound to the credit of the Republican candidate. Further repetition might be possible 'if there were no danger of encouraging bold bad men ... who are eager for something new upon which to base new misrepresentations – men who would like to frighten me, or at least, to fix upon me the character of timidity and cowardice. They would seize upon almost

51. Wells, *Douglas: The Last Years*, p. 256; Parks, *Brown*, p. 109.

any letter I could write, as being an "*awful coming down*".
Whatever Lincoln's stance would be, it would be resolute.[52]

But resolution would confront hysteria – always a combustible
mixture. Lincoln was stigmatized, on the evidence of his 'House
Divided' speech, as an abolitionist: 'a fanatic of the John Brown
type; the slave to one idea, who, in order to carry that out to its
legitimate results, would override laws, constitutions, and
compromises of every kind', and as such, would weaken the
institution of slavery in the states. Though there were conservative
northerners who sympathized with slavery, chatter and fanaticism
would 'render slave property so precarious as regards its tenure,
that it would become valueless to its owners'. That the time factor
in this regard was ignored is a measure of how infrequently cool,
sober calculations entered southern heads, *even if* Lincoln was the
kind of politician they conjured up, which he was not.
Nonetheless, there can be no doubt that the policy of hemming in
slavery within its exiting boundaries would have profound
implications for its enduring vitality. But whether this warranted
the kind of action that the South was now contemplating was quite
a different matter.[53]

Before the election results were known, doubters like Brown
were already preparing their ground. He wrote a message to the
Georgia legislature recommending that retaliation be invoked
against those states whose 'personal liberty laws' had cancelled out
the workings of the Fugitive Slave Act. When asked by the
Governor of South Carolina what action he would take if Lincoln
was elected, Brown replied that a convention of all the slave states
would be required so that they could 'take common action for the
protection of the rights of all'. Lincoln's defeat, he predicted
correctly, was unlikely.

> Should the question be submitted to the people of Georgia
> whether they would go out of the Union on Lincoln's election
> without regard to the action of other states my opinion is they
> would determine to wait for an *overt act*.

Stressing the limits of action, and the limits of the possible, he
pointed out that unless the South made a 'respectable show' of

52. Quoted in McPherson, *Battle Cry of Freedom*, p. 231.
53. Arthur C. Cole and J. G. de Roulhac Hamilton, 'Lincoln's Election an
Immediate Menace to Slavery in the States?', in Sidney Fine and Gerald S. Brown
(eds) *The American Past: Conflicting Interpretations of the Great Issues* (New York:
Macmillan, 1961), I, pp. 531–66. See also Michael Davis, *The Image of Lincoln in the
South* (Knoxville: University of Tennessee Press, 1971), Ch. 1.

resistance' it might not be possible to mobilize support for it again in the future. 'Already the people of the North taunt us with inability and cowardice'. A concern with such moral imperatives drew politicians to act even though they had not thought out the object and compass of their acts or their consequences very systematically. But even sceptics were anxious to show that they were prepared for action of some kind and agreed that whatever was undertaken should be consonant with the action of other southern states and coordinated jointly with them.[54] But the policy of waiting on events surrendered more of the initiative to the 'ultras', offered even less space for manoeuvre, and rendered the final act, when it came, a colossal gamble.

The presidential election of 1860 is also significant because of the splintering of the Democratic Party, the sole remaining political grouping which straddled the two sections. The Democratic Party was not only a national institution, but also a political force that was allied with, and drew much of its strength from, the South. The issues of the election did not revolve around the continuance of slavery in the states, only its restriction there. By refusing to accept the protection of northern Democrats, the southern pro-slavery party unwittingly (and in some cases wittingly) shattered that political grouping best able to defend their peculiar institution. They sought to replace it with a purely southern political structure which, if it sought to safeguard slavery outside the Union, would have to rely on force. This was a huge risk, for it staked the survival of slavery in the *southern states* on the southern ability to defend it. This had not been an issue in the election itself. By their precipitate and rash conduct, the secessionists dramatically increased the stakes of the contest and risked all that they held dear.

The election confirmed the political authority and electoral support of the Republican Party in the North. It confirmed in the most hard and fast manner possible that the two sections voted predominantly for different candidates on different issues. One of those sections now refused to accept that the majority vote as represented in the electoral college and the election of a Republican president was binding on the South because its message and candidate had been so thoroughly and wholeheartedly rejected there. Such an attitude not only challenged the continuance of the democratic process in the

54. Parks, *Brown*, p. 108.

United States – which was central to the health of American nationalism and was the very essence of an evolving concept of American national identity and uniqueness – but also would represent a flagrant challenge to the authority of the central government. Could such a challenge be ignored? And if it could not, could the crisis be resolved without resort to force? Abraham Lincoln did not exaggerate when, on leaving Springfield, Illinois, to travel to Washington DC to take up his presidential burdens, he admitted that he faced a 'task before me greater than that which rested upon Washington'.[55]

---

55. *The Lincoln Reader*, p. 309.

CHAPTER SEVEN

The Secession Crisis: Southern Challenges, Northern Responses

[Of] calamities and misfortunes which may greatly afflict us . . . and to fortify our minds against the attacks of these. . . . The only method of doing this is to assume a perfect resignation to the Divine Will, to consider that whatever does happen, must happen; and that, by our uneasiness, we cannot prevent the blow before it does fall, but we may add to the force after it has fallen.

THOMAS JEFFERSON, *Jefferson Himself*[1]

Without a party a statesman is nothing. He sometimes forgets that awkward fact.

RONALD SYME, *The Roman Revolution*[2]

President-Elect Lincoln's problems, as he sat musing in the parlour of his Springfield home, were indeed the most unenviable and intractable ever placed before a prospective chief executive of the United States. The course of the secession crisis resembled a menacing minuet. Clearly, the southern states, as they had indeed threatened, would make the first move; but the outcome of that move would be determined by the response of the Federal government; which, in turn would shape the next step. The northern response clearly is as important in determining the outcome of this crisis as southern behaviour. We should never forget A. J. P. Taylor's injunction that it takes two sides to make a war.[3] Here the behaviour of the Federal government is just as

---

1. Thomas Jefferson, quoted in *Jefferson Himself*, ed. Bernard Mayo (Charlottesville: University Press of Virginia, 1970), p. 13.
2. Ronald Syme, *The Roman Revolution* (Oxford: Clarendon Press, 1939), p. 60.
3. A. J. P. Taylor, *From Napoleon to the Second International: Essays on Nineteenth Century Europe*, ed. C. Wrigley (London: Hamish Hamilton, 1993), pp. 224, 321.

decisive in leading to the fateful steps resulting in civil war as the action of southern insurgents. And in tracing this process, attribution of blame for provoking a conflict is a minor consideration when set beside the need to evaluate the chain of causation. Contemporaries were very free in allotting blame at the time, as we shall see, and most of this fell on the shoulders of the hapless President Buchanan; but even the most well-meaning statesman can trigger off a series of events which results in catastrophe. Wars have frequently resulted from a series of well-intentioned acts, and such was the case in 1861.

One important obstacle, which all northern participants in the crisis were powerless to overcome, was the four months' interlude prescribed by the Constitution before Lincoln could be inaugurated as president. The Founding Fathers had assumed that American democracy would not encounter a crisis of such magnitude in which drastic action would be required. Or, even if this was threatened, that such a crisis would not be so immediate or coincide with a change of chief magistrate. This long period of time stymied dramatic initiative and was an embarrassment to both Buchanan and Lincoln. The latter could not assume office until 4 March. If Lincoln made announcements, it would set in train a deluge of speculation and denunciation which he could not silence by action; if Buchanan took action, which he was temperamentally ill-disposed to do, it could founder with one word from the president-elect. The dilemma was insuperable. Lincoln decided to keep his own counsel and say nothing. The expedient he had employed during the presidential election was employed again during the period of transition. If Washington Irving was right in thinking that American government was nothing but the unadulterated government of words, then the government of the United States ground to a halt in the early months of 1861. Fortunately, there were many others who were willing to fill the breach with talk, but they had no responsibility for action. There is no better example of the age-old problem of equating power and responsibility. Buchanan had power, though it was diminishing, but had no responsibility beyond March 1861; Lincoln had awesome responsibility but no power. He had political authority as president-elect but whether he could do anything constructive with it was quite a different matter. Buchanan (like Douglas) was also sensitive to the need not to make any move which might endanger the return of a Democrat to the White House, which would need southern votes. This additional calculation lent a certain prudence to the moves of a politician not inclined to antagonize the South.[4]

At any rate, the long period of waiting, if it did not inaugurate a president, inaugurated a protracted period of manoeuvring which attempted to influence the policy of the incoming Lincoln Administration. The Republican Party, more than most, was a coalition of groupings that had little in common with one another. The attempt to discern the policy of the party once it was in government became a major objective. But one characteristic of all these warring factions was that they underestimated the president-elect. They all assumed, on no evidence but a wish that he would prove compliant, that he would have no views of his own and that he would follow the advice of the more distinguished members of his party in a docile and respectful manner. More attention will be devoted to this foolish and unfortunate attitude in the next chapter. Suffice it to say that this presumption, defended by William H. Seward's biographer on the grounds that Lincoln was untested, only added to the muddle in policy which was exacerbated by structural rigidities, such as the long transition between administrations. On the contrary, the chief executive they would have to deal with, though initially diffident, had already developed tremendous skill in manipulating and cajoling men. He would choose his own cabinet, but would do so without alienating the various factions which were manoeuvring about him. Lincoln posed as a humble man, and he was, in any case, winning, affable and kindly. But he did not underestimate his own capacities, which, in truth, were greater than those of the men around him. But it would take *time* for this to have an effect on the formulation of policy. Lincoln simultaneously had too much of this and too little; too much time in Springfield, yet too little in Washington DC. In view of his peculiar and unprecedented difficulties, it is possible that Lincoln's silence contributed to the sense of uncontrollable drift. But he could *do* nothing. Leadership without action is as pointless as cars without petroleum. Lincoln was surrounded by men who thought that they had all the answers to his problems if only they were in his place. 'Hindsight makes us

4.   The reduction of the period of transition from 4 March to 20 January did not come until the Twentieth Amendment in 1933, when urgent legislation was required with the onset of the New Deal. See Gary Wills, *Reagan's America: Innocents at Home* (London: W. H. Allen, 1988), pp. 64–5.

admire him [Lincoln] even more', writes Marcus Cunliffe with characteristic acuity, 'for his honest bewilderment'.[5]

Forming the Lincoln Administration

The structure of the Lincoln Administration would determine the Federal government's response to the crisis. Lincoln himself, even to prominent members of his own party, was an unknown quantity and he lacked the customary alliances and networks which would allow observers to predict in advance his cabinet. The result was a prolonged bout of shadow boxing in which various individuals and factions jostled for influence. The most prominent of these was Seward. Since the Chicago Convention Seward had nursed the illusion, no doubt a sop to his wounded vanity, that he would be left to run the Administration. Seward was devious and rather conceited. It never occurred to him that he would not be the centre of decision-making in the new Administration. Lincoln did not formally become president-elect until 5 December when the presidential electors of Illinois and other states met to confirm the decision of the electorate a month before. Here was a prime example of the inertia of the presidential-making machinery. Lincoln had not wasted this month; he devoted a lot of time, when not importuned by callers, to considering his course of action. He was already providing evidence for those with a mind to see it that he would behave as chief executive in substance as well as in style. The office of the presidency is very personal and may be moulded to fit the character of the incumbent. Lincoln would *lead* but in his own individual way. He had already discerned from the manoeuvres of Thurlow Weed, Seward's alter ego, that Seward would try and dominate the new Administration, and he took action immediately to try and counteract this overweening effort. In a series of adroit and complex measures, using correspondence dispatched via the vice president-elect, Hamlin, he sought to ensure that Seward would decline an offer of secretary of state before it was actually tendered. He also felt unable to accept Weed's invitation to visit Seward at his home at Auburn, New York.

5.   See Herman Hattaway and Archer Jones, *How the North Won* (Urbana and Chicago: University of Illinois Press, 1983), pp. 4–5; Glyndon G. Van Deusen, *William Henry Seward* (New York: Oxford UP, 1969), pp. 248–50, 283; Marcus Cunliffe, 'The Struggle in Prospect', in H. S. Commager, M. Cunliffe and M. A. Jones (eds) *Illustrated History of the American Civil War* (London: Orbis, 1976), p. 146.

Finally, he sent word to the Republican congressional leaders, telling them not to entertain suggestions of compromise with the South. Henry Villard of the New York *Herald*, the best informed of the watching correspondents, reported that 'The result of the secession conventions will be awaited. . . . No difficulty will be experienced in choosing the representatives of the free states in the cabinet'. But would this include a southerner? He predicted, 'a "coming together" seems a rather remote contingency'.[6]

During these days Lincoln was often accused of 'a grotesque joviality' in his attitude. Those who met him socially gained the opinion that he considered the threats of secession nothing more than bluff. He was asked by Villard to make a public statement. To meet this demand in November he had written out two paragraphs which would appear in a speech by Senator Trumbull. This was a clever move because the sentiments were not binding on the president-elect, having been uttered by Trumbull. Lincoln wrote, 'all of the states will be left in complete control of their own affairs . . . and at perfect liberty to choose and employ, their own means of protecting property and preserving peace and order within their respective limits, as they have ever been under any administration'. Perhaps the crucial passage illustrating (as he saw it) the moderate intent of the Lincoln Administration and the hollowness of southern threats, was:

> Disunionists *per se*, are now in hot haste to get out of the Union precisely because they perceive they cannot much longer maintain apprehension among the southern people that their homes, and firesides, and lives, are to be endangered by the action of the Federal Government. With such '*now or never*' is the maxim.

Throughout, Lincoln had maintained an optimistic frame of mind. Two months earlier he had predicted that 'In no probable event will there be any very formidable effort to break up the Union'. In reaching this judgement he relied on 'many assurances' he had received from southern correspondents, who

6.	William E. Baringer, *A House Dividing: Lincoln as President Elect* (Springfield, IL: Abraham Lincoln Association, 1945), pp. 17, 78–9, 87, 89, 95–6, 99, 100–1, 106–7; Van Deusen, *Seward*, p. 239. David Potter, *Lincoln and his Party in the Secession Crisis*, 2nd edn (New Haven, CT: Yale UP, 1942, 1962; New York: AMS Press, 1979), p. 156. On pp. 80–2, Potter claims that Seward's capacity for leadership during the interregnum would have been greater if he had not been so concerned with cultivating his influence with the new administration. But Potter is too intolerant of the difficulties posed by the electoral system, and his pro-southern bias is pervasive. Furthermore, as the Sumter crisis would show, it is by no means certain that had Seward been given his head war would have been avoided.

included too many individuals 'of good sense and good temper to attempt the ruin of the government rather than see it administered as it was administered by the men who made it. At least so I hope and believe'.[7]

But Lincoln's studiedly optimistic stance was also the product of a knowledge of the fragility of the Republican Party which had to be held together. This could be achieved by adopting an attitude which imposed the minimum stress on its fissure-ridden surface of unity. To take one example, the Indiana Republican Party lay at the centre of Lincoln's political base. Like his home state, Illinois, Indiana included in its southern counties many citizens originally from the South. The Republican Party there lacked a number of basic principles acceptable to this diverse constituency. Some acquiesced in secession. 'Of what value will a union be that needs links of bayonets and bullets to hold it together?' Other conservative Republicans, although they were doubtful whether the allegiance of the Deep South could be held, believed that the Upper South could be divided from their more militant allies. The Indianapolis *Journal*, for example, proposed that liberty laws be passed that allowed slaveholders to take their slaves through the free states, and the introduction of popular sovereignty in the territories. That is to say, they advocated an abandonment of the very *raison d'être* of the Republican Party itself. There was hostility to the views of Republicans in New England, 'fanatical, abolitionised, canting, hypocritical New England States', whose views on tariff and banking matters were also abhorrent. Could secession spread to the North itself? In the southern counties, some Indianans muttered darkly. 'I cannot obliviate the fact that our interest is with the South', wrote one, 'and I cannot reconcile the separation'. This was a measure of Lincoln's problem, and he was criticized for keeping silent.

Under these circumstances, Lincoln's sunny disposition, smiling, making pleasant homilies, receiving enthusiastic crowds with unexceptional sentiment, kissing little girls, and behaving as if he was still on the hustings, had a tactical significance. But Lincoln had to respond to the thousands of moderate Republicans, who though lukewarm if not downright hostile to Negroes themselves, refused to concede an inch on the slavery extension issue. There could be no compromise like that of 1850. To do so would sacrifice the success of the Republican Party just at the moment

7. Baringer, *A House Dividing*, pp. 32–3, 42–3.

when it had gained power. 'The Republicans', wrote one loyalist, 'have nothing to take back. . . . We knew the man we voted for; understood his principles, and, be the consequences what they may, are determined to give him 'aid and comfort' in carrying out those principles'. Another claimed, surely rightly, that if the Republicans cowered to the South after bellowing so much 'anti-slavery bluster' it was obvious that 'Republicanism is a dead dog'. How could Lincoln straddle these contradictory currents within his own party and yet present a firm but conciliatory policy to the southern states?[8]

One ploy was to award cabinet posts to men who might be acceptable to the South, like Edward Bates and John M. Botts, the Virginia Unionist. Lincoln at this stage was reluctant to appoint Seward not only for personal reasons, but also because he would enrage the South – his exaggerated radical image still prevailed – and 'alarm and dissatisfy' conservative Republicans. Indeed he pondered on the possibility of making Bates his secretary of state. But he could not do so until Seward had declined the position. Predictions of Lincoln's conservatism at the Chicago Convention were more than vindicated by these initial moves. Indeed he was prepared in principle to include a southerner in his cabinet. His old Whig ally, Botts, might fit this bill. But Lincoln was under no illusions, given the stream of vituperation frothing from the South, that such an appointment would end the crisis. Indeed when Thurlow Weed mentioned the need to have no fewer than two southerners in his cabinet, Lincoln replied sternly, asking whether these men could be trusted if their states seceded? When Weed assured him that they could and offered to vouch for them personally, Lincoln snapped caustically, 'Well, let us have the names of your white crows'. Even the most committed recent defender of Upper South Unionism, Daniel W. Crofts, concedes that unconditional Unionism was not a sentiment shared by the majority at this date. Lincoln was right to tread with caution.[9]

This remark is indicative of a major development on the northern side in the crisis. The longer it went on, the less inclined was Lincoln to compromise. He still hoped to gain the open

8. Kenneth M. Stampp, *Indiana Politics during the Civil War* (Bloomington: Indiana UP, 1949, 1978), pp. 50–9.

9. Willard L. King, *Lincoln's Manager: David Davis* (Cambridge, MA: Harvard UP, 1960), p. 168; Baringer, *A House Dividing*, pp. 109–10; Potter, *Lincoln and his Party in the Secession Crisis*, pp. 147–8; Daniel W. Crofts, *Reluctant Confederates: Upper South Unionists and the Secession Crisis* (Chapel Hill, NC: University of North Carolina Press, 1989), p. 134.

support of men who had proved enthusiastic for Douglas and Bell, but whatever the press of everyday manoeuvring, he would not compromise the basic tenets of Republicanism. In December 1860 he issued an invitation to Thurlow Weed, as Seward's emissary, to visit him in Springfield. Seward was anxious to know the policy of the president-elect, because if he joined his cabinet and found that he disapproved of the policy, he would have lost his freedom of action as an influential member of the Senate. Weed himself favoured territorial compromise; Seward was more equivocal, but would latch on to this if it offered a viable solution to the crisis. Weed took back to New York three resolutions which encapsulated the president-elect's views at this stage; that the Fugitive Slave Act should be enforced; that all state laws inconsistent with those of Congress should be repealed; 'That the Federal Union must be preserved'. He made no mention of territorial compromise.[10]

During his talks with Weed (and let it be remembered that Weed was only one of a host of visitors including David Wilmot), Lincoln heard a lot of criticism and ridicule of Seward's rivals for possible cabinet positions. The final list of names included, Salmon P. Chase, Gideon Welles, Simon Cameron and Montgomery Blair from the defecting wing of the Democratic Party, with three Whigs, Seward, Bates and one other – possibly a southerner. Weed announced that he could count four Democrats but only three former Whigs. The balance of patronage was always uppermost in his thoughts. 'You seem to forget', Lincoln reminded him, 'that I expect to be there; and counting me as one, you see how nicely the cabinet would be balanced and ballasted', and as for Simon Cameron, he was 'not Democrat enough to hurt him' – and the same could also be said of Salmon P. Chase. But Weed's comment is interesting in revealing the preoccupation of powerful agents within the Republican Party with themselves and their own views. This had the unfortunate effect of writing out the leading actor from the script. Yet Lincoln had already asserted leadership and control over the cabinet-making process; but he did this not by striking attitudes and revelling in bombast but by giving the impression to the various warring factions that he was taking *them* into his confidence. He then reduced the more exposed issues by some judicious refining of the language employed. It took a man like Lincoln, a politician who had never

10. Potter, *Lincoln and his Party in the Secession Crisis,* pp. 164–70; Baringer, *A House Dividing*, pp. 117–20; Van Deusen, *Seward*, pp. 240–2. These ideas were incorporated into the first inaugural.

held an executive office of any kind, to teach the Republican Party, whose short life had been spent in passionate and perpetual opposition, the disciplines of government.[11]

Yet the illusion persisted, perhaps in spite of rather than because of Lincoln's style, that one figure would be 'premier' in the new Administration. This phrase had been banded about in the Buchanan Administration but had no substance. The jockeying for position around Lincoln was so fevered because the various groups thought that they could capture this position, and enthrone a kind of surrogate president. Although Joshua Leavitt, an ally of Chase, thought that Seward's seniority and 'age entitles him to his choice', Chase's other allies thought that 'the post of 'Premier' can be secured' for him if he would allow the effort to be made.[12] Chase at first declined the post offered to him of Secretary of the Treasury. Simon Cameron wanted this position; Thurlow Weed wanted to keep Chase out, because as Treasury Secretary, he would control patronage in New York. Neither Chase nor the Blairs were very keen on being placed subordinate in the cabinet to Seward as 'premier'.[13] Such selfish wrangling, which drew much critical comment both from contemporaries and modern historians,[14] should be set against the unprecedented crisis and the outbreak of panic on the New York money market which brought calls for an appeasement of the South. Such agitation left Lincoln unmoved, and again he brought his speeches to his correspondents' attention.

Then in December 1860, Lincoln sent Weed, doubtless so he could pass it on to Seward, a forthright statement of his policy. Lincoln made no concession on the territorial question on which Weed had urged the president-elect to give ground. It was an issue that Weed did not think worth the life of a single New York dragoon. On the contrary, Lincoln now made it quite clear that

> I will be inflexible on the territorial question; that I probably think either the Missouri Line extended, or Douglas's and Eli Thayer's

11.　Baringer, *A House Dividing*, pp. 121–2; Roy F. Nichols, *The Stakes of Power, 1845–1877* (London: Macmillan, 1965), pp. 92–3; Crofts, *Reluctant Confederates*, p. 246.

12.　In November 1860 Chase expressed a commonly held view: 'Would to Heaven we had a President equal to the emergency. Imbecility, now, works as treason' (quoted in Baringer, *A House Dividing*, p. 66). Chase could never bring himself to consider Lincoln a candidate of stature worthy of respect. See Frederick J. Blue, *Salmon P. Chase: A Life in Politics* (Kent, OH: Kent State UP, 1987), p. 214.

13.　Van Deusen, *Seward*, pp. 239–40.

14.　For example, Stampp, *Indiana Politics during the Civil War*, p. 49.

popular sovereignty, would lose us everything we gained by the election; that filibustering for all south of us, and making slave States of it would follow, in spite of us, under either plan.

Also that I probably think all opposition, real and apparent, to the fugitive-slave [clause] of the Constitution ought to be withdrawn.

Lincoln had referred to this latter requirement in the three resolutions that he handed to Weed when he left Springfield. As to the so-called 'right' of secession, Lincoln claimed that 'no State can in any way lawfully get out of the Union without the consent of the others; and that it is the duty of the President and other Government functionaries to run the machine as it is'.[15] Lincoln also began to study Andrew Jackson's edict, the 'Proclamation to the People of South Carolina', which had been promulgated almost thirty years before.[16] In conversation with some Kentucky unionists, Lincoln made some shrewd observations on the differences in the southern position over those thirty years. Whereas in 1832 'the South made a special complaint against a law of recent origin. Now they had no new law, or new interpretation of old law to complain of'. Lincoln apparently remained 'serene and good natured' throughout this interview, but it was clear that underneath this facade was a resolute and steely heart, one which deplored 'the naked desire to get out of the Union' which underlay the wholly 'false' secession crisis. Certainly, he was successful at conveying an air of calm amidst overwhelming waves of southern hysteria. And, like other Republican leaders, he was prone to treat this as bluster, and he expected that the secessionists would give ground and then collapse if the new Administration refrained from making concessions.[17]

Thus by December 1860 Lincoln still had no cabinet and though his views were forming on how to treat the South these were not articulated except to a number of individuals. In a sense they had already formed. Lincoln remained inflexible on the Chicago platform and the non-extension of slavery. By that date, Lincoln had drawn up a list of cabinet members and this had resisted the importunate inspection of the leaders of a number of pressure groups. Lincoln had changed his mind as to the

15. Quoted in John G. Nicolay and John Hay, *Abraham Lincoln: A History* (New York: Century, 1890), III, p. 253. Here Lincoln was more closely aligned with Thaddeus Stevens, Sumner and Chase, than with Seward and Weed. His conservatism can be exaggerated. See Blue, *Chase*, p. 135.

16. For this Proclamation, see above, pp. 58–60.

17. Baringer, *A House Dividing*, pp. 51–2, 57, 62.

desirability of keeping Seward out of the cabinet, probably reflecting that it was more advantageous to have him inside the executive branch rather than outside of it, intriguing and doubtless criticizing with magisterial senatorial authority. Thus he had decided on Seward (State), Chase (Treasury), Bates (Attorney-General), Welles (Navy), Smith (Interior) and Blair (Postmaster-General); at a later date, and somewhat reluctantly, the Pennsylvania debt was discharged, by allowing Simon Cameron (War) to take up a portfolio. Lincoln took the audacious step of filling the cabinet either with those who had been his rivals for the nomination, or who had been actively involved in securing it for him – men, in short, who did not need encouragement to take a lofty view of their accomplishments by comparison with his.

Shortly after Lincoln's arrival in Washington, Seward and his supporters attempted to seize control of the cabinet and displace the three former Democrats, Chase, Blair and Welles. Seward and Chase were rivals for both the vaunted position of 'premier' and for the patronage of the state of New York; Lincoln's own relations with Chase were personally very tense; there was little love lost there. Seward sought to replace them with C. F. Adams, Henry Winter Davis and a former Whig senator from North Carolina, George E. Badger. Clearly, if this coup had succeeded the policy of the administration would have followed the path of appeasing the South. It would also have greatly reduced the effectiveness of the Republican Party as a governing party, because it would have alienated the non-Whig elements. It was also symptomatic of another emotional reaction to the crisis, namely, that if only *one* particular path of action was adopted (usually to do with appointments), then the whole problem would pass. If only Lincoln would take my advice on forming the cabinet, was a repeated cry, if only Lincoln would appoint Crittenden to the Supreme Court, and so forth. There was a general reluctance to make a clear-cut choice between not using force, and using force, and instead a faith was evinced that some magic formula could be alighted on to spirit away all unpleasant difficulties.

But Lincoln was utterly determined that attempts by one or other group to seize control of the cabinet should be thwarted. Or, as he put it, 'I can't afford to let Seward take the first trick'. He hinted mischievously that he might appoint William M. Drayton of New Jersey to the State Department while leaving Chase at the Treasury. This provoked Seward to move out of the undergrowth. He threatened to resign unless Chase was removed from the cabinet list, and did so, overplaying his hand. Leaks that Seward had actually resigned began to appear in the newspapers, and with them the danger that Seward would lose the New York patronage to Chase, with severe implications for his re-election as a senator. With Seward effectively prostrate over a barrel, Lincoln requested him to 'countermand the withdrawal', which Seward did hurriedly but good naturedly after the inauguration ceremony was over. Here was clear evidence that the will of the chief executive could not be flouted with impunity and that Lincoln was determined to maintain cabinet unity during the secession crisis. Only in this way could he secure his northern power base and develop a robust policy towards the South.[18]

The president-elect's resolution, however, remained concealed. Indeed for the three months prior to Lincoln's inauguration, the activities of Senator Seward were to dominate public discussion of these vexed issues. Seward's policy was based on four premises: first, that the South should be conciliated without abandoning Republican principles – this would prove an intractable formula, for it indicated a desire for the ultimate extinction of slavery which agitated southern nerves; secondly, that Lincoln's three propositions as handed to Weed should be at the forefront of policy; thirdly, that secessionists were impulsive hotheads whose ardour would soon cool once the enormity of their action became obvious, cooler and more restrained counsels would come to the fore and the secessionist thunder clouds would dissipate as rapidly as they had formed; finally, a core of southern Unionism remained that would reassert itself when (and if) conditions were right. By 12 January 1861 these general principles assumed a more concrete form. Northern personal liberty laws would have to be weakened to accommodate southern fears; a constitutional amendment was necessary to ensure that no power could interfere with slavery in the states (Lincoln was prepared to concede this); and finally, New Mexico and Arizona should be admitted as slave states. This sounded well in theory, but was it practicable? Could it be passed? Would it enjoy unanimous *Republican* support, and if this could not be secured, would the passage of such legislation redound to the credit of the governing party? On these three counts Seward's policy does not carry conviction. But it overlooked

18. Baringer, *A House Dividing*, pp. 326–9; Nicolay and Hay, *Lincoln*, III, pp. 170–1; Potter, *Lincoln and his Party*, 21, 35–6, 57, 141–2, 224, 237, 245; Crofts, *Reluctant Confederates*, pp. 226–9, 290; Crofts reflects the 'magic solution' approach, see pp. 353–5.

the uncomfortable reality, which loomed in an ever more menacing fashion in the months November 1860 to January 1861, that the basic northern and southern positions were irreconcilable. This did *not* make civil war inevitable, but it made compromise on the model of 1850 impossible.[19] But more than that, the policy was based on fallacious notions about southern aspirations. Both Seward and his associate, Charles Francis Adams, in the opinion of the latter's son, 'dwelt in a fool's Paradise. . . . We knew nothing of the South, had no realising sense of the intensity of feeling which there prevailed; we fully believed it would all end in gasconade'.[20] Yet the president-elect himself had once proclaimed, 'The *probability* that we may fail in the struggle *ought not* to deter us from the support of a cause we believe to be just; it *shall not* deter me'.[21] His ingenuity would be put to the test when, only three weeks after his election, he received news of the secession of the Lower South.

As for the man still holding power, historians have agreed, almost unanimously, that President Buchanan was not a man well equipped to deal with a crisis of this magnitude. By this stage of his presidency, a lot of opprobrium had been heaped on his head. Among historians he ranks among the least admired chief executives; in various polls of historians who were asked to list presidents in order of ability and achievement, Buchanan and Pierce are invariably found lurking at the bottom of the roll. Taken in the round, Buchanan was probably more sinned against than sinning. Peter Parish is surely right in suggesting that he deserves less censure for the conduct of the last days of his presidency than he does for earlier blunders, for example over Lecompton. Buchanan had a proud record of reconciliation and negotiation to his credit; he had been predicting a sectional crisis for thirty years, warning against the consequences of northern hostility to slavery.[22] He also brought to the crisis a measure of

19. David Donald, *Charles Sumner and the Coming of the Civil War* (New York: Alfred A. Knopf, 1965), p. 372; Bruce Collins, *The Origins of America's Civil War* (London: Edward Arnold, 1981), pp. 138–40.

20. Charles Francis Adams, Jr, *An Autobiography, 1835–1915* (New York: Chelsea House, 1974, 1983), pp. 69–70; Potter, *Lincoln and his Party in the Secession Crisis*, p. 80, quotes this extract in full as evidence of 'Republican short-sightedness', though he assumes this to be a northern monopoly when it was more evident in the South.

21. Quoted in Edmund Wilson, *Patriotic Gore: Studies in the Literature of the American Civil War* (New York: Oxford UP), p. 108.

22. For Buchanan, see James G. Randall and David Donald, *The Civil War and Reconstruction*, 2nd edn (Boston, MA: D. C. Heath, 1969), pp. 142–3; Avery O. Craven, *The Coming of the Civil War*, 2nd rev. edn (Chicago UP, 1957), pp. 429–30; Peter J. Parish, *The American Civil War* (London: Eyre & Spottiswoode, 1975), pp.

administrative skill and political insight, and of course four precious years' experience as chief executive; he was certainly not overawed by his cabinet.[23] Yet the nature of his early predictions of sectional strife provides the vital clue for his eventual failure. He put the secessionist crisis down entirely to northern anti-slavery agitation; by his account the South was blameless. He had no conception that so much of the northern annoyance with the South was provoked by the inflammatory language so hysterically and dogmatically expressed by southern spokesmen.[24]

In his annual message to Congress in December 1860, Buchanan argued that all that was necessary to maintain sectional peace, 'and all for which the slave States had ever contended, is to be let alone and permitted to manage their domestic institutions in their own way'. But it was not so simple, and the maintenance of the peculiar institution demanded that slave states exert powers over the citizens of free states. He viewed the recalcitrance of some northern states over enforcing the Fugitive Slave Act as unconstitutional. Liberty laws – these 'obnoxious enactments' – were the root cause of so much discord. Thus if the aggrieved states had exhausted 'all peaceful and constitutional means to obtain redress' they were justified in employing 'revolutionary resistance' to the Federal government. Buchanan, in an adroit circumlocution, then appeared to curry favour with secessionists by appearing to justify secession *if* it took the form of a revolutionary measure to overcome oppression rather than a valid constitutional mechanism open to all states when they chose to use it. Such an approach could hardly hearten southern unionists and it annoyed northerners who could notch up yet another example of the malign influence of the slave power over the Federal government.[25]

71–2; Elbert B. Smith, *The Presidency of James Buchanan* (Lawrence, KS: University Press of Kansas, 1975, 1988), p. 143; compare this with Elbert B. Smith, *The Death of Slavery: The Limited States, 1831–65* (Chicago UP, 1967) p. 169.

23. Roy F. Nichols, *The Disruption of American Democracy* (New York: Macmillan, 1948), pp. 76–8; Allan Nevins, *The Emergence of Lincoln*, II (New York: Scribner's, 1947), p. 342.

24. Smith, *Buchanan*, p. 148; see above, pp. 95–7.

25. Smith, *Buchanan*, pp. 149–51.

Southern secession: the first phase

The secession of South Carolina brought to the surface the festering sore of southern separatism. Because of an outbreak of small pox in Columbia, the state capital, the ordnance of secession was passed unanimously in Charleston on 20 December. This unilateral and precipitate act confirmed that city's (somewhat undeserved) reputation as the raging source of secessionist fever. This move was to launch a crisis that would last for the next five or six months. The phenomenon of secession needs to be studied generally, drawing connections between states and tracing oscillations within the secessionist movement. These events should not be allotted to compartments. Yet there has been a tendency by historians to ascribe secession to 'peace' and examine it in terms of politics, which are the exclusive preserve of the 'political historian'. Conversely, when treating events after April 1861, arbitrary divisions between 'peace' and 'war' (which is where the military historian takes over) are of little value. The secession movement was inextricably linked with preparations to use force, and it cannot be adequately understood purely in political terms. Thus we must perceive this whole crisis as one period of political upheaval during which at one point organized violence broke out. The secession crisis continued after the firing of the first shots. If we consider these general trends, and the failures of secession as well as its successes, then three distinct waves of secession may be detected, exhibiting various degrees of enthusiasm for the secessionist cause – ardour diminishing the further the cause moved away from its viral focus in the Deep South. The first occurs from December 1860 to March 1861 and sweeps South Carolina, Georgia, Alabama, Mississippi, Louisiana, Florida and Texas. The second wave occurs after the *casus belli* at Fort Sumter in the second week of April 1861 and represents a reaction to the 'coercion' of the slave states. It includes the most populous, wealthy and industrially advanced southern states, Virginia and Tennessee, as well as North Carolina and Arkansas. Without these states the infant Confederacy would have had little hope of creating a viable national unit.

The third stage occurs as a direct result of Lincoln's call in April 1861 for 75,000 volunteers to put down unlawful combinations, and involves insurrection and controversy in Missouri, Kentucky, Maryland and Delaware. Secessionist progress in these states is halted and crushed by the use of federal military power. Indeed, secessionist progress is reversed; the Confederate tide is turned back by the rapid occupation of the non-slaveholding counties of western Virginia in June 1861. Their representatives, meeting at Wheeling, had announced their desire to 'secede' from the rebellious state of Virginia. Military forces were marched quickly into these counties to protect citizens loyal to the Union (West Virginia became a separate state of the Union in 1863). A similar move into the loyal Unionist counties of eastern Tennessee was continually urged on his military commanders by President Lincoln, though it was not successfully mounted until December 1863. Whatever the strength of the legal or constitutional arguments, ultimately these were of secondary importance. The eventual success or failure of their revolutionary movement depended entirely on the ability of the secessionists to bring *force* to bear to extend or protect their territories from the armed forces of the Federal government in Washington, and correspondingly, on the capacity and the will of the federal authorities to use armed force to stamp secession out. It is no coincidence that secession was strongest in those areas far distant from the District of Columbia, and least successful in those states contiguous to it, notably in Maryland, or in areas, such as Missouri, where federal military power was partly mobilized. The political and constitutional factors obviously have influence (especially in providing a pretext for action), but it cannot be emphasized too strongly that secession was a revolutionary movement and ultimately rested on the sanction of force. It is striking how these important features of the crisis are frequently overlooked in accounts of the secession crisis, which tend to focus on its political or constitutional nature.[26]

Of course, this should not be overlooked either, because the political and constitutional issues provided the motivation for the precipitating the crisis in the first place. It is perhaps convenient at this point to summarize the issues that have emerged in the previous chapters. The secessionists held that any power that was *delegated* to the central authorities was bound to increase. To provide a sturdy hedge against such a development, they argued that it was necessary to provide statutory protection for property rights. Slavery had preceded the drafting of the constitution and

26. Allan Nevins, *The War for the Union*, I, *The Improvised War* (New York: Scribner's, 1959), pp. 140–4.

safeguarding its expansion in the years 1820–60 should become the major priority. Such a rectification would further nurture the peculiar institution within the Union, not least in the territories. Republican critics of the resurgent 'slave power' held that the territories were the common possession of the United States, not of individual sovereign states. Both sides fought this constitutional battle, soon to be transferred to the battlefield, within Congress. Both sides supported congressional intervention in this matter. The South demanded congressional protection for slavery; the North demanded congressional legislation to restrict slavery to its current limits within the slave states. Few, mainly Radical Republicans, objected to the sanction of congressional protection being extended to slavery within the slave states; very few were prepared to see such protection cloak slavery in the territories. Moderate northern Republicans and some Democrats would not acknowledge that slavery was founded on the common law; they refused to countenance establishing it by statute. Hence the South's fervent denunciation of Douglas because popular sovereignty did away with the need for a common foundation of statutory regulation.

The major change during the 1850s was the attempt to coordinate southern action in pursuit of their objectives. The Memminger Resolutions passed by the South Carolina legislature in 1859 called for a southern convention to defend southern interests. Increasingly strident secessionist voices based their appeal on several arguments. The first claimed that the North was motivated by a passionate hatred of the southern people (indicated by their willingness to unleash servile war). Secondly, its proponents argued that secession should be regarded as an *alternative* to civil war, or a servile revolt provoked by northern controversialists. Thirdly, they claimed their approach was fundamentally defensive. They were protecting themselves, not attacking others. James M. McPherson calls this 'pre-emptive counter-revolution'. Many wars have been sparked off by both sides claiming that they were acting defensively. A defensive action confronting another defensive move, in an atmosphere of intense mutual suspicion, however, is sufficient to cause a war. Two defensive moves may amount to an offensive in the eyes of one (or both) parties. Defensive insecurities accounted for the fears harboured by many secessionists that non-slaveholders would not stand by a united South; such divisions would provoke serious strife and perhaps, in a confrontation with the North, restrict civil commotion to the southern states, greatly to the detriment of the peculiar institution. Hence, too, a desire to take the struggle to the enemy, thus concealing potential southern divisions. This might explain a reluctance to accept compromises – even take heed of blandishments to consider offers of constitutional amendments to protect slavery in the states. The North could not be trusted; compromise solutions might be a ploy to stir up disaffection and incipient Unionism in the South. Here such fears were more than justified. Almost all the members of the Lincoln Administration who counselled caution and conciliation argued that Unionism in the seceded states would revive and overwhelm secession.[27]

Of course, it was clear by December 1860 that aside from Yancey, Senator Hammond and the younger 'fire-eaters', there was a wide spread of opinion on how the South should achieve its objectives, and beyond the 'defence of southern rights', what those objectives involved. Should they be attained within or outside the Union? Southerners who opposed unilateral, individual state secession were termed 'co-operationists'. They were essentially an indistinct group, and any political movement has difficulty rousing followers if its appeal is negative or blurred. Unlike secessionists they desired to follow up offers of compromise, but their ultimate goals were by no means agreed. Some southern Whigs, for instance, acknowledged the need to discuss further southern co-operation; others seemed to accept the logic of separatism; an influential group actively spoke out against secession, and expressed great faith in the political value for the South of pursuing their constitutional rights within the Union. They believed that the majority of northern leaders would respect these rights. Some others called for the meeting of a constitutional convention; the proposals emanating from this should be dispatched to the governors of all the northern states; if these were rejected then the South, having exhausted the constitutional process, had the moral right to secede. A further group was even more cautious. They preached prudence and were prepared to wait until the new Republican Administration committed some bellicose and outrageous act that would justify war of some kind. The only problem with this prognosis is that caution was not a striking facet of southern statecraft. At any rate, all these diverse

27. Dwight, L. Dumond, *The Secession Movement, 1860–1861* (New York: Macmillan, 1931), pp. 3–6, 8–19, 21, 26–8, 30, 107–19; e.g. Van Deusen, *Seward*, p. 247; James M. McPherson, *Battle Cry of Freedom: The Civil War Era* (New York: Oxford UP, 1988), ch. 8.

groups were united in opposing impulsive secession by individual states without an agreed structure of cooperation before withdrawal from the Union. Unionist caution was strongest in the Upper South, especially in Tennessee and Virginia, because though they might dread slave emancipation, politicians from these states feared rightly that they would suffer most from the ravages of war in their reluctant role as strategic bulwarks of the Deep South. Elections called in February 1861 resulted in overwhelming defeats for secession in these two states and in North Carolina.[28]

Secessionists, needless to say, defended the right of *peaceable secession*. Governor Joseph E. Brown was especially voluble on this point. But it is one thing to assert such a right, quite another to carry it out if it is unacknowledged by the side who must acquiesce in the act of secession. The likelihood of war, and the southern need to fight to defend their independence, was an omnipresent feature of the frantic discussion of secessionist rights. This raises the major problem of discerning the kind of interest that secession was designed to protect; the reasons behind the South's willingness to fight. Although there were very real differences of a political nature between the North and South, the cultural divergences have been exaggerated. It is striking when comparing American commotions in the mid-nineteenth century, with European upheavals of about the same date, in Italy, Hungary, Poland and in Ireland, all asserting cultural, nationalistic, and separatist claims, the issues agitating North and South revolved around slavery and a threatened social system rather than cultural oppression. And, moreover, how extreme emotions were so rapidly engaged to react to enormities of a very mild kind, especially in connection with hypothetical, conditional threats. The power of the Federal government was conspicuous by its absence in the slave states. The South was not persecuted, either politically or culturally. Southern schools were not being closed because they taught a different language, cultural values or a separate history; on the contrary, they gloried in the same triumphs as the North. Southern students, exclaiming a love of their country, were not prosecuted by vicious judges and officious police; on the contrary, the Supreme Court was consistently pro-southern. Southern middle-class men and women did not cower before an alien

28. Dumond, *Secession Movement*, pp. 119–25; Crofts, *Reluctant Confederates*, pp. 149, 164–94.

military presence – although they were to bring military occupation on themselves in a very mild and limited form after 1865. In short, the South lacked any coherent sense of national identity, based on ethnic convergence, cultural tradition and political roots *vis-à-vis* the North. This may help to explain the vigour and exaggeration of the language used by southern spokesmen who posited some kind of cultural conflict by 1860 which served as the basis for a broader life and death political struggle. 'I believe that the northern people hate the South worse than the English people hated France; and I can tell my brethren over there [on the Republican side]', warned Senator Iverson of Georgia in December 1860, 'that there is no love lost upon the part of the South'. Jefferson Davis tried to give the South a feeling of identity in his inaugural, with talk of an 'agricultural people' and 'homogeneity'. But a North American example reveals even more starkly how shallow these claims were. If southern appeals to separate nationhood are set beside those of the *Québecois* in Canada, they look like hyperbole.[29]

If secessionist action, then, provoked so much hyperbole, can we identify any rational purpose for secession? Even if secession ordinances were advocated by foolish leaders and supported by an ignorant electorate, whose fears had been raised to fever pitch by rabble-rousing, we can still discern the influence of the political and social factor that unquestionably differentiates the South from the North, chattel slavery. If the defence of slavery – indeed its further nourishment – was the prime component of secessionist ideology, then clearly political action which advanced secession can be justified in rational terms by the extent to which slavery was protected by separatist action. Secession can be regarded as an act of self-preservation under certain circumstances. In the words of Eugene D. Genovese, 'the slaveholders recognized in other than an abstract way their existence as a ruling class and as self-appointed guardians of a way of life'. They believed their dominance was being challenged and they moved dramatically to reassert their hegemony; to preserve that way of life, the economic structure that sustained it, and the system of race relations that bound it together.

Such an analysis has much to commend it, but to borrow one of Professor Genovese's terms, we cannot, and should not, consider

29. Quoted in Kenneth M. Stampp, *And the War Came: The North and the Secession Crisis, 1860–1861* (Baton Rouge: Louisiana State UP, 1950), p. 1.

secession in 'an abstract way'. Whatever the professed intentions of
the secessionist leaders, they were undertaking a political act, not
arguing a legal brief, and this political act carried with it the
strong risk of civil war. Indeed, given the manner in which they
comported themselves, whether this was true or not in the abstract
is irrelevant, *the manner in which they pursued secession unavoidably led
to civil war.* War of any kind was fatal to the health and stability of
plantation slavery. Acts of secession, therefore, which were
designed not to avoid war were suicidal. Thus, however much we
may judge the act of secession in rational terms, it was justified
and carried out in a wholly headstrong, short-sighted, irrational
and self-defeating manner.[30]

The 'revolutionary' character of secession has some bearing on
this matter. Secession was revolutionary only in a political sense. It
sought to drastically reorder the governmental arrangements of
the slave states and overthrow by force if necessary the existing
structure of government. It was certainly a rebellion in these
terms. But the object of this action was to conserve and further
the existing social and economic system of the southern states, not
to alter it. It was justified by reference to the defence of
'community'. Those who seek to arrest the momentum of such a
political movement, even when the social upheaval envisaged was
minimal, need to argue a cogent case and do so convincingly. The
American 'Tories' during the Revolution, despite their numbers,
failed to halt the revolutionary fervour that led to the break with
Great Britain in 1775–76. The 'co-operationists', especially in the
Deep South, were similarly stymied because they were divided in
their aims and interests. 'Those who favour moderation are
branded as cowards or traitors', complained the Whig moderate,
Alexander H. Stephens. He believed that Providence had frowned
on the co-operationist cause. On the day Georgia voted for the
setting up a secessionist convention, he believed a rain storm had
cost them 10,000 votes.[31] But whatever the exigencies of fate,
whose importance can never be underrated, surely the most
important factor in sustaining secessionist fever in all the states of
the Deep South, and not just in Georgia, was the inability of the
co-operationists to agree on a consistent programme and
communicate it effectively. They muttered vague pleas but came

30. Eugene D. Genovese, *The World the Slaveholders Made* (New York: Pantheon,
1969), pp. 94–5.

31. Michael P. Johnson, *Toward a Patriarchal Republic: The Secession of Georgia*
(Baton Rouge: Louisiana State UP, 1977), pp. 6, 24–5.

up with nothing sufficiently appealing which would provide a viable, alternative programme to secession; perhaps given the prevailing mood such a programme was a seductive but an unattainable mirage. The only question on which the co-operationists could agree was their opposition to the unilateral, individual secession of states; the dangers of this did not loom large in the thoughts of secessionist sympathizers. And the majorities secessionists achieved in the votes cast for establishing secession conventions left their critics little to denounce but the procedure used to elect them – hardly an exciting line of attack. The secessionists urged action; many agreed that action was above all things required, but action in pursuit of what?[32]

The secession movement

The object of secession was two-fold: to remove the external threat to slavery and secure the conservative revolution at home by conciliating slaveholders with non-slaveholders. In addition, there were less concrete issues, a passion to avenge 'insults', avoid 'humiliation', assert 'manliness' and defend 'honour'; the importance of these fiery emotions should not be underestimated. A conciliation of these diverse aims was to be achieved by elevating the Constitution, suitably amended, and venerated by most southerners like a Greek Orthodox icon. The most important part of this process was the expropriation and reinterpretation of the symbols of the American Revolution in favour of liberty based on enslavement. George Washington and the southern Founding Fathers, the Declaration of Independence, and the Constitution itself, 'the precious heritage of 1776', were cast in a new light. It is indicative of the weakness of secessionist ideology in particular, and southern national identity in general, that they were forced to seize the national symbols of the nation-state from which they were seceding and which they were prepared, if necessary, to fight. Secessionists perhaps realized that an appeal based exclusively on the defence of slavery was in itself insufficient to carry the revolutionary weight they were forcing it to carry. It had to be developed in two ways. First, the essentially conservative drift of southern thought had bequeathed the notion that, by 1861, the

32. Dumond, *Secession Movement*, pp. 144–51; Johnson, *Patriarchal Republic*, pp. 26–7; Crofts, *Reluctant Confederates*, pp. 344–5.

American system of government was 'too democratic'. Southern critics focused on the evils of the spoils system, which in truth agitated many Americans from all parts of the country. The second party system had thus failed to provide strong and incorruptible government. It was too prone to interfere in matters detrimental to the South's interests. Secondly, by 1860–61 the South had persuaded itself that it was 'losing' the constitutional struggle over slavery. If nothing was done to reverse this position, then future dangers would multiply and overwhelm the peculiar institution. In the secessionist argument, the South must face up to Republican 'tyranny' which was characterized by an irrational fear and ignorance of slavery. Slavery was actually 'benign', and the slaves themselves happy and contented. This was a terribly weak argument, because southern slaveholders were so sensitive to the mildest complaints about their treatment of slaves, and dreaded servile revolt.

Thus expropriation of the rhetoric and symbols of the American Revolution concealed the weaknesses and contradictions of the southern position under a warmly glowing, hazy and sentimental veneer. The 'Black' Republicans could be anathematized as resembling 'George III' and British 'tyranny'; secessionist, and later Confederate leaders, could be held up as the true servants of the revolutionary heritage. Most of the revolutionary leaders, after all, had been southerners and slaveholders. The repeated emphasis in secessionist rhetoric was on unity, harmony, unanimity, and the spurning of party spirit. 'Our whole social system is one of perfect homogeneity of interest, where every class of society is interested in sustaining the interest of every other class', claimed Governor Brown in November 1861. But if it was so unified, so blessed in thoughtful consideration for the interests of others, why was it so urgent to take dramatic action? There was one unfortunate, indeed catastrophic, consequence of giving revolutionary symbols such a prominence in secessionist rhetoric. Because the Revolutionary War was viewed in sentimental terms, repeating the experience of a Second Revolutionary War was viewed with equanimity, if not downright enthusiasm. Southern leaders failed to give priority to avoiding war; secession and the need to fight were increasingly considered as interchangeable aspects of the struggle for independence (very few grasped the reality that they would need to wage a protracted conflict). Southern leaders would prevail as George Washington had done before them. No further thought needed be given to the problem. But a lot more thought was needed, and a great deal less complaisance.[33]

It was a measure of the true insecurity felt by the champions of the South's peculiar institution that they feared the spread of the Republican Party into their stable and benign homeland. It could be nourished by use of the patronage power. As always, the secessionists demanded nothing less than absolute, unconditional obedience to their dictates. Use of presidential patronage might signal the beginnings of the blockade of slavery which so alarmed secessionist propagandists, with the South 'under siege' from 'abolitionists' outside. Yet they did not make much of this argument. The reason was that some prominent southern spokesmen were of the view that 'slavery [was] much more secure in the Union than out of it'.[34] Had this theme been exposed more fully the basic fallacy of 'peaceable secession' might have been brutally exposed (though one suspects that the argument had much to commend it in hindsight). But this is not to suggest that it would have offered the co-operationists an alternative programme to rapid and immediate secession. In a bellicose atmosphere, pleas for peace sound more like craven submission than sound sense.

An important influence shaping the fevered and panicky atmosphere was the southern press. The influence of press reporting is a perennial problem: to what extent do the opinions of newspaper editors directly influence the views of their readers? Or is the opposite true? Do newspaper editors merely reflect the prejudices and preferences of public opinion? The answer is probably a compound of the two, in inexact and oscillating quantities. Nonetheless, press opinion can decisively shape the atmosphere is which pressing decisions are taken, and the various alternatives discussed. Mere repetition of a point of view however absurd can create its own reality. Outright secessionist newspapers, notably in the Lower South, accepted without question that the election of a Republican president justified secession. 'For our part', affirmed one, 'we would prefer to strike the blow this very hour than to wait for the morrow'.[35]

---

33. Emory M. Thomas, *The Confederacy as a Revolutionary Experience* (Englewood Cliffs, NJ: Prentice-Hall, 1971); Johnson, *Patriarchal Republic*, pp. 28–30, 32–5, 37–8, 40–1; Crofts, *Reluctant Confederates*, pp. 95–9.

34. Quoted in Johnson, *Patriarchal Republic*, p. 45.

35. Donald E. Reynolds, *Editors Make War: Southern Newspapers in the Secession Crisis* (Nashville, TN: Vanderbilt UP, 1966, 1970), pp. 14–16.

Other newspapers were less strident. They dedicated themselves to helping the formation of a coordinated southern action which would permit secession *at a later date en bloc.* They also dedicated themselves to fostering closer southern economic integration.[36] In any case, the press tended to undermine the cooperation case by indiscriminately linking Republicanism with abolitionism – a pernicious consequence of John Brown's raid.[37] They also inflicted wounds on the co-operationists by branding them as 'submissionists'. There was no heated debate over the merits of secession, only over its timing and the measure of prudence required of southern political leadership. In this sense, the margin of disagreement between southern radicals and their more moderate critics was only one of tone; the divergence of opinion was indeed marginal.[38] Reducing further the space for manoeuvre between these two groups was surely the major contribution of the southern press to the secession crisis. All accounts stress the role played by the newspapers in arousing fear, hatred and suspicion, spurning compromise and creating a combustible atmosphere in which eventually, all southern states accepted the inevitability of war. In short, southern newspapers in general, and not just those tied to secessionist sympathizers (which were few), exerted power and carried awful responsibility. The press was politically dependent and very much a creature of local partisan identities.[39]

But the deep feelings of insecurity reflected in press opinion and which lay at the heart of southern bellicosity, could not be expressed in a political vacuum. Still, the political form they assumed was very odd. The South tilted at windmills. The further its fears wandered from real concrete political issues, assuming only hypothetical form, the firmer these spectres of some future threat loomed in the southern psyche. And these fears seemed to be agitated by constant and remorseless repetition. 'Hear the words which were repeated day after day', one historian has written of the secessionist fervour in South Carolina, 'in

36. Ibid., pp. 17–18, 44, 143–4.
37. Stephen A. Channing, *Crisis of Fear: Secession and South Carolina* (New York: Simon & Schuster, 1970), pp. 77–8, 87–9, 93.
38. Reynolds, *Editors Make War*, pp. 23–7, 127, 131, 136. See also ibid., p. 58 for grotesque racial slurs.
39. Ibid, pp. 116, 142. Reynolds notes (p. 146) that some Whig newspapers thought that Lincoln's image might improve over time once his essential conservatism became obvious, but time was not on their side. See also Bruce Collins, *White Society in the Antebellum South* (London, Longman, 1985).

newspapers, in stump speeches, at Sunday barbecues and Sunday sermons, from soap boxes to pulpits, an unrelenting stream of emotional reinforcement from June to December [1860]'. But what was the threat? At bottom, it was not anxiety over the growing strength of northern economic and industrial power, or the assertion of northern influence in Congress. Secession was another magical formula by which future hold over Negro slaves could be ensured; after its incantation slavery could never be abolished.[40]

In the states of the Deep South the tides of enthusiasm for secession rose to a level which would guarantee the passage of a series of individual state secession ordinances. This was not the ideal way to set up an alternative government to that sitting in Washington DC. It underlines that no coherent programme underpinning the move towards southern independence existed. There was certainly no agreed form on the character of any secessionist government. On the eve of the presidential election, Robert Barnwell Rhett wrote with confidence about the imminent disruption of the Union to Edmund Ruffin. But he stopped short once disunion had been achieved. 'We wait however to give Alabama and Mississippi and Georgia every opportunity to lead'. This remark illustrates the piecemeal and quite unconsolidated approach to secession adopted by the states in the Deep South. Secessionists like Rhett had devoted so much thought to achieving secession from the Union that their thoughts stopped short of considering what would follow the disruption. The Deep South made all the running. Why did they exert such command in the crisis rather than the more populous and slightly more industrialized states of the Upper South?[41]

In South Carolina, Alabama and Georgia were heard the most strident voices, and emotive cries can generate much misdirected activity – 'an irresistible motion towards disunion', as Channing calls it. On receiving news of Lincoln's election, the most senior federal officials in South Carolina resigned their posts, followed by the announcement of Senator Chesnut's resignation from Congress. Then on 9 November followed a meeting in Charleston

40. Channing, *Crisis of Fear*, pp. 213–214, 236–7. In Henry Adams's opinion, 'The Southern secessionists were ... unbalanced in mind – fit for medical treatment, like other victims of hallucination – ... mentally one-sided, ill-balanced and provincial to a degree rarely known'. *The Education of Henry Adams* (New York: Modern Library, 1931), p. 100.
41. Channing, *Crisis of Fear*, p. 246.

in which outraged emotion, exultation and a lack of proportion misdirected logical deduction from a false premise. Charleston's most influential citizens 'in burning phrase, counselled immediate secession, declared the Union was even now dissolved. As they uttered their fierce words, the multitudes rose from their seats, waved their hats in the air, and thundered forth resounding cheers'.[42]

In South Carolina the sense of insecurity – and arguably the distance from reality – was greatest, and the irritation, the mood of discontent, most virulent. It was not that these elements were absent from the Upper South, they were most certainly present, but in the Lower South, and especially in South Carolina, a fatal combination of hysteria and a lurking fear that any loosening of the bonds of slavery would result in a catastrophe, led to a mobilization of public opinion, and a frantic increase in those prepared to take the radical step of leaving the Union.[43] There was also a further, and significant difference between the Lower and Upper South: in the latter secessionist fervour was undermined by the persistence of two-party politics which had disappeared from the Deep South by the mid–1850s. Consequently, voters were distracted from secessionist appeals by inter-party disputes *within* states. Secessionists in South Carolina, Alabama and Mississippi were assured of their headstrong path because of the assurances they received from northern conservatives – and in South Carolina's case, letters – which, in effect, validated their policy with supine assurances that no effort would be made to force the seceded states to return to the Union.[44] States in the Upper South were inclined to follow this powerful lead, if reluctantly and slowly, because they feared that if they remained in the Union they would become a harassed minority at the mercy of northern abolitionists.[45]

How then was this political revolution carried out, involving the manipulation and exploitation of public opinion? First it must be made absolutely clear that the southern states did not behave as a political unit, despite a significant degree of unanimity on the need to defend their common institutions.[46] For example,

42. Quoted in ibid., pp. 250, 261.

43. William L. Barney, *The Secessionist Impulse: Alabama and Mississippi in 1860* (Princeton UP, 1974), pp. 27–9.

44. Channing, *Crisis of Fear*, pp. 268, 274–5.

45. See Dumond, *Secession Movement*, p. 215; Michael F. Holt, *The Political Crisis of the 1850s* (New York: Norton, 1978, 1983), pp. 244–50.

46. Southern historians are prone to blur this point, see Dumond *Secession Movement*, pp. 107, 124, 209–210.

Alexander H. Stephens did not deny that theoretically the South could secede. But he was concerned that the slave states should act in concert and meet in convention to resist any laws hostile to the South's institutions. Such action would also secure much greater bargaining power *vis-à-vis* the northern states. He was not convinced that any unfavourable laws would be forthcoming, mainly because Congress was still controlled by an anti-Lincoln majority. This majority was endangered by rash southern action, as immediate secession would result in the withdrawal of southern congressional representatives. The secessionists, for their part, spurned a convention because it weakened their authority as the revolutionary vanguard. Thus the conventions that convened to take their unprecedented decisions (Florida on 3 January 1861, Mississippi and Alabama on 7 January, Georgia on 16 January, Louisiana on 23 January, and Texas on 28 February) were individual *state* conventions that then took unilateral action. This was their clear aim. In November 1860 in Mississippi at a private meeting of the state's congressional delegation, L. Q. C. Lamar, Jefferson Davis and Brown argued for a joint, coordinated secession to take place immediately after Lincoln's inauguration; they were out-voted by their colleagues, who demanded that separate secession begin immediately. This stress on unilateral action was ironical because frequently secessionists argued in the electoral campaigns waged before the meeting of the state conventions, that their programmes involved southern cooperation. But the states were sovereign, they now argued, and some had to act first to ensure that the others would follow. This contradiction at the heart of the secessionist case – that the unity of the new slaveowning republic should come out of fragmentation – would be fatal to its eventual, admittedly bleak prospects of attaining independence without war.[47]

The secessionist conventions were dominated by men of some means (they were either 'fire-eaters' themselves, or influenced by them) who were politically experienced, and exerted considerable sway over their lesser brethren. The more influential and powerful planters assumed that they were the rightful 'voice' of their people and were generally opposed to putting their decisions, particularly those pertaining to secession, to the test of a referendum. (The secessionists were opposed in principle to these on the grounds

---

47. Ibid., p. 178; Ralph A. Wooster, *The Secession Conventions of the South* (Princeton UP, 1962), pp. 3, 14, 74–5; Barney, *Secessionist Impulse*, pp. 195, 197.

that they would slow down matters that urgently needed to be put to the proof.) There is also, despite some variation between states, a fair measure of uniformity of membership of these conventions. The average age was about 42, usually slightly younger than their co-operationist opponents, with lawyers and farmers as the dominant occupational interests. They were characterized by a passionate desire to defend the *existing status quo*, so that ambitious members of these assemblies could emulate the richest members and rise to the summits of society as they knew it. Representatives of traditionally Democratic counties were secessionist in sympathy, confirming the disruption of that last national organization. Some former Whig counties were inclined towards 'co-operationism', as in Florida, though in Alabama and Louisiana there appeared to be no disagreement between either former Whigs or Democrats over the desirability of secession. All of these groups developed highly tuned techniques in playing on the prejudices of the lower orders, notably the illiterate and dispossessed, who were appalled by the possibility that blacks might be jostling with them for jobs and trades.

One item of evidence that seems to indicate a measure of prudence in an otherwise combustible and impulsive atmosphere, is that areas in Mississippi where the slave population consisted of more than 62 per cent of the total, tended to be far less sympathetic towards secession than those with a population ranging 25–62 per cent. These members may have sensed the danger that secession might represent to existing social and race relations; that the cure might be worse than the disease; that chattel slavery was a delicate organism which should not be tampered with casually. But this would appear to be a minority sentiment, because generally throughout the Lower South, those counties with the largest slave populations were secessionist without reservation.[48]

Neither was secession as popular in Louisiana as in other states of the Deep South. The popular vote for the convention ranged from 20,448 for the immediate secessionists and 17,296 for the co-operationists (which included those who favoured conditional unionism), electing 80 and 44 delegates respectively. The ordinance of secession did not reflect this less than broad endorsement however, being passed 113 to 17, and hailing that

48. Wooster, *Secession Conventions*, pp. 20, 24, 31, 34–5, 42–4, 54–5, 62, 64–5, 78–9, 85, 94–5, 105–7, 110, 112, 113–14, 118–19, 126–7; Johnson, *Patriarchal Republic*, pp. 70–1, 82–3, 110; Barney, *Secessionist Impulse*, pp. 44–6, 88–93.

Louisiana was 'a free, sovereign and independent power'. As with other states, the convention then appointed six delegates to attend a further convention meeting at Montgomery, Alabama, to set up a southern Confederacy. This was done *after* the state had seceded, and not before. The Louisiana convention pursued the commonplace opposition to referenda, delegating to itself all powers vested in the people of the state. A motion in March 1861 urging that the Confederate constitution be put to the people was voted down 74 to 26; the state convention then voted 109 to 7 to ratify this document. Those historians who see in this process a harking back to the authoritarian methods of the Federalist Party would seem to be right.[49]

There was unanimity among the state governments and their supporters, whether former Whig or Democrat, as to the desirability of some form of secessionist activity – only the pace and intensity of this activity spawned dissent. The support of the state governors (as commanders in chief of their various militia and volunteer forces) was of enormous import in generating pro-secessionist sympathy and securing installations vital for self-defence. Texas was the exception to this pattern. Here the administration, led by the redoubtable Governor Sam Houston, adamantly opposed the secessionists. Although Houston was forced to acquiesce in the secession of the state, he refused to swear allegiance to the Confederate States of America. In what amounted to a coup, the secessionist convention declared the office of governor vacant and Houston's election void, and the Lieutenant Governor, Edward Clark, took his place. This was another example of the disruption of democracy itself when it suited the secessionists' interests, a disruption that led Lincoln to argue that the very existence of the democratic process in North America was at stake. Yet, ironically, Texas was the only state in the Deep South that sought popular ratification of the ordinance of secession.[50]

Southern opinion

But how united was the South in this ill-directed stampede to leave the Union? Earlier historians, such as Dwight Dumond, were of

49. Wooster, *Secession Conventions* pp. 101, 104, 111–12; Johnson, *Patriarchal Republic*, p. 168.

50. Wooster, *Secession Conventions*, pp. 115, 121, 135; Barney, *Secessionist Impulse*, pp. 191, 201.

the opinion that the secession of the Lower South was 'not a triumph of one party over another but rather a demonstration that the lower South was finally united'. He reflects in this passage the anti-party stance of so many of the participants in the secession crisis.[51] Congress had made no concession to this haphazard grouping, though it was to consider doing so. The president-elect had said nothing; the incumbent president had signalled that the Federal government would continue to hold such installations as still lay under the flag of the United States. Of the seven states that had seceded, Georgia was the wealthiest and most populous. The separatist movement now led by South Carolina was stronger than the stand made by one lone state in 1832–33, South Carolina herself, in her struggle with the Jackson Administration. But this was not an impressive combination, and perhaps some optimists might have been forgiven for thinking that it might yet come to its senses and return to the Union. It had no agreed policy, no detailed plan of action, no agreed course of action; its very future depended on enticing further states to take the same hurried and uncoordinated action which had characterized the first phase of the secession crisis – hardly a blueprint for orderly, measured and above all, prudent, political action. Unilateral secession had created *anarchy*, those conditions ripe for foreign intervention and war. Yet this Confederate grouping lacked experienced officials and an agreed system of governing; it lacked an army, though many southerners had a high opinion of their martial prowess: one southerner could lick five Yankees (or was it ten?); it lacked a foreign policy or indeed basic contacts with foreign powers – whose attitude indeed would be crucial to the success of this whole experiment in secession. Southern unity was fragmentary and was being hastily assembled, like a pre-fabricated house, as each state seceded, and this process was far from complete. Unity of action was essentially a mask; one slip, one adverse vote, and the 'momentum' working in favour of secessionist fever might have ground to a halt or even gone into reverse. Secession had not been arranged according to any plan, but improvised unilaterally and in great haste.[52]

The wealthier and more advanced states with a putative industrial base held back. The secessionists egged on the Upper

51. Dumond, *Secession Movement*, pp. 209–10, 214.
52. David M. Potter, *The Impending Crisis, 1848–1861*, completed and ed. by Don E. Fehrenbacher (New York: Harper, 1976), p. 500.

South by exhorting it to follow the example of the Lower South. The argument that the South should present a solid front within the Union carried greater weight in Virginia. Here a secession convention was elected on 7 January 1861. The western counties, as already noted, felt that any threat was greatly exaggerated and their first loyalty was to the Union. They were annoyed by decades of under-representation and neglect by the planter interests and were outraged that their loyalties had been trampled on in this high-handed manner. The strength of this feeling undoubtedly swayed opinion in the Tidewater that every effort should be made to seek redress within the Union. This forced the secessionist sympathizers to shift ground and emphasize the impossibility of patching up the Union, as in 1850, and that the forces surging to create a southern Confederacy were at high tide and inexorable. They repeated a noisy chorus of exhortation and nagging. 'For heaven's sake,' one delegate cried, 'give us a little more time – one short day's time at least – to ponder over these great questions, the most important ever presented for the reflection of American freemen'. After the rejection of the Crittenden Compromise[53] on 16 January, ten Virginian congressmen and senators circulated a letter to their constituents, arguing that constitutional redress was now impossible. This act provoked a stinging counter-attack from Unionists, whose voice carried greater authority than in the Lower South. On 4 February in an election for a state convention those advocating immediate secession without referring to the people of Virginia were defeated by 145,697 votes to 45,161. The action of the state convention was thus referred to a popular referendum. Delegates to the convention who supported continued Union amounted to 120 out of a total of 152. The secessionists had appeared to overplay their hand; their cause had received a major setback. Yet this victory was rather more conditional than it appeared. The electors had rejected 'precipitate secession', not secession *per se*, and were in favour of restoring the Union in favour of the South.[54] Yet this vote, and similar defeats in Arkansas, Tennessee (on 9 February, when the people voted against calling a convention 69,675 to 57,798 and secessionist candidates were drubbed by 91,803 to 24,749) and North Carolina (on 28 February when the bill calling for the meeting of a secessionist convention was defeated 47,323 to 46,672 and 78 of

53. See below, pp. 280–1, 285, 287
54. Wooster, *Secession Conventions*, pp. 100, 120, 142; Henry T. Shanks, *The Secession Movement in Virginia, 1847–1861* (New York: AMS Press, 1934, 1971), pp. 125, 128, 137, 141, 148, 152–3, 154.

the 120 delegates were Unionists) stalled the seemingly relentless momentum of secessionist success. So North Carolina voted for delegates but refused to allow them to meet in a convention. Was the first phase of the secession crisis going to be its only phase?[55]

But a number of factors operating in favour of the southern secessionists cannot be ignored. Unlike the rabid revolutionary, the southern secessionists sought to secure, not overthrow, the existing economic, social and race relations of their states. They sought rather to modify the jurisdiction of central authority in relation to the individual states and slavery. The *universal* nature of the ideals of the Declaration of Independence and the Constitution as interpreted by the North, and especially northern liberals, was rejected in favour of a *particularist* interpretation of those documents. The secessionists, therefore, argued that they should take their goods and chattels out of the Union and create a polity that would protect them; their title to their property was unquestioned – here was no revolutionary secessionist movement involving huge sequestration of property; their claim to the federal property within their native states was more questionable. Nonetheless, the southern secessionist case rested ultimately on the charge of discriminatory redistribution. That is to say, northern tariffs drained the South of specie, and northern political movements endangered the very foundations of that wealth and placed in jeopardy the very lives of white southerners by provoking servile war. If necessary, white southerners would be justified in fighting to preserve their unique culture from the depredations of the Yankees.[56]

A persuasive case can be made that southern secession *was* justified. The argument of discriminatory redistribution was made to justify the secession of the United States from the British Empire. Irrespective of the morality of slavery, the South could make the case that like the Thirteen Colonies, the trade policy of the central government was designed to increase its wealth rather than the region from whence it came. But a major difference between the South and the Thirteen Colonies was that the former enjoyed both taxation *and* representation. Still, southern representatives argued that this would be reduced to impotency

55. Dumond, *Secession Movement*, p. 228; Wooster, *Secession Conventions*, pp. 180, 192–3.

56. Allen Buchanan, *Secession: The Morality of Political Divorce from Fort Sumter to Lithuania and Quebec* (Boulder, CO: Westview, 1991), pp. 8, 10, 12, 41, 56, 104–5, has been an invaluable guide here.

because of the steady reduction of the South's influence within the Congress, and especially in the House of Representatives, which had been felt as early as the Missouri Compromise.[57] The strongest argument on the southern side, moreover, was that for a war of independence to be regarded as just it should enjoy *popular support.* That is to say, secessionist leaders must represent those citizens they were presuming to lead. And there can be no doubt that though very few voters in the South would have supported an unconditional, untrammelled call for disunion, public opinion did eventually support withdrawal from the Union. Southern opinion, moreover, did not hesitate to endorse the unconstitutional methods used to strip Governor Sam Houston of Texas of his office and the use of force to overawe persistent Unionists.[58]

These constitutional arguments, however, cannot exist in a political or military vacuum.[59] In the first instance, no states in peacetime in practice form themselves on the basis of company law, governed by limited contracts or limited liability. Secondly, there is no *right* of secession, so that components of states can secede unconditionally and unilaterally when they choose. Various degrees of right may be accorded individual cases. This is merely a restatement of the old Unionist argument that the South was quick enough to support the Federal government and criticize those who disagreed with it, when it *suited* the South. It only flouted the Constitution when it saw electoral shifts moving against slavery. Finally, did the South's cause, or the occasion, warrant the risks, at the very least anarchy, but more likely civil war or subordination to a foreign power, inherent in the great gamble on which it had embarked? In both cases, the answer must be in the negative. Slavery was a morally abhorrent cause, much as southern apologists themselves attempted to conceal its importance in the move to secede from the Union, and apologists for the South abroad connived in this concealment. The North, irrespective of the legal position, could suppress secession as an *act of policy*. The grounds for supporting such a move were strong. The South was to make them stronger.[60]

57. Ibid., pp. 69–70.
58. Michael Walzer, *Just and Unjust Wars: A Moral Argument with Historical Illustrations* (Harmondsworth: Penguin, 1977, 1980), pp. 86–94, 104–8; Martin Ceadel, *Thinking About Peace and War* (Oxford UP, 1987), p. 49. This argument serves also as a justification for foreign intervention on the southern side.
59. Which is the main criticism to be directed at Buchanan's *Secession*
60. Ibid., pp. 36, 99, 158.

Efforts at compromise

All previous crises of the Union had ended with some final effort at compromise which succeeded. Although the state of affairs in the early months of 1861 were much graver than in 1850 or 1820, many hoped and others worked for the imposition at the last minute of a compromise solution which would be acceptable to both parties and avoid the outbreak of civil war. Hopes were raised because the American system of government was adept at resolving conflict; indeed some historians have stressed that a pragmatic spirit bereft of ideological dogmatism constitutes the 'genius' of American politics. That contemporaries expected the forces of compromise to prevail is not surprising, neither is the praise lavished on these efforts by historians, but whether such proposals were workable is quite another matter.[61]

Early attempts at compromise tended to focus around two congressional committees: the Senate Committee of Thirteen and the House Committee of Thirty-Three. All measures designed to solve the secession crisis were put to these two bodies. The Senate Committee of Thirteen simply broke up without agreement. The House Committee of Thirty-Three at least enjoyed a modicum of cooperation among its members. The most promising measure was the Crittenden Compromise reported to the Senate on 18 December 1860. In essence it required the passage of six Constitutional Amendments. The most controversial was that all territory held 'or hereafter acquired' prohibited slavery north of the line 36°30′, and recognized and protected this institution south of it; secondly, that Congress would have no power to abolish slavery in the areas where it already existed; thirdly, this limitation on congressional prerogative applied to the District of Columbia; fourthly, Congress could not interfere with the inter-state slave trade; fifthly, slaveholders were to receive compensation if they were unable to recover their property due to violence; and sixthly, these amendments were perpetual – they could not be modified in any shape or form by later amendments. These six amendments should be accompanied by congressional

---

61. See Daniel J. Boorstin, *The Genius of American Politics* (Chicago UP, 1953). The standard account of compromise efforts, Robert G. Gunderson, *The Old Gentlemen's Convention: The Washington Peace Conference of 1861* (Madison, WI: University of Wisconsin Press, 1961), p. v, dilates on 'the American genius for compromise, for adjustment, and for conciliation'.

resolutions declaring that the Fugitive Slave Law *was* constitutional and that personal liberty laws passed by individual northern states were to be declared null and void. These latter resolutions provoked much harsh comment, though they secured support from the anxious and beleaguered spokesmen of northern business interests.[62]

On 4 February 1861, at the request of the Virginian General Assembly, which gave voice to this widespread hope that the inherent mechanisms working towards compromise would now come into play, 132 representatives of 21 states gathered at Willard's Hotel in Washington DC to seek a solution to the secession crisis. This worked in parallel with the two congressional committees. Forces urging compromise had gathered a head of steam because of the need to keep the Border states quiescent. Crittenden had already advanced his compromise and this would be the focus of discussion at this 'Peace Conference'. The only difficulty with Crittenden's otherwise neat solution – of prohibiting slavery above 36°30′ – was that moderate Republicans, including the president-elect, were adamantly opposed to any further slavery extension, which would be permitted as southerners would be able to take their slaves into the New Mexico territory. Congressman Charles F. Adams, a friend of Seward, urged that New Mexico be allowed to join the Union after a vote by its citizens on the desirability of slavery; that is to say, popular sovereignty would be rekindled in the territories. Most compromise proposals were based on prescriptions that were hardly new. Buchanan had favoured a constitutional amendment, similar to that advocated by Crittenden, which would protect slavery in the areas where it currently existed, or in the areas where it would subsequently spread. But it was overlooked by such enthusiasts that Breckinridge's similar platform in the 1860 election had been very vague, and spoke only in terms of refusing to sanction the eviction of private property from the territories, and even this formula had virtually no northern appeal. To develop it into an amendment which would cloak slavery with moral approval was an impossible task.[63]

Indeed the conference convened in Washington had the air of 'yesterday's men' offering up to urgent problems which they had failed to solve in their own day, advice based on yesteryear's failed

62. Kenneth M. Stampp, *And the War Came*, pp. 129–30; Crofts, *Reluctant Confederates*, pp. 196–213.

63. Smith, *Buchanan*, p. 151; William C. Davis, *Breckinridge: Statesman, Soldier, Symbol* (Baton Rouge: Louisiana State UP, 1977), pp. 231, 234, 264.

solutions. This impression is indicated by the average age of the venerable but admittedly distinguished delegation, chaired by former President John Tyler. Only seven of the delegates were under 40. The remainder had long since said farewell to middle age. Twelve were over 70, thirty-four were sexagenarians, and seventy-four were over 50. Radical and moderate Republicans were opposed to any attempt at divorcing the secession crisis from the passions that had provoked it by examining its ramifications with a presumed air of detachment. 'These venerable old gentlemen are no more fit to be intrusted with . . . guidance than a bull is fitted to keep a china shop,' claimed the *Tribune.* Secessionists dismissed them as rambling old fools. Only conservatives looked to the conference as 'the hope of the century'. The conference was predominately Whig in sentiment and outlook, particularly in the expectation that a balanced, moderate course should prevail. Above all, conservatives denounced demagoguery, and believed that the people would have the sense to spurn crude emotionalism and turn to their experienced, distinguished and patrician, natural leaders. They deprecated 'the perverted mediums of stump speeches, partisan diatribes, [and] buncombe resolutions'.

Delegates who were convinced that all that was needed to solve the crisis was prolonged rational study and a strong dose of common sense were perplexed by the agitated state of the country. 'I cannot comprehend the madness of the times,' Tom Corwin admitted, 'Southern men are theoretically crazy. Extreme northern men are practical fools. The latter are really quite as mad as the former'. Those who called for a 'preventive war' sanguinely believed that 'one campaign in the slave state states would settle the matter'. It might all be over before the autumn: all finished, one claimed, 'before haying time'. Perhaps the deliberations of the peace conference might have compelled respect if contemporaries had enjoyed a more realistic understanding of the nature of the impending civil war. Instead an unthinking, gesture-ridden, extravagant rhetoric prevailed. Lincoln, for instance, 'should maintain the integrity of the Union if it costs enough blood to fill Charleston harbour'. The signs of preparation for war on both sides were unmistakable. Georgia had set aside $1 million for weapons; South Carolina a mere $100,000. Tension had increased in Charleston harbour; the federal garrison had moved from Fort Moultrie to Sumter.[64]

64. For the significance of this and other secessionist attempts to seize federal installations, see below, pp. 313, 335.

Munition shipments heading for southern ports were causing alarm. Even southern states, like North Carolina, which had rejected secessionist blandishments, moved towards a war footing. North Carolina's Governor, John W. Ellis, was convinced that Lincoln would attempt to 'coerce' the seceded states back into the Union. North Carolina must prepare for the contingency. A Military Commission to oversee all martial preparations was set up. The state prepared to organize 20,000 volunteers, and $300,000 was set aside to arm them. The scale of these preparations alarmed Virginia moderates, who feared the country was degenerating into anarchy, a breeding ground for civil war and revolution. 'The desire of some for change,' one observed fearfully, 'the greed of many for excitement, and the longing of more for anarchy and confusion, seemed to have dethroned the reason of men, and left them at the mercy of passion and madness'. The majority of delegates to the Peace Conference were determined to obviate this regrettable release of popular passions. By concerning themselves with this matter, many delegates failed to realize that it was unilateral action by individual states that was the root of anarchy, and thus violence, not movements of popular opinion.[65]

Northern governors, too, were re-examining their military institutions and readying themselves for civil war. The Governors of Maine, New York, Pennsylvania, Massachusetts and Ohio met in New York and signalled their desire to fill any interregnum caused before Lincoln took office by stating their unequivocal intention to see the laws enforced. Governor John A. Andrew examined how to move Massachusetts militia regiments to Washington in the shortest possible time; he needed no encouragement to heed General Winfield Scott's request 'to look up their arms and have them taken care of'. Through the good offices of Senator Seward, Scott urged Governor Morgan of New York to put together 'a force of 5000 to 10,000 men in readiness at 48 or even 24 hours notice'; Seward enjoined that 'no publicity' should be given to this measure. Efforts were made, moreover, to improve the readiness of central government for a possible military struggle with the seceded states. On 18 February there began prolonged controversy in Congress over an attempt to extend the Militia Act of 1795 to cover possible 'insurrections against the authority of the United

---

65. This and the preceding paragraph are based on Gunderson, *Old Gentlemen's Convention*, pp. ix, 5–6, 13–16, 23, 31. Whiggish echoes deprecating 'passion' may be found in the coda of Lincoln's first inaugural address.

States'. President Buchanan had warned that the existing Act permitted the use of the militia only to assist a US marshal to execute the due processes of law or 'disperse hostile combinations'; it could not be used to suppress a general rebellion. Some northern senators believed that an extension of the Militia Act would help deter the South from precipitate action; others that it would only inflame southern passions. Those who argued for an overhaul of the Militia Act were optimistic given the disuse into which the militia had fallen over the previous two decades. But though this measure was debated on a number of occasions, it was not put to the vote. Several other efforts were made to give the chief executive increased powers to enforce a naval blockade. Representative John A. Bingham put forward a measure which would permit the collection of customs from the decks of warships, and the protection of customs officers by the army or navy should they face intimidation. This bill was also discussed but not put to the vote. Such discussions, therefore, which continued throughout the three weeks in which the Peace Conference was in session, failed to reach a definitive settlement of the problem of military preparation: local measures were improved; central authority still remained dormant.[66]

Passions were simmering among the more extreme groups. Companies of Minute Men and Wide-Awakes glowered at one another in the cities of the Border states. The Superintendent of the New York City police was so angered by the circulation of leaflets criticizing the Republicans that he demanded the governor legislate against treason 'and kindred offenses'. The president-elect, warned by Seward that the North would not endure a long civil war, continued to mutter that he would not make concessions in order that he could have 'the privilege of taking possession of the government'. Chase summed up the prevailing mood of the new Administration in waiting: 'Inauguration first, adjustment afterwards'.[67]

The atmosphere slowly but surely darkened, and the prospects for any compromise seemed less favourable. Moderates anxious to avoid civil war began to express themselves forcibly. But the strong language used by conservatives tended to conceal that the moderates in the North, as in the South, were disorganized and

66. Gunderson, *Old Gentlemen's Convention*, pp. 19–21; Stampp, *And the War Came*, pp. 117–20.
67. Blue, *Chase*, p. 134; Gunderson, *Old Gentlemen's Convention*, pp. 21–2.

badly led. Many newspapers sounded strident clarion calls for better leadership and a clear aim. It was, however, so much easier to make glib demands for a compromise, so much harder to find common ground for reconciliation when the topography was treacherous and unpredictable. Even small gains were apt to be lost in local landslides, and any edifice might be constructed on sand concealed by a thin layer of rock; all could be hazarded by an unstoppable avalanche. The process of conciliation was painfully slow. The first suggestions for a compromise convention had surfaced in the summer of 1860; further proposals were discussed by Buchanan's cabinet in November. A resolution embodying an invitation to slave and free states to discuss their 'present unhappy controversies' did not emerge from the Virginian legislature until January 1861; then a minority suggested that it should meet not in Washington DC but in the mooted capital of the fledgling Confederacy, Montgomery, Alabama. This indicated in the most explicit form a recurring feature of attempts at compromise. *Those moderates in the slave states who were most vociferous in calling for a peaceful resolution of the secession crisis on southern terms were inclined, in the final resort, to favour the secessionists and acquiesce in revolution.*[68] If accepted such a decision would have weighted the convention decisively in favour of the secessionist case. Agreement to meeting in Washington was achieved by urging acceptance of the Crittenden Compromise and demanding that Buchanan refrain 'from any and all acts calculated to produce a collision of arms'. But the date, 4 February, was selected because it was the same day on which the seceded states had planned to meet and organize themselves at Montgomery. Virginia sent a delegation to observe this process. This ominous coincidence underlines the inability of all those inclined to seek a compromise solution to bridge the yawning sectional gap which had developed over the issue of slavery. If this gap could not be closed by the summer of 1860 – indeed it had widened during the presidential election – then there were fewer expedients remaining on which to base a workable compromise. In short, the Peace Conference of February 1861 was meeting too late to have any dramatic or emollient effect. Hence the more frenzied calls for action may be

68. For instance, Bell had declared 'Give me disunion' when confronted with the possibility of a Union bound by force rather than by an acknowledgement of the rights of states. See Davis, *Breckinridge*, p. 242. Of course, Crittenden himself was a conspicuous exception to this generalization.

gauged as a measure of frustration that the capacity to take action had been reduced. Charles Francis Adams Jr wrote later that 'The simple fact was that the ship was drifting on the rocks of a lee shore; nothing could save it; this, however, was something none of us could bring ourselves to believe'.[69]

Because conciliation tended to involve making yet further concessions to secessionists, many Republicans feared that the conference would do nothing but compromise the integrity of the Republican Party. Here the stalwart role of Lincoln was vital in strengthening the party's resolve. It could 'be *smashed into a thousand fragments*', warned a correspondent of Senator Trumbull. In the various state caucuses, the middle Atlantic states (and especially New Jersey) were the most enthusiastic supporters of the conference; the Border states were enthusiastic, too, though some secessionist sympathizers tried to send delegations to Montgomery. In New England, however, Sumner tried to prevent Massachusetts sending a delegation; Governor Andrew had been warned by Stanton, the Attorney-General, that any attempt at compromise might lead 'to . . . a Provisional Govt. which was to take possession of the Capital and declare itself a nation'. Despite such exaggerated fears (for Tyler was not a Clay let alone a George Washington), delegates from the seceded states were conspicuous by their absence. Therefore, that all-important grouping which would have to be party to any workable compromise did not submit itself to the conference's deliberations. It had no chance of succeeding from the first day. '*Southern friends . . .*', Governor Alexander Randall of Wisconsin declared ironically during the continuing struggle in his state as to whether to send a delegation, '. . . have dictated and browbeat long enough'. This attitude was to gather in strength rapidly in the North during the next two months. So did the realization that the secession crisis was something more serious than a debilitating bout of fever which would pass out of the body politic as quickly as it had come.[70]

The conservatives likened the proceedings of the Peace Conference to the Constitutional Convention of 1787 which was more an indication of aspiration rather than achievement. Southern delegates, outnumbered 2:1 (because of the secessionist

---

69. Gunderson, *Old Gentlemen's Convention*, p. 32; Adams, *Autobiography*, pp. 75, 85.

70. Donald, *Sumner and the Coming of the Civil War*, p. 376; Gunderson, *Old Gentlemen's Convention*, pp. 33–4, 35–6, 38–9, 41; Potter, *Impending Crisis*, pp. 508, 546–7; Crofts, *Reluctant Confederates*, pp. 215–16, 233–4, 242.

boycott), implored that something be done to propitiate the South. But even though some delegates were inclined to agree, a soporific torpor overcame the conference. Most of the delegates were past their prime; others liked the sound of their own voices; they would 'babble us all to eternity', complained one delegate. Attempts to restrict the length of discussion failed. Republicans pursued a strategy of delay, and this was supported by Seward and Weed, who thought this might deliver some kind of compromise at a later date after Lincoln was inaugurated, and he (Seward) was in charge. Many different groups, but especially the Republicans, had much to gain from this inertia. The interminable negotiations ensured that the infection of secession would not spread to the Border states, ensured that Congress remained in quorum, and allowed the counting of the electoral college votes. But the policy of masterly inactivity risked alienating, rather than reconciling, both the Border states and the more radical Republicans, both of whom wanted something to be done though they differed as to what action should be taken. Others took the view that southern unity would soon fragment. 'If the South was let alone, its own disagreements will soon block the operations of the fire eaters'. But this, too, was a risky strategy, threatening to alienate southerners who were not yet committed to secession. 'The Abolitionists will continue to amuse us with hopes of Compromise without any real purpose to make a substantial Settlement,' warned Governor John W. Ellis of North Carolina. 'They are seeking time in which to find grounds on which to get control of the army and navy and the power of the government'. But attempts to gain time in order to find grounds on which to secure a *modus vivendi* risked losing it, as the Sumter crisis would demonstrate two months later.[71]

What were the attitudes of the political leaders to this process of discussion and expiation? Lincoln had already declared his opposition to any accommodation based on the Crittenden Resolution. He arrived in Washington on 23 February while the Peace Conference was still in session. Douglas, who had previously denounced southern rashness and the 'Rebellion' over dinner with Tyler, urged him to do everything to prevent a dissolution of the Union. Douglas was of the view that, if Republicans in the conference would help him, and Lincoln gave his presidential blessing to Seward's call for a national convention, then some

---

71.   Gunderson, *Old Gentlemen's Convention*, pp. 51–2; see below, pp. 322, 331–4, 349

progress might be made. Lincoln made no effort to apply any pressure on the Republican delegations at the conference. He listened 'respectfully and kindly' to Douglas's assurances that he would not make personal, political capital out of the crisis, but he failed 'in getting Lincoln to a point on the subject'. The president-elect continued to keep his own counsel. But he dropped a hint as to his future course some days later, when he was asked what concessions he was prepared to make to avoid civil war? He replied rather enigmatically that war was not always the worst evil that could be inflicted on a nation; he would do all in his power to avoid it, but he refused to 'neglect a Constitutional duty'. Here was an early clue to Lincoln's technique of following contradictory courses with two possible outcomes, and then decisively switching to the most appropriate at the correct moment. During the secession crisis this technique was misconstrued as weakness.[72]

One of the striking features of the Peace Conference's debate was its fervent rejection of 'party spirit'; indeed, it was widely assumed that this had brought the crisis on a neglectful nation which had fallen into the hands of wicked and selfish politicians. 'Your patriotism', Tyler assured the Conference with an air of smug superiority, 'will surmount the difficulties, however great, if you will but accomplish one triumph in advance, and that is, a triumph over *party*'. But Tyler equated partisanship not with his own viewpoint, but with that of the Republican Party. His chairman's address precipitated a wave of similar denunciations; but the only effect of a sweeping moral denunciation of the other side's 'party spirit' while assuming a monopoly of moral rectitude in one's own, is to limit the *practical* effect of any proposals made; such accusations lead to a *complete* rejection of the proposals offered for review by the side which is denounced. Thus the only long-term effect of these denunciations was to undermine further any hope of securing a workable basis for compromise.[73]

The Virginia Convention assembled on 13 February and invested a great deal of hope in a successful report from the Peace Conference. Tyler was also a member of this convention and so there was some measure of overlap between the two organizations. But both were equally deluded. After three weeks of discussion,

---

72.   Robert W. Johannsen, *Stephen A. Douglas* (New York: Oxford UP, 1973), pp. 835–6, 841–2; Baringer, *A House Dividing*, p. 307.

73.   Gunderson, *Old Gentlemen's Convention*, pp. 45–6.

the conference put forward a seven part amendment to the Constitution not greatly different from the Crittenden Compromise. A pregnant elephant had given birth to a mouse. Senator James Guthrie presented the conference's recommendations on 27 February, dispatching them to Congress a mere four days before the end of the legislative session. It contained seven sections adumbrating the main proposals. First, Section I called for a compromise based on the Missouri Compromise line, which protected slavery south of it but prohibited the institution north of it. Secondly, no new territories were to be acquired, under Section II, without a four-fifths ratification by the Senate; such territories were a source of strife and their significance must be reduced. Thirdly, Congress was not to interfere either with the workings of slavery in the states where it already existed or in Washington DC without the consent of the state of Maryland; clearly the symbolic importance of the peculiar institution in the District of Columbia touched nerves on both sides of the sectional divide. Fourthly, Section IV required that the Fugitive Slave Act should be rigorously enforced. Fifthly, the external slave trade was prohibited. In Section VI those prohibitions and articles pertaining to slavery in the Constitution were judged inviolate; they could not be altered without the agreement of all the states. Finally, slaveholders would be allowed compensation for any damage to their property (or themselves) incurred in recovering it. The general thrust of this document favoured the South and would have permitted some measure of slavery expansion. The Peace Conference, in short, fell back on the expedients of the Compromise of 1850. Any 'middle' course would thus favour the institution of slavery.

J. A. Seddon advocated a minority report consisting of the resolutions of the Virginia General Assembly. These demanded that the South exercise nothing less than a veto over all executive and legislative appointments; secondly, that all free blacks should be disenfranchised and prevented from holding office; and thirdly, that all states should be granted the right of secession. There were also calls from John B. Baldwin and other Whigs for a national convention. This was a cry very much favoured by southern radicals because the assembly of such a body would take time. Delay allowed them to consolidate their strength in the seceded states without making the slightest concession.[74] Secessionists

---

74. The manoeuvres around calls for such a convention illustrate how the restriction of slavery was the moot issue. Blue, *Chase*, p. 135.

dismissed the majority report as consisting of 'wishy washy resolutions that amounted to nothing' and could find nothing in it worth giving up the strong position that secession had already granted them. Once these irreconcilable differences at the Peace Conference had surfaced, there followed six days of chaos accompanied by incongruous outbreaks of the kind of unseemly brawling that had disfigured congressional debates. Much of the discussion focused around the relative power of the sections *vis-à-vis* one another over the next decade, whether the seceded states remained in or out of the Union. Some contemporaries then, and some historians later, have claimed that in these heated discussions, slavery was a mere 'incident' in this struggle for relative power upon which future stability would rest. What really counted, claimed James B. Clay of Kentucky, was 'the old question of the balance of power between the different sections and different interests'. In his account of the Peace Conference, Gunderson describes slavery as an 'emotionally charged symbol for rhetorical and political manipulation'. Obviously, the struggle for relative influence over the Union's political institutions during the next decade was not irrelevant, but slavery was much more than a symptom or symbol of this sectional struggle. The relative condition of the peculiar institution, the width of its geographical spread, and the breadth of its support and influence in the legislative and executive branches of government, would determine the future character of the Union. It was therefore not only a central consideration in any debate over the future direction of United States economic and social development, but a pervasive and unavoidable issue.[75]

The failure of compromise

Any attempt to evade the differences over this issue was futile. This was one of the prime reasons why the Peace Conference was doomed to failure. Indeed Republicans manoeuvred in a way that would have been deplored by Tyler. They tried to ensure that the 'Union-savers' as they were sarcastically called, both northern and southern Democrats, did not reunite to vote them down. The president-elect held firm consistently to the theme of the 1860

75. Gunderson, *Old Gentlemen's Convention*, pp. 62–6. Gunderson's comment is found on p. 66. See Thomas J. Pressly, *Americans Interpret their Civil War* (Princeton UP, 1954), pp. 61–2, 68, 244–5, 247–8, 280.

presidential campaign. Attempts to extend the Missouri Compromise line were unacceptable. Lincoln's consistency was not applauded by those who condemned political expediency; they deplored it. The truth was that Tyler and other Whigs who criticized 'party' spirit could do so only because they were convinced of the rectitude of their own political position and could see no good, or integrity, in an opposite point of view; but there was more than one point of view on this vexed issue. Political manoeuvring and lack of coherent principle were not a monopoly of the Republicans. Secessionist sympathizers, for instance, were offering increasingly dogmatic pro-southern amendments in a transparent effort to justify later outright secessionist moves. Lincoln's response to these efforts, while visiting some of the leaders of the Conference was to admonish them against 'any concession in the face of menace'. The Constitution he reiterated must be 'respected, obeyed, enforced, and defended, let the grass grow where it may'.[76]

The Peace Conference then stuttered to a halt at the moment when it should have been at its most dynamic – as the votes were cast by the various state conventions on the seven sections of the proposals. The call for a national convention was defeated. Tyler revealed his own true sympathies by vacating the chair and canvassing for Seddon's minority report; this, too, was defeated. Discussion then revolved around the acceptance of the Missouri Compromise line. The southern radicals disliked this because, unlike the Crittenden Compromise, it would not apply to territory acquired in the future. They joined with the Republicans to vote Section I down. Without unity on this all-important clause, the efforts of the Peace Conference were disembowelled. Despite calls from Chase that the Conference should vote on the entire document as a whole, Tyler (now back in the chair), sent the seven sections to the Senate without any formal vote on them at all. They were presented as the Thirteenth Amendment to the Constitution. It represented the views of the moderate pro-southern lobby as to how the secession crisis should be resolved. For the radical southern secessionists it did not go far enough.

In the Congress this effort at compromise did not fare well. In these frantic last weeks before the session came to an end, it had

---

76.   Baringer, *A House Dividing*, p. 307; Gunderson, *Old Gentlemen's Convention*, pp. 84–5. The reference to grass concerned Lincoln's future responsibility for grass growing in the streets of American commercial cities.

to compete for consideration of other efforts at compromise, like
those of Crittenden. Controversy immediately arose as to whether
the House should suspend its rules before receiving the
proposition of this putative constitutional amendment. Southern
representatives were keen to follow this course so that they could
vote it down. But although a majority favoured suspension, it was not
large enough to secure a two-thirds majority, and so the House
refused even to receive the arduous labours of the Peace
Conference. It was forwarded to the Senate on 27 February, where
it lay idle and unread for three days. A spur of activity marked the
closing hours of the session with Crittenden's desperate decision
to replace his own effort at compromise with that of the Peace
Conference. This was a move not calculated to please the South, the
very section Crittenden was most concerned to placate. Only seven
senators supported this move, while twenty-eight were opposed.
There was also a noticeable hardening of the southern position
during these frenetic days. Those delegates who had sceptically
smiled on the deliberations of the Peace Conference, now spurned it.
For example, George Davis of North Carolina, a state which had not
shown any marked enthusiasm for secession, now warned that 'he
could never accept the plan adopted by the "Peace Congress" as
consistent with the rights, the interests or the dignity of North
Carolina'. His state must now align with the rest of the South or
face the unenviable fate of being 'the tail-end and victim of a
Free-Soil North'. Again, southern political leaders, even those who
disapproved of secession, seemed to be more impressed by something
vague and potentially awful which might occur at some unspecified
date in the future, than by the immediate threat of civil war.[77]

The effort at compromise had failed. The president-elect had
not endorsed the efforts of Crittenden or the Peace Conference.
He was determined to unite his party around a policy that insisted
on the restriction of slavery to its present limits. The efforts at
compromise mounted by Baldwin, Crittenden, Guthrie and Tyler
that sought, at the very least, to permit an extension of the
Missouri Compromise line, were doomed to fail if they could not
gain the adherence of the governing party. Given the refusal of
the southern moderates to accept this restriction, there would
appear to have been no realistic basis for a meaningful and
enduring compromise. Perhaps the Peace Conference played a
useful role in assisting the southern moderates in the February

77. Gunderson, *Old Gentlemen's Convention* pp. 86, 91, 94–7; Crofts, *Reluctant Confederates*, pp. 156, 193–4, 196–9, 200.

elections, which postponed the second, and in some respects more dangerous wave of secession ordinances in Virginia, North Carolina, Tennessee and Arkansas, until after the resolution of the Sumter crisis in April 1861. The South, let alone the Upper South, was not a monolith. It may also have helped keep the Border states in the Union, and although individual delegates opposed General Scott's measures, the conference proceedings helped contribute to the peaceful inauguration of Lincoln. 'We have thus far done all in our power to procrastinate', Thurlow Weed reported, 'and shall continue to do so, in order to remain in session until after the 4th of March'.

But we cannot avoid the question why compromise was possible in 1850 but not in 1861? The most obvious reason was that the whole psychological ambience of these days was hostile to the placatory, accommodating and forbearing attitude required to bring forth a compromise. This was true despite the obviously desperate efforts by many to broker such a settlement, a deal which would have enjoyed a great deal of public support. This does not negate, however, the harsh reality that the longer the representatives of the slave states negotiated with those of the North, the more such transactions resulted in a firmer rationalization of their competing positions. There were those who believed earnestly that such polarized positions should be set aside and appeals made to the more elevated, patriotic sentiments of men on both sides; but such calls were rarely as disinterested as they seemed, and were often implicitly, and sometimes explicitly, pro-southern in their connotations. Upper South Unionists steadfastly refused to believe that the Lower South could maintain its independence; they stood out for a 'compromise' based on the 'Border State Plan', which simply resurrected the Missouri Compromise. To Republicans this was not a compromise at all. Any pro-slavery hints were liable to increase the determination of many Republicans to stand by the platform of 1860. Consequently, there was no unanimity among the 'great' congressional leaders to sponsor anything like the Compromise of 1850. When amendments were proffered, they were offered piecemeal and soon sank into oblivion among the quicksand of congressional procedure. They also suffered from the odour of decay. There is something fittingly symbolic that the two politicians, Crittenden and Douglas, who strove most frantically to revive the corpse of the second party system, the republic of Calhoun, Webster and Clay, were both mortally ill.[78]

If the northern response was occasionally feeble, there can be no doubting the vigour and stridency of the southern secessionist position. It had, of course, gained in confidence and bellicosity since John Brown's raid in 1859. It was not very well thought out, neither logical nor judicious, but it certainly carried conviction among the great majority of slave states. This was the crucial difference between 1861 and the Compromise of 1850. Then secessionist sentiment was a spurned minority view, and regarded as somewhat eccentric, impulsive and risky. Eleven years later secessionist cries had attained not only respectability, but also, because of the limited coordination of southern action, practicability. Setting up a slaveowning republic seemed a real, and to many, a sensible alternative. Secessionists had 'momentum' and moderates, previously sceptical of its allure, now hurried to guard their exposed political flanks and modify their views. With his call for a slave code for the territories, Jefferson Davis, a respected former Secretary of War, had signalled the surrender of the moderates, whose cause he had until very recently upheld, and their adherence to the radical view. But given this combustible compound of overweening belligerence and short-sighted rhetoric, which overlooked the catastrophic dangers facing the South if it joined wholeheartedly in a Gadarene plunge towards the secessionist precipice, it is unlikely that any concessions on the part of either the Buchanan or the Lincoln Administrations would have persuaded the seven seceded states to return to the Union, or placated the six that were contemplating this hazardous step.[79]

There was, in short, no overwhelming desire for a compromise. The somewhat sentimental, patriotic loyalties, especially to the holy relics of the Revolution, including the revered memory of George Washington, were insufficiently compelling to overcome the southern passion for setting up a republic dedicated to chattel slavery. On the contrary, these symbols were expropriated by the new Confederacy to justify its standpoint on political, economic

78. Douglas died at 9 p.m. on 3 June 1861. The doctors were mystified by his symptoms. His purported last words were: 'Tell my children to obey the laws and uphold the Constitution'. Damon Wells, *Stephen Douglas: The Last Years, 1857–1861*, (Austin: University of Texas Press, 1971), p. 289; Crofts, *Reluctant Confederates*, pp. 232–3, 259, 287.

79. Smith, *The Death of Slavery*, p. 171. Smith is in error, however, in thinking that the Compromise sponsored by the Peace Conference was passed by the House of Representatives by a two-thirds majority.

and constitutional developments in the new republic. There is, in any case, something rather unreal and scholastic in the long and intricate legal discussions over constitutional amendments and their exegesis which preoccupied so many in the days before the firing on Fort Sumter. Yet these had succeeded a decade previously. If Paris was worth a mass, alas, the Union could not be saved by hair-splitting over legal niceties. They could no longer establish a consensus on the fundamental slavery problem. Such discussion was in part designed to conceal the harsh reality that with the Republican victory in 1860, the South had lost some of its power (though not all, and perhaps temporarily) over the Federal government. The southern extremists could not and would not accept this loss; they would not make the slightest accommodation which would cover a graceful retreat. They spoke in terms of an 'insult' delivered to the South and in inflammatory language warned of the perils of a resurgent and overpowering industrialism. Hence the contemporary stress on the cultural chasm that separated the two sections. At the end of the Peace Conference, Seddon accused northerners of nursing hatreds: 'You have educated your children to believe us monsters of brutality, lust and ingenuity'. That contemporaries accepted the existence of an unbridgeable cultural divide, and that this was due to the way political anti-slavery attitudes had worked their way into popular culture and the social and intellectual fabric of the North, is evinced by President Lincoln's celebrated comment in 1862, on meeting Mrs Harriet Beecher Stowe at the White House, 'So this is the little lady who made this big war?'[80]

An unwillingness to accede to any accommodation with the South is sometimes put down to the prevalence of mean-spirited and wholly selfish, political partisanship. Politicians' thoughts were on their own advancement, not on saving the country from civil war. This did exist; politicians and ambition are rarely separated. And certainly politicians on both sides underestimated the dangers they were facing. If the North was prone to underestimate the potency of the secessionist appeal, then the South completely misunderstood the forces that would shape the North's rather laggard response to any attempt at separation. Southern leaders surveyed the threat of war with smug casualness. In any case, the Republican Party could hardly surrender its partisan interests and remain a viable governing party. It was not a realistic alternative

80. Quotations taken from Gunderson, *Old Gentlemen's Convention*, p. 101; D. W. Brogan, *American Aspects* (London: Hamish Hamilton, 1963), p. 178.

for Republicans to abandon the advantages that had accrued from the political system when their rivals found reasons not to follow their noble example. 'Compromise' ten years before had resulted in an extension of the slavery system; this was now quite unacceptable. To have embraced the 'patriotic' stance suggested by former President Tyler would have resulted in the Republican Party negating its first presidential victory and all its finest, cherished ideals. For better or for worse, politicians were stuck with the political arrangements they had fashioned and had to work with them. The spoils system forced on them a mode of behaviour and they could not operate in any other way.[81] Consequently, because it diverted energies and distracted the attention, the spoils system contributed to those conditions that resulted in the Civil War. But that is not to suggest that an enduring settlement, accommodating both North and South, would have emerged without it.

In truth, for a compromise – defined by the *Concise OED* as 'the settlement of a dispute by mutual concession' – to work it needed an agreement on all sides, extending to the bits of the argument with which all concurred. This was not forthcoming in the early months of 1861. A compromise settlement denotes a desire by all parties to reach agreement. But if that desire is absent on one side let alone both, then such efforts are futile and doomed to fail. It is easy for those who have never known the suffering, misery and sacrifice of a great war to ridicule the well-meaning efforts of those intent on avoiding it. Nonetheless, if it takes two sides to make a war, then it takes at least two sides to keep the peace. The general failure to achieve any accord after the 1860 presidential election led to a fatalistic acceptance of the coming of war. In December 1860 Lincoln had commented, 'If the tug has to come better now than later'. Three months later this view had hardened, and 'traitors' were excoriated in the press. 'Let this intolerable suspense and uncertainty cease!' wrote Horace Greeley in the *Tribune*. 'If we are to fight so be it'. Historians have frequently commented on the unendurable tension that statesmen feel before the outbreak of a war, and the relief felt, almost a meaningful release, when a decision is finally taken that political disputes must be resolved by war. The men who felt that some kind of conflict was inevitable after February 1861 would perhaps

81.   For an assessment of the significance of distributing the patronage during the Sumter crisis, see below, p. 342.

have shown a good deal more prudence if they had known what kind of war was about to overwhelm them. It was one thing for politicians to accept the necessity of fighting a war, another for their constituents to fight it. To convince northern public opinion that this was a case deserving of their commitment and sacrifice was a major challenge. This problem was resolved by the behaviour of the seceded states during the Sumter crisis.[82]

The Montgomery convention

A convention of the first six seceded states, followed by Texas a couple of weeks later, began the work of forging a slaveowning republic on 4 February 1861 in Montgomery, Alabama. On 9 February, Jefferson Davis, on the strength of his previous distinguished career rather than on the consistency and strength of his secessionist fervour, was nominated in caucus as provisional president of the Confederate States. He eventually faced an unopposed presidential election for a single six year term in November 1861. Alexander H. Stephens was nominated as vice president. The secessionist ideologues, once the movement they had championed had secured its objectives, lost influence, and Yancey, Rhett and Hammond fell almost into political oblivion once the Civil War began. They were essentially wizards of words rather than men of the less mercurial but firmer timbre needed to run great departments of state. This confirmed the extraordinary paradox that characterized the leadership of the Confederacy, namely, that those who strove to secure southern independence and destroyed their careers in this delusive quest, had not been keen enthusiasts for the cause in the first place. This is true of the two civilian officials, Davis and Stephens, and the two generals that commanded the South's principal field armies, Robert E. Lee and Joseph E. Johnston. All four men had opposed secession in some shape or form, and acquiesced in it only once its momentum appeared unstoppable. But once they had thrown themselves into the cause their loyalty was never in doubt. Indeed, although their loyalty to the 'lost cause' was slower in forming, it was surer and

82. Lincoln to William Kellogg, 11 Dec. 1860, *The Collected Works of Abraham Lincoln* (New Brunswick, NJ: Rutgers UP, 1953–5), 9 vols, IV, p. 150; Gunderson, *Old Gentlemen's Convention*, p. 102; Brogan (*American Aspects*, p. 142) points out that relative to population, the United States suffered greater casualties in the four years of the Civil War than did Great Britain in 1914–18. See above, pp. 186–7.

steadier, and less flashy and idiosyncratic, than that of the ideologues of secession.[83]

Stephens was only the most articulate spokesman of those southerners who urged that the new government 'be modeled as nearly as possible on the basis and principles of the late government of the United States'.[84] The delegates at Montgomery claimed to be the *true* apostles of 1775 and 1787, and simply modified the Constitution of the United States in accordance with their convictions. It says a lot for the legalistic bias of American political culture in the nineteenth century that immediate priority was allotted to perfecting this provisional document instead of taking practical measures to secure southern independence, working out a viable policy towards the Upper South, and establishing a satisfactory foreign policy and the means to implement it. After all, less than half of the slave states had so far seceded, and the Confederacy was behaving as if its independence was an established fact. In this otiose constitutional document, as if its formulation rather than *policy* would guarantee the operation and security of the new republic, states rights was strengthened. The right to secede was passed over in silence, confirming the unionist suspicion that the South had indulged in a riot of special pleading after the presidential election. The powers of the central government were reduced. Slavery was enshrined and protected at the heart of the new constitution: 'the new Government . . . rests upon the great truth', Stephens affirmed, 'that the Negro is not equal to the white man; that slavery – subordination to the superior race – is his natural and normal condition'.

Slavery was protected in the Confederate territories and representation in Congress was based on the three-fifths ratio adopted in 1787.[85] The Confederate system of cabinet government was identical to that of the United States save that a Department of Justice was created and replaced the Interior. There would, however, be one major change in the style of Confederate government – party spirit would be banished. Though applauded at the time as a means of eradicating narrow selfishness and wicked tricks from the political scene, such a move resembled the

83.   Craig L. Symonds, *Joseph E Johnston* (New York: Norton, 1992), pp. 93–5; Alan T. Nolan, *Lee Considered* (Chapel Hill, NC: University of North Carolina Press, 1991), p. 36; Paul D. Escott, *After Secession: Jefferson Davis and the Failure of Confederate Nationalism*, (Baton Rouge: Louisiana State UP, 1978), pp. 31–4.

84.   Johnson, *Patriarchal Republic*, p. 155.

85.   See above, pp. 25–6.

proverbial search for a mirage. It also contributed decisively to the dullness and lack of creativity in Confederate politics – 'sterility' is William Brock's word – which became increasingly personalized. But given the enormity of the task before it, the adaption of the United States Constitution and imitation of methods and styles of government, and even discussion as to whether the United States flag should be 'kept' (though it was agreed this would constitute a 'political and military solecism' and the Confederacy must have a flag of its own), these efforts express the essential provincialism voiced by the southern secession movement. And that parochial spirit was given firm shape by the institution of slavery. The Confederacy was not a vital nationalist movement, but a profoundly provincial one.[86]

In the wider world, the provincial leadership of the Confederacy floundered. What was to be its policy? There seemed to be much bravado in a number of public statements. 'There will be no war in our territory,' Jefferson Davis explained *en route* to Montgomery. 'It will be carried into the enemy's territory'. How could any policy be convincingly framed while the most powerful slave states remained obdurately in the Union? 'The man and the hour have met!' Yancey declared with a typically melodramatic flourish, when he first introduced President Davis to a rapturous Montgomery crowd. Davis was in no doubt of the enormity of the task before him. He led nothing more than a fragment of the slave states. He faced the dilemma produced by a series of unilateral, individual state secessions. A policy could not be pursued because the slaveowning republic remained in pieces that still needed to be stitched together. He struck a self-confident, perhaps bombastic note in his remarks. 'The time for compromise has now passed,' he announced. 'The South is determined to maintain her position, and make all who oppose her smell southern powder and feel southern steel'. This was hyperbole. Writing privately to his wife four days later, Davis complained: 'We are without machinery, without means, and threatened by a powerful opposition; but I do not despond, and will not shrink from the task imposed upon me'.[87]

86. Parish, *American Civil War*, pp. 211–13; Johnson, *Patriarchal Republic*, pp. 135–6; W. R. Brock, *Conflict and Transformation: The United States, 1844–1877* (Harmondsworth: Penguin, 1973, 1978), p. 228; Randall and Donald, *Civil War and Reconstruction*, pp. 244–6.

87. Davis to Varina Davis, 20 Feb. 1861. Jefferson Davis, *Private Letters, 1823–1891*, ed. Hudson Strode (New York: Harcourt Brace, 1966), p. 123; William C. Davis, *Jefferson Davis: The Man and his Hour* (New York: HarperCollins, 1991), p. 305.

Davis was a narrow, stern, conscientious but forbidding and aloof man, who lacked a sense of his true priorities. He coupled dread of conflict with a fatalistic acceptance of its inevitability. 'Civil war has only horror for me, but whatever circumstances demand shall be met as a duty and I trust be so discharged that you will not be ashamed of our former connection or cease to be my friend', he wrote to former President Franklin Pierce. 'When Lincoln comes in he will have but to continue in the path of his predecessor to inaugurate a civil war', he averred. Davis's thoughts seemed to revolve rather too automatically around war rather than its avoidance; he, after all, preferred a field command in the Confederate army to high political office. But Davis did not consider in his rigid, complacent way, when reflecting on future federal policy, that he had a prime responsibility for and a supreme interest in, avoiding war, too.[88]

Davis's inaugural address was less bellicose than his earlier remarks. War would come only if the North began it, he promised. Perhaps some northern states would wish to join the Confederacy, he surmised, not an altogether fanciful suggestion as it turned out. At any rate, unless he misunderstood 'the judgement and will of the people, a reunion with the States from which we have separated is neither practicable nor desirable'. Davis proclaimed Jefferson's 'right of revolution' for all southerners. Yet he then denied that a 'revolution' had taken place. The Confederacy merely asserted the right which the Declaration of Independence considered 'inalienable', that is to say, the methods of government are not immovable and that 'government rests on the consent of the governed, and that it is the right of the people to alter or abolish them'.[89] In fact, the 'consent of the governed' had not been asked, as no ordinance of secession had been confirmed by popular vote, and secession had been decided by 854 men selected by their legislatures (of which 157 had been opposed). There was not a single mention of slavery in the address. 'We have changed the constituent parts, but not the system of government', he claimed. On five separate occasions he addressed directly the likelihood of war with the North. The whole thrust of his address was that the South had been forced to take itself out of the Union

88.   Davis to Pierce, 20 Jan. 1861; Davis, *Private Letters*, p. 122; Davis, *Jefferson Davis*, pp. 303–4.
89.   William W. Freehling, *The Road to Disunion: Secessionists at Bay* (New York: Oxford UP, 1990), p. 7.

because of 'wanton aggression'. This defensive posture would determine all its future actions, he argued. 'If we may not hope to avoid war, we may at least expect that posterity will acquit us of having needlessly engaged in it'. But he was prepared to submit to the test of the sword if Confederate rights or territory were abused by the 'lust of dominion' of the northern states. Trade must be kept 'free', and Davis hinted that as southern cotton was 'required' by many of the world's manufacturing countries, they might intervene to break any Union blockade of southern ports. The auspices, as without doubt the Lord smiled down upon the southern people, were good. 'We may...look forward to success, peace, and to prosperity'. But all this depended on avoiding war. Could this be achieved?[90]

Lincoln's first inaugural address

By contrast with Jefferson Davis's comparatively smooth installation as Confederate president, Lincoln's arrival in Washington DC in February 1861 had been an embarrassment to him. Advised by the Pinkerton Agency of an assassination bid in Baltimore, he was prevailed upon to leave Mrs Lincoln and take an earlier train which would arrive in Washington at the dead of night. Given Lincoln's eventual fate, it would have been criminally careless of his advisers to ignore such threats. But his arrival *incognito* did little to elevate the dignity of his office at a time when citizens looked for evidence of resolution and vigorous leadership. It also reinforced the impression, in a city which was nervous and panicky, that Lincoln was a weak and ineffectual nonentity, a ninny, who would make a fool of himself whatever he did; or, that his thoughts and actions were of such little account that they were not worth taking seriously.[91] This was unfortunate. The air of long-running farce was confirmed by the failure of Lincoln's son, Robert Todd Lincoln, to look after the precious copies of the president-elect's inaugural address on the train, and it was nearly

90. William C. Davis, *Jefferson Davis*, pp. 307–10; 'Inaugural Address', in Jefferson Davis, *Rise and Fall of the Confederate Government* (London: Longmans Green, 1881) I. pp. 232–6.
91. See David Donald, *Lincoln Reconsidered*, 2nd enlarged edn (New York: Vintage, 1989), pp. 3–4, 112. On Washington's nervous state, see Potter, *Lincoln and his Party*, pp. 254–5, 256–7, 266, 280.

lost. Lincoln carried a copy himself when he arrived in Washington. Met by Congressman Washburne, an old though not intimate ally, he was conveyed to Willard's Hotel, to meet the Secretary of State (designate), William H. Seward, and, in the opinion of many, to be embraced in his hypnotic clutches. In a city lacking many salubrious hotels, Willard's was the natural place to base the president-elect until he could move into the Executive Mansion. That Lincoln found Seward's lively and amusing company convivial (they shared a common delight in story-telling) reinforced the latter's faith that he could bewitch and beguile the chief executive and exercise his chief's prerogatives himself.[92]

One of Lincoln's first acts was to hand Seward a copy of his inaugural address for comment. Such documents attempted to enshrine a statement of intent at the beginning of an Administration. They had become symbolic statements of sentiment as much as of policy. Clearly, in Lincoln's case the symbolism was two-fold: he was the first Republican president to take the oath of office; and secondly, the very taking of that oath coincided with the most abrupt and well-organized challenge to the process of presidential transition yet encountered in the short history of the United States. Thus Lincoln's inaugural would have to embrace a diplomatic appeal which was unprecedented. Many of Lincoln's finest state papers are short and concise to a remarkable degree; he was a great believer in the dictum that brevity is the soul of wit. It was this acuity and cogency which so many of his contemporaries, schooled in the expansive and voluble tradition of public speaking of a Gladstone or a Calhoun, found so puzzling. This helps to explain why his public utterances lacked contemporary appeal, yet have the protean elevation which has been cherished by successive generations ever since. Lincoln's first inaugural is a good deal longer than many of his later state papers. Seward found the last paragraph of the first draft rather too blunt. It concluded,

> In your hands, my dissatisfied fellow-countrymen, not in mine, is the momentous issue of civil war. The Government will not assail you. You can have no conflict without being yourselves the aggressors. You have no oath registered in Heaven to destroy the Government, while I shall have the most solemn one 'to preserve, protect and defend it'.

92. Baringer, *A House Dividing*, pp. 294–304.

He suggested to Lincoln that he sandpaper its rather abrasive edge with an appeal to common traditions and wells of patriotism. Lincoln accepted this advice, though he ignored, in Seward's draft, references to his lack of ability when compared with George Washington, James Madison, Jackson and Clay. Adding on to the draft a new paragraph, Lincoln transmogrified its sentiments into his majestic prose from Seward's somewhat strained and stilted draft. The inaugural address was now complete.[93]

Lincoln was to be the target of numerous assassination threats; Washington DC was filled with pro-Confederate sympathizers (Varina Davis was widely quoted by many that she was looking forward to returning to the Confederacy's natural capital within a few months); it was possible that the inauguration would be disrupted. General Winfield Scott made thorough preparations to ensure that the ceremony would not be interrupted and that the process of government would continue. On 4 March Lincoln called on President Buchanan and together they travelled to the steps of the Capitol, its great dome still not in place, and the building covered with scaffolding. Lincoln delivered his address first before taking the oath of office from the Chief Justice, Roger B. Taney. Also symbolic was Stephen A. Douglas's gesture of holding Lincoln's top hat while he delivered his address.[94] Lincoln's inscrutable and mournful expression gazed out over a large crowd and he spoke in a pleasing tenor voice. He began by stating yet again that the election of a Republican Administration would not have the slightest effect on the institution of slavery in the southern states; he could think of no reason, save mischief, why that issue should have been raised.

> There has never been any reasonable cause for such apprehension. Indeed the most ample evidence to the contrary has all the while existed and been open to their [southerners'] inspection. . . . I only press upon the public attention the most conclusive evidence of which the case is susceptible, that the property, peace, and security of no section are to be in any wise endangered by the now incoming administration.

Indeed towards the end of his speech, Lincoln signalled that he would not object to a constitutional amendment enshrining the

93. William H. Seward, 'Suggestions for a Closing Paragraph', Robert Todd Lincoln Collection of the Papers of Abraham Lincoln, Library of Congress, Washington DC; *The Collected Works of Abraham Lincoln*, ed. Roy P. Basler (New Brunswick, NJ: Rutgers UP, 1953), IV, pp. 261–2n99.

94. Johannsen, *Douglas*, p. 843.

principle that the Federal government 'would never interfere with the domestic institutions of the States' – that is to say, slavery. Lincoln also urged that the Fugitive Slave Act remain operative, brushing aside as irrelevant the dispute as to whether this should be enforced by federal or state agencies. But he did take a swipe at the exercise of the 'slave power' over the civil rights of northerners by suggesting that future legislation might be required to protect their immunities and privileges as free men while the Act was enforced.[95]

Promising not to exercise authority or construe laws in a hypocritical spirit, Lincoln then turned to examine the unprecedented crisis which was his unhappy lot to inherit – his 'great and peculiar difficulty'. 'A disruption of the Federal Union, heretofore only menaced, is now formidably attempted', he declared. Immediately, Lincoln turned to elaborate the major premise of his speech and subsequent policy. Secession could not be admitted as valid and would not be acknowledged as a legal or political fact. There could be no compromise with its perpetrators or a tacit acceptance of a *de jure* right to secede.

> I hold, that, in contemplation of universal law and of the Constitution, the Union of these States is perpetual. Perpetuity is implied, if not expressed, in the fundamental law of all national governments. It is safe to assert that no government proper ever had a provision in its organic law for its own termination.

The Union could not be destroyed 'except by some action not provided for in the instrument itself'. Lincoln argued that the Union could not be broken by one party without the assent of the others, even if the right to break it was assented to. But Lincoln then disposed of this possibility by arguing that the Union was older than the Constitution, and that all the elements cementing the Union, the Articles of Association (1774), the Declaration of Independence, the Articles of Confederation (ratified in 1781) and the Constitution itself (1787) also sought to create 'a more perfect Union' forged *perpetually*. This was an astonishingly bold – if necessary – claim. But it is doubtful if many northerners would have accepted the assertion that the Continental Congress had established a 'perpetual' Union. Unabashed, Lincoln went on:

> It follows from these views that no State, upon its own mere motion, can lawfully get out of the Union – that *resolves* and

95. Lincoln, *Collected Works*, IV, 'First Inaugural Address – Final Text', pp. 262–3, 264, 269–70.

ordinances to that effect are legally void; and that acts of violence, within any State or States, against the authority of the United States, are insurrectionary or revolutionary, according to circumstances.[96]

Here was the core of Lincoln's case; unilateral action by states *within* the Union to its detriment could never be acknowledged; unilateral action by the elected officials of the Union to safeguard its security was justified. Such action would strengthen the Union if it was directed against political forces *outside of it*. But if states directed unilateral action towards the legitimate government of the *United* States then the results would be calamitous. Lincoln developed this point by emphasizing, in a sentence added to the final draft at the last minute, that

> in view of the Constitution and the laws, the Union is unbroken; and to the extent of my ability I shall take care, as the Constitution itself expressly enjoins upon me, that the laws of the Union be faithfully executed in all the States.[97] ... I trust this will not be regarded as a menace, but only as the declared purpose of the Union that it *will* constitutionally defend, and maintain itself.[98]

In a more placatory tone Lincoln observed that 'Where hostility to the United States' was 'so great and so universal' there would be no attempt to offer the patronage in the president's gift to those (such as abolitionists or Republicans) who objected to slavery: 'there will be no attempt to force obnoxious strangers among the people' – those who would agitate against the institution of slavery while domiciled in the southern states. 'The mails, unless repelled, will continue to be furnished in all parts of the Union'. The president stressed that life would continue as it had always done; the charge that his Administration involved a violent break with the past could then be gently laid aside.

> In doing this there needs to be no bloodshed or violence; and there shall be none, unless it be forced upon the national authority. The power confided to me will be used to hold, occupy and possess the property and places belonging to the government, and to collect the duties and imposts; but beyond what may be necessary for these objects, there will be no invasion – no using of force against or among the people anywhere.

96. Ibid., pp. 264–5; Kenneth M. Stampp, *The Imperiled Union: Essays on the Background of the Civil War* (New York: Oxford UP, 1986), pp. 3–36.
97. Marginalia by A. Lincoln, Draft of First Inaugural Address, Lincoln Papers.
98. Lincoln. *Collected Works*, IV, pp. 265–6.

Lincoln was here expounding a policy that the United States government would not seek the means to *implement its policy by force should it not be given a reason for doing so*. 'So far as it is possible, the people everywhere shall have that sense of perfect security which is most favourable to calm thought and reflection'.[99]

It is difficult to imagine a more pacific line announced by a head of state when confronted by such flagrant and provocative defiance. In the initial draft written at Springfield, Lincoln had set down an intention to 'reclaim' the public places and property already purloined by the rebels. Orville Hickman Browning persuaded him to alter this to 'hold, occupy and possess' those installations. Seward and Francis Preston Blair had between them ensured that any statements of resolve concerning federal authority were diluted and attempts at reconciliation were accentuated. Benjamin P. Thomas does not exaggerate when he claims that the speech was as 'indulgent as he could make it without renouncing his constitutional duties'.[100] Yet there can be no doubting the consistency of Lincoln's position since the 1860 presidential campaign, and many of the statements in the inaugural had been made in previous speeches.[101]

There are several references in the document to the need for careful, calm thought and reflection. This rested upon the strong and widespread sentiment that the secessionists would come to their senses after they had thought through the consequences of their actions, and perhaps that Unionism would reassert itself. Lincoln acknowledged that there were numerous outright, dogmatic and irreconcilable secessionists on whom his words were wasted. Yet he addressed a plea to those, mainly in the Upper South, of a more moderate and doubting disposition.

> Will you hazard so desperate a step, while there is any possibility that any portion of the ills you fly from, have no real existence? Will you, while the certain ills you fly to, are greater than the real ones you fly from? Will you risk the commission of so fearful a mistake?

Here was a strong statement that many of the issues raised in the presidential election resulting in the hysterical and ill-informed

---

99. Ibid., IV, p. 266.

100. Benjamin P. Thomas, *Abraham Lincoln* (London: Eyre & Spottiswoode, 1953), p. 160.

101. As Lincoln observed at the beginning of the Address, Lincoln, *Collected Works*, IV, pp. 262–3.

clamour which dominated the secessionist conventions, were fallacious and in a very real sense, unreal. The secessionists were boxing with shadows. But there exists a warning throughout the speech, despite so many explicit placatory appeals, that the gloves would be peeled off if the secessionists blatantly flouted or lashed out at federal authority. Certainly, Lincoln would shortly discover that moderate southern opinion, even that which even recently had been Unionist in sentiment, would not call a halt to the secessionist march. His other observation, namely, that there was a stark possibility that the institution of slavery was more vulnerable outside the Union than within it, was more than realized after April 1861.[102]

An interpretation of the speech in which Lincoln invokes an image of uninterrupted 'normalcy' as a contrast to the uncertainty, panic and squabbles which would attend the unknowns of secession and revolution, is supported by the last part of the address. Here the president praises American democracy – the source of 'that truth and justice, [which] will surely prevail, by the judgment of this great tribunal, the American people'. Obviously, the more haunting and apocalyptic notions advanced since the election of a Republican president with a Republican majority in Congress could be safely ignored. 'While the people retain their virtue, and vigilance, no administration, by any extreme of wickedness or folly, can very seriously injure the government, in the short space of four years'. Nothing had fundamentally changed, Lincoln assured his audience.[103]

> Such of you as are now dissatisfied, still have the old Constitution unimpaired, and, on the sensitive point, the laws of your own framing under it; while the new administration will have no immediate power, if it would, to change either.

He then made a vain appeal for stocktaking and prudence: 'Nothing valuable can be lost by taking time'. He upheld the importance of all using their intelligence and relying on 'patriotism, Christianity, and a firm reliance on Him who has never yet forsaken this favoured land', factors that 'are still competent to adjust in the best way all our present difficulties'.[104]

Then Lincoln, after a beautifully composed but essentially constitutional exegesis, brought the speech to an unexpected, though quite logical and noble climax in a quite sublime passage:

102. Ibid., IV, pp. 266–7.
103. Ibid., IV, p. 270.
104. Ibid., IV, pp. 270–1.

I am loth to close. We are not enemies, but friends. We must not be enemies. Though passion may have strained, it must not break our bonds of affection. The mystic chords of memory, stretching from every battlefield and patriot grave to every living heart and hearthstone all over this broad land, will yet swell the chorus of the Union, when again touched, as surely they will be, by the better angels of our nature.

That a man who could write such a passage was written off as a nonentity must be put down to the giddiness and agitation attending momentous and hazardous events, and the ceaseless and ill-informed chatter which accompanies them. When clever but self-satisfied men are determined to see a fool, they will see a fool even if a sage returns their stares.[105]

Yet the import of the inaugural address was unambiguous. Lincoln had made every effort to conciliate the southern states. He had conceded as much as he could on the slavery issue. Southern fears about the future of slavery in the states received great attention, and Lincoln had underlined that he would not oppose a constitutional amendment protecting it there indefinitely. He was not markedly enthusiastic about this. Such an initiative was superfluous as slavery was already protected within the states. The only dispute of substance related to its extension. The apostles of slavery were of the view that unless the institution grew it would ultimately wither and die. They chose to use force to ensure this growth. No longer would they have the patience to rely on the negative, protective influence of labyrinthine congressional procedures and the deliberations of the Supreme Court. Indeed Lincoln was of the opinion that the Federal government could not continually defer to the Supreme Court and permit it untrammelled power in this matter, because it would abdicate democratic procedures leaving them in the hands of non-elected judicial officials. The democratic mechanism must be given an unfettered right to decide grave questions unchecked by threats of secession: 'the central idea of secession is the essence of anarchy'.

Lincoln thus offered the choice of a heart-warming presidential embrace, continuing with the Union as before, with slavery protected but restricted, or the cold and harsh winds of isolation and uncertainty if the embrace was spurned. The South would inhabit an inhospitable environment which might batter slavery to

105. Ibid., IV, pp. 271.

pieces. By cleverly placing the onus on the secessionists to make the next move, however, Lincoln had set in place another strand of the policy which he hoped would deter the secessionists from rashness: that the power of the Federal government would *force* the secessionists to return to the Union if they failed to take counsel of patriotism and common sense. Charles Francis Adams was to describe the dual elements in Lincoln's policy by reference to 'Napoleon's simile of "a hand of iron and a velvet glove" '.[106] Lincoln adverted to the dangers of collision, should the seceded states carry on regardless in their headstrong way. 'Physically speaking, we cannot separate. We cannot remove our respective sections from each other, nor build an impassable wall between them. . . . They cannot but remain face to face; and intercourse, either amicable or hostile, must continue between them'. On returning to a cold, dingy Executive Mansion, much in need of redecoration, Lincoln's first act was to read documents which indicated that such a collision seemed to loom sooner rather than later.[107]

106. Adams, *Autobiography*, p. 98.
107. Lincoln, *Collected Works*, IV, p. 269.

CHAPTER EIGHT

The Final Crisis: Fort Sumter

[Hay] had come to think of Lincoln as a beleaguered fortress, with cannons firing at him from every direction; a fortress waiting to be relieved by. . . . But Hay did not know by what. No one knew what was in Lincoln's mind.

GORE VIDAL, *Lincoln: A Novel*[1]

In his inaugural address, President Lincoln claimed that the secession of the Lower South constituted the 'essence' of anarchy. The anarchical elements of southern separatism have been one of the main themes of this book. In setting out to answer the two questions posed at the beginning – why did the Lower South secede in 1860–61, and why was that act followed so quickly by civil war? – we must now turn our attention to tracing in detail the passage of events that resulted in the firing of shots by southerners on fortifications sheltering northerners. It should be made clear at the outset that this event does not stand like a lighthouse, with the tranquillity of peace on one side and the surging fury of the tides of war on the other (which is the impression given in some accounts), but full square in the middle of the secession crisis. The order to open fire given at Fort Sumter on 12 April 1861 is only the culmination of a stream of violent acts that had begun in the mid-1850s and was to escalate gradually until the onset of punitive war by the autumn of 1862. In this perspective, the main significance of this final crisis is to signal the onset of organized violence. The anarchical condition affected small matters as well as great; indeed, it was a breakdown over the minor, if significant, legacy of secession, namely, the status of a handful of federal forts, that precipitated the Civil War, rather than the momentous act of

1. Gore Vidal, *Lincoln: A Novel* (London: Grafton, 1985, 1990), p. 46.

310

seceding from the Union. Thus, the act of secession itself did not lead inevitably to war. Secessionist acts do not intrinsically carry the seeds of civil war (although there are few secessions carried out peaceably: the withdrawal of Belgium from the kingdom of the Netherlands in 1830 is perhaps one, but that settlement was guaranteed by two great powers, Britain and Prussia, in the Treaty of London in 1839). The real cause of organized violence *was the way that secession had been carried out*. The seceded states were unconsolidated, uncoordinated and ill prepared for independence materially and psychologically. The same was true of the northern states and the Federal government. The South was weak and belligerent simultaneously – a fatal combination. The strength and capacity of the Confederate armies in 1862–63 is one indication of the kind of power that the South could have brought to bear in 1861 if her attempt to gain independence had been agreed, thought out, and carefully prepared for. The Confederacy might have been successful in deterring war. Be it remembered that relative strengths, and opinions about comparative military power currently prevailing, are a powerful factor in the calculations that statesmen make before deciding for war.[2]

To recapitulate: the eruption of the American Civil War in April 1861 is just the culmination of a stream of violent acts arising from unstable political conditions, verging on anarchy, that went back well before 1858, though it had been particularly strong since that date. But the precipitate rush to full-scale hostilities needs to be explained. As the decision on both sides represents a balancing of competing forces and an estimate of relative strengths, such a correlation needs to be assessed strategically, using methods of strategic analysis, not of politics. Earlier historians have attempted to reduce the manoeuvres of the early months of 1861, as they should be, to a 'strategy', for example, Kenneth M. Stampp's 'strategy of defence'. Certainly the last fifty years have demonstrated beyond any doubt that methods of strategic analysis can increase our understanding of a political problem in peacetime. Even when the participants in a given crisis or confrontation themselves do not think in terms of strategic language, they may act in ways which are consistent with it. This chapter will be the second in which the structure and relationship of events will be analysed by employing a 'model'. But before

---

2. Geoffrey Blainey, *The Causes of War*, 3rd edn (London: Macmillan, 1988), pp. 67, 264, 293.

proceeding further with an investigation of this kind, the political
context of the last crisis must be established.

The political context

The most intractable aspect of the whole crisis was that both sides
were concerned first and foremost with principles rather than with
the more mundane but amenable lesser issues of day-to-day
political intercourse. The South, or a part of it, sought its
'independence'. The North sought to maintain the 'integrity of
the Union'. It would have been difficult enough to have reached
any kind of 'deal' to accommodate these elevated sentiments, even
if their proponents had been of a mind to seek and accept one,
which they were not. Because of this an asymmetry of political
relations developed between the two sides which contributed to
the misunderstandings and errors that occurred. The South acted
and behaved like an independent country; northerners continued
to treat its emissaries as fellow citizens with a shared culture and
values – even when they were engaged in 'secret' diplomacy over
the future of the Union. They often acted at cross-purposes
because of this difference. Matters were also confused because of
the chaos on the southern side. In the first stage of the developing
crisis over the forts, the government of South Carolina was the
'sovereign' power negotiating with the United States; after 12
February it was the Confederacy. Opinion was inflamed on the
southern side, because the pro-southern tenor of Buchanan's
administration led them to believe that he would continue to
acquiesce, if not sympathize, with their aspirations. When it
became clear that he did not, the southern reaction, like a jilted
lover, was bitter, and Buchanan was accused of despicable
double-dealing.[3]

Here were two sides, both of whom claimed to be acting
defensively. The South sought, as all legitimate states should, to
protect its territorial integrity and security; the North attempted to
protect the Constitution from the depredations of a handful of
mischief-making insurgents who had stampeded their states into
defying the verdict of a presidential election; it also sought to
defend its property, and prevent any addition to Confederate

    3.   Elbert B. Smith, *The Presidency of James Buchanan* (Lawrence, KS: University
of Kansas Press, 1975), pp. 182–3, 186.

military power, however small. Yet this attitude, which was so important to both sides in sustaining the somewhat mythical(and over-strained) time-honoured tradition that Americans behave only defensively, *never* aggressively, was in one very profound sense irrelevant. If principles were at the forefront of everybody's mind, then the symbolism pervading the confrontation could easily be extended to the forts in question. This was what happened to Fort Sumter, which became a symbol for both sides. It also became a symbol that both sides were pursuing their objectives defensively. Yet two defensive attitudes may produce an offensive act in the same way that two negative poles make a positive.[4]

What were they arguing about and why did these properties assume a symbolic significance? The four properties offering the most blatant provocation were those found in the environs of Charleston, South Carolina. They included Fort Sumter (still unfinished but dominating Charleston harbour because of its location on a tiny island in the harbour entrance) and Fort Moultrie, Fort Johnson and Castle Pinckney, all nestling in the basket of secessionist vipers. Less exposed was Fort Pickens, near Pensacola, Florida. Pickens was less vulnerable, mainly because it lay outside any harbour, while Castle Pinckney, Fort Johnson and Fort Moultrie not only were weak and undermanned fortifications (Castle Pinckney boasting a garrison of one quartermaster sergeant) but also could easily be isolated from relieving naval forces. Even Sumter could not easily be succoured because any vessels coming to its rescue could easily be fired on from shore batteries (see maps).[5] These forts were held by virtue of a contract or sometimes a conditional cession from the parent state. There were obviously ways of securing legal redress for the loss of such installations *if* the Federal government was prepared to recognize southern independence. But this was begging the question. Not only did Charlestonians believe that the forts should and must belong to the Palmetto state but they served as a bellwether of Union intentions towards the secessionist movements − not as yet consolidated, of course, into a unified rival republic.[6]

4.   Ken Booth and Moorhead Wright (eds) *American Thinking about Peace and War* (Brighton: Harvester, 1978).

5.   The fullest account is still W. A. Swanberg, *First Blood: The Story of Fort Sumter* (New York: Scribner's, 1957) who (p. 134) suggests that 'As it stood, Sumter could easily have been taken by a few hundred men with scaling ladders'.

6.   Smith, *Buchanan*, pp. 168, 170. Smith's book is a useful corrective to Swanberg's severe strictures on the weakness exhibited by the Buchanan Administration. See Swanberg, *First Blood*, pp. 72, 92.

The major change in the political climate in which Buchanan (and later Lincoln) had to operate, was the tremendous and sudden shift in northern public opinion concerning the range of measures available to deal with the South. In January 1860 northern public opinion, in so far as it can be measured, seemed to smile on the Crittenden Compromise. In New York City alone 63,000 people signed a petition supporting the passage of the Compromise. A further petition included another 14,000 female signatures. St Louis addressed to the president a list of names 100 pages long shrouded in an American flag. Business in the north eastern states quivered at the thought of losing $150 million in southern debts let alone double that sum lost in lucrative business with the South. Wall Street feared the onset of 'creeping economic paralysis'. 'To the very last', complained George W. Julian, 'the old medicine of compromise and conciliation seemed to be the sovereign hope of the people of the free states'; this is not very surprising, since the great majority of peaceful citizens, if given a choice, tend to prefer the continuation of the arts and prosperity of peace to the danger, uncertainty and discomfort of war.[7] There were, however, only three alternative solutions to the northern dilemma: first, to acquiesce in secession; secondly, to attempt to use force; or thirdly, what Kenneth Stampp calls the 'escapist formula' of masterly inactivity advocated (and pursued) by Seward and Bates.[8] Over a period of two months, northern public opinion shifted significantly from supporting the first and third positions, to believing that the Federal government needed to 'stand up' to the secessionists, so that by July it supported preventive war. (Admittedly, we cannot test public opinion rigorously in this period, but collections of constitutents' letters support this contention.) This was a shift in opinion comparable in its suddenness and intensity to that experienced in Great Britain between the German occupation of Prague in March 1939 and the following September, when opinion resisted further concessions at the expense of Poland.[9]

Most of Buchanan's admirers were based in the South and he was unwilling to upset them. As proof of his good intentions he

7.   George W. Julian, *Political Recollections, 1840 to 1872* (Chicago: McClurg, 1884), pp. 186–7.

8.   Kenneth M. Stampp, *And the War Came: The North and the Secession Crisis, 1860–61* (Baton Rouge: Louisiana State UP, 1950), pp. 49, 124, 131–2.

9.   See P. M. H. Bell, *The Origins of the Second World War in Europe* (London: Longman, 1986), pp. 264–6.

accepted the demands of his South Carolinian Assistant Secretary of State, William H. Trescot. He did not send reinforcements to the Charleston forts, as requested by Lieutenant General Winfield Scott in a controversial document called his 'Views', which was later published. And he relieved of command of Fort Sumter, Colonel John Gardner, who was too energetic and masterful in the pursuit of his duties for southern tastes; he also instructed that the forty muskets, acquired by Gardner to strengthen his garrison, be returned to the Charleston arsenal from whence Gardner had spirited them. It is symptomatic of the muddle and anarchy prevailing at this date, with central authority crumbling under an Administration that represented the only national party political institution remaining, the Democrats, that Buchanan seemed to be negotiating with members of his own administration over the future of the Charleston forts rather than with the central authority of another power. It says much for the arthritic state of the Federal government's response to this crisis that the officer who replaced Gardner, Major Robert Anderson, a 56-year-old Kentuckian, who because of his pro-slavery views was considered more 'acceptable', was referred to by his septuagenarian commanding general, Scott, as 'young Anderson'.[10]

Yet by 8 January 1861 in his State of the Union Address, Buchanan had made clear his view that 'the right and the duty to use military force defensively against those who resist federal officers in the execution of their legal functions, and against those who assail the property of the federal government, is clear and undeniable'. Buchanan, with that iron determination and steadfast stubborness, which he had inherited from his Scottish forebears, and which he had expended in many a wrong-headed cause, at last directed his undoubted talents in defence of a worthy one. It was thanks to him that these last outposts of federal authority were held against the Confederate tide and left as bridgeheads for a relieving counter-attack. Buchanan received no thanks for this during his lifetime. The overall effect of his contribution was nonetheless negative. He held the line, and rather than solve the problem itself, he bequeathed it intact to his successor. The situation can hardly be described as the maintenance of the *status quo*. (In view of what had occurred between November 1860 and March 1861.) But he could have made it worse; he could have left Lincoln in a weaker position *vis-à-vis* the South by tolerating a *force*

---

10.   Swanberg, *First Blood*, p. 84; Smith, *Buchanan*, pp. 154, 169.

majeure, which would have left Fort Pickens an isolated and exposed outpost of federal authority. Washington's prestige, would probably never have recovered from the loss of the Charleston forts. At all events, Buchanan struggled obstinately, though unheroically, not to make Lincoln's intractable difficulties even worse than they already were.[11]

It is against this chaotic background, of an embryonic polity struggling to assert a right to independence yet lacking a cohesive central form, and a timorous Federal government in Washington feeling its way cautiously, with some of its members representing the rebels more vociferously than the rebels themselves, that we need to understand certain key terms used as the final crisis unfolded. These are often placed in apposition but ultimately, because of misunderstandings, they were placed in opposition. What was the difference between 'enforcing the laws' and 'coercing a sovereign state'? Here we return to the semantic argument of who was the aggressor? This, needless to say, depended on whether 'peaceable secession' was a feasible proposition; or whether, even if the act of secession could be carried out peaceably, the Federal government would simply sit back passively and make no effort to impede or resist it? It cannot be reiterated too firmly, especially when considering a society whose political life was dominated by the legal process and governed by lawyers, that this issue rested on *policy* and not judicial rights, and in the last resort, politicians acted on both sides in accordance with this view. There were two alternative explanations of the prevailing formulae, which acted as a cloak, or pretext, for the pursuit of policy.

1 The 'enforcement of the laws' meant the collection of the duties and imposts, and the administration of all the other commercial and judicial regulations pertaining to the federal government, including the holding of all federal property. The end of the crisis would see the North, supported by public opinion, demanding compliance with a proper and untrammelled enforcement of federal law.

2 The 'coercion of a sovereign state' was the subjugation and invasion of a state which had chosen the right of self-determination (as a later generation would put it), or the threat thereof which amounted to intimidation of the most brutal

11. Stampp, *And the War Came*, pp. 75–82; Smith, *Buchanan*, p. 164.

kind. It also involved the forcing of states to send their representatives to Congress and enjoy the privileges of a political system against their will, and which they wished to leave.

Now clearly these standpoints were not unrelated, in the sense that they were different sides of the same American coin. Yet they provide evidence of an unbridgeable gulf between the two interpretations North and South, which no amount of adjudication by benches of judges, or refinement by politicians in their speeches, could bridge. One or other had to prevail and this could be achieved only by force. But to the North secessionists were the aggressors because, not only did they flout the judgement delivered by the electors in 1860, but also they sought to change the structure of the existing political relationships, and do this in a blustering and bellicose manner. The *status quo* was threatened, and the North needed only to uphold the symbols of the Union's power to keep this *status quo* intact. The onus of drastically altering this could be placed on the South. This had long been recognized, and the argument itself was familiar, though the means of carrying it out were not. For example, Stephen Douglas outlined with admirable clarity in 1858 the strategic dilemma facing the Lincoln Administration in March 1861. Should it come to secession, Douglas argued,

> Our true policy is to put the disunionists in their real light before the country. We must put them in such a position that when the break comes, as come it must, they will be in the position of insurgents; instead of letting them create a situation, as they wish to do, in which *we* must revolt. We will let them be the rebels. Then the army and the power of the nation will be against them.[12]

The only difficulty with this strategy was, did the South mean what it said? There can be no doubt that if Lincoln chose to adopt this course (and we have no way of knowing whether Lincoln knew of Douglas's views or whether he made them clear to Lincoln in discussion) it was very risky. One error, one slip, and the Federal government would be branded as a reckless and callous aggressor. Yet if it is borne in mind that the Federal government was faced only by a rebellious fragment of the slave states, calling their bluff did not seem a bad bet, though it would have to be done cautiously. The Federal government could be seen to be well

12. Quoted in Allan Nevins, *The Emergence of Lincoln* (New York: Scribner's, 1950), I, pp. 261–2.

within its rights in attempting to collect the revenues owed to it, or to reinforce, or at least re-supply, its forts, *so long as the Federal government still existed and it continued to enjoy the loyalty of a majority of the citizens of the United States.* That is to say, even a president as supine and compliant in the face of southern demands as James Buchanan was not prepared to admit that the Federal government had ceased to exist or lost its prerogatives. Thus 'peaceable secession' was an illusion of the cruellest kind, for it led southerners to paint a mental picture of chalk, which would soon be washed away once their ambitious plans met with a firm *douche.*

Nonetheless, it should be made clear that the 'coercion' that secessionist sympathizers referred to – one of those words which was repeated so often by southerners that it became a mantra – was different in kind from the visions they summoned up of a large army advancing remorselessly, stamping out their liberties and prosperity; for such an army did not exist (unless one counts John Brown's pathetic foray, which was designed to create a slave army, but this would hardly have been of a Napoleonic order). And under such conditions, a spirited effort at resistance in southern eyes, could be viewed by the North as an act of flagrant aggression; an act of aggression, moreover, of such wantonness that it would provoke the creation of that huge army that would stamp on southern hopes. Often the dividing line between 'peace' and 'war' is an artificial one, as these conditions are so closely related. In the same way that a lack of proportion and prudence had characterized southern actions in those months before secession, so they characterized southern behaviour on leaving the Union, and the result was war. The South, as usual, was its own worst enemy.[13]

The problem of interpretation

Certain common features have characterized the large literature on the outbreak of the American Civil War, even if (and largely because) historians from the two sections have approached the question of who was responsible from opposite directions. Historians have tended to assume that the reactions of leading figures in the Sumter crisis took the form of a game of chess on a grand scale. Their accounts have been written in a manner which

13.   Stampp, *And the War Came,* pp. 31–44.

identifies each side in the confrontation with one individual – the political leader. It is his motives, aspirations and calculations that count.[14] Such considerations, of course, are not inconsequential. But it is the underlying theme of this chapter that an undue focus on motives in evaluating the Sumter crisis is misleading; it underrates the importance of *how* decisions are carried out, and the effect of these decisions on the overall environment in which action is taken – which might be quite unexpected and unprepared for. Taking decisions and having them carried out is not a game of chess. The assumption that action in a great crisis can be controlled as in a game neglects the enormous physical and moral obstacles to fulfilling the will of a leader and gaining acceptance of his executive instructions. A later chief executive, President Harry S. Truman, realized this and predicted that the victorious Republican candidate in the 1952 presidential election, General Dwight D. Eisenhower, a military man used to giving orders, would experience considerable frustration. 'He'll sit here, and he'll say "Do this! Do that!" *And nothing will happen.*'[15]

The approach adopted in this chapter reflects Truman's shrewd remarks. It argues that mishaps, miscalculations and misfortunes characterized the manoeuvres that prefaced the Civil War in 1861 just as much as they dominated the conduct of military operations that followed the first shots at Fort Sumter. 'Few indeed are the occasions', wrote Sir Harold Nicolson, 'on which any statesmen sees his objective clearly before him and marches towards it with undeviating stride; numerous indeed are the occasions when a decision . . . which at the time seems wholly unimportant, leads almost fortuitously to another decision which is no less incidental, until, little link by link, the chain of circumstance is forged'.[16] And in reaching these decisions emotion was just as important as calm reasoning, illusion and wishful thinking as persuasive as realistic deliberation, and error and doubt just as potent as resolution and

---

14. The controversy over the responsibility for firing the first shot was related to a similar controversy after 1941 as to Franklin D. Roosevelt's responsibility for 'exposing' the US Pacific Fleet to Japanese attack. See Richard N. Current, *Lincoln and the First Shot* (New York: Lippincott, 1963) and Current, *Secretary Stimson: A Study in Statecraft*, 2nd edn (New York, 1970). The most critical book on Lincoln's policy is John S. Tilley, *Lincoln Takes Command* (Chapel Hill, NC, 1941: 2nd rev. edn, Bill Coates, 1991).

15. Quoted in Marcus Cunliffe, *American Presidents and the Presidency*, 2nd edn (London: Fontana, 1972), p. 272.

16. Harold Nicolson, *The Congress of Vienna* (London: Constable, 1946), pp. 17–18.

determination. In a hazardous crisis statesmen may seek to exert maximum control over events and their baleful consequences; but their capacity to do this depends on the relative state of technology – and communications technology especially.[17] Once we stop treating the Sumter crisis like a criminal trial which seeks either to condemn or to exculpate various actors in the drama, then we may be able to analyse it without reference to polemical (and often sectional) controversies. This requires, more than anything else, a reappraisal of the evidence on which traditional interpretations rest.

The Sumter crisis has usually been viewed, and quite rightly, as the culmination of the general political crisis of the 1850s. Once the first shots rang out at Fort Sumter 'the war' began and so ended the political crisis. This view is represented in David Potter's survey, *The Impending Crisis, 1848–1861* (1976). His final chapter is entitled, 'Fort Sumter: End and Beginning'. Strategy begins, according to this view, when politics comes to an end. Such an approach ignores the fundamental continuities which run through the crisis and characterize both the last days of peace and the first days of war. These events cannot be treated convincingly when they are studied in artificial compartments.[18] The crisis at Fort Sumter cannot be understood adequately unless it is viewed *strategically*. The actions of both the Buchanan and Lincoln Administrations must be analysed in relation to the decision-making machinery available to nineteenth-century presidents. The crisis was from the first a military clash and it is only by making full use of strategic analysis that we can make sense of it within the broad political and social context which has been emphasized by earlier historians. In the nineteenth century presidents lacked the executive means to assert the enormous latent resources of the United States in peacetime. The executive branch was small; the presidency gradually lost influence and prestige after 1840. During the 1850s the initiative for policy-making came either from independent-minded cabinet members, like Franklin Pierce's Secretary of War, Jefferson Davis,

---

17.   Under rather similar circumstances over a century later during the Cuban Missile Crisis in October 1962, President John F. Kennedy attempted to centralize decision-making as much as possible. See Robert F. Kennedy, *Thirteen Days: A Memoir of the Cuban Missile Crisis* (New York, 1969), pp. 62–3, 105–6.

18.   David M. Potter, *The Impending Crisis, 1848–1861*, completed and ed. by Don E. Fehrenbacher (New York: Harper, 1976), pp. 555–83; Stampp, *And The War Came*, pp. 190–2, 284–5.

or from Congress.[19] By James Buchanan's presidency both the will and the means for organizing an energetic policy to oppose secession was lacking. Throughout, Buchanan argued that only Congress had the right and authority to settle the matter of seeking a peaceful settlement or sanctioning the use of force in the defence of federal installations.[20] Contemporaries were inclined to believe that Buchanan only lacked the will. Thus when Lincoln's friend, Orville Hickman Browning, lamented 'how easily by promptness, energy and honesty of action, this government could have been maintained. The men who had the power and means to maintain it, and failed to use them, deserve death', we should be aware that no executive machinery existed to implement the energetic measures that he demanded.[21]

By the time that Lincoln as president-elect arrived in Washington DC on 22 February 1861, he had already received papers from General Scott including his 'Views' written in the previous October, and he had studied Jackson's Proclamation of 1832. Lincoln had declared at Philadelphia while *en route* that 'there will be no bloodshed unless it be forced upon the Government, and then it will be compelled to act in self-defense. [Applause]'. But by then all of the crucial decisions had already been taken. During the early months of 1861 the southern states had occupied all federal installations within their frontiers save for the three forts, Sumter, Moultrie and Pickens. The commander at Sumter and Moultrie, Major Anderson, was denied clear and incontrovertible instructions from the Secretary of War, the timorous and deceitful Confederate sympathizer, John B. Floyd. On 9 December 1860 Anderson discussed with the visiting Assistant Adjutant General, Captain Don Carlos Buell, the possibility of moving his tiny garrison of seventy-three men (plus over two hundred obstreperous workmen) from the exposed and indefensible Moultrie to Sumter.[22] Buell agreed that Moultrie

19. M. J. Heale, *The Making of American Politics, 1750–1850* (London: Longman 1977), pp. 108–12, 115; John M. Belohlavek, *'Let the Eagle Soar!': The Foreign Policy of Andrew Jackson* (Lincoln and London: University of Nebraska Press 1985), pp. 32, 39–40.

20. Smith, *Buchanan*, p. 161, 189.

21. Orville Hickman Browning to Abraham Lincoln, 26 Mar. 1861, Robert Todd Lincoln Collection of the Papers of Abraham Lincoln, Library of Congress, Washington DC (hereafter Lincoln Papers).

22. William E. Baringer, *A House Dividing: Lincoln as President Elect* (Springfield, IL: Abraham Lincoln Association, 1945), p. 291; Memorandum of Verbal Instructions to Major Anderson, 1st Artillery, Commanding at Fort Moultrie, South Carolina, 11 Dec. 1860, *The War of the Rebellion: A Compilation of the Official Records of the Union and Confederate Armies*, 128 vols (Washington DC: Government Printing Office, 1880), series 1, I, p. 89.

could not be held but urged caution as Floyd was anxious to avoid 'any measures which might add to the present excited state of the public mind, or which would throw any doubt on the confidence . . . that South Carolina will not attempt, by violence, to obtain possession of the public works or interfere with their occupancy'.[23]

Anderson had also discussed his dilemma with a South Carolinian officer, Benjamin Huger, his former West Point classmate, who now commanded the Charleston arsenal. He, too, urged Anderson to shift his garrison to Sumter.[24] Huger justified his behaviour later by an argument that would be repeated many times during the crisis. 'My counsel and influence would be given by all honourable means to gain *time* and not to commit any act tending to a civil war, which none of us may see the end of.'[25] But each attempt to gain time ended by increasing the time pressures on the garrison and those seeking to extricate them, closing off space in which to manoeuvre. On 26 December Anderson moved his garrison after dark from Moultrie to Sumter under the noses of the South Carolinians. Anderson's decision, more than any other, shaped the pattern of the subsequent crisis. 'Cut off from all intercourse with my Government', he explained, 'I have been compelled to act according to the dictates of my own judgement'. The only instructions he received from Floyd were contradictory. Anderson was ordered 'to hold possession of the forts in the harbor of Charleston and, if attacked, to defend yourself to the last extremity'. But he was not expected 'to make a vain and useless sacrifice of your own life and the lives of the men under your command, upon a mere point of honor'. Anderson was assured: 'This is far from the President's intentions. You are to exercise a sound military discretion on this subject'. Even after Lincoln's inauguration Anderson was neglected by his political masters. He wrote many missives detailing Confederate activities but was unaware of the administration's policy until the very end, and then he disapproved of it.[26]

23. Smith, *Buchanan*, pp. 171–2.
24. Jeffrey Rhoades, *Scapegoat General* (Hamden, CT: Archon 1985), pp. 18, 22, 25.
25. Swanberg, *First Blood*, pp. 32–3, 41–3, 46.
26. Anderson to General Scott, 1 Apr. 1861, Anderson Papers, General Correspondence, 11, Library of Congress; John B. Floyd to Anderson, 21 Dec. 1860, *Official Records*, I, p. 103; Swanberg, *First Blood*, pp. 5, 49–51; David Potter, *Lincoln and his Party in the Secession Crisis* (New Haven, CT: 1942, 1962; New York: AMS Press, 1979 reprint), pp. 268–72.

A delegation of commissioners from South Carolina visiting Washington to seek a resolution of the crisis (and which Buchanan had agreed to see as 'private gentlemen') was enraged by Anderson's move. They believed that he had violated an informal truce which had prevailed at Fort Pickens and was extended to Sumter. The existence of this 'truce' had not discouraged a demand made on 20 December by the Governor of South Carolina, William Pickens, for the surrender of Fort Sumter. The Confederates had agreed not to carry out any hostile acts so long as the *status quo* was maintained. Buchanan tried to placate them and for several days dithered over whether to order Anderson to return to Moultrie. Yet in January under pressure from the increasingly hawkish members of his cabinet, especially the new Secretary of War, Joseph Holt, and the new Attorney General, Edwin M. Stanton, Buchanan agreed to dispatch the *Star of the West*, a merchant vessel, to revictual Sumter. The South Carolinians fired on her and she withdrew at the first sign of hostility.[27] But the results of this ill-fated expedition were profound. By taking the risk of sailing into Charleston harbour, and then not pushing on to Sumter while the Confederate works were weaker than they would be four months later, the *Star of the West* incident committed the dual sin of provoking the Confederates while not attaining the aim of re-supplying Sumter. Furthermore, it increased the pressure of time on the Lincoln Administration which took office on 4 March 1861. As Lincoln was soon to discover, Anderson could not possibly hope to hold out beyond the middle of April 1861. Thus the stalemate was cemented.[28]

The prime concern of the Buchanan Administration was to leave office without provoking war. Buchanan believed that, although secession was illegal, the Federal government had no power to resist it. He was prepared to excuse political disruption in the South as 'revolution', which was somehow condonable; secession was not, because Buchanan could not agree that the slave states could pass ordinances 'by virtue of an inherent constitutional right'. Secession would also be a temporary rupture. If the Administration showed itself conciliatory, and slavery was not endangered, the erring southern sisters would return to the

27. Allan Nevins, *The Emergence of Lincoln* (New York: Scribner's, 1950), II, pp. 366–74; Roy F. Nichols, *The Disruption of American Democracy* (New York: Macmillan, 1948), pp. 428–35.

28. Smith, *Buchanan*, pp. 178–9.

Union in time to elect another Democratic president in 1864. Consequently, no attempt was made to extend the instructions formerly issued by Floyd. Holt merely affirmed that Buchanan believed that the truce would continue: 'there will be no immediate attack on Fort Sumter; and the hope is indulged that wise and patriotic counsel may prevail and prevent it altogether'. Buchanan had placed especial faith in the deliberations of the Peace Congress in Washington; and 'the presence of that body here', Anderson was assured, 'adds another to the powerful motives already existing for the adoption of every measure, except in necessary defence, for avoiding a collision with the forces that surround you'. And indeed, throughout these months the besiegers (now commanded by Anderson's West Point pupil, General P. G. T. Beauregard) were at pains to avoid a *casus belli*.[29] This reflected the increasing hold the new Confederate government at Montgomery was exerting over the crisis, which was determined not to allow the South Carolinians to plunge the South impulsively and needlessly into war. Thus the stalemate and tedium continued to wear on until the inauguration of President Lincoln.[30]

In his earliest statements on the issue Lincoln had declared his determination to '*hold* or *retake* the forts, as the case may require, at and after the inauguration'. This deceptively simple statement (which concealed a number of insurmountable difficulties) guided Lincoln's policy throughout the crisis. He adhered to a determination to enforce federal law. But, despite his more belligerent tone, Lincoln moved as cautiously as Buchanan. Nonetheless he held to the basic policy announced in the inaugural address of wishing to 'hold, occupy and possess' the forts but refraining from invading any state. But the most important decisions which decided the fate of the garrison had already been taken, and all of these had led to a reduction in Lincoln's freedom of manoeuvre.[31]

Lincoln and his cabinet met four times to discuss the crisis, 9, 14 (two sessions in morning and afternoon), 28 and 29 March.

---

29. Holt to Anderson, 23 Feb. 1861, Anderson Papers; T. Harry Williams, *P. G. T. Beauregard: Napoleon in Gray* (Baton Rouge: Louisiana State UP, 1955, 1989), pp. 8, 54–7.

30. Smith, *Buchanan*, p. 150.

31. *The Collected Works of Abraham Lincoln*, ed. Roy P. Basler (New Brunswick, NJ: Rutgers UP, 1953), IV, pp. 262–71; see also John G. Nicolay and John Hay, *Abraham Lincoln: A History* (New York: Century, 1890), III, pp. 250, 256–7; Lincoln resisted pressure from Seward to remove this statement from the address, see Nevins, *Emergence of Lincoln*, II, p. 456.

After 14 and 29 March meetings the president required the cabinet to put their views in writing (and during the last meeting they actually set them down 'in cabinet'). The cabinet was divided into two groups, former Democrats led by the Secretary of the Treasury, Salmon P. Chase, and former Whigs led by the Secretary of State, William H. Seward. Lincoln was resolved to carry both these factions with him, whichever policy was decided on. At the second meeting and in the subsequent memoranda produced on 15 March, only one member, Montgomery Blair, the Postmaster-General (and not, as was expected, Chase) was unconditionally in favour of succouring the garrison. Over the course of the next fortnight opinion gradually hardened. On 29 March Lincoln eventually decided on a limited provisioning of Fort Sumter of which the Governor of South Carolina would be informed as the ships set out. A detailed consideration of how Lincoln reached this decision will be presented shortly. Already suspicious of these moves because of the promises given privately by Seward, that the Sumter garrison would be withdrawn, the Confederate government decided that the fort would have to be eventually taken. This decision was taken rather lightly considering the momentous consequences; but most figures involved in the crisis were convinced that if civil war did break out, then it would be short.

But if we view the Sumter crisis very much as the product of muddle, confusion and error just as much as of forethought and consideration, this should not be surprising. The methodology adopted to discuss it, therefore, should reflect such an overall perspective. It is important to relate each of the multifarious aspects of the crisis to a general interpretation. It was quite evident that throughout the crisis the Confederacy conducted itself like an independent state dealing with another foreign power (as the state of South Carolina had behaved before joining the other slave states in the Confederacy). Therefore, whatever the reality of the South's pretensions and its claims to separate nationhood (not only politically but also socially and culturally), for the purposes of this discussion the two sections are treated as distinct polities, even though the attempt to create a southern republic introduced anarchy to North America. In seeking to analyse the methods used by the Buchanan and Lincoln Administrations, a 'model' will be deployed to explain them, and one that owes little to the methods of political history. Therefore, in discussing crisis-management the 'model' will rest on three interrelated strategic elements: *space, time* and *direction*. This 'model', adapted from military theory, seeks to adumbrate those *conditions* that shaped decision-making. According to Clausewitz, the object of strategy is 'the employment of the available means for the predetermined end'.[32] The elements of the 'model' may be fitted into this framework. Space is the overall geographic framework in which a decision-maker operates, time is the factor which determines the pace of his decisions, and direction the manner in which they are carried out. This kind of analysis is equally applicable to the confrontations of peace as to those of wartime. These three elements will be related to the political issues and institutions which governed the crisis. In his treatise, *On War*, Clausewitz observed that

> The political object – the original motive for the war – will thus determine both the military objective to be reached and the amount of effort it requires. The political object cannot, however, *in itself* provide the standard of measurement . . . . We can therefore take the political object as a standard only if we think of *the influence it can exert upon the forces it is meant to move*. The nature of these forces therefore calls for study.

In his famous formulation, so frequently quoted but so imperfectly understood, Clausewitz declared 'that war is not merely an act of policy but a true political instrument, a continuation of political intercourse, carried on with other means. What remains peculiar to war is simply the peculiar nature of its means'. But he also reminds us shrewdly that, 'Man and his affairs, however, are always something short of perfect and will never quite achieve the absolute best'. This insight led him to expound the importance in any kind of conflict of 'friction', of which Lincoln's secretaries became acutely aware as they lived through the Sumter crisis. Those 'Countless minor incidents – the kind you can never really foresee – [which] combine to lower the general level of performance, so that one always falls far short of the intended goal'.[33]

In this analysis of the outbreak of a civil war, in which the two parties were divided by very clear geographical boundaries and formed distinct physical units (unlike in many earlier civil wars,

32. For the theoretical underpinning for this chapter, see Brian Holden Reid, 'The Crisis at Fort Sumter in 1861 Reconsidered', *History* 77 (Feb. 1992), p. 10.
33. Carl von Clausewitz, *On War*, ed. Michael Howard and Peter Paret (Princeton UP, 1976), I, i, pp. 7, 78; I, i, pp. 11, 81; I, i, pp. 24, 87; I, vii, p. 119; see Nicolay and Hay, *Abraham Lincoln*, III, p. 96, on organizing relief expenditures: 'It is the almost universal fate of such enterprises to encounter unforeseen difficulties and vexatious delays'.

such as the French Wars of Religion or the English Civil War), it was therefore possible for the rebel section to behave towards the Federal government as if it was an independent power. Consequently, the focus in this analysis will be just as much on the results of actions taken as on the intentions prompting them. This emphasis follows from an application of Clausewitz's concept of friction to the Sumter crisis. Just as the revolt of Great Britain's North American colonies in 1775–83 was greatly aided by the exploitation by the rebels of the enormous distance separating them from the government in London, so in 1861 did it appear likely that a rebellion against the authority of the Federal government in Washington DC would be greatly aided by the immensity of the distances that needed to be traversed if the rebels were to be coerced (especially while the Confederate government sat at Montgomery, Alabama). Moreover, it would take a government wholly unprepared for war a long time to mobilize sufficient strength to bring the rebels to heel. 'The outbreak of war', writes Evan Luard, 'depends not only on the motives of states but on their actions: on the specific decisions their governments reach at a certain moment to achieve their ends through war'. If we accept that the *way* decisions are reached is just as important as the underlying motives, then it is important to assess the kinds of decisions that were taken during the Sumter crisis. The influence of space and time will be considered first, before turning to an examination of the direction exerted by the president, not only over the general development of the crisis, but also the influence he enjoyed over the cabinet, the Congress, and the mechanisms of the executive branch itself.[34]

Space

The impact of the sheer size of the North American continent frequently exercised the imagination of early American political publicists. Thomas Jefferson was of the opinion that republics could not continue to expand indefinitely, and if they grew too large they would split asunder. During the early 1840s a school of expansionist writers held that technological innovations, especially the telegraph, would enable the United States to overcome the

34. Evan Luard, *War in International Society* (London: I. B. Tauris, 1986), pp. 18–20.

problems of communication and dominate the North American continent. Clearly, coordinating action and relating it to policy when such great distances were involved presented a major problem for the Federal government during the secession crisis. But this was not the only problem. An independent Confederacy would dominate strategic points in the Gulf of Mexico and along the eastern seaboard that were detrimental to the interests of the United States. As the Attorney General, Edward Bates, argued, 'the port of Charleston is, comparatively a small thing . . . the real struggle will be at the mouth of the Mississippi, for it is not politically possible for any *foreign* power, to hold the mouth of that river, against the people of the middle and upper valley'. The immense importance to American security and prosperity of this enormous basin was to figure prominently in Lincoln's calculations. It included forty-two tributaries, a total of 12,498 navigable miles. Mid-westerners, including Lincoln, did not wish to see this river system divided. Yet it had already fallen into rebel hands. The enormous size of this theatre of war meant that the North could not *conquer* the South very easily; indeed to many it seemed a hopeless task. The crisis at Fort Sumter, therefore, was the strategic symptom of a general geopolitical problem, and one which crippled the ability of the Federal government to react quickly. It would become clearer later in the crisis that if Sumter was given up, then the Confederacy would demand the surrender of Pickens and thus effectively exercise sovereignty over the Gulf of Mexico. The United States would lose all control over this region.[35]

This problem was further complicated by Lincoln's anxiety that another eight states might secede from the Union, should the United States government act to coerce their seceded sisters at Fort Sumter. These states included Tennessee, Kentucky, Virginia, and Maryland. Should the last two leave the Union, then Washington DC would be surrounded by the territory of a hostile power. 'Without some . . . benign measure, the remaining slave holding states will, probably, join the Montgomery confederacy in less than sixty days,' cautioned General Scott, 'when this city being included in a foreign country would require a permanent Garrison of at least 35,000 troops to protect the Government within it.' Jefferson Davis was quite confident in predicting that 'It is scarcely

---

35. Thomas R. Hietala, *Manifest Design: Anxious Aggrandizement in Late Jacksonian America* (Ithaca, NY: Cornell UP, 1985), pp. 196–7; Edward Bates, Memorandum on the Desirability of Reinforcing Fort Sumter, 15 Mar. 1861, Lincoln Papers.

to be doubted that for political reasons the US govt. will avoid making an attack so long as the hope of retaining the border states remains'.[36] This view was confirmed in the last days of the Buchanan Administration, when the Secretary of the Interior, Jacob Thompson was sent by the government of Mississippi to discuss secession with North Carolina. This mission was approved by President Buchanan. However, Thompson's view, as reported to cabinet, namely, that North Carolina would not secede unless some flagrant act of 'coercion' was committed, provoked a barrage of criticism. The northerners argued that the proper relationship between the Federal government and the states was not based on force; the threat of force came from the South. The President could not fail to notice a shift in northern opinion, a shift his successor could not ignore.

On 18 March Lincoln requested from Bates his opinion whether the president was constitutionally justified in collecting duties on board ship, offshore if normal procedures were disrupted. 'This would include the question of lawful power to prevent the landing of dutiable goods, unless the duties were paid'. Here, and in Lincoln's further letter to the Secretary of the Treasury, Salmon P. Chase, seeking views on whether ships 'could be effectively used to prevent such importations' was an effort to enforce the writ of the Federal government on recalcitrant states. The opinions of both Chase and Bates were later to serve as the legal basis for the blockade of the Confederacy which was organized very swiftly in April. Lincoln saw such methods as a more indirect way of applying pressure on the southern states. This policy was favoured by Seward (and other former Whigs) who preferred to 'defer military action on land until a case should arise when we would hold the defence'. Seward justified his position by a superficially persuasive case.

> I would not initiate a war to regain a useless and unnecessary position on the soil of the seceding States. I would not provoke war in any case *now*. I would resort to force to protect the collection of the revenue, because this is a necessary as well as legitimate Union object.[37]

36. Scott to Seward, 3 Mar. 1861, Lincoln Papers; Grady McWhiney, 'The Confederacy's First Shot', in John T. Hubbell (ed.) *Battles Lost and Won* (Westport, CT: Greenwood, 1975).

37. Lincoln to Bates, 18 Mar. 1861; Lincoln to Chase, 18. Mar. 1861; Seward to Lincoln, 15. Mar. 1861, The President submits to me the following question etc. (a memo of 28 pages), Lincoln Papers. Allan Nevins, *The War for the Union* (New York: Scribner's, 1959), I, p. 46, sees these letters as evidence that Lincoln 'leaned' towards Seward's views. Evidence on this point can never be conclusive because of

He preferred to rely on naval power to enforce this action, but such a method required time, and this Lincoln did not have.[38]

But the sheer practical difficulties of mounting an expedition to relieve Sumter bore down heavily on the president and his advisers. 'The influence of distance,' Roger Beaumont has observed, 'time lag and filtering through the levels within a communication system are factors that lie outside of presidential control.' The problem of moving even a small force a great distance would tax Federal resources. 'A projected attack, in large force', wrote General Scott justifying his own caution and pessimism as the crisis deepened, 'would draw to this Harbor [Charleston] all the available resources, in men and material, of the contiguous States'. The rebels could move larger forces by land than the Federal government could by sea (even allowing for poor southern road and rail communications). 'Charleston harbour would be a Sevastopol in such a conflict and unlimited means would probably be required to ensure success before which time the garrison of Fort Sumter would be starved out'. And, if this was not bad enough, how could it be possible, as Seward asked repeatedly, to prepare an expedition to sail to Charleston harbour *secretly*? 'In this active and enlightened country,' the Secretary of State warned, 'in this season of excitement with a daily press, daily mails and incessantly operating telegraph, the design to reinforce and supply the garrison must become known to the opposite party at Charleston as soon, at least as preparation for it should begin.' Far from acting as a means of binding the Union, the telegraph served as an efficient way of aiding its enemies. The telegraph could not be used to communicate with ships at sea, but could be used to communicate news of their movement to land-based forces. Consequently, the president would lose all control over any expedition once it had put out to sea, while those who sought to impede its progress would make ready to resist it. Clearly, in spatial terms the odds favoured the Confederate government; they held the initiative. This was not an equation that favoured the

the absence of material in Lincoln's hand; nonetheless, it is safer to conclude that the letters were more consistent with his inaugural address and its determination to enforce federal law and dues. Potter also argues (*Lincoln and his Party*, p. 358) that 'The supposed necessity of evacuating Sumter was the formative factor of all administration policy during March'. But this is too sweeping and ignores the missions of Hurlbut and Gustavus Fox as important contributions to the development of the president's thinking.

38. Smith, *Buchanan*, p. 176.

Lincoln Administration as it pondered an insoluble dilemma and March turned to April and time seemed to be running out.[39]

Time

In his first inaugural address President Lincoln declared that nothing could be lost 'by taking time'.[40] All Unionist participants in the crisis attempted to take their time but in vain. Before 4 March President Buchanan played for time by not deigning to reach a decision on any matter unless his hand was forced. The result of his indecisive and halting policy was that secession advanced without hindrance. Not only was the Administration on the defensive and forced to react to the secessionists' moves but also it was rendered almost defenceless. Thus the logic of making further concessions appeared inexorable. Time was marching with secession.

Lincoln had hoped that time would be his ally; instead it became his greatest enemy. 'He had counted on the soothing aid of time; time, on the contrary,' Nicolay and Hay recalled, 'was in this emergency working in the interests of the rebellion'.[41] Gaining time had two distinct advantages. First, it permitted, or so it was claimed, the emergence of wiser, more prudent counsel in the slave states. Secondly, by encouraging the growth of Unionist sentiment the Federal government could be seen to be doing *something*, no matter how innocuous. This belief – which was central to Seward's policy and guided the military advice tendered by General Scott – was also shared by Edward Bates who felt that the South was full of Unionists who would make their influence felt if given time. 'A reaction has already begun, and, if encouraged by wise, moderate, and firm measures. . . . I persuade myself that the nation will be restored to its integrity, without the effusion of blood'. Seward's policy, therefore, enjoyed a wide measure of support among the president's intimate advisers. But it, too, demanded time, and this was in short supply.[42]

39. General Scott, Memorandum Concerning the Reinforcing of Fort Sumter, 28 Feb. 1861; Seward to Lincoln, 15. Mar. 1861, Lincoln Papers; Smith, *Buchanan*, pp. 170–1; Roger A. Beaumont, 'Epilogue', in Joseph G. Dawson III (ed.) *Commanders in Chief: Presidential Leadership in Modern Wars* (Lawrence, KS: University Press of Kansas, 1993), p. 168.

40. Lincoln, *Collected Works*, IV, p. 270.

41. Nicolay and Hay, *Abraham Lincoln*, III, pp. 38, 75, 378.

42. Scott to Seward, 3 Mar. 1861; Bates to Lincoln, 15 Mar. 1861, Lincoln Papers. For a defence of Seward, see Daniel W. Crofts, *Reluctant Confederates: Upper South Unionists in the Secession Crisis* (Chapel Hill, NC: University of North Carolina Press, 1989), pp. 92, 124, 134, 214, 246–7, 254–8, 295–6, 356–9.

Events would soon confirm that such calculations were based merely on self-delusion, even wishful thinking. For, as Montgomery Blair, the most vociferous champion of resupplying Fort Sumter declared, secession had already gained a momentum which it would be difficult to check. 'Every hour of acquiescence in this condition of things', he warned, 'and especially every new conquest made by the rebels strengthens their hands at home and their claim to recognition as an independent people abroad'. Blair also raised another issue – the moral factor. Blair was quite right to argue that earlier failures of decision had encouraged rebellion. The Federal government therefore had to make a moral stand and Sumter was its symbol. Contempt for the Buchanan Administration was not the only factor promoting secessionist feeling. Blair warned that the secessionists assumed '*that the northern men are deficient in the courage necessary to maintain the Government*'. It was this confidence that encouraged secessionists to make increasingly ambitious claims. Blair felt that conciliatory moves were hopeless because demagogues had insinuated that the object of the Republican Party was to abolish slavery and introduce racial equality. Thus any policy which lacked firmness, in his view, 'so far from tending to prevent collision [will] ensure it unless all the other forts are evacuated and all attempts are given up to maintain the authority of the United States'. Conciliation could not work when it was treated by one party with contempt.[43]

This kind of argument undermined the advice being proffered by Bates and Seward, especially Seward. They both believed that Sumter symbolized no great national interest. Its possession would not allow the Federal government to collect the revenue or enforce rights of commercial navigation. In Bates's opinion, Lincoln could 'in humanity and patriotism safely waive the point of pride, in the consciousness that we have the power, and lack nothing but the will to hold Fort Sumter'. This point touched on a particularly sensitive nerve analysed very perceptively by Blair. Increasingly Lincoln felt pressure from his constituents and Congress, especially Republicans of a radical persuasion, that Sumter must be held to demonstrate the resolve of the Administration. Lincoln's postbag was full of letters from constituents and old friends calling for resolution. Yet Seward remained convinced that 'even in South Carolina, devotion to the

43. Montgomery Blair to Lincoln, 15 Mar. 1861, Lincoln Papers; on the general question of northern resolve, see Michael C. C. Adams, *Our Masters the Rebels* (Cambridge, MA: Harvard UP, 1978), pp. 56–60, 68–70.

Union is a profound and permanent national sentiment' which if sustained by conciliation would ultimately triumph and rally citizens to reverse the ordinance of secession. Thus if the Disunionists were denied an excuse to begin a civil war, their claims and anxieties would be rendered superfluous. Seward's policy was to hold Sumter 'so long as it can be done without involving some danger or evil greater than the advantage of continued possession'. But time was not on the side of such a waiting game, and abandonment of Sumter without a struggle would have detonated a political explosion almost as dangerous to the Lincoln Administration as an attempt to re-supply it.[44]

Lincoln sensed this strongly during the last-minute negotiations with Virginia unionists held in Washington during the first two weeks of April. At his first meeting on 4 April with a member of the Virginia Convention, John B. Baldwin, Lincoln flew a kite concerning the possible withdrawal of the Sumter garrison out of 'military necessity' to see what he could get in return. His most significant remark was that it was almost too late. Baldwin hectored him on the need to give up both Sumter and Pickens and give in to all southern demands. The price was too high – it guaranteed maximum concessions on the one side and the minimum on the other: 'you Virginia people are good Unionists, but it is always with an *if*' Lincoln observed later. Four days later he met with John Minor Botts, a former Whig. Lincoln repeated the details of the discussion with Baldwin concerning the possibility of evacuating Sumter in return for the adjourning of the Virginia convention, and stressed its inconsequential conclusion. When Botts urged that he repeat the offer, Lincoln replied, 'It is too late now'. Virginia Unionism was too flimsy an edifice on which to construct any durable compromise. Too much hope and resolution had been invested in Sumter to give it up, even for the sake of a fading hope that Virginia – a state of immense strategic importance – might remain neutral in the confrontation off Charleston harbour. Lincoln would not allow the Sumter garrison to be starved into submission.[45]

44. Bates to Lincoln, 15 Mar. 1861; Seward to Lincoln, 15 Mar. 1861 Lincoln Papers; Current, *Lincoln and the First Shot*, pp. 56, 78; Glyndon G. Van Deusen, *Seward* (New York: Oxford UP) pp. 276–85; see also Potter, *Lincoln and his Party*, pp. 144, 211–13, 227–31, 272, 286–7, 318; and Robert W. Johannsen, *Stephen A. Douglas* (New York: Oxford UP, 1973), p. 849.

45. Bates acted as an intermediary here. See Bates to Lincoln, 5 Apr. 1861, Lincoln Papers. Current, *Lincoln and the First Shot*, pp. 94–6, 111–13; Potter,

It was in complicating the vexing problem of re-supply that the failure of the *Star of the West*'s mission in January 1861 was so significant. It would have been comparatively easy to reinforce Sumter in January. General Scott estimated that 'The difficulty of reinforcing has now been increased 10 or 15 fold'. It increased the pressure of time and the necessity of taking a decision. Then, on 4 April the president received a letter from Anderson telling him that unless the labourers (who were working on the defences and were unluckily trapped when Anderson occupied Sumter) were released he would run out of provisions within four to six days. It was later claimed that this missive came as a shock to the Administration. But the president had already received a letter from Anderson on 4 March indicating that his supplies were low, which he hastened to pass on to Joseph Holt, who was standing in for the indisposed Cameron as Secretary of War, and was a valuable strand of continuity with the previous administration. When Lincoln enquired on 9 March how long the Sumter garrison could hold out, Scott replied categorically that he had sufficient flour and rice for twenty-six days and salt pork for forty-eight days. In other words, Lincoln was already aware that Anderson could not hold out beyond mid-April. It was for this reason that Lincoln eventually turned for advice to Gustavus Fox, an intrepid former naval officer (and Montgomery Blair's brother-in-law); he urged on the president a plan to relieve the fort. On 21 March Fox was dispatched to Sumter to get fresh intelligence. After discussion with Anderson, Fox came to the conclusion, broadly agreeing with Scott, that Sumter could hold out only until 15 April. Thus Anderson's letter could not have come as a shock to the president, even though in a later message (actually drafted by Lincoln but sent out under Simon Cameron's signature), the new Secretary of War reported that his letter 'occasions some anxiety to the President'.[46]

Impending Crisis, pp. 510–12; Nevins, *War for the Union*, I, pp. 46–7, 52–3; Potter, *Lincoln and his Party*, pp. 354–8, is less dismissive of these attempts but relies heavily on a reading of John Hay, *Lincoln and the Civil War in the Diaries and Letters of John Hay*, ed. Tyler Dennett (New York: 1939; Da Capo; 1988), p. 30 (entry for 22 Oct. 1861). But it is significant that Lincoln here dismissed the Virginians as 'pseudo-Unionists'. He evidently placed little faith on their long term loyalty, and rightly so. See also Crofts, *Reluctant Confederates*, pp. 301–6.

46.   Lincoln to Scott, 9 Mar. 1861; Winfield Scott, Fort Sumter, 11 Mar. 1861, Lincoln Papers; Cameron to Anderson, 4 Apr. 1861, Anderson Papers; Current, *Lincoln and the First Shot*, pp. 57, 71–2, 100–1; Nevins, *Emergence of Lincoln*, II, pp. 461–2.

Direction

It is possible to suggest, therefore, that Anderson's letter was used by Lincoln as a bombshell in an attempt to galvanize activity, and persuade the doubters that Sumter must be held. But in so doing, he brought to a head all the muddles, contradictions and sheer chaos inherent in the development of this crisis – especially in the improvised decision-making machinery with which he attempted to direct it. That is to say, Lincoln's efforts to resolve the crisis were hampered at every turn by the means at his disposal. Anderson's courageous and single-minded conduct throughout had transformed him into a public hero. His former commanding officer, John A. Dix, briefly Secretary of the Treasury in the Buchanan administration, having reported, after leaving Lincoln's inaugural, on the widespread demoralization in Washington and commented that 'the country turns with a relief . . . to the noble example of fidelity and courage presented by you and your gallant associates'. Anderson's plight therefore served to heighten determination in the North that he should not be left to his fate and served to fix attention on his beleaguered garrison. The incident which inflamed most feeling against treason among federal office-holders was the earlier surrender by General David E. Twiggs on 16 February of the United States arsenal and barracks at San Antonio, Texas (followed by all other military posts under his command two days later and his defection to the Confederacy). Dix considered 'The cowardice and treachery of General Twiggs is more disheartening than all that has transpired since this disgraceful career of disloyalty to the government commenced'. His act cast doubt on the loyalty of all serving officers, especially, if like Anderson, they were southern born (he was from Kentucky and his wife from Georgia). Anderson always believed that if his garrison needed help, 'it would be sent promptly, and in full force'. But he had always hoped that the crisis would be resolved peacefully. Either a settlement of outstanding issues would somehow be negotiated, or, most attractive prospect of all, his garrison would be evacuated honourably. In this suspicious climate, doubts about Anderson's loyalty surfaced in the newspapers, which reported rumours of his secessionist sympathies.[47]

47. Dix to Anderson, 4 Mar. 1861, Anderson Papers; Twiggs's Report, 19 Feb. 1861, is in *Official Records*, I, pp. 503–4; Swanberg, *First Blood*, p. 159; clipping of *New York Herald*, 22 Mar. 1861, Anderson Papers.

This distrustful atmosphere was a product of the last days of the Buchanan Administration, and it is necessary to go back in time to review once more its closing months. The Sumter crisis splintered the Buchanan Administration and it threatened to do the same to Lincoln's cabinet. Indeed it was a feature of the Civil War that the president's domination of his cabinet depended crucially on the progress made to suppress the Confederacy. The upsurge of Confederate support in 1861 threatened to engulf Lincoln as it had his predecessor. Buchanan was a wily politician, and an able diplomatist; but he was so attuned to dissimulation that he often failed to recognize when it was realistic or prudent to stop, and *act* rather than talk. His cabinet had included a number of Confederate sympathizers, Floyd, Howell Cobb (Georgia) and Jacob Thompson (Mississippi), none of whom was above dispatching privileged information to the South. These fissures were revealed starkly in the crisis arising from South Carolina's occupation of all federal installations (except the Charleston forts) in December 1860 and General Scott's call in his 'Views' that all southern forts should be reinforced. Scott later claimed in correspondence with Lincoln that he had been bullish at this stage. He argued that President Buchanan should either allow 'succour be sent by means of ships of war fighting their way to the fort, or 2. That the Major [Anderson] should ameliorate his condition by the muzzles of his guns – that is, enforcing supplies by bombardment'. There can be little doubt that Scott exaggerated his earlier preference for the use of force in December 1860, once he was weighed down with gloom in March 1861. On 28 December 1860 Buchanan met with the South Carolina Commissioners, who urged him to send Anderson back to Moultrie. That night the cabinet discussed the alternatives open to them. Buchanan sat like old Mr Woodhouse in Jane Austen's *Emma*, huddled in a dressing gown by the fire.[48] When Thompson called for an evacuation, the cabinet almost erupted into fisticuffs.

48. This account broadly agrees with that of Elbert Smith (*Buchanan*, p. 144) that the fifteenth president was not the enfeebled and hysterical puppet of his cabinet as portrayed in Nevins, *Emergence of Lincoln* and Nichols, *Disruption of American Democracy*, ch. XXI. I have hesitated using again the analogy with Mr Woodhouse as in 'Sumter Reconsidered', p. 18, until I noticed in Tony Tanner's commentary on the novel that he actually considered Mr Woodhouse, for all his infirmities and whining, a dominating character – as Buchanan certainly was. So I have left it in the text.

Stanton shouted: 'no administration. . . can afford to lose a million of money and a fort in the same week'.[49]

In an attempt to keep the peace Buchanan drafted a reply to the South Carolina Commissioners, which the southerners thought too hostile to South Carolina, and Stanton and his ally, Jeremiah Black, the new Secretary of State, too conciliatory. With Buchanan's agreement they drafted a further reply. Stanton and Black restated the view that the Charleston forts belonged to the government and that its authority should not be trifled with. They threatened coercion of South Carolina. They also required of Buchanan a denial that he had at any time given an informal pledge to evacuate the forts. Otherwise his presidential oath to 'preserve, protect and defend' the constitution and faithfully oversee the laws, which was continually being reiterated by Lincoln, was meaningless. But whatever Buchanan's private sympathies, he was too canny to succumb to southern pressure unconditionally, and consistently for the rest of his term he sought to find ways of revictualling the fort. It was at this point that Buchanan had sanctioned the *Star of the West* expedition. Thompson telegraphed to warn the Governor of South Carolina, Pickens, of the relief attempt. A squadron of four small steamers from the Coastal Survey, and a company of marines aboard the sloop, *Brooklyn*, were held offshore with instructions not to move unless Sumter was attacked. But the firing on the *Star of the West* broke Buchanan's nerve, and further preparations were stymied by half-measures and inconsistency. Attempts at accommodation were also counter-productive, especially the informal agreement to maintain the *status quo* – what Scott derided as 'something like a truce established between the President and a number of principal seceders'. Actually, the agreement at Sumter was reached between Anderson and Governor Pickens of South Carolina. At Fort Pickens, the agreement was reached between Buchanan and a group of southern senators sympathetic to secession. This established an important link between the two forts that could not

---

49. Benjamin P. Thomas and Harold M. Hyman, *Stanton: The Life and Times of Lincoln's Secretary of War* (New York: Alfred Knopf, 1962), pp. 93–4, 96–9, 100–5; Winfield Scott. Remarks of Lt-Gen. Scott on the within (Holt to Lincoln, 5 Mar. 1861), Lincoln Papers. Stanton's reference to losing a million dollars concerned the criminal carelessness of John B. Floyd in managing finances which was made public at the same time as the crisis took this grave turn. See Nichols, *Disruption of American Democracy*, pp. 423–7; on Thompson, see Thayer to Davis, 6 Jan. 1861, in Martin Crawford (ed.) 'Politicians in Crisis: The Washington Letters of William S. Thayer, December 1860–March 1861', *Civil War History* XXVII (Sept. 1981), p. 236.

be broken easily. Though Pickens was much the more defensible of the two posts, Anderson was nonetheless assured that if he needed reinforcements 'a prompt and vigorous effort will be made to forward them'.[50]

Buchanan's efforts at appeasing the South had the unexpected result that his cabinet was increasingly dominated by Unionists. His attitudes bent accordingly. In his special message to Congress on 8 January, he signalled his determination 'to collect the public revenues and protect the public property'; though he recommended that the Missouri Compromise line of 36°30' should be extended to the Pacific. This proposal was, of course, in line with the Crittenden Compromise which Buchanan despaired of ever being passed by Congress. Buchanan had also placed great faith in the Washington Peace Conference. Anderson was accordingly informed that 'The Secretary [of War, Holt] entertains the hope that nothing will occur now of a hostile character'. Indulging these hopes had the disadvantage of not forcing Holt (or the president) to face the uncongenial task of working out detailed instructions for Anderson's guidance.[51]

Although there were differences in style and direction under Lincoln, it is striking how many features of the Buchanan Administration carry over during Lincoln's first months in office. Notwithstanding differences in personality, a number of these unhappy features reflect basic structural cavities in the executive branch. These had identical results in both administrations despite major contrasts in attitude. In his first major public address in 1832 Lincoln had declared that 'Reason, cold calculating, unimpassioned reason, must furnish all the materials for our future support and defence'. As a Washington outsider, Lincoln absorbed advice silently in his ruminative, calculating manner. He did not commit himself to paper. Lincoln was as secretive as Buchanan and no less wily. But unlike Buchanan he had not had the benefit of executive experience before taking the presidential oath. Lincoln always remained calm and level-headed. He had a very clear sense of his political priorities. Yet we know little of his innermost calculations, as he did not live to write his memoirs. He

50. Remarks of Lt-Gen. Scott on the within, Lincoln Papers; Smith, *Buchanan*, pp. 177–86.

51. Nichols, *Disruption of American Democracy*, pp. 423–9, 447–50; Nevins, *Emergence of Lincoln*, II, pp. 365–72, 376–80. Holt to Anderson, 22 Feb. 1861, Anderson Papers, urged him to 'act with that forebearance which has distinguished you, heretofore, in permitting the South Carolinians to strengthen Fort Moultrie and erect new batteries for the defence of the harbor'.

is the embodiment of Roger Beaumont's dictum that 'We know much of what the presidents have said and done but far less of what they thought'. But although his handling of the crisis was a great advance on Buchanan's equivocation, the effect on the crisis was the same. By taking time to consider his position, Lincoln used up room in which to manoeuvre. He was forced back on the stark alternatives of either reinforcing Sumter or abandoning it.[52]

This led to another problem that Buchanan had already encountered. Because of the ramifications of the actions that were being taken, the slightest tactical error, or accident, could have the most momentous consequences. Hence so many of the entanglements of the crisis were the results of the caprice of fate, like the failure of the captain of the *Star of the West* to push on to the fort, or the fact that the draught of the *Brooklyn* was too low to pass over the bar at Charleston. But it was because the military alternatives open to the Lincoln Administration were now so restricted that the Sumter problem could not be resolved. Yet these military possibilities continued to be studied. The longer the crisis continued the more hazardous it became to employ force. And the capital invested in Sumter's symbolic significance continued to multiply in value. Lincoln was faced with a Catherine wheel of vicious circles.[53]

Because he gave the *impression* of dallying, contempt for Buchanan was soon transferred to Lincoln. This was not very surprising after his furtive entry into Washington, which was hardly a public relations triumph, and the attitudes that currently prevailed towards him; he seemed to be a figure out of the same mould as his predecessors. He was the available man at the Chicago convention in 1860, as Buchanan had been in 1856. He was eager to please, affable and considerate, and written off as a compliant nonentity like Franklin Pierce. Much of this criticism reflected a frustrated desire for *reassurance*, a not uncommon wish in a democracy during a crisis. 'Any distinct line of policy,' wrote Carl Schurz, 'be it war or a recognition of the southern Confederacy would be better than this uncertain state of things'. Francis P. Blair, frustrated with the perplexing ambiguities

52. Nicolay and Hay, *Abraham Lincoln*, III, 256–7, 318; Daniel Walker Howe, *The Political Culture of the American Whigs* (Chicago UP, 1979), p. 270; Beaumont, 'Epilogue', p. 171.

53. J. G. Randall, 'Lincoln's Sumter Dilemma', in Randall, *Lincoln the Liberal Statesman* (London: Eyre & Spottiswoode, 1947), p. 98; Current, *Lincoln and the First Shot*, p. 57.

surrounding the crisis, asked for a statement to reassure southern states against invasion, reconcile the Border states and also appeal to the North: 'I think there never was an occasion when a logical appeal by the President to the people like that of General Jackson in the crisis of 1832, could be of more use'. He actually lost his temper at the seemingly languid Lincoln and hastened to apologize via his son, Montgomery.

> I may have said things that were impertinent and I am sorry I ventured on the errand. . . . I said that the surrender of Fort Sumter "was virtually a surrender of the Union". . . . If I said anything which has left a bad impression on the President you must contrive some apology.

Old Frank need not have worried. His forthright, if ill-tempered, diatribe chimed with Lincoln's own instincts (and the president was not one to hold a grudge) as he moved towards ordering his thoughts on how the crisis could be resolved.[54]

But the example of the Nullification Crisis of 1832–33[55] was of little help to Lincoln because too much time had already been wasted for him to act quickly and decisively. As Scott reminded him, Jackson had issued a proclamation denying the validity of the Ordinance of Nullification immediately. He relied on an Act of 3 March 1807 'authorising the employment of land and naval forces'; he rushed reinforcements to Moultrie and dispatched the *Natchez* to Charleston. Scott himself arrived the day after the issue of the Ordinance to overawe its citizens. But the major difference between the crises of 1832 and 1861 was that in the former South Carolina had been isolated. In the latter she enjoyed the support of six other states, and any attempt at coercion could see at least a further six states rally to her cause – and perhaps many more (even in the North).[56]

How could Lincoln assert federal authority? What force was available, and how could he direct it? Lincoln was commander in chief of the armed forces but he had no military staff to advise him. Lincoln seems to have consciously pulled all the reins of power into his own hands, so that he alone could tightly control

54. Schurz to Lincoln, 5 Apr. 1861; F. P. Blair to M. Blair, 12. Mar. 1861, Lincoln Papers; Nevins, *War for the Union*, I, pp. 47–8; Fehrenbacher (*Impending Crisis*, p. 558) stresses that, whatever his public face, Lincoln was determined not to show 'weakness' and be 'scared into anything'.

55. See above, pp. 62–3.

56. Winfield Scott, Southern Forts, 30 Mar. 1861, Lincoln Papers; Lacy K. Ford, *Origins of Southern Radicalism* (New York: Oxford UP, 1988), pp. 141, 145.

the way decisions were made. But the machinery of government became clogged. Lincoln had only the services of his two secretaries, John G. Nicolay and John Hay, to help; he lacked the counsel of a general staff. On taking office Lincoln attempted to rationalize the relationship between the president, the Secretary of War and the general in chief. But this did not help him over much. The Secretary of War designate, Cameron, was indisposed for most of the crisis. Lincoln also faced a major difficulty with the rank of general in chief of the army.

The general in chief actually commanded nothing. He did not preside over an organized general staff. His position was not acknowledged in either the Constitution or in law. The relationship between the general in chief and the Secretary of War was vague, and if the secretary was determined to assert his prerogatives, as Jefferson Davis had been during the Pierce Administration, then the general in chief lacked a role. He neither commanded an army in the field nor directed a general staff. The heads of the bureaux, the quartermaster general, the chief engineer, the adjutant general, and so forth, reported to the Secretary of War, and not to the general in chief. Indeed in 1854 Scott had taken himself off to New York in a huff, and nobody appears to have missed him. He returned to Washington only after the secession of South Carolina in December 1860. Lincoln then instructed Scott to provide him with daily reports on strategic matters. He relied heavily on Scott's experience and advice.[57] But Scott was elderly and ill, and did not try to conceal his maladies. He could not be regarded as an energetic source of dependable military advice. The other senior generals were almost as old as Scott.[58]

The military power that Lincoln could assert was equally arthritic. The regular army of 16,215 men was scattered along the 79 posts of the frontier. Of the 1,033 graduates of the US Military Academy at West Point, 275 (or 26.6 per cent of those engaged in the Civil War) had so far resigned their commissions and gone with their states. Of the 93 officials in the War Department, 30 had

57. Baringer, *A House Dividing*, pp. 47–8; Smith, *Buchanan*, pp. 167–8; Nichols, *Disruption of American Democracy*, pp. 380–1, are highly critical of Scott and suggest that his reputation never recovered from the appearance of his 'Views', but the evidence suggests that Lincoln relied heavily on him.

58. Russell F. Weigley, *Quartermaster General of the Union Army: A Biography of M. C. Meigs* (New York: Columbia UP, 1959), pp. 215–17; on Lincoln's failure to appoint any officers to his staff, see *The Diary of Edward Bates*, ed. Howard K. Beale (vol. IV of the Annual Report of the American Historical Association, 1930; Washington DC: Government Printing Office, 1933), p. 220 (entry for 31 Dec. 1861).

resigned. Scott had stated his requirement for coercing the South: a force of 5,000 additional regular troops and 20,000 volunteers which he estimated would take eight months to raise. 'The President cannot call, direct for volunteer companies, or battalions', Scott reminded him, 'but Governors of States frequently substitute volunteers to make up the quota called for, in lieu of regular militia drafts'. Mobilization was in the hands of the state governors. Lincoln was to ignore some of these restrictions later when flexing his elastic authority under the war powers, but such latitude was possible only once a *de facto* state of war existed after the firing on Fort Sumter. In March and April 1861 Lincoln found that the enormous power frequently alluded to by his critics lacked a coherent institutional base. He was powerless to reduce the great local superiority the South enjoyed in Charleston harbour. And such a 'correlation of forces' would be a crucial calculation in choosing when and if shots were to be fired.[59]

Lincoln was, furthermore, worn down throughout the crisis by the immense burden of distributing the patronage. The range of offices requiring allocation was enormous, from the Librarian of Congress to the coiner of mint at San Francisco. Lincoln was attacked for spending so much time on place. But as the first Republican president, this was a paramount duty he could not shirk. James K. Polk was an example of a war president who was later plagued by a failure to exploit patronage opportunities fully. The magnitude of the crisis and the feebleness of the federal machinery available to the president in his attempt to solve it, forced him to select his priorities and the patronage was high on his list. Without doubt the cohesion and strength of the Republican Party was more important than the misguided prejudices of public opinion. Yet Lincoln paid a price for spending so much time on a relatively thankless task: it made possible the temporary ascendancy of William H. Seward.[60]

Seward's interference, combined with executive institutional weakness, accounts for much confusion during the last days of the crisis. But it is as well to recall that the pattern of a divided cabinet

59. James M. McPherson, *Battle Cry of Freedom: The Civil War Era* (New York: Oxford UP, 1988), p. 313; Winfield Scott, Fort Sumter, 11 Mar. 1861; Winfield Scott's Daily Report no. 5, 5 Apr. 1861, Lincoln Papers; Allan G. Bogue, *The Congressmen's Civil War* (Cambridge UP, 1989), p. 45.
60. Nevins, *War for the Union*, I, pp. 32–5; Hietala, *Manifest Design*, pp. 222–4; David Donald, *Lincoln Reconsidered* 3rd edn (New York: Vintage, 1989), pp. 72, 76.

with one senior member pursuing his own line unknown to other members had been foreshadowed during Buchanan's last months. Then, Stanton (a Democrat) had actually crossed party lines to keep Senator Charles Sumner and Seward himself informed of traitorous conduct in the Buchanan Administration. Such was the impact of the secession crisis that it threatened to overturn established executive institutions. Since November 1860 Seward had cherished the illusion of his singular importance to the Administration. Seward was headstrong, locquacious, crafty, quick-witted and subtle. He was supremely confident in his own ability to settle the crisis in sixty days, if only he was given the power to do it. Lincoln's preoccupation with the patronage, a widespread feeling (certainly shared by Seward) that Lincoln was a mediocrity, plus Seward's zeal and certainty that he would be 'Premier', left an unmistakable impression that he was the real power standing behind the president's desk – as he had been, albeit briefly, before Zachary Taylor's sudden death in 1850. Thus Scott, an old Whig ally, wrote, on welcoming Seward to the State Department, that Lincoln was 'an honored successor of the great Washington – with you as Chief of his Cabinet'. It was widely believed that Seward had drafted Lincoln's inaugural address. This speculation was endlessly, and inaccurately, reiterated.

Seward had made some progress in dominating the Administration by April 1861. Lincoln was a lazy and disorganized administrator. And considering the intolerable burdens he was carrying, it would surely be less than human for a man so beset with woe not to turn for support to a man more experienced in the ways of Washington than he was, and one so willing and able to offer advice and take on additional duties. Seward suggested that the cabinet meet in an informal manner regardless of whether all members were present or whether an agenda had been circulated. Lincoln agreed. Seward interfered in the affairs of other departments, and his advice was solicited on a range of patronage appointments (especially in the state of New York) affecting other cabinet members. Secretary Chase refused to acquiesce in this interference. An acrimonious exchange resulted which involved Lincoln himself. The president soon began to formalize cabinet meetings, which checked Seward's meddling. The president was also very careful to ensure that his cabinet members put their views on the Sumter crisis in writing. The disruption that had destroyed Buchanan's cabinet was only just avoided, though Lincoln had yet to resist one further attempt at disturbing established cabinet procedures.[61]

The consequences of this unhappy though temporary ascendancy were that not only did Seward meet with first the South Carolina Commissioners and then (after 3 March) deal with Confederate emissaries and make promises about the evacuation of Sumter that he was in no position to keep, but also that his views on evacuation were disseminated down the military chain of command via Scott. Anderson was misled into thinking that the garrison would be evacuated. Welles recalled after the cabinet meeting on 15 March at which (apart from Blair) all the cabinet were opposed to succouring Sumter, that Lincoln 'appeared to acquiesce in what seemed to be a military necessity, but was not disposed to yield until the last moment, and when there was no hope of accomplishing the work if attempted'. But over the course of the next two weeks Lincoln's disinclination to give way before professional military advice was transformed into a steely resolve not to abandon the fort. There are two items of evidence which indicate how he reached this decision. The first was a long report written by Stephen Hurlbut after his return from a fact-finding mission to Charleston with Lincoln's friend, Ward H. Lamon. He effectively demolished Seward's assumption that Union sentiment would ultimately prevail, even in the Deep South.

> Separate Nationality [Hurlbut wrote] is a fixed fact – that there is a unanimity of sentiment which is to my mind astonishing – that there is no attachment to the Union – that almost every one of these men who in 1832 held military commissions under secret orders from General Jackson . . . are now as ready to take arms if necessary for the southern Confederacy.
> . . . The Sentiment of National Patriotism always feeble in [South] Carolina, has been extinguished and overridden by the acknowledged doctrine of the paramount allegiance of the State.

He warned that the South was a *de facto* nation-state exercising its prerogatives and privileges. He was sure that any vessel carrying provisions for Sumter would be stopped by force if necessary. If Sumter was abandoned, Hurlbut counselled, 'Undoubtedly this will be followed by a demand for Pickens and the keys of the Gulf'. No policy, he concluded, however framed or restricted,

---

61. *The Diary of Gideon Welles*, ed. Howard K. Beale (New York: Norton, 1960), I, pp. 6–9; see Chase to Lincoln, 28 Mar. 1861, and Seward to Lincoln, 28 Mar. 1861, Lincoln Papers, over the marshalship of the northern district of New York.

could guarantee avoiding an armed collision. 'At all hazards and under all circumstances . . . any Fortress accessible by the Sea, over which we still have dominion should be held, if war comes, let it come'.[62]

The second item of evidence is Lincoln's reaction on 29 March, to a memorandum circulated by Scott advocating withdrawal from both Sumter and Pickens. This infuriated him. Furnished with Anderson's letter of 4 April, he was galvanized into action. At last by 28 March the majority of the patronage appointments had been made and he could turn his full attention to the Sumter crisis. That day the Senate passed a resolution reminding the president sternly that he must enforce federal law. Republican Party pressure to make a stand at Sumter was also felt. The cabinet met to consider its position. It regarded the coming of war gravely but not fearfully, so long as the South opened fire first on United States forces. Lincoln now more secure than he had been two weeks earlier, ordered the preparation of two expeditions, one to re-supply Sumter, the other to reinforce Pickens. But it was one thing for the president to reassert control at this level, quite another for him to direct its execution. He had already ordered weeks before, both orally and in writing, that the warship *Brooklyn* be sent to Pickens on 5 March (repeated on 11 March), but these orders had not been carried out (mainly because the naval commander, fearful that he would provoke civil war, refused to obey an order signed by General Scott rather than the Secretary of the Navy). The two expeditions ordered on 4 April met a similar fate. Seward regarded the Pickens expedition very much as his own. Enlisting the aid of Captain M. C. Meigs, he organized an expedition without the knowledge of the Secretary of the Navy, Welles, who had in the mean time prepared orders for the *Powhatan*, one of the strongest ships in the US Navy, to set out for Sumter. But because Lincoln had signed orders without looking at them, and with no military or naval staff to lighten his burden, this ship was assigned to both expeditions. Lincoln was simply trying to do too much and the result was foolish errors which reflected little credit on the efficiency of American decision-making machinery in

---

62. Nevins, *War for the Union*, I, pp. 42–3, correctly describes Scott as Seward's 'echo'. Hurlbut to Lincoln, 27 Mar. 1861, Lincoln Papers; Nevins, *War for the Union*, I, pp. 53–4. Note Hurlbut's confidence that a re-provisioning expedition would be stopped.

a crisis of such a magnitude, with which it was pathetically ill-prepared to cope.[63]

But despite this muddle, the entire episode illustrated Lincoln's working methods. When Welles came to the White House to protest against Seward's interference, Lincoln revealed a beguiling lack of self-confidence, beguiling because it is such a refreshing contrast when compared with the bombastic and pompous striking of attitudes so characteristic of American politicians of this period. He asked: *'What have I done wrong?'* The president could perhaps have asserted himself more strongly in these opening weeks, though Americans then (as they still do) attached far too much importance to the impression created in the first three months of a president taking office. If a leader is taking stock, as Lincoln was, then it was better to act cautiously. Nicolay and Hay wrote that Lincoln's 'life-long habit was to listen patiently to counsel from all quarters . . . [and] followed the practice of holding his convictions open to the latest moment, and of not irrevocably committing himself to specific acts till the instant of their execution'. Lincoln showed supreme skill in following a contradictory course (or keeping a dual option open to the last minute) and then switching decisively to adopt the right course at the most opportune moment. The Sumter crisis saw him do just this, though perhaps more hesitantly than later. He had manoeuvred himself into a position (in spite so many handicaps) that by 12 April he gained, whatever action resulted. If the southern forces in Charleston harbour allowed the victualling expedition to pass, Lincoln would have seized the initiative from the secessionists who had enjoyed it since December 1860; if they resisted and fired on federal ships, then by declaring war on the Federal government they would have given up the moral high ground and *given themselves* the guise of aggressors. It was typical of the distractions under which Lincoln laboured that as the Sumter expedition left New York harbour he was forced to turn his attention to the appointment of matron to a Maryland hospital.[64]

The muddle over the *Powhatan* also occurred within a few days of an offer the president had received from Seward to take the

63. J. G. Randall, *Lincoln the President: From Springfield to Gettysburg* (London: Eyre & Spottiswoode, 1947), I, pp. 337–42; Weighley, *Meigs*, pp. 142–9, 153; Current, *Lincoln and the First Shot*, pp. 103–7. Seward's acquiescence in the face of Lincoln's anger on 29 March demonstrates how hollow his pretensions to being 'Premier' were.

64. Welles, *Diary*, p. 17; Nicolay and Hay, *Abraham Lincoln*, III, pp. 256–7, 318, 440.

weight off his shoulders – which he found no difficulty in declining. On 1 April he had received Seward's 'Some Thoughts for the President's Consideration', in which Seward offered, in view of the president's supposed failure to evolve a coherent policy, to shoulder the burden of executive duties. 'It is not in my especial province. But I neither seek to evade nor assume responsibility'. This document is not a sustained memorandum but a series of somewhat disjointed and discursive assertions. Seward claimed that the issue during the secession crisis must be changed from slavery to Union or Disunion, from a party question 'to one of Patriotism or Union'; evacuating Sumter would be a way 'of changing the issue'. One way of securing a revival of Union feeling, Seward suggested, was by provoking a war with Spain and France. It is likely that Seward calculated that an attack on Cuba would tempt the South to intervene to prevent the abolition of slavery there. If so a northern attack would increase southern hatred of the North and provoke war with the Confederacy in Cuba, not lead to an upsurge of Unionism. By reasserting his authority (either by letter or in a quiet conversation with Seward is still not clear, probably the latter), Lincoln managed to keep his cabinet together. It was therefore able to stand united behind his own cautious policy. But the most charitable interpretation that could be placed on Seward's effrontery in producing his 'Thoughts' was that he had sipped too much brandy during its composition. For the alternative suggestions are that he was either drunk with delusion or he had lost touch with political reality. It was traditional for American presidents in the first half of the nineteenth century to concentrate on domestic affairs – foreign affairs were a low priority. Yet Seward's agenda for solving the greatest domestic crisis in American history required the president to reverse his priorities to an unprecedented degree and concentrate on foreign affairs, with Seward's ineffable advice to guide him. The presumption of Seward's 'Thoughts' might have been excusable if they were right, but though some of this document's elements did indeed come to pass, doing what Seward suggested when he suggested it would have been reckless folly.[65] But the true significance of this incident transcends personal ambition. The

65. Some Thoughts for the President's Consideration, 1 Apr. 1865, Lincoln Papers; Van Deusen, *Seward*, pp. 280–5; Benjamin P. Thomas, *Abraham Lincoln* (London: Eyre & Spottiswoode, 1953), pp. 164–5; Peter J. Parish, *The American Civil War* (London: Eyre Methuen, 1975), p. 77; for a defence, see Crofts, *Reluctant Confederates*, pp. 298–300.

dispatch of Seward's 'Thoughts' was a measure of the extent to which the Sumter crisis threatened to subvert the workings of American political institutions.[66]

Resolution

These three factors, space, time, and direction, dominated the resolution of the crisis. As the climax neared so did the muddle surrounding its resolution become more acute. Indeed, some explanation for Seward losing his head in a characteristically rash gambit and offering to take control of the Administration may be found in his dealings throughout March with Confederate emissaries (chosen and dispatched to Washington within two days of Davis's inauguration and superseding the earlier South Carolina delegations). On 15 March Seward assured the Confederate delegation that Sumter would be given up within five days. He did not meet them himself but made his unauthorized promises through two southern intermediaries, Associate Justices of the Supreme Court, Samuel Nelson and John A. Campbell. Seward claimed that Lincoln's inaugural did not convey adequately the true flexibility of the Administration's attitude. The Commissioners informed the Confederate government that 'We are sure that within five days Sumter will be evacuated. We are sure that no steps will be taken to change the military status'. This pledge (without the time limit) was repeated on 22 March and placed in writing by Campbell.[67] The Confederate Commissioners, Crawford, Forsyth and Roman, had accepted at face value the informal assurances of a cabinet member who had no authority to make them. But this evidence was confirmed by the congressional rumours that Senator Wigfall continued to report to Davis until he resigned his seat after the secession of Texas.[68]

This behaviour casts little credit on the diplomatic skill of the Confederate government. They found indirect dealings with Seward congenial because his policy suited their own

66. A convincing reconstruction of what form a possible meeting might have taken can be found in Gore Vidal, *Lincoln: A Novel* (London: Grafton, 1985), pp. 152–7.

67. Ludwell H. Johnson, 'Fort Sumter and Confederate Diplomacy', *Journal of Southern History* (1960), pp. 452–3, 457, 459–61.

68. William C. Davis, *Jefferson Davis: The Man and his Hour* (New York: HarperCollins, 1991), pp. 320–1.

preconceptions and determination to secure Confederate independence. In view of later Confederate claims that Seward had misled them, it is salutary to note that they quite cynically exploited Seward's delusions about a resurgence of southern Unionism for their own ends. They, too, sought time. As Forsyth mentioned earlier, 'We are playing a game in which time is our best advocate, and if our Government could afford the time I feel confident of winning. . . . Our policy is to encourage the peace element in the fight, and at least blow up the Cabinet on the question. The outside pressure in favour of peace grows stronger every hour'. There was no doubt, either, that the Commissioners thought in terms of progressing step by step, achieving one object at a time (vindicating Montgomery Blair's warning against piecemeal appeasement). Thus when Seward observed that 'the evacuation of Sumter is as much as the administration can bear', they were of the opinion that this was the first of several concessions that would culminate in recognition of Confederate independence.

The optimism of the Confederate Commissioners was also supported by other outspoken and unauthorized remarks, such as those of Lincoln's empty-headed friend, Ward H. Lamon, who had visited Charleston with Hurlbut, and had remarked on leaving that he would return in a few days to escort Anderson's garrison home. Such statements were believed because the Confederacy wanted to believe them, not because they represented authoritative Administration opinion. Governor Pickens telegraphed the Confederate Commissioners inquiring why Lamon had not returned on 30 March to attend to this obligation. The telegram was passed via Campbell to Seward. He again reiterated that Sumter would be evacuated, but said that he could not reply to the telegram until 1 April – the day he confidently expected the president to delegate to him the authority he had assumed so rashly on his behalf. Seward had told his wife that he expected to have to seize power, and was forced to do so at a time when he was losing his grip over both the Administration's policy and the reaction of the secessionists to its formulation. When Campbell called on 1 April for the expected reply to Pickens's telegram, Seward shifted ground. He now merely confirmed that 'the President may desire to supply Fort Sumter, but will not undertake to do so without giving notice to Governor Pickens'. This was evidently in accordance with Lincoln's rebuff. So almost two weeks before the relief expedition actually set out the Confederates were given notice, via Seward, of the method by which Lincoln would try and resolve (perhaps prolong) the crisis.

Yet the Confederates now refused to believe a source whose blandishments they had earlier accepted with alacrity. 'This is not the course of good will', wrote the Confederate president, 'and does not tend to preserve the peace'. Of course, the Confederate government had been assured by Campbell that the undertakings of 15 and 22 March were still valid. It is here that space – the great distance between Washington and Montgomery – became important again. The paucity of the information placed before the Confederate cabinet and its lack of a professional, skilled diplomatic corps redounded on the quality of the decisions taken. While before 1 April reports emphasize federal inactivity, after that date they become more suspicious and querulous, and greatly exaggerate the scale of renewed federal activity. The Confederate Secretary of War, Walker, wrote to Beauregard that 'The Government has at no time placed any reliance on assurances by the Government at Washington in respect to the evacuation of Fort Sumter' – this was untrue, but not inaccurate in its import, for the Confederate government had received no such assurances. It was a cardinal error committed by the Confederacy to accept assurances that were *not* made by the US government, but by a member of it whom they *presumed* was its leader. Never was there a better example of rumour and press tittle-tattle by constant repetition creating their own reality, and never has that habit proved so disastrous.[69]

The Confederacy now feared 'coercion'. This was another term endlessly repeated. But what did it mean? It was a synonym for invasion of the southern states by the Federal government, which Lincoln had promised would not be levied on them in his first inaugural address: 'The government will not assail you, unless you first assail it'. To the Confederate cabinet the hapless garrison at Fort Sumter was an instrument of blatant coercion and Lincoln's obstinacy in refusing to give it up a naked act of aggression. This position rather lacked a sense of proportion. This may be confirmed by recalling that it made sense only within the context of the South's long-term political insecurity; the language used was the same as that of the Missouri Crisis of 1820. Lucius Q. Washington reported that the Administration had 2,600 troops

---

69. Ibid., pp. 464–5, 467; Nevins, *War for the Union*, I, pp. 50–1.

poised to strike, 'and nearly every available ship in the Navy had been ordered to prepare for service'. Actually, the Federal government had an entire force of eight companies garrisoning Washington and seven at Fort Monroe. These were needed to defend the city which remained virtually defenceless for another month. The expedition ordered by Lincoln to revictual Sumter consisted of the *Pawnee, Pocahontas* and the *Harriet Lane* (300 sailors and 200 soldiers) but minus the *Powhatan*. Without the fire-power of the latter, had matters come to the proof, it is unlikely that the expedition could have fought its way through to the fort even at night. By comparison, South Carolina could muster 7,000 men in the port of Charleston. Yet Lucius Washington's imagination soared. Sumter was to be relieved 'by means of a combined movement by sea and by land, taking Beauregard's batteries in rear with infantry and field artillery etc while their ships press up the bay'. Such fantasy would be typical of what passed for strategic thinking in the South over the next few months.[70]

This attitude of mind seemed to indicate that a decision was about to be made. Napoleon once advised that in war (or when contemplating war) 'A general should never paint pictures [of a given situation]; his intelligence should be as clear as the lens of a telescope'. During the final stage of the crisis, southern leaders, fretting over the possible loss of Charleston, seemed to lose all sense of perspective. They never seemed to ask *for what end* were they launching a fratricidal war? Opening fire on Sumter was justified on the grounds that the fort might assist the Union fleet by opening fire on their batteries – in the totality of the crisis, a very minor consideration. But *their* bombardment would alter the *status quo* very dramatically. It ignored the great local superiority Confederate forces enjoyed in Charleston harbour. It ignored the importance they had attached to maintaining the *status quo* earlier and the pressure this placed on the Federal government to react to their moves. Anderson had not opened fire to aid the *Star of the West*, and four months later his position had deteriorated markedly. The Confederate government seemed determined to view the Sumter expedition as a mortal threat. News of the sailing of the expedition had been sent to Montgomery despite great secrecy, by the US Minister to Portugal designate, a native of

70. Stampp, *And the War Came*, p. 31; Johnson, 'Sumter and Confederate Diplomacy', p. 473; Nevins, *War for the Union*, I, pp. 58, 67.

South Carolina, James E. Harvey. What is striking when their deliberations are examined, as Allan Nevins, the greatest historian of the subject, observes, is an absence of the agonizing prevailing in Washington. The decision, in his opinion, 'was an act of rash emotionalism'. Just as the South fell victim to its own propaganda after the presidential election of November 1860, indulging its worst fantasies about 'Black Republicans', 'racial amalgamation' and the abolition of slavery, so in April 1861 it was swept off its feet by swirling rhetoric about 'coercion' and lashed out indiscriminately at its enemies. The South precipitated a conflict for which it was unprepared and which sealed its doom. In terms of direction, the Confederacy reached decisions more quickly than the Lincoln Administration, but they were imprudent, ill-considered and entirely predictable in a narrow sense.[71]

Indeed, impatience to resolve the matter as quickly as possible seems to have been the key factor in the southern decision to open fire. It was determined to seize Sumter at the earliest moment because the Confederate government calculated that it could use force with impunity. Interception of Anderson's mail revealed the increasingly vulnerable plight of Sumter. An attempt to seize Fort Pickens, by comparison, was a much riskier proposition. The Confederate commander there, General Braxton Bragg, advised President Davis that the only way to break in to Pickens would be by 'an escalade of ladders. My troops are eager and will risk anything to avoid a long investment on this sand beach. Ignorant in a great degree of the danger they would go at it with a will, and with ordinary good luck would carry the point. Our greatest deficiency', he concluded, 'is the want of means to reach the Island properly and secretly'. This did not sound very encouraging to Davis and he turned his attention back to Sumter.[72]

A great deal of relief had been felt in February when the Confederate government had taken over responsibility for negotiating for Sumter. Many felt that a more prudent and responsible body had taken over from the bombastic and rash South Carolinians. Governor Pickens urged that they demand the

---

71.   Quoted in J. F. C. Fuller, _The Conduct of War, 1789–1961_ (London: Eyre & Spottiswoode, 1961), p. 45; Swanberg, _First Blood_, pp. 146–9; Nevins, _War for the Union_, I, p. 73; material quoted in Johnson, 'Sumter and Confederate Diplomacy', p. 477, supports this argument but the thrust of his article is essentially a defence of Jefferson Davis and his cabinet.

72.   Grady McWhiney, 'The Confederacy's First Shot', in Hubbell, _Battles Lost and Won_, pp. 80–2.

surrender of the fort while Buchanan was still president in January, thus presenting Lincoln with a *fait accompli*. Pickens was inclined to the boastfulness characteristic of South Carolinians. William Howard Russell recorded in his diary that Pickens began one of his speeches with the modest claim that he was ' "Born insensible to fear" ', yet Russell 'was amused by a little middy who described with much unction the Governor's alarm on his visit to Fort Pickens, when he was told that there were a number of live shells and a quantity of powder still in the place'.[73] But in fact there was little difference in the style of negotiations adopted by the Confederate government, which was marked by an unthinking belligerence.

The Confederate government and its emissaries pursued a consistent object and were determined to delude members of the Lincoln Administration so long as it suited them. They shared the common error that the president would be of little account in the Administration by comparison with his lieutenant, Seward, and simultaneously typecast him as a Black Republican devil intent on evil doings. His confidants urged Davis to 'make up your account *for war*'. A commissioner from South Carolina, Isaac Hayne, predicted that 'if the attack on Sumter is delayed a week, our harbour may be in the possession of a fleet'. As the weeks wore on the Confederate president, despite his inability to assess authoritatively the extent of preparations for war, was inclined to the view that Union activities were not peaceful in intent. 'This is not the course of good will and does not tend to preserve the peace', he said of reports that Lincoln intended to revictual Sumter. There was one personal factor of an undefinable but omnipresent quality. Davis's sense of his 'honour' and that of the new Confederacy demanded that the issue be resolved. Not to act was to admit defeat and humiliation.

On 8 and 9 April the Confederate cabinet met to discuss what to do. They knew of Lincoln's plan to revictual the fort and believed that Anderson was preparing to resist a bombardment; but they had also intercepted a letter from Anderson indicating his desire to evacuate and detailing his parlous state. Davis wanted to bombard the fort, and other cabinet members supported him. Only Robert Toombs, the Confederate Secretary of State (who

73. William Howard Russell, *My Diary North and South*, ed. Eugene H. Berwanger (New York: Alfred A Knopf, 1988), p. 94 (entry for 19 Apr. 1861).

disliked Davis) dissented. He considered such an act 'suicide'. 'It is unnecessary, it puts us in the wrong, it is fatal'. It does not seem to have occurred to the Confederate cabinet that if they declined to fire on Sumter and stopped the relieving force, yet failed to attack it, they could compel the Union squadron to open fire should it persist in forcing its way through to Sumter. Under these circumstances, the Confederacy could justly claim that it was acting defensively. But calm consideration did not prevail. An excitable Wigfall telegraphed from Washington, 'Lincoln intends war. . . . Let us take Fort Sumter'.

At the last minute a solution to the crisis seemed to recommend itself. On 8 April Beauregard ordered Sumter's mails cut off. He informed Anderson that the Confederate government had not asked for the surrender of the fort previously because they believed that it would be evacuated. Now that an expedition to provision Sumter had set sail 'the Confederate States can no longer delay assuming actual possession of a fortification commanding the entrance of one of their harbours and necessary for its defence and security'. He concluded laconically, 'I am ordered by the Government of the Confederate States to demand the evacuation of Fort Sumter'. Anderson indicated that the garrison would be starved out anyhow but in further discussion he would not agree to an unconditional evacuation. Davis's patience was hardly endless. He had already indications of strong support from North Carolina, Virginia, Tennessee, Missouri, Kentucky, and Maryland. Persuading them to leave the Union was not an unimportant consideration in taking his decision. For example, secessionist sympathizers had penetrated pro-Confederate mobs and the militia in Richmond and stirred up a 'clamour'. 'They have been trimming and blindfolding in Washington,' Davis claimed. 'We have been patient and forbearing here'. He deduced therefore that 'Nothing was left for us but to forestall their schemings by a bold act'. On 12 April 1861 under the watchful eyes of an enormous Charleston crowd, the bombardment began. 'The shells were bursting,' Mrs Chesnut remembered. 'In the dark I heard a man say "waste of ammunition" '. The bombardment lasted for 34 hours, and no US soldiers were actually killed during its course, though one was killed during an accident at the general salute after the surrender on the 13 April. Davis briefly hoped this happy outcome – 'There has been no blood spilled more precious than that of a mule', he claimed – would persuade Lincoln that the bombardment was *not* an act of war but an assertion of legitimate rights.[74]

But it is important to note, given the considerable quantity of special pleading advanced on behalf of the South by many distinguished (often southern) historians, that the *casus belli* was an unprovoked attack on the fort itself, and *not*, as during the *Star of the West* incident, an attempt to repulse the forces seeking to *relieve* the beleaguered garrison. In considering why war came when it did, we must return to Clausewitz's 'political object' and its relationship to the decision-making machinery. Earlier writing has tended to focus on motives. The main emphasis in this analysis has been on the *way* decisions were arrived at, or their results, rather than on what prompted them. A good deal of this earlier writing has arisen from the paucity of evidence at our disposal as to the calculations underlying Lincoln's moves. Under such circumstances 'conspiracy theories' tend to spring up. The most scholarly was advanced by the southern historian, Charles W. Ramsdell. He argued that Lincoln 'manoeuvred' the South into firing the first shot with the 'bait' of the revictualling expedition.[75] A sustained analysis of the primitive decision-making machinery employed during the crisis demonstrates that no attempt to organize and control such an elaborate plan was even remotely possible. Lincoln's objective was far simpler – to enforce federal authority, without appearing provocative, and in accordance with his constitutional duties, while avoiding any recognition of the independence of the rebellious states. As the pursuit of these aims required him to adopt an increasingly stern and uncompromising tone, Lincoln never once trespassed beyond the limits set by northern public opinion which was itself in a state of flux if not outright muddle. The employment of military force at any stage in a given crisis is an expression of *power*, an ability to enforce a fiat. This power might be channelled, or restricted, by the environment in which statesmen and soldiers operate. In this chapter, three factors of a strategic 'model' have been advanced as a means of

74. Beauregard to Anderson, 11 Apr. 1861, Anderson Papers, Library of Congress; Davis, *Jefferson Davis*, pp. 320–25; C. Vann Woodward (ed.) *Mary Chesnut's Civil War* (New Haven, CT: Yale UP), pp. 45–6 (entries for 7, 12 Apr. 1861); Daniel W. Crofts, *Reluctant Confederates* (Chapel Hill, NC: University of North Carolina Press, 1989), p. 320.

75. Charles W. Ramsdell, 'Lincoln and Fort Sumter', *Journal of Southern History* III (1973), pp. 259–88; for the southern bias of interpretations of this period, see Thomas J. Pressly, *Americans Interpret their Civil War* (Princeton UP, 1954), pp. 239–53.

understanding how this environment acted to advance, or retard, the aspirations and activity of harassed men taking decisions, the ramifications of which they barely discerned. In any case, Davis ordered shots to be fired on the fort, and not the expedition that Lincoln dispatched, and this important distinction reveals the weakness of Ramsdell's special pleading.

By April 1861 Lincoln recognized the importance of *defending* the *status quo*. As his confidence grew, especially in deciding what was valuable and what was misleading military advice, he determined that the *status quo* must not be allowed to change (as had happened so many times during the Buchanan Administration) in the secessionists' favour. He sent two emissaries to warn Governor Pickens that the expedition to Fort Sumter would land only food, not weapons and ammunition. This gesture was later ridiculed by Jefferson Davis. But it was typical of the Confederate government's determination to accept only what it wanted to hear, that it welcomed the informal blandishments of a member of the cabinet, Seward, when it suited them, and yet rejected the warnings of the president's messenger. This was the only direct contact between the chief executive and the rebels throughout the entire crisis; yet they had earlier generalized about his attitude towards Sumter with all the confidence of architects who constructed their castles on clouds. The Confederate government was equally determined to uphold southern independence. The two sides often acted at cross-purposes. To the Lincoln Administration, merely upholding federal law and installations was continuing its legitimate, peaceful business; to secessionists, obstinately set on securing their independence, this attitude was tantamount to a declaration of war. In these combustible circumstances, the only question remaining was: which side would resort to force first?[76]

It is in this context that the immense political significance of firing the first shot – in securing the moral high ground and galvanizing northern opinion to strike at southern 'aggressors' – should be understood. Lincoln was operating in a political culture which accepted stoically, as Richard N. Current has written elsewhere, that 'the decision for peace or war is up to the other side; we ourselves have no choice'. Hurlbut had warned the President that vessels sent to reprovision Fort Sumter 'would be

76. Jefferson Davis, *The Rise and Fall of the Confederate Government* (London: Longmans Green, 1881), I, 237; Johnson, 'Sumter and Confederate Diplomacy', pp. 474–6.

stopped and refused admittance'.[77] But Lincoln could not have possibly *known* that the other side would fire on the fort rather than on the relieving squadron. It was a remote possibility, though not a certainty. As Gideon Welles summed up the consensus which the cabinet had now reached under Lincoln's patient prodding:

> armed resistance to a peaceable attempt to secure provisions to one of our forts will justify the government in using all the power at its command to reinforce the garrison and furnish the necessary supplies ... and the time has arrived, when it is the duty of the government to assert and maintain its authority.[78]

Lincoln was attempting to reverse the pressure of time on his Administration and ensure that whatever shape the crisis might assume he would keep his cabinet united. Previously the time factor had worked in favour of the Confederacy, and Buchanan's cabinet had splintered under the pressure of events. Throughout the crisis the Confederacy had retained the initiative, and Lincoln had merely *reacted* to their moves. Should the Confederacy lash out and be provoked into firing the first shot then, in the event of war, the president had placed himself in an advantageous position. But if they stood aside and allowed a peaceful revictualling then the pressures of time could be exerted on *them*, and not the Federal government, and Lincoln would have seized the initiative. He had placed himself in a position to gain whatever action resulted. It is as an illustration of this remarkable gift (and not some sordid, nebulous conspiracy) that a terse entry in Browning's diary should be read:

> He himself conceived the idea, and proposed sending supplies, without an attempt to reinforce giving notice of the fact to Gov. Pickens of South Carolina. The plan succeeded. They attacked Sumter – it fell, and thus, did more service than it otherwise could.[79]

Lincoln had begun to overcome the enormous 'friction' inherent in handling this crisis; yet the dividend on his skill was not a happy one – the outbreak of civil war. But did Lincoln, or Davis, 'decide' for war in the manner conveyed in so many books? The answer is an emphatic *no*. Lincoln was determined to conduct the crisis in as conciliatory a manner as possible consistent with his constitutional position; he would not compromise this; nobody should presume

77. Current, *Stimson*, p. xvi; Hurlbut to Lincoln, 27 Mar. 1861, Lincoln Papers.
78. Welles to Lincoln, 29 Mar. 1861, Lincoln Papers.
79. Orville Hickman Browning, *Diary*, eds Theodore C. Pease and James G. Randall (Springfield, IL: Illinois State Historical Library, 1925), pp. 475–6 (entry for 3 Jul. 1861).

to encroach on his presidential prerogatives, as Seward discovered. But if the South would not respect these, then he was prepared to fight to safeguard the constitution and the integrity of the Union. But he did not positively decide for war. He and the members of his cabinet were prepared to fight one – the distinction is subtle but important. His attitude was best summed up in Hurlbut's observation 'if war comes let it come'. As for Davis, he thought an energetic exercise in belligerence would frighten the North and allow him to assert Confederate rights and territorial integrity without loss of life. He calculated wrongly, even though the bombardment of Fort Sumter led to a significant accretion of Confederate power, the secession of the Upper South. Yet even at this late stage, Davis confided to his wife that he had not given up hope that some kind of compromise or reconciliation could be reached with the North. 'Separation is not yet of necessity final'; some way might yet be found to accommodate southern rights in a looser federation. If that hope was sincere, then the actions of the Confederate government belied it and cleared the way for an unrestrained use of force. But neither leader expected, nor wanted, the outbreak of a general war.

Northern outrage followed the firing of the first shots at Sumter. The South chose the one method, as Toombs feared, that would antagonize the other section. From January onwards the northern state governors had made their influence felt. On 12 January 1861 Ohio had passed a resolution demanding that the federal government refuse to permit secession and pledged the resources of the state to the defence of the Constitution. Six days later Maine passed similar resolutions; on 21–24 January Wisconsin, Minnesota and Pennsylvania did likewise, and Michigan on 2 February. Thus Lincoln could call upon northern resources to put down secessionists in arms against the legitimate government. But would the states of the Upper South and on the 'Border' between the sections show a comparable unconditional loyalty? This would test to the uttermost the unionism of Virginia and North Carolina On 15 April Lincoln issued a proclamation calling for 75,000 volunteer militia for three months to suppress the rebellion. In William Brock's view, he used 'words reminiscent of a county sheriff summoning a posse to deal with outlaws'. This is exactly right: for Lincoln expected the war to be a short police action, and he used similar powers to those employed by Andrew Jackson in raising a *posse comitatus*.[80] Lincoln stressed his

80. See above, p. 60.

determination 'to suppress said combinations [of rebels] and to cause the laws to be duly executed'. In pursuing his object, he promised that 'the utmost care will be observed . . . to avoid any devastation; any destruction of, or disturbance of peaceful citizens in any part of the country'. The total number of volunteers asked for by Lincoln is often ridiculed in the context of the great war on which he now unknowingly embarked. Neither side were aware of the kind of war they were unleashing on their fellow citizens. But in the context of a police action, and by comparison with the small numbers of troops raised by the United States in her earlier wars, Lincoln was asking for a very large force.[81] He had made it abundantly clear on 13 April to the Virginian convention that 'I shall, to the very extent of my ability, repel force by force' and that if necessary 'I shall hold myself at liberty to re-possess if I can, like places [to Sumter] which had been seized before the Government was devolved upon me'. The request for volunteers was dispatched to *all* state governors. Would they all comply?[82]

Southern secession: the second phase

From Lincoln's point of view, the least desirable result of the firing on Fort Sumter was the secession of four states of the Upper South, Virginia, Tennessee, North Carolina and Arkansas, and their adamant refusal to participate in the 'coercion' of their sister states of the Deep South. The first two were of inestimable importance to the Confederacy because with their population and industrial capacity they made a southern republic a more viable proposition. There was also a further, perhaps more desirable, result. The passage of secessionist ordinances in these states revealed precisely where allegiances lay. In retrospect, it is now abundantly clear that even if a way could have been found to solve the impasse at Sumter, it would have been resolved only on terms that would have created a section within a nation-state. The Federal government would have been continually obliged to defer

---

81. William R. Brock, *Conflict and Transformation: The United States, 1844–1877* (Harmondsworth: Penguin, 1973), pp. 202–4.

82. By the President of the United States, A Proclamation, 15 Apr. 1861; The President's Reply to the Preamble and Resolution of the Virginia Convention, 13 Apr. 1861, Lincoln Papers, Library of Congress; see also Brian Holden Reid, 'First Blood to the South: Bull Run, 1861', *History Today* 42 (Mar. 1992), p. 21, and Dwight L. Dumond, *The Secession Movement, 1860–1861* (New York: Macmillan, 1931), pp. 230, 253–62.

and pander to it; and these four states would have continued to look for advice and succour from, and certainly sympathized with, the Confederacy in its rivalry with the Union. In other words, the Sumter issue would not have gone away; it would have been transferred to another spot in another state, and after each concession the Federal government would have been in a weaker and weaker position. There was also the problem of federal installations in these four states. Doubtless before too long, the Confederacy would have made special demands on these, for example, that they be demilitarized. What the attitude of the four state governors would have been to such demands is possible to reconstruct. Their speeches before Sumter were consistently pro-Confederate (though this by no means reflected majority opinion in their states), and it is safe to predict that they would have favoured the Confederacy with their support, and actively worked for such a demilitarization. The shots fired at Sumter, and Lincoln's proclamation, settled these issues once and for all and both sides knew where they stood. The real problem for the Lincoln Administration lay in the possibility that secession would extend into a third phase involving Missouri, Kentucky, Maryland and Delaware. If this was allowed to succeed, then the Federal government itself could no longer be maintained in Washington DC.

The Virginia convention had assembled on 13 February 1861. The delegates feared that Lincoln would persist in holding the forts; gradually a latent pro-secessionist outlook came to dominate its proceedings. Only a concession on the crucial issue of Sumter would have bought their loyalty and that would not have been unconditional. It was a price that Lincoln (or Buchanan) were not prepared to pay. The 'moderates', or conditional unionists, favoured secession once the reaction of the Federal government to the firing of the first shots had been gauged. William B. Preston placed the ordinance before the convention meeting in camera on 16 April. The votes were 88 in favour and 55 opposed; an attempt to put the vote to the people or call a convention of Border states was voted down. Secessionist sentiment was less striking in the Whig counties, and more vibrant in those with the heaviest slave population; though it is perhaps an interesting contrast that individually, the very wealthiest slaveowners, with most to lose from upheaval or war, were far more cautious about the supposed joys of secession. The ordinance was placed before the voters for ratification on 23 May, although the decision of this vote was pre-empted by the moves to raise an army and join the

Confederacy. It was passed by 125,950 to 20,373. By this vote, Virginia volunteered herself for the front line in any civil war.[83]

That sentiment was a factor not to be discounted in the secession crisis may be seen by reference to the experience of Arkansas and North Carolina. In both these states the more ardently expressed view of southern states rights had never enjoyed much of a hearing. In Arkansas a proposal was passed, after the initial defeat of the secessionist cause in the convention called in February, that in August an election would be held in which the electors would choose between cooperation or secession; the convention then adjourned until these results were known, although it could be recalled in event of a crisis. Lincoln's proclamation was judged such an event: 'the members of the Arkansas convention meant to be on the side of their brothers of the South', concludes Ralph Wooster. Arkansas's ordinance of secession was a gesture of solidarity with other slave states and a steadfast refusal to assist in action whose aim was to crush the government of any sister state whose basic aims and aspirations were compatible with its own. In North Carolina Lincoln's request for troops was considered an insult to the honour of the state. Opinion had been moving towards the secessionist position for some weeks. The Sumter incident provided a convenient scapegoat for closing the inconsistent gap between the unionist victory at the polls in the February election for the secession convention, and an increasing sympathy for the Deep South and a wish to see its territorial integrity remain inviolate. 'In North Carolina the Union sentiment was largely in the ascendant and gaining strength until Lincoln prostrated us', wrote Jonathan Worth somewhat optimistically. A coalition of former secessionists and former unionists gave this movement the added respectability of a non-partisan flavour. The original secession ordinance was framed in terms of North Carolina's right to leave the Union as the result of a 'revolutionary' act. This was withdrawn eventually, but is ominously indicative of the lurking danger that secessionist fervour in North Carolina was miles wide but less than half an inch thick.[84]

Secession might have been motivated by economic self-interest or legalistic sentiment but ultimately, like all revolutionary

83. Ralph A. Wooster, *The Secession Conventions of the South* (Princeton UP, 1962), pp. 142–8, 151–4.
84. Ibid., pp. 155, 164–72, 194, 199–203; Crofts, *Reluctant Confederates*, pp. 330–3.

movements, it rested on the efficacy of force (or at the very least
the threat of force). The case of Tennessee is instructive in this
regard. The whole process was guided, not by a special
convention, but by the state legislature; the state governor also
played a more prominent role than in other slave states.
Tennessee had not voiced radical views on the states' rights or
slavery questions, even when the southern convention was held at
Nashville in 1850. The Tennessee legislature went into special
session on 7 January 1861; its composition resembled the basic
pattern of secessionist conventions in the South, with an average
age of about 43, with lawyers and farmers predominating. A
unionist coalition gained victory over the secessionists in February,
but became more persuaded of the secessionist cause, as first the
Washington Peace Conference terminated fruitlessly, and then
Sumter demanded of them an unconditional obedience to the
demands of the Federal government. Despite opposition from East
Tennessee the secession ordinance, was passed eventually on 7
May by 14 to 6 in the state senate, and 45 to 16 in the state house.
Public opinion sanctioned this 104,913 to 47,238; in the east of the
state 32,923 (as against 14,780 for) were opposed to withdrawal
from the Union. Governor Isham Harris had resolutely set his
mind against complying with Lincoln's request for troops.[85]

Governor Harris had developed a rather sly strategy of placing
Tennessee in an isolated but exposed position; although the state
had not seceded in February, relations with the Federal
government were rather tense. Eventually Harris hoped that the
voters would see that the security of Tennessee required her to
join the Confederacy. Between April and July 1861 a state army of
more than 100,000 men was organized. If this independent 'state'
was menaced by 'coercion' then Harris could advocate all-out
adherence to the Confederate constitution. This process was not
complete until at least July 1861, as the Confederate government
was very slow in assuming responsibility for the defence of
Tennessee. This left the state not only exposed but also prone to
an ill-coordinated, brash and reckless policy. Thus in September
1861 Tennessee violated the neutrality of Kentucky quite
gratuitously, even though no defences of any substance existed on
her northern border.

85. Crofts, *Reluctant Confederates* pp. 173–5, 176, 184, 188–9. For the use of
'vigilance committees' against unionist sympathizers in North Carolina and
Mississippi, see Charles C. Bolton, *Poor Whites of the Antebellum South* (Durham, NC:
Duke UP, 1994), pp. 146, 166–7, 172–5.

From April to August 1861 Harris's attitude to the treatment of persistent unionists in eastern Tennessee was tolerant, mainly because he felt he needed their votes to secure re-election. After this had been achieved in August (even though he had lost the east by 12,000 votes) he decided upon a new 'decided and energetic' policy, which included the arrest and even execution of loyalist 'Tory' leaders and their sympathizers. In October and November 1861, the unionists rose in revolt. Harris's inconsistent policy, first toleration then suppression, had probably provoked the rebellion. It was typical of the rash belligerence, and a lack of coherent policy stamped on the region by the Confederate government, that the state of Tennessee had extended its military commitments outside its borders, without any reference to some higher plan or thinking. Inside the state, Harris had provoked an uprising by a group who were militarily powerless but who refused to accept the political action taken in their name. Perhaps it was entirely predictable in this intense, 'localized' political culture, secessionists could not tolerate the thought that their actions were less popular than they assumed they were; when they were flouted they did not hesitate to use force brutally.[86]

Concluding reflections

Amid this great dramatic crisis we must now confront the unavoidable question, *why* did the South secede? The answer to this question must take into account the inconvenient fact that the secession 'movement' was very disparate; the 'impulse' towards secession had three different motives. In the first instance, there was a strong measure of defiance against a political system that had allowed a candidate who was a perceived threat to southern institutions and liberties to walk through the door of the White House. Since 1848 the South had grown used to presidents who appeared sympathetic to her plight and counter-balanced the critics of the South, the most voluble of whom could be found in the Senate chamber. Thus to protect those liberties and institutions, whose unifying characteristic was a reliance on chattel slavery, seven states claimed they had the power to leave the Union if their interests so demanded it. Most had exercised this

86. Thomas L. Connelly, *Army of the Heartland: The Army of Tennessee, 1861–1862* (Baton Rouge: Louisiana State UP, 1967, 1986), pp. 26–7, 40–3.

right and achieved their aim in the incredibly short period of some three weeks at the beginning of 1861. Eugene Genovese has suggested, as a development of this case, that 'the South' left the Union to further a policy of slavery expansion, which would augment not only the wealth and power of a republic based on slavery but of individual slaveowners who felt hemmed in and frustrated in an ungrateful Union. There is, surely, a good deal of truth in this assertion. If the South had secured her independence there can be little doubt that she would have attempted to extend southern influence over the entire Caribbean basin, for the Confederacy would have been first and foremost a Caribbean power. The whole American experiment had been based on *expansion* of one kind or another, and the South had been in its van. There seems to be no reason to exclude the Confederacy from this pattern simply because it had become independent. On the contrary, under the stimulus of competition with the confederacy's northern neighbour, this 'scramble' for outposts and new territories would have become more frantic.

But does this argument apply equally to the Upper South, whose slave population was declining though rather patchily (there were some increases in the non-plantation areas). This seems much less likely. Thus one may conclude that Genovese's thesis is much more applicable to the Deep South than to the states of the Upper South or the Border states (who had yet to secede). It is only necessary to reiterate here that historians, when they refer to the South, tend to refer exclusively to those attitudes or policies, whose most vociferous spokesmen came from the Deep South. There are many 'Souths', but the Deep South has the loudest shout and the most menacing grimace.

Secondly, the secessionists claimed to be acting defensively – in every sense. They sought to defend their unique way of life and institutions, and they defended these steadfastly against the 'coercion' of their enemies in the North. Once violent action was decided on, this in effect forced the states of the Upper South to decide where their loyalties – and their self-interest – lay. Some Virginians were impressed by arguments that the Old Dominion (whose main exports were still tobacco, wheat and livestock) had much more to gain by obtaining admission to southern markets than she possibly could by selling those same products in the North.[87] A similar argument had been used to stir up secessionist

87. Henry T. Shanks, *The Secession Movement in Virginia, 1847–1861* (New York: AMS Press, 1934, 1971), p. 167.

activity in other states reliant on the Mississippi River for their commerce, such as Indiana and Illinois, and sympathy for the Confederacy in New York City, although not in New York State.[88] The slavery argument clearly has no relevance here. Yet the enormous growth of the American economy throughout the nineteenth century had been dependent on building new types of government, admittedly in the various territories, as the frontier was penetrated and economic bounty was seized and exploited. The sense of excitement at the kind of challenge offered by southern secession, with the prospect of new markets and new opportunities and settlements, should not be discounted. And there was a good deal of boasting accompanying it, claiming that once the yoke of the Federal government was thrown off, Charleston would become a second New York.

But one looks in vain among the innumerable editorials and speeches made during the short period (of only four months) of the secession crisis, for many statements adumbrating a coherent policy of slavery expansion. However much political action may be governed by an underlying economic or social motive (and obviously these are not irrelevant in the slavery case), such action is rarely expressed in anything other than political language. Here was a section of the United States that had felt itself abused and undervalued for at least twenty years (something like one-quarter of United States history). Secession was a political answer, or reaction, to this abuse, real or imagined. Independence was its aim and it drew on the appeal of the southern contribution (and example) during the American Revolution. The theory of states rights had just as long, and just as respectable a history as the theory of the Union (indeed its theory was more fully developed). In April 1861 the occasion and the date fused in an *opportunity*, the benefits of which beckoned some but appalled others.

Thirdly, Americans prided themselves on their pragmatism. If one expedient fails, another is tried in its place, until progress is made. There is a danger of treating the whole secession process too rationally and earnestly. It was essentially a highly provincial and perhaps insubstantial 'movement' led by excitable men who espoused a highly emotional appeal. They stirred up a cause which enjoyed an abundance of enthusiasm but rather less loyalty. Success generates its own momentum in American politics, as

88. See e.g. Kenneth M. Stampp, *Indiana Politics during the Civil War* (Indiana UP, 1949, 1978), pp. 12–13, 78, 113.

elsewhere, and professional politicians always seek to be on the winning side; often they get their calculations wrong. The excitement and drama of secession had, for a while, an irresistible appeal. The whole of American history had witnessed the glamorization and idealization of revolutionary mores within a conservative setting; the South had developed her own version of those mores, and sought to protect them by revolutionary means – that is, military action. Southerners saw that they had the opportunity to gain their independence; they felt they had the power, they thought they had the resolution; they were not far wrong.

But these points tend to ignore the question which lies at the heart of the problem of secession. Why did so many secessionists accept the risk of war so casually in pursuing their policy in April 1861? This is the real question that needs a convincing answer, not endless quibbling over value judgements as to whether their cause was rational or irrational, expansionist or defensive, or motivated by economic aggrandizement. The whole policy of the Confederate government, and the individual states that jostled in anarchic disorder, depended on force, or the threat of force. The decision to fire on Fort Sumter was taken so lightly because of an overconfident belief in the efficacy of force. Southern leaders believed they could intimidate the North into accepting a *fait accompli*. Bluster and belligerence, it was unthinkingly assumed, would secure their independence because northerners lacked the resolve, which southerners enjoyed in abundance, to hold on to what they wanted. They could be cowed into submission. On such fragile and flimsy bases are the decisions which launch great wars often founded.

Secession itself was a rather negative act. The South left a coherent grouping and did so rapidly and decisively, but not completely. Something had still to be created to replace the Union. Genovese and other scholars who emphasize the logic which underlay secession overlook the possibility that the act of leaving a political unit does not automatically lead to its replacement by a coherent structure. The conditions prevailing after secession were anarchic; there is no more dangerous condition in the affairs between nation-states than the combination of unguided belligerence and inertia. Drafting a constitution, no matter how delicate the legal refinements, does not make a nation. A sensible policy might have been a start in the right direction, but even before this could be worked out, the infant southern polity brought a war upon itself.[89]

The act of founding a new nation-state brings to the very fore the question of the creation of armed forces because nation-states are differentiated from one another by their capacity to organize and use force: to maintain peace and order at home and secure liberty from attack from abroad. The creation of the Confederacy launched a massive programme of army-building, the largest that North America had yet seen. All commentators visiting parts of the southern states commented on it. In the pursuit of southern rights – which in the case of the Upper South involved a desire to be on the Confederate side in the fight to resist the *potential* danger of a dismantling of the southern system of race relations – force was used in a rash, thoughtless and self-defeating manner. Secession could not be made peacefully even if the North acquiesced in it, which she did not; secession was based on force, not legal right, and was justified by the use of force. Secessionist forces were consolidated and extended by the act of striking at Fort Sumter. Yet the movement to create a slaveowning republic in the southern states contained a fatal contradiction. The one force that could overwhelm slavery and the rationale for the Confederacy was war, and it was war that southerners relished and brought upon themselves.

89. Michael F. Holt, *The Political Crisis of the 1850s* (New York: Norton, 1983), pp. 256–7.

CHAPTER NINE

The Origins of a Punitive Civil War: Why Did the War Not Spread?

[We may] conquer the seceding states by invading Armies. No doubt this might be done in two or three years by a young and able general, a Wolfe, a Desaix, or a Hoche with 300,000 disciplined men – estimating a third for garrisons and the loss of a yet greater number by skirmishes, sieges, battles and southern fevers. The destruction of life would be frightful – however perfect the moral discipline of the invaders.

GENERAL WINFIELD SCOTT to WILLIAM H. SEWARD, 3 March 1861, Lincoln Papers

The tragedy of the Civil War as a bloody, fratricidal conflict – brother set against brother, fathers against sons, and in the case of J. E. B. Stuart, son-in-law against father-in-law – invariably engages the attention of United States historians and shapes their approach to the war.[1] This depiction is rather overdrawn, and usually applies only to the Upper South or Border states. And on various fields of battle Union regiments from Kentucky, Tennessee and Western Virginia (which entered the Union as a separate state in 1863) were drawn up opposed to Confederate regiments from the same states, including friends and neighbours who had chosen to rally to their states rather than to the Union. Nonetheless, the Civil War for all its emotional impact on American society must be viewed in a wider perspective. Indeed, the American Civil War should be interpreted as one part of a general crisis in North America. The halting of United States expansion while the Union

---

1. Emory M. Thomas, *Bold Dragoon: The Life of J. E. B. Stuart* (New York: Harper & Row, 1986), p. 95. Major General Philip St George Cooke, although of a distinguished Virginian family, remained loyal to the Union. Stuart nursed the romantic hope of taking him prisoner. 'I married his daughter, and I want to present her with her father; so let him come on'.

was engulfed in civil commotion, along with similar upheavals in Canada and Mexico, introduced a period of prolonged instability on the continent which invited intervention by other powers. When President Polk invoked the Monroe Doctrine during the Oregon Crisis in December 1845, he signalled the desire of the United States to exclude European influences from North America. The coming of the Civil War and the creation of another American republic hostile to the United States which sought alliances with Great Britain and France threatened to reverse the process initiated by Polk (but which had its origins in the Monroe presidency). During the American Revolution a regional conflict in North America had expanded into a 'world' war involving all the great powers. Campaigns waged in the Carolinas and Virginia were relative 'sideshows' compared with those waged by European armies and navies in Europe and the Caribbean.[2]

This chapter will consider three themes. First, it will assess the failure of the third phase of secession and Union success in securing the Border states. Secondly, it will discuss the place of slavery and emancipation in expanding the nature of the war. And thirdly, it will consider the crucial question of whether the conflict would expand from a civil to an international war. From April to July 1861 it was very unclear what kind of war had broken out. By September 1862 it was very clear, though it was quite different from what had been anticipated. There was a paradox here. The war had become much greater in scope than expected, but also more limited in one important respect. It had not expanded into an international war involving the great European powers, Great Britain and France. The reasons for this fundamental limitation need to be explored.

In 1861 it appeared likely that the pattern of the Revolutionary War would repeat itself. Seward even saw war with foreign powers as a solution to the ghastly schism of secession. If the European great powers had intervened in the Civil War then United States dominance would probably have been destroyed and replaced by a balance of power between competing North American republics. General Scott had acknowledged this possibility in a memorandum when he predicted that the United States might divide into four regional republics, North, South, North West and South West. Such a development would increase the influence of Mexico and

---

2. Piers Mackesy, *The War for America, 1775–1783* (London: Longman, 1968), pp. 180–6.

Canada within a North American states system previously dominated by the United States. It would also have opened the door of opportunity for increasing European influence and intervention. This was foreshadowed by Napoleon III's attempt to install his client, Maximilian, as Emperor of Mexico. Thirty thousand French troops were garrisoned in Mexico by 1862. Spain intervened in San Domingo to crush the Negro rebels, a matter that disturbed Lincoln and Seward during the Sumter crisis. Indeed Seward was so worried by these grave developments that in his 'Thoughts for the President's Consideration' he advocated a most energetic if rash response. 'I would demand explanations from *Spain* and *France*, categorically at once. I would seek explanations from Great Britain and Russia and send agents into *Canada*, *Mexico*, and *Central America*, to rouse a vigorous continental *spirit of independence* on this continent against European intervention'.[3]

Seward's somewhat frantic and extreme reaction was nevertheless in line with the overall trend of United States policy to its North American neighbours. The break-up of the Union, a continental republic which dominated the region, would introduce a mechanism resembling the European balance of power between smaller, competing states. 'But a balance of power', Professor Connell-Smith argues, 'was precisely what the United States would not permit in the Americas. She was determined to maintain an imbalance which was so markedly – and increasingly – in her interests'. Thus a major question that needs to be answered is *why* the American Civil War remained a local conflict? Why did it not spread into a wider conflagration, particularly given its length and intensity? Related to this issue was the manner in which the war developed into what the twentieth century calls a 'total' war. The destruction of the Confederacy, the abolition of slavery and the military occupation of the southern states until 1877 prevented any extension to North America of a balance of power. In 1895 President Grover Cleveland's Secretary of State, Richard Olney, boasted that 'Today the United States is practically sovereign on this continent and its fiat is law upon the subjects to which it confines its interposition'. This was possible,

---

3. W. L. Morton, 'British North America and a Continent in Dissolution, 1861–71', *History* XLVII (June 1962), pp. 139–56; Scott to Seward, 3 Mar. 1861, Lincoln Papers; 'Some Thoughts for the President's Consideration', 1 Apr. 1861, ibid.; Geoffrey Blainey, *The Causes of War*, 3rd edn (London: Macmillan, 1988), p. 59.

Olney explained, because the United States' 'infinite resources, combined with its isolated position render it master of the situation and practically invulnerable as against any or all other powers'. The firing at Fort Sumter presented an opportunity for preventing such an accretion of power and strategic invulnerability.

The attitude of the United States to foreign powers was conditioned largely by progress on the military front. The danger that a European power might intervene was most urgent when Union armies were routed and Confederate forces invaded northern soil. The thorny problem of war aims is also related to the fate of northern and southern arms. What were the two sections actually fighting about? To what extent did military success (or failure) modify these aims? How were these aims perceived by foreign powers, not least Great Britain? Why did the Civil War remain confined to the United States? Seward was later to pay the British Prime Minister, Lord Palmerston, a guarded and convoluted tribute. He 'could have been sustained by his countrymen in placing his Government in an attitude more unfriendly and more directly hostile to the United States'. But, Seward wrote, he resisted this imprudent temptation and 'prevented our deplorable civil strife from becoming a universal war'.[4]

Such views emphasizing endurance were comparatively rare in these heady, optimistic days, on both sides. The illusion of a short war was pervasive. The prime consideration appeared to be striking at the political focus of the rebellion – the Confederate capital which was moved to Richmond, Virginia in May 1861. The Confederate Congress agreed to meet there on 20 July. Once this city was occupied and its rebellious body dispersed, the rebellion would be crushed.[5] There was little appreciation in these early days of the strength of secessionist feeling. The widespread illusion evident during the Sumter crisis that Unionism would assert itself once the extremities of the dangers to which the South was exposing herself became evident, was still influential.

At first there was a great reluctance to accept this political imperative. But it was forced on northern leaders because

4.   Gordon Connell-Smith, *The United States and Latin America: An Historical Analysis of Inter-American Relations* (London: Heinemann, 1975), p. 78; Gerald G. Eggert, *Richard Olney: Evolution of a Statesman* (University Park, PA: Pennsylvania State UP, 1974), p. 206.

5.   Richard S. West, Jr. *Lincoln's Scapegoat General: A Life of Benjamin F. Butler, 1818–93* (Boston, MA: Houghton-Mifflin, 1965), pp. 73–4.

southern war aims complemented their own. The South demanded nothing less than recognition of her independence, not only by the Federal government, but also by foreign powers. The longer she survived, the greater the likelihood that such an acceptance would be forthcoming. The North had to be persuaded that the immense effort required to subjugate the South was futile and debilitating. Foreign powers were to be encouraged to intervene and deliver the beleaguered Confederacy.

The secession crisis: the third phase

Secessionists hoped that by creating a southern polity all slaveowning states (whether they accepted the 'right' of secession or not) would be attracted to join it, like an irresistible magnet. First the Upper South then the Border states would be dragged into the new confederation. For all its disadvantages, the series of unilateral state secessions operated to disintegrate the Union piecemeal, so that individual states would see that it was inexpedient to remain in the Union, isolated and friendless. A week before the firing on Fort Sumter, a Confederate Commissioner, John Forsyth, was boasting that within sixty days the Confederacy would include all the states, including Washington DC, south of New York. 'That said states could cut off those damned puritan states east, and never let them in [the Confederacy].' The prime fault with this strategy was that it now had to confront federal military power. Secession in the Deep South had occurred in an area completely bereft of federal coercive influence: the further north it occurred, the less likely secession could occur successfully with impunity.[6]

By 20 April, however, it appeared likely that the Federal government would no longer be able to maintain itself in Washington. On the day before, the 6th Massachusetts Volunteers, hurrying to the relief of the capital, had been attacked by a secessionist mob in Baltimore while attempting to take street cars to the station. Sixteen were killed, twelve civilians and four soldiers. The Baltimore militia were called out to deter the federal authorities from taking reprisals. Lincoln was so alarmed that

6. William Howard Russell, *My Diary North and South*, ed. Eugene H. Berwanger (New York: Alfred A. Knopf, 1988), pp. 48–9, 55; General Scott's Daily Report no. 5, 5 Apr. 1865; Col., Charles P. Stone to Seward, 5 Apr. 1861, Lincoln Papers.

further violence would provoke Maryland's secession that troops moving to Washington were diverted from Baltimore. This incident illustrates the widening scope of violence after Sumter. The writ of habeas corpus was suspended along 'the military line . . . used between the city of Philadelphia and the city of Washington'. This was justified on the grounds that 'in Cases of Rebellion or Invasion the public safety may require it' – but the Constitution was ambiguous as to which federal agency could exercise this power. The initial suspension aroused little comment. Indeed this whole period demonstrates the reluctance in many quarters to accept that a civil war had erupted. Violence was fitful and intermittent but gradually growing in ferocity. Two thousand stands of arms arrived in Baltimore – a gift from the secessionists of Virginia. One citizen, Joseph Spencer, was arrested for claiming that secessionist rioters 'had done right'.

On 22 April Governor Thomas Hicks called a special session of the Maryland legislature which met four days later. The prospects looked grave. But within days the secessionist bubble in Maryland was pricked. Its popular support was nebulous: even without opposition ten secessionist candidates nominated to fill vacancies on the Maryland legislature scraped only 9,200 votes. Lincoln had considered suspending the meeting, but he prudently declined because 'they have a clear legal right to assemble; and we can not know in advance, that their action will not be lawful and peaceful', and as it turned out the meeting was harmless. But Lincoln was ready to take brutal measures to suppress rebellion in Maryland if necessary, including 'the bombardment of their cities'. Such action was unnecessary. The Maryland legislature acknow- ledged that it lacked the constitutional authority to pass an ordinance of secession; the issue was a dead letter by the time it adjourned on 14 May. There was no burning reason why Maryland should take such a hazardous step. The number of slaves had dropped significantly as a proportion of the total population: in 1800 slaves accounted for 100,000 out of a total population of 350,000; by 1860 this number had fallen to 87,000 but Maryland's population had increased to 680,000. And such action as Baltimore had already taken, especially the blockade of Washington, had severely damaged her commerce. On 7 May the Mayor of Baltimore acknowledged that 'the authorities of the city fully recognise and admit their obligations to submit to the lawful authority of the government of the United States'.

This was an action of the greatest significance. If Maryland had seceded Washington would have been untenable and the prestige of the Federal government might have been dealt a mortal blow. But on 9 May 2,500 volunteers from Pennsylvania passed through Baltimore without incident. Five days later the 6th Massachusetts returned to the city to cheers. Without authority General Benjamin F. Butler took command and prohibited assembly, drilling, the hanging of Confederate flags, and confiscated the property of those sympathizing with the rebellion – a portent of his attitude to slavery. Under the suspension of the writ of habeas corpus, John Merryman, a wealthy secessionist, was arrested. A writ of habeas corpus was issued on 27 May in the district court of Baltimore, by an unhappy coincidence presided over by Roger B. Taney, the Chief Justice of the Supreme Court. With much indignation, bustle and display of otiose legal learning, Taney instructed Butler's replacement, General George Cadwallader, to appear before him; Cadwallader refused. There was, of course, some legal weight to Taney's judgment. He argued that Lincoln had subverted the Constitution; the president had impugned the separation of powers and had failed to uphold his inaugural oath to 'faithfully execute the laws if he takes upon himself the legislative power by suspending the writ of habeas corpus – and the judicial power also by arresting and imprisoning a person without due process of law'. But in this instance, as in so many others, secessionists (or those who acquiesced sympathetically in secession) eyed a rich, iced cake and sought to devour it simultaneously. Secession could never be an exclusive exercise in judicial rights however cleverly interpreted, because ultimately it rested on force. Lincoln had demonstrated at Sumter that secession could not be attained peaceably. In Maryland he demonstrated that the Federal government would exercise its power and protect its security by force if necessary. Revolution would be challenged by counter-revolution, and the Chief Justice's response may be set aside as only so much bleating because it failed to take account of the immense political changes which had occurred since December 1860. These placed Taney's sombrely worded judicial warnings at a severe discount.[7]

Once the capital was secure and federal forces had made their way into it rather like a surge of refreshing water pouring into a

---

7.   Mark E. Neely, *The Fate of Liberty* (New York: Oxford UP, 1991), Dean Sprague, *Freedom Under Lincoln* (Boston, MA: Houghton-Mifflin, 1965), pp. 2–3, 5–14, 25–38, 39–41.

dried up reservoir, then confidence began to return that the rebellion would be crushed quickly. Professor Blainey has argued that a belief in a short war is a reflection of confidence in an overwhelming superiority.[8] In terms of material strength the North had a preponderant advantage. The total northern population (including Kansas) was 18,907,753 compared with that of 8,726,644 in the Confederate states. But this latter figure included over 3,900,000 slaves who in 1861–62 were not considered suitable material for soldiers. In the vital category of white men of military age (15–40) the North could draw upon a population of 4,000,000 while the South had only a quarter of that figure, 1,100,000. The population of the Border states was 3,588,729 – if they had enthusiastically embraced the southern cause, then the North's margin of superiority would have been significantly reduced. The margin of industrial production was even greater. The individual value of industrial goods produced by the states of Pennsylvania and New York was double the entire production of all the Confederate states. A striking indication of this is revealed by the number of locomotives (19) built by the South in the year ending 1 June 1860; the North built 451.[9] Predictions that a war is likely to be short are based on three main propositions. First, they rely heavily on faith in economic resources, especially financial prosperity. The South despite the paucity of its resources was buoyed up by the expectation that a Confederacy would inaugurate a new age of free trade with Europe which would transform Charleston into another New York. The Secretary of the Treasury, Chase, took pleasure in informing Lincoln on 2 April that as bids for a federal loan were over-subscribed four times that 'All this shows decided improvement on finances and will gratify you'. Two weeks previously Chase had gloomily advised against re-supplying Fort Sumter. It would require 'the enlistment of armies and the expenditure of millions I cannot advise it . . . in the present condition of the national finances'. This sudden upturn encouraged many to believe that the South could not withstand the sheer weight of resources that the North could turn against her, especially in the sophistication and quantity of her weapons technology.

Secondly, predictions that wars will be short are often based on

8.   Geoffrey Blainey, *The Causes of War* 3rd edn (London: Macmillan, 1988), pp. 35–6, 41, 51, 56.

9.   Peter J. Parish, *American Civil War* (London: Eyre Methuen, 1975), pp. 107–10.

rash and highly emotional forecasts. Even Stanton, who had taken great political risks to cross the party divide during the last days of the Buchanan Administration to feed Republican colleagues with information, thought the war would be short. 'Nor indeed do I think hostilities will be so great an evil as many apprehend,' he informed Senator Dix. 'A round or two often serves to restore harmony; and the vast consumption required by a state of hostilities, will enrich rather than impoverish the North'.[10] Certainly Russell was of the opinion that both sides in 1861 were prone to boast about their untried martial prowess and underestimate the resources and skill of their opponents. Thirdly, those who are confident of early military success expect victory to come *soon*; misplaced optimism frequently prefaces wars.[11]

This belief in speed and decisiveness was strengthened by the suddenness by which the secessionist tide was turned. Firm, belligerent action by Nathaniel Lyon prevented secessionists seizing 21,000 muskets in Missouri and he defeated their militia, capturing numbers of them before occupying the state capital. Jefferson City. The result of his action enabled the Federal government to maintain control of most of the state, though other parts degenerated into guerrilla war. Three-quarters of all Missourians who fought in the Civil War fought for the North (as did two-thirds of all Marylanders). The loyalty of Delaware (with only 2 per cent of its population as slaves) was never in doubt. The western counties of Virginia 'seceded' from the Confederacy, and were swiftly occupied by Union forces commanded by George B. McClellan. The only area of doubt was in Kentucky. Lincoln said, 'To lose Kentucky is nearly the same as to lose the whole game'. In May the state declared 'a position of strict neutrality'. In fact, this aided the Confederacy immeasurably. A neutral Kentucky shielded the southern heartland better than a Confederate army. Lincoln declined to recognize this neutrality but agreed to respect it and did not extend any form of blockade to Kentucky's land frontiers. In June the Unionists won in excess of 70 per cent of the votes in a special election. The Confederacy then rashly violated Kentucky neutrality in September, and solved Lincoln's problem

10. Chase to Lincoln, 16 Mar., 2 Apr. 1861, Lincoln Papers; Benjamin P. Thomas and Harold H. Hyman, *Stanton: The Life and Times of Lincoln's Secretary of War* (New York: Alfred A., Knopf, 1962), p. 120.

11. Glyndon G. Van Deusen, *Horace Greeley: Nineteenth Century Crusader* (Philadelphia, PA: Pennsylvania State UP, 1953), pp. 275–6, 276–8; Russell, *My Diary North and South*, pp. 25, 27, 61–2, 66, 80, 82 (entries for 3–15 Mar., 5 Apr., 8 Apr., 16 Apr.).

by occupying this important state. In November an ordinance of secession was passed by a convention, but Confederate troops occupied only the south western corner of the state. The hard hand of war hit Kentucky and this state did experience a 'brothers war'. But such a precipitate move opened up the Confederate heartland to invasion.[12]

The problem of slavery

Of course, as slavery was inescapably part of the issues which had led to the rupture of the Union and the recourse to physical force to resolve them, it was inextricably linked with the form assumed by those military activities. This development was complicated by the determination of the executive branch not to use military force to alter either the parameters of political discussion after April 1861 or permit any change in the status of slavery in the southern states. Congress, moreover, subscribed to a similar view of war aims. On 22 July the House of Representatives passed a resolution supporting the presidential stance; the Senate three days later resolved that the war was not for oppression, conquest or subjugation, 'nor for the purpose of overthrowing or interfering with the rights or established institutions of those [seceded] States' but to preserve the Union and its laws, and 'as soon as these objects are accomplished the war ought to cease'. But as federal armies moved on to Confederate soil, adherence to this position became more burdensome. Once begun, organized violence generates its own momentum. To secure the desired ends those agencies resorting to violence must exercise a tight control over this political instrument; such control was impossible to maintain under the plural military and political system adopted by the United States. When Benjamin F. Butler's troops occupied Fort Monroe in Virginia in May 1861, they welcomed Negro slaves into their camps who were set to work on Union works. Butler declared them 'contraband of war', that is to say, property used for warlike purposes. Butler justified his action on military grounds, and it was endorsed by the War Department. 'In a state of rebellion', Butler argued, 'I would confiscate that which was

---

12. James M. McPherson, *Battle Cry of Freedom: The Civil War Era* (New York: Oxford UP. 1988), pp. 284–301; Stephen E. Wordworth, ' "The Indeterminate Quantities": Jefferson Davis, Leonidas Polk, and the end of Kentucky Neutrality, September 1861', *Civil War History* 38 (Dec. 1992), pp. 289–92.

used to oppose my arms – and take all that property which
constituted the wealth of that state, and furnished the means by
which the war was prosecuted, besides being the cause of the war'.
Butler took no action which redounded on the status of Negroes
as slaves. For under the Fugitive Slave Act, commanding officers
were obliged to return escaped Negroes as property to their
rightful owners. This raised the possibility that the Union army
could be transformed into a judicial arm of an Act which was
execrated in New England. The resulting controversy gave the lie
to the notion that somehow the war did not involve the slave
question or race relations.[13]

This was a problem that could not be concealed. On 30 August
General John C. Frémont, the former Republican presidential
candidate and now commander of the Department of the West,
promulgated in grandiose language from his headquarters at St
Louis, a 'proclamation' that declared a state approaching martial
law. Frémont would 'assume the administrative powers of the
State: any citizen caught possessing arms would be court-martialled
and shot if found guilty; the property of those opposed to the
government would be confiscated, including their slaves 'hereby
declared as freedmen'. Its incendiary effects on the Border states
were obvious. Joshua F. Speed commented to Joseph Holt that 'we
could stand several defeats like that at Bulls run [sic], better than
we can this proclamation if endorsed by the Administration'. It
also rather bombastically (if naively) usurped executive authority.
Lincoln could not permit one local commander to issue piecemeal
declarations which had effects on government policy over a whole
range of matters.

Frémont's position was also open to attack on other grounds.
His administration in Missouri was foolish and careless. (A useful
informant on these matters was Seward's nephew, Samuel S.
Seward.) Lincoln argued that the terms of the proclamation were
'purely political'. The status of property should 'be settled
according to laws made by lawmakers and not by military
proclamations'. Frémont received a mildly worded reproof from
Lincoln, which he did not deign to obey. An official investigation

---

13. Quoted in Hans L. Trefousse, *Andrew Johnson: A Biography* (New York:
Norton, 1989), p. 144; Benjamin F. Butler, *Butler's Book: A Review of his Legal,
Political and Military Career* (Boston, MA: Thayer, 1892), p. 258; *Private and Official
Correspondence of Benjamin F. Butler*, ed. Jesse A. Marshall (privately issued, Norwood,
1917), I, p. 232; Parish, *American Civil War*, p. 234; Thomas and Hyman, *Stanton*,
p. 232.

of Frémont's administration revealed all kinds of petty irregularities. A Californian crony was paid $191,000 to build forts at St Louis – at three times the usual cost. To Frémont's annoyance, officers from Washington were sent out to observe his activities. The formidable Mrs Frémont, the daughter of Thomas Hart Benton, travelled to Washington to lobby the president personally on her husband's behalf. Boisterous and indignant, she received the crushing reproof of which Lincoln was more than capable: 'You are quite a female politician'. Orders for Frémont's dismissal were issued in October 1861. This caused a furious uproar. Frémont had enjoyed public applause because he seemed to be doing something to break the torpor which was paralysing the Union war effort in the autumn of 1861. As George Templeton Strong, hardly a radical but a man who was increasingly impatient with laggard methods, wrote in his diary, Frémont's declaration 'looks like war in earnest at last. . . . A most significant step in the right direction, though it may weaken the national cause in Kentucky' – but this looked like a risk well worth taking.[14]

But there can be no doubting the correlation between enthusiasm for liberating the slaves and voices calling for an energetic prosecution of the war. Those who counselled caution and prudence were usually men who wished to preserve slavery in the South, or like Charles P. Stone, were slaveholders themselves. Ethan Allen Hitchcock, a former army officer who would soon be called to Washington to advise the Secretary for War, had advocated evacuating Sumter on the grounds that it would be a prudent strategic withdrawal. 'Take the Major [Anderson] away and employ the Navy in collecting the revenue'. He (wrongly) thought that the president would attempt to avoid any occasion for war. 'I would abandon the public property. I would not spike the guns'. But when it came to standing behind the guns, Hitchcock revealed a marked lack of enthusiasm for the task. 'Many friends urge my return to the Army. But I have no heart for engaging in Civil War. . . . If fighting could preserve the Union (or restore it) I might consider what I could do to take part – but when did fighting make friends?' Sherman wrote candidly that civilians were much keener than soldiers not only to start a war

14. McPherson, *Battle Cry of Freedom*, pp. 284–301; Wordworth, ' "The Indeterminate Quantities": Jefferson Davis, Leonidas Polk, and the End of Kentucky Neutrality, September 1861', pp. 289–92.

but also to prosecute one, 'and so it appears now'. General John M. Schofield, who had a distinguished military career, commented on this gap in martial enthusiasm in his memoirs:

> Men who have been fighting most of the three or four years generally become pretty cool, while those in the rear seem to become hotter and hotter as the end approaches. . . . They must in some way work off the surplus passion which the soldier has already exhausted in battle.

This 'surplus passion', which was frustrated by early failures, influenced profoundly the character and development of the war. Although military operations commenced with the firing at Fort Sumter, the origins of a war to emancipate slavery lie in these early failures. Conservative generals, who found a leader in the new commander called by Lincoln to take command of the Army of the Potomac in July 1861, George B. McClellan, could not understand that their failure to achieve the decisive victory which public opinion cried out for led to an increase in the influence of the Radicals. Furthermore, this slow transition in the character of the war was determined by the democratic process (what Clausewitz called 'popular passions') which had contributed to the political crisis assuming a military form. This elementary point is obscured by the many accusations that the hysteria generated by political intercourse was of material assistance to the Confederacy.[15]

Each step forward in the war, each acceleration in its intensity, had been preceded by an outburst of popular enthusiasm or fury. The channels of democratic procedure and intercourse had directed the velocity of military force aimed at the Confederacy, as before First Bull Run. But after that battle, despite the shock attendant on an unexpected defeat, political conservatism had reasserted itself. In both the congressional resolutions on war aims, in presidential use of the war powers (and the nomination of McClellan to command the Army of the Potomac, though his political views were less obvious than they would be three months later), and in the passage of the First Confiscation Act of 6 August 1861, war aims remained strictly limited. The First Confiscation

15.   Ethan Allan Hitchcock, *Fifty Years in Camp and Field*, ed. W. A. Croffut (New York: G. P. Putnam, 1909), p. 430; Lloyd Lewis, *Sherman: Fighting Prophet* (New York: Harcourt Brace, 1929), p. 142; John M. Schofield, *Forty-Six Years in the Army* (New York: Century, 1897), p. 314; Brian Holden Reid, 'General McClellan and the Politicians', *Parameters* XVII (Sept. 1987) pp. 102–3.

Act, which confirmed Butler's actions at Fort Monroe, simply declared that slaves employed to support military measures against the United States were declared forfeit – but not free.

But the alternative interpretation, favoured by Hans L. Trefousse, that there was much common ground between the Administration and its congressional critics, and that they managed to establish a working partnership, signally fails to take into account the impact of military failure on politicians who had been persuaded to expect a quick and decisive military victory. Some enthusiastically agreed with the radicals that the war effort must be revitalized. Others reluctantly agreed that the only way this could be achieved was by removing constraints on discipline and foraging, and by striking at the very heart of the southern social system and property rights – the emancipation of slavery. But many who were eager to root out traitors were less keen to contemplate the social consequences of more drastic measures. Indeed Browning was soon complaining in November 1862 when he heard that Union troops in the West were 'doing an immense deal of wanton mischief, as well as mercenary plundering. That they rob and steal for private gain, and burn and destroy through malice or wantoness, utterly regardless of the loyalty and disloyalty of the person depredated upon'. The firing at Fort Sumter had, in short, released a two-way political process. The war reflected the political system that had produced it; yet that political system, and the views aired in its institutions, were profoundly influenced by the course of military operations; these two elements could not be separated. Any interpretation of party politics in the American Civil War which fails to take this omnipresent reality into account is partial and incomplete.[16]

The making of the Emancipation Proclamation

The main problem that Lincoln faced in the first year of the war was that the North had not resigned itself to the kind of long,

16. This interpretation seeks to cut across the long-running controversy over the nature of Republican Radicalism. See the two essays by David Donald and T. Harry Williams in Grady McWhiney (ed.) *Grant, Lee, Lincoln and the Radicals* (Evanston, IL: Northwestern UP, 1964), pp. 79–91, 92–117. Also see Hans L. Trefousse, *The Radical Republicans*, (New York: Alfred A. Knopf, 1969), p. 167. Browning's views may be found in his *Diary*, eds Theodore C. Pease and James G. Randall (Springfield, IL: Illinois State Historical Library, 1925), pp. 538, 585 (entries for 2 Apr., 20 Nov. 1862).

arduous conflict which we readily associate with the American Civil War. The popular expectation was a massive northern victory by the summer of 1862. Seward informed Senator Sumner that he had been passed 'authentic information from Virginia that the Rebellion will be over there in 4 weeks'. On 3 April in what has been rightly judged a monumental blunder, Stanton closed all recruiting offices. The indecisive Battle of Shiloh in April was a portent of things to come, a portent confirmed by the great disappointment of McClellan's failure in the Seven Days Battles of June 1862. These general engagements indicated that, far from a prompt suppression of rebellion, the Federal government would have to brace itself to wage a full-scale Civil War. This was a slow process which took just over twelve months from the firing of the opening bullets at Fort Sumter. It may be gauged by the increasing attack on private property. The defence of private property is, after all, one of the prime duties of a nation-state. Once such a duty is jettisoned, however gradually, then it is clear that all pretence at harmony between conflicting polities has been abandoned. All barriers to the escalation of organized violence and brutality have been swept away until the end of 'total' victory has been achieved. The July 1861 resolution passed by the House of Representatives had stated that soldiers were under no compulsion to return runaway slaves. The Confiscation Act of 6 August declared that any slaves found undertaking military labour for the enemies of the United States would be forfeit. Such measures did not impugn the Fugitive Slave Act because they were worded in such a way as to avoid reflecting on the liberty of the broad mass of slaves.

Whereas the first six months of the war had seen only one great battle, First Bull Run, the period of six months from 31 March 1862 had seen a clutch of great battles, Shiloh, Seven Days, Second Bull Run, and then in September 1862, Antietam. Only the battles in the East had great political consequences because it was these that agitated the thoughts of politicians in Washington. Not only did these battles transform the face of war in North America but also the unprecedented scale of death and destruction inflicted on American society had important political consequences. Their very indecisiveness led to a recourse to 'total war' measures. After Lee's withdrawal to Maryland, on 22 September Lincoln presented to his Cabinet the text of the Preliminary Emancipation Proclamation. This august occasion was enlivened by Lincoln reading an amusing passage from Artemus

Ward's the 'High Handed Outrage at Utica', which affronted the sensibilities of the pompous Salmon P. Chase, who thought it inappropriately frivolous for such a solemn occasion. Turning more gravely to the necessity he had been forced to confront, Lincoln observed, 'I think the time has come. I wish it were a better time. The action of the army against the rebels has not been quite what I should have best liked'. Nonetheless, Antietam had driven Lee from northern soil and restored some credit to the northern cause.[17]

The entire document was justified as an exercise of the presidential war powers. The reference to the president as commander in chief which prefaces it did not appear in the proclamation calling out the militia in April 1861. All slaves held as chattels in states 'in rebellion against the United States' from 1 January 1863 were 'then, thenceforward, and forever free'. All federal agencies were to recognize this freedom and not discourage chattel slaves from seeking it. If the Confederate states returned to the Union, however, then Lincoln would ensure that loyal slaveowners would 'be compensated for all losses by acts of the United States, including the loss of slaves'. If they remained outside the Union then they risked losing all. For the Preliminary Emancipation Proclamation applied only to areas not occupied by Union forces. Those occupied by Union troops would be able to keep their slaves, at least for the time being, and would receive compensation after a due process of gradual emancipation. Blair and Seward were still worried about the Border states; but Lincoln now felt confident in their loyalty. The Federal government 'must make the forward effort. . . . They [will] acquiesce, if not immediately, soon'. This emphasis on the 'forward movement' is significant. Lincoln realized that a means had to be found, now that the war had moved into a second phase, of striking at the Confederacy rather than sitting back and allowing the South to strike at the Union, which it had done rather successfully over the previous two months. Given the adamant Confederate refusal to make any concessions, Lincoln now realized that he had no choice if he was to achieve a reunion of the states but to wage a punitive war against the South and its social system. He was candid in agreeing that after 1 January 1863 'the character of the war will

17. David Donald (ed.) *Inside Lincoln's Cabinet* (New York: Alfred A. Knopf, 1954), pp. 149–52 (entry for 22 Sept.).

change. It will be one of subjugation. . . . The [old] South is to be destroyed and replaced by new propositions and ideas'.[18]

The fearful cost of the war, which would be multiplied many times before it came to an end, not only supported those who called out for more drastic war measures, but also lent credence to an increasingly strong cry that the South be punished for bringing the curse of fratricidal conflict on the United States. The North, furthermore, should be punished by providence for tolerating the evil of slavery for so long. Even those soldiers who had objected to the Emancipation Proclamation realized as they advanced on to southern soil how slavery bound together and sustained its war economy. By striking at slavery Lincoln aimed to root out the fundamental cause of the war: the paramount issue which had tempted the South to seek its independence. Yet conservative members of his cabinet, one of whom, Seward, was considered a radical in 1861, were still fearful that the outbreak of a servile rebellion in the Confederacy would tempt foreign intervention. How and why this had not occurred despite the comparative success of southern arms we must now turn to consider.[19]

The illusions of the South

The South, like the North, was prey to a number of illusions after the firing of the first shots at Fort Sumter. The first of these was that the war would be won with ease and without bloodshed. The second was that southern independence would be won with the assistance of foreign powers. The third was that the British felt a deep sympathy for their 'Cavalier' kith and kin in the South based on indefinable racial and cultural links. There was a dangerous contradiction lurking at the heart of these calculations. Great Britain in the South's eyes was both sentimental and mercenary. The Confederacy consciously modelled itself in the style of the American Revolution. In 1780–81 France had made an important contribution to achieving American independence. Southerners

18.   John Hope Franklin, *The Emancipation Proclamation* (Edinburgh UP, 1963); James G. Randall and David Donald, *Lincoln the President: From Springfield to Gettysburg*, 2 vols (London: Eyre & Spottiswoode, 1947), II, pp. 162–5; McPherson, *Battle Cry of Freedom*, p. 558.

19.   See Peter J. Parish, 'The Instruments of Providence: Slavery, Civil War and the American Churches', in W. J. Sheils (ed.) *The Church and War* (Oxford: Basil Blackwell, 1984), pp. 291–320; Glyndon G. Van Deusen, *William Henry Seward* (New York: Oxford UP, 1969), pp. 330–34.

had convinced themselves that they could exploit Great Britain's mercenary interests and compel her to intervene, thanks to the power of 'King Cotton'. This strategy began to assume the hypnotic power of an article of faith. An overweening belief in the economic power of the South became evident in the early 1850s. By 1861 most southerners, quite ignorant of the world outside their own states, parroted ill-thought-out notions of the long reach of King Cotton. William Howard Russell had numerous conversations with southerners who seemed to consider the British Empire

> as a sort of appanage to their cotton kingdom. 'Why, sir, we have only to shut off your supply of cotton for a few weeks, and we can create a revolution in Great Britain. There are four millions of your people depending on us for their bread, not to speak of the many millions of dollars. No, sir, we know that England must recognise us', etc.

Most southerners were comforted by the sight of cotton bales piled up on the docks of Charleston. 'All these gentlemen to a man are resolute that England must get their cotton or perish'.

Great Britain would break the illegal Union blockade in her frantic search for cotton. The Confederacy held that the federal blockade was illegal because blockades were declared between nations at war, which the South claimed to be, while the Federal government insisted that it was suppressing an insurrection. This was an inconsistency that the Lincoln Administration worried about in private but did not acknowledge in public. Recognition of Confederate independence would then follow, with British military and naval assistance in the war against the North. This kind of thinking was therefore mutually supportive. The war would be short because the South would be victorious in a single great battle with few casualties ('a whippin' '), and victory would be consummated at a stroke by British intervention. Both these points did nothing to reduce southern conceit. The Governor of Mississippi, Pettus, seemed to labour under the misconception that his state cut a greater figure on the world stage than the British Empire. Russell quotes him as announcing that 'England is no doubt a great country, and has got fleets and the like . . . and may have a good deal to do in Eur-*ope*, but the sovereign state of Mississippi can do a great deal better without England than England can do without her'. Such voices were guilty of the sin of what Napoleon called 'making pictures'. They drew a sketch of the world as they would have liked it to appear, rather than how it actually appeared, and they lacked the imagination and the knowledge to grasp the hard realities of international affairs. Consequently, southern illusions fed on one another. As even an educated southerner wrote home to his wife, 'I believe the war will not last long. . . . England's interest unerringly points to an issue with them [the North], and it will surely come. Let us adhere closely to our policy. Let us keep our cotton and let not a single bag go, except in exchange for necessary articles'. [20]

Thus Confederate policy was governed by this *idée fixe*. In July 1861 the Confederate vice president, Alexander H. Stephens, claimed confidently that the blockade would be broken 'or there will be revolution in Europe. . . . Our cotton is . . . the tremendous lever by which we can work our destiny'. The self-imposed blockade of cotton worked most efficiently, supervised by local committees of public safety. During the first twelve months of conflict after Fort Sumter, European importation of cotton was but 1 per cent of its normal level. No official embargo was declared in case this risked European wrath rather than their intervention. But despite this initial success the European great powers did not intervene to slake the thirst of their cotton mills for cotton. In the first place, the massive crops of 1857–60 had permitted British mill-owners in particular to build up large stocks. Working off these, as James M. McPherson points out, was actually a commercial 'blessing in disguise' despite some gloomy forebodings from British ministers. Therefore, *pace* southern expectations, there was little pressure from commercial lobby groups to take action against the northern blockade. The same factors operated in the smaller French cotton industry. Also, the main impact of unemployment postdated the highwater mark of southern military success in the summer of 1862. This too had the unfortunate consequence that when the South struck after the Seven Days her blow missed its mark in Europe. Nonetheless, the Confederacy was determined to achieve recognition from European powers, especially Great Britain. The activities of her emissaries brought the United States to the brink of war with Great Britain and a step

20. Allan Nevins, *The Ordeal of the Union* (New York: Scribner's, 1947), I, p. 471; Francis B. Simkins, *The South, Old and New: A History, 1820–1947* (New York: Alfred A. Knopf, 1949), p. 221; Russell, *My Diary North and South*, pp. 130, 178, 195 (entries for 7 May, 2 and 14 June 1861); Randall, *Lincoln the President*, II, pp. 33–6; *The Granite Farm Letters: The Civil War Correspondence of Edgeworth and Sallie Bird*, ed. John Rozier (Athens, GA: University of Georgia Press, 1988), p. 53; Brian Jenkins, *Britain and the War for the Union* (London and Montreal: McGill and Queen's UP, 1974), I, p. 207, shows Palmerston's determination not to permit intervention for cotton.

nearer fulfilling the Confederate goal of widening the war to involve European powers.[21]

Anglo-American crises and their resolution, 1861–62

The first step which encouraged the South was the British recognition of belligerent status for the Confederacy as part of the declaration of neutrality on 13 May 1861. France followed this British initiative on 10 June. These moves set the pattern for the crisis. France followed the British lead and would not act without her. These declarations provoked a great deal of hostile northern comment but had in fact been conceded by Lincoln with the levying of the blockade. Therefore, it was with an optimistic air that on 12 October 1861, in accordance with their policy of gaining foreign recognition, the Confederate government dispatched two emissaries, James M. Mason (Virginia) and John Slidell (Louisiana), to Britain via Havana, Cuba. They took the British packet, *Trent* bound for St Thomas in the Danish West Indies, where they planned to take ship to Southampton. They were intercepted by the USS *Jacinto*, commanded by the intrepid Captain Charles Wilkes. Wilkes boarded the *Trent*, removed the two envoys, arrived back in the United States on 15 November where he was greeted by rapturous applause, and incarcerated them in Fort Warren, Boston. On 29 November the British Cabinet met in emergency session and agreed that Wilkes had violated the law of nations; and the following day, the British Ambassador, Lord Lyons, demanded the return of Mason and Slidell and an apology for an aggressive act. With the British press agitating for the dispatch of a naval expedition to break the federal blockade, war between Britain and the United States looked likely. But behind the bellicose demands of the press, on both sides of the Atlantic, was a determination not to take precipitate action. The French note supporting the British was phrased so as not to give unnecessary offence. This desire to avoid confrontation more than any other factor explains the avoidance

---

21. Frank L. Owsley, *King Cotton Diplomacy*, 2nd edn (Chicago UP, 1959), pp. 5–23; Parish, *American Civil War*, pp. 397–403; McPherson, *Battle Cry of Freedom*, pp. 382–7; John D. Pelzer, 'Liverpool and the American Civil War', *History Today* 40 (Mar. 1990), pp. 46–52.

of conflict between the United States and Great Britain and why the Civil War remained restricted to the United States.

Queen Victoria interceded in the affair. Anxious to avoid war, she persuaded the dying Prince Albert, who could hardly hold his pen, to tone down the second note delivered by Lyons rendering it much less offensive to the Lincoln Administration. The British government demanded that Mason and Slidell be returned within seven days; if the United States failed to comply then diplomatic relations would be severed. A number of warlike preparations were undertaken: reinforcements were dispatched to Canada; the fleet was mobilized; and an important Union order for saltpetre – an essential compound in the manufacture of gunpowder – was cancelled. But behind this warlike smokescreen, both sides played for time. Formal demands were presented on 19 December in a more conciliatory spirit. A further four days' grace was granted to the Lincoln Administration by not conveying written demands until 23 December; a reply was not required for seven days after this. In the meantime, Seward, having now abandoned his earlier bombastic and belligerent stance, wrote to the American minister in London, Charles Francis Adams, on 30 November, 'I trust that the British Government will consider the subject in a friendly temper, and it may expect the best disposition on the part of this Government'.

Again, it was in the interests of both sides to come to some kind of accommodation. The Lincoln Administration was in no position to risk war with Britain. By December 1861 the United States Navy had still not effectively blockaded southern ports. The Royal Navy could break this blockade with ease, inflict damage on the US merchant marine, and replace a Union blockade of southern ports with a British blockade of northern ports. The effect of this on the putative northern war effort need hardly be stressed. Seward's position was that Wilkes had acted without the knowledge or instructions of his government. The prisoners should be regarded as contraband of war. As the *Trent* was a merchant ship it could be lawfully searched, and was unmolested once the contraband had been identified and removed. But Seward then conceded that contraband should have been subject to the jurisdiction of a prize court; as this procedure had not been followed, the United States government was content to release Mason and Slidell. Indeed, in line with the existing 'short war' mode of thought, Seward now asserted that the issue was unimportant because of the 'waning character of the rebellion' which he was sure would crumble in the spring of 1862. This line was agreed at a cabinet meeting on 25 December, even though the president took some persuading to give up the Confederate emissaries. Thus the crisis was brought to an end as quickly as it had blown up. Within months the two countries had signed a treaty suppressing the Atlantic slave trade. By appearing conciliatory the Lincoln Administration had wriggled out of a triangular trap in which, no matter how hard it might have struggled, it could not have broken free by force.[22]

Anglo-American relations had been improved by the *Trent* crisis. Throughout the summer of 1862 Great Britain acquiesced in some stringent enforcement of the rules of blockade. British merchant ships, notably the *Bermuda*, had their cargoes confiscated because they were headed for the Confederacy. They were placed before a prize court, and in the case of the *Bermuda* she was bought by the United States Navy and put to work enforcing the blockade. These actions put Great Britain in a tricky dilemma. The United States and Great Britain had gone to war in 1812 mainly because of a British determination to enforce identical regulations in her own blockade of Napoleonic France. The United States, then a neutral, claimed they did not apply to her. The United States had refused to recognize the Declaration of Paris (1856) which upheld the right of any blockading power to search and confiscate contraband *en route* to a belligerent state. But on 24 April 1861 the United States had no choice but to accede to the Declaration of Paris because under international law, to be legal and binding a blockade had to be *effective*, and this entailed asserting all the rights and powers that the American government had previously found so obnoxious. The readiness of the United States government to concede ground on this contentious issue reversed earlier confrontations, with Britain dealing with an American blockade and not vice versa. Unless the British government was determined to declare war and enter on the side of the South in the Civil War, she would be setting a most unfortunate precedent.

22.   Cecil Woodham-Smith, *Queen Victoria: Her Life and Times* (London: Hamish Hamilton, 1972), I, p. 442; Van Deusen, *Seward*, pp. 308–20; McPherson, *Battle Cry of Freedom*, p. 390, points to the importance of the saltpetre order in forcing Lincoln to resolve the crisis; Randall, *Lincoln the President*, II, pp. 33–53; Jenkins. *Britain and the War for the Union*, I, pp. 194–9, 202–3, 211–14, 216, 224, 226–9, 235–6; Allan Nevins, *The War for the Union: The Improvised War, 1861–1862* (New York: Scribner's, 1959), I, pp. 387–94; Llyn M. Case and Warren F. Spencer, *The United States and France: Civil War Diplomacy* (Philadelphia, PA: Pennsylvania State UP, 1970), pp. 59, 122–3, 201, 217–20, 230; D. P. Crook, *The North, the South and the Powers* (New York: Wiley, 1974), p. 111, shows that despite the jubilation in the North at the seizure of the *Trent*, there was *anxiety* at Britain's reaction.

Breaking the blockade would be tantamount to inviting the United States to side with Britain's enemies in a future hypothetical conflict which could endanger the British Isles. This was a risk which the British government felt that it could not take, however inviting short-term advantages might appear if she entered the American conflict in 1862.[23]

This whole question of weighing future security needs against the short-term benefits of intervention dominated British and French deliberations during this first year of the Civil War. The longer the war continued the greater the chance that the South would survive *if* she defended her territorial integrity successfully. As Lord John Russell pointed out in May 1861, with a territory of some 700,000 square miles, an organized government machinery and a number of powerful armies at her command, the belligerent rights of the Confederacy were a question of fact. If she sustained herself intact then intervention might follow under certain conditions, but it could not be expected as a virtual right as many southerners seemed to demand. It is impossible not to be amazed by the casual way southerners treated foreign affairs and the running of the Confederate State Department in the opening months of the Civil War. Indeed southern efforts in this area were contradictory, and the 'King Cotton' policy almost self-destructive. The South could gain her independence only by force: this was after all, in the final resort, the motive behind secession. Therefore she should have employed all her resources, military, diplomatic and financial to securing that aim. Belligerent rights did permit her to raise loans abroad and this could have been done, and munitions purchased by the use of her undoubted cotton wealth. But by indulging in the 'King Cotton' self-imposed blockade the Confederacy denied herself the ability to make use of this financial strength in the first year of the war. Her ability to field strong, well-equipped armies was accordingly reduced, as was her power to seek the victory which would have attained independence. The South seemed to think that intervention would follow a declaration of independence like day follows night. Southerners probably read too much into the history of the American Revolution.

23. This issue is explored in detail in Ephraim D. Adams, *Great Britain and the American Civil War* (London: Longman, 1925) I, pp. 256–67, 268–73; see also Van Deusen, *Seward*, pp. 293–5; E. Merton Coulter, *The Confederate States of America, 1861–1865* (Baton Rouge: Louisiana State UP, 1950), p. 191, likens the South to 'a silly child, looking across the big water expecting the British lion with one bound to leap the Atlantic and with a mighty thrust of its paw crush the blockade'.

Intervention would have followed consistent and sustained military success; but this eluded the South.[24]

Yet in the summer of 1862 it looked momentarily as if the Confederacy would defeat Union armies in the field. A succession of military victories, Seven Days, Second Bull Run and the invasion of Maryland, indicated that intervention was more likely than hitherto. And the Confederate commander, Robert E. Lee, was of the view that the South would have to advance and *win* her independence and not wait passively for another power to join the struggle, and help her attain it. Yet, for all their triumphs, southern armies had an annoying habit of failing the Confederacy at crucial moments. In August 1862, as Lee advanced into Maryland, Lord John Russell prepared a memorandum cautiously advocating joint mediation in the struggle with France and Russia; this fell somewhat short of the outright recognition that the South hoped for; only if the North abruptly rejected his overtures would recognition be proffered. Napoleon III prepared to intervene but would not do so without British support. Russell's plan was tentative and probing. If the South was victorious at the Battle of Antietam then he would place the plan before the British Cabinet on 23 October. News of Lee's withdrawal from Maryland after Antietam effectively shelved it. The issue of the Preliminary Emancipation Proclamation also undercut Russell's efforts to continue with his mediation policy. Moreover, Britain did not interfere in the American conflict because she assumed (and hoped) that the South would win. It was regarded as a 'lesson' of history that a large, compact, homogeneous unit would win its independence by the weight of its own exertions. Gladstone's famous speech when he declared that 'the South had made a nation' was a typical viewpoint. But it by no means followed that because Great Britain hoped the Confederacy would win that she would relish intervention on her behalf; wanting something to happen and doing something about it are far from identical states of mind. In 1861–62 Great Britain offered the South all aid short of physical help.[25]

---

24. As Mason observed of the northern penetration of the Mississippi Valley in February 1862, 'The late reverses at Forts Henry and Donelson have had an unfortunate effect upon the minds of our friends'. Quoted in Adams, *Great Britain and the American Civil War*, I, p. 294; see also Parish, *American Civil War*, p. 401.

25. Howard Jones, *Union in Peril* (Chapel Hill, NC: University of North Carolina Press, 1992), p. 8; Henry Blumenthal, 'Confederate Diplomacy: Popular Notions and International Realities', *Journal of Southern History* XXXII (1966), pp. 151–71; Case and Spencer, *United States and France*, pp. 338–45; Crook, *The North, the*

Why then did Great Britain not intervene in a conflict when the short-term benefits would have been enormous? Such an intervention would have shattered United States dominance in North America and replaced a continental republic with a number of smaller American republics which would have greatly increased British influence in the region. The answer is quite simple: there was no overwhelming motive for entering the war. Great Britain was actually profiting from the war, and the Lancashire MP, John Watts, wrote that 'all good and honourable men spoke of the cessation of the most terrible war of modern times as a thing to be dreaded'. Whereas in 1860 the cotton industry had entered a crisis, with bankruptcy common, by 1862 trade was booming. This was not simply because war enabled cotton mill owners to use up tons of stored cotton. They were able to sell tons of manufactured goods which had previously languished in warehouses. Within a year of Sumter these were sold at a profit of $200 million. Banking interests objected to intervention. They had joined in cotton speculation; peace would bring cheap cotton 'and that meant Judgement Day'. The same was true of the linen and woollen industry: they 'waked to life again and recaptured much of their lost ground, and reaped a golden harvest'. In the former, profits were $14.5 million in excess of normal levels for the five years prior to the war. In the latter, profits increased by $30 million and more workers were employed.

The North and South spent, at a conservative estimate, $100 million on munitions (including powder, lead, steel plates and rails, knives, sabres and bayonets), exclusive of tents, shoes, leather goods and the ships built for the Confederacy, like the famous commerce raider, the *Alabama*. Enormous profits were also made from blockade-running. Only one in eight blockade-runners were caught, and 1.5 million bales of (smuggled) cotton were sold at inflated prices. Another great boon brought by the American Civil War was the almost complete destruction of the United States merchant marine either by Confederate privateers or by Washington's own action. The American fleet was 'grounded' and Britain purchased the best ships of the fleet at the bargain price of $42 million. Before 1860 the United States had been Britain's only major rival in the carrying trade, indeed had surpassed her in the

South and the Powers, p. 224, argues that even if the South had been victorious at Antietam, it was by no means inevitable that British intervention would have followed.

direct trade between Britain and America. Before 1860 the United States had 2,245,000 tons of merchant shipping to Britain's 940,000. By 1863 this rival was destroyed indefinitely. Britain was not prepared to go to war to hazard her own merchant marine, let alone her now guaranteed supremacy. This was another factor that the 'King Cotton' preoccupation had not taken into consideration. Wartime developments could not be taken into account by a rigid *idée fixe* that had been formulated under peacetime conditions.

Far from being coerced by the South into intervening, Great Britain had made enormous profits. Far from being thrown into chaos she had been rejuvenated. In 1860–64 her foreign trade had increased from $374 million to $509 million. Nevertheless, Great Britain wished to see the Union permanently split; it would certainly favour British interests in the New World and decisively weaken her only rival in the western hemisphere. But Great Britain did not interfere in the American Civil War because the short-term economic motive of benefiting from the conflict while remaining neutral outweighed the political motive of weakening a strategic rival. That is to say, the political-economic situation was the exact reverse of that forecast by the 'King Cotton' doctrine. Besides Britain shied away from setting a precedent by interfering in fratricidal struggles. It would also make little sense in losing her best customer in exchange for the Confederacy, one whose economic potential simply did not begin to compare with the United States. British investments in the North in railroads, banks, mines and companies exceeded those in the cotton industry.[26]

The South hoped to extend the war by inviting British intervention on her side by two-fold means, by coercion – by withholding cotton – and by sentiment – the affinity that the British upper class would feel for the patrician southern planter class. These expectations were not fulfilled because the South grossly overestimated the power of cotton and the likelihood of intervention. Britain and France, for a variety of reasons, were not prepared to enter the American Civil War. Fundamentally, the Confederacy blundered because it staked all on a theoretical economic argument wholly irrelevant to European power politics. The supposed cultural bonds, though they cannot be dismissed completely, were not strong, and failed to pull Britain towards the

---

26. Jones, *Union in Peril*, pp. 111–15; Owsley, *King Cotton Diplomacy*, pp. 542–52; Crook, *The North, the South and the Powers*, p. 269, also demonstrates British dependence on northern grain imports. Imports of US wheat, flour and maize on average rose to 33.3 per cent of total British imports in the years 1860–65.

brink of intervention on the South's side. As a factor in practical politics they were more apparent than real. The British government had no intention of endangering British prosperity to save English-speaking gentlemen from a 'motley crew of Germans and Irish'. 'King Cotton' diplomacy served only to isolate the Confederacy and increase its vulnerability to the military power now being mobilized against southern forces.[27]

Thus by the autumn of 1862 the American Civil War had assumed the character that we have come to associate with it. It remained a *civil* war, and the likelihood of European intervention decreased – gradually (even during the dark and troublesome months of December 1862 to June 1863 which saw a major cabinet crisis and a second Confederate invasion of the North), and then markedly after July 1863. Therefore the conflict begun at Fort Sumter in April 1861 did not escalate into a vast international conflict resembling that of 1775–83 involving all the great powers, concluding, with perceptible inevitability, with the independence of a second North American polity. The *Trent* crisis was the first major landmark of the war. As other powers were excluded, the North could concentrate on attaining a decisive victory over the South. It appeared more receptive, and in some quarters positively enthusiastic, in adopting punitive methods to crush the South. The Emancipation Proclamation was the second important landmark pointing towards punitive action because it permitted, and eventually justified, the rapid passage to measures that attacked private property and dispensed with the formalities of military discipline. Crushing the southern people and their institutions would be just as much the object of northern generals as southern armies. General Butler urged such a course in 1863 before the Joint Committee on the Conduct of the War. He carried forward the strategy which he had begun tentatively at Fort Monroe two years before. He wanted an army to 'supply itself ruthlessly from the country . . . organising . . . Negroes into troops with which to go to Richmond the other way'. Warming to his theme, which would correctly predict General Sherman's course a year later, he suggested that 'to take away all the producers, to

---

27. Pelzer, 'Liverpool and the American Civil War', pp. 46–50, shows the strength of sympathies with the South; but see Max Beloff, 'Great Britain and the American Civil War', *History* 37 (1952), pp. 44, 47; also W. D. Jones, 'British Conservatives and the American Civil War', *American Historical Review* LVIII (1953) p. 543; H. Blumenthal, 'British Sympathies in the American Civil War', *Journal of Southern History* 33 (1967), pp. 356–67.

stop the production of the country and everything else contributing to the power of the Confederacy . . . will be such a movement as would determine our strength and the weakness of the Confederacy, for it is but a shell'. And such views, expressed by a general with a mediocre record of field command, indicate that the strategies eventually adopted the following year were already part of the common currency of political discussion, and not the unique fruit of military genius.[28]

Pursued to a decisive and victorious conclusion, the American Civil War ended any possibility that the balance of power would return to North America; liberal democracy, based on unified and durable social and political institutions was sustained. The American system dominated by the United States would not just survive but thrive. The Civil War, and the issues which gave it shape and form tested, as Lincoln said, 'whether that nation or any nation so conceived, and so dedicated can long endure'. But only he, whose hopes had been raised prematurely, as they were dashed so frequently, by promises of imminent and rapid victory, sensed the true cost of the punitive war upon which he had so reluctantly embarked.[29]

28. Morton, 'British North America and a Continent in Dissolution', p. 149; Butler, *Butler's Book*, pp. 582–3.

29. Morton, 'British North America and a Continent in Dissolution', p. 145; Randall, *Lincoln the President*, II, p. 310.

Conclusion

I fear if S[outh] C[arolina] and some of the other states are hurrying our whole country into civil war. I fear if S.C. takes Fort Sumter, by force, and gives the first shot, then the *South* will commence the war, and if there is any war, I want the North to have all the blame.

MILDRED SAYRE to EDMUND RUFFIN, 4 February 1861[1]

This book has been concerned with broadening the usual, rather narrow, political approach to discussing the origins of the American Civil War. It has argued that we should treat this complex question in relation not only to political events, important though these are, but also to geography, social and cultural forces, economic vicissitudes, and how men thought and acted towards the possibility of war. The study of war origins cannot be divorced from the military factors that give wars their shape and finally precipitate them. Thus close attention must be accorded to the immediate origins of the conflict because it is only these that actually produce war at a given date in a specific form; the more distant origins of conflict – which, as this book has argued, may be traced back to the very foundation of the American Republic – are significant in establishing the vital preconditions that render war possible. But they provide no answer to the tricky question of why war broke out when it did. Only the immediate origins can provide the answer to this question, and military considerations come to the fore. So at what point did civil war in 1861 become likely?

1. Mildred Sayre to Edmund Ruffin, 4 February 1861, quoted in David F. Allmendiger, Jr, *Ruffin: Family and Reform in the Old South* (New York: Oxford UP, 1990), p. 133.

Let us first review the distant origins to give perspective to the discussion. It was inevitable that in a country like the United States, its 'destiny' would be the subject of much discussion and disagreement. The Hartford Convention (1814) and the Nullification Crisis (1832–33) indicated that such discussion had the potential to generate armed conflict. This was accentuated by the 'unstable pluralism' of American democracy, the tiny size of the Federal Administration, an over-reliance on legal niceties and interpretations, and the weakness of the central government *vis-à-vis* the states. The Federal government could not deter the threat of rebellion by force because it had no force to mobilize. This did not have severe repercussions until the southern states began to act in concert, especially after 1850.

The Compromise of 1850 was a *conditional* compromise. It demonstrated that compromises with the southern states were invariably pro-slavery in character. The Democratic Administrations of Franklin Pierce and James Buchanan were dedicated to protecting the Compromise. Their policy was, therefore, consistently pro-southern and alienated large sections of northern opinion who believed that the price extracted by those pro-slavery compromises was too high and that the growth of the 'slave power' had important, serious implications for the continuance of northern liberties. The Pierce–Buchanan policy was counterproductive and contributed to a profound sense of domestic 'political crisis'. The Kansas-Nebraska Act was perhaps the most significant political manoeuvre of the decade: the year 1854 was a major turning point, and most southerners were eager to turn.

But which way should the South turn? The South was far from being a coherent, unified entity; it was the Deep South that forced the pace, the Upper South was reluctant to follow. The 1830s had seen the development of a pro-slavery ideology which argued that the South's peculiar institution was a positive good. By the 1850s these ideas were generally accepted and widely popularized. This ideology increasingly bound the slave states together. It sought the modernization of slavery, so that it could compete more effectively with free labour. The institution of slavery was central to the sense of cultural divergence between the North and South, even if this has been exaggerated. Certainly this sense of cultural separateness was accentuated by large-scale immigration to the North after 1840. Hence the attempt to coordinate action among southern states. If we accept that centrifugal tendencies – separatism – were inherent in the American experiment, this does not mean that they inevitably led to civil war and at a particular date. Certainly a sense of confrontation was sharpened by the rise of the Republican Party after 1854, even though its origins had far less to do with the slavery controversy, and much more to do with ethnic-cultural tensions within the North, than earlier historians believed.

Nonetheless, the rise of a sectional, northern party dedicated to the *restriction* of slavery, not only gave point to differences over the peculiar institution and the tariff question, but also signalled an end to a desire to compromise on a basis that secured, or prolonged, the evolution of slavery in North America, in contradistinction to all other western, liberal opinion. By 1850 slavery survived elsewhere only in Brazil, Cuba and Puerto Rico.[2]

All of these factors contributed powerfully to the disintegration of the Second Party System and its replacement with one that responded to sectional interests. But the import of these events essentially provides an *indirect* explanation of the origins of the American Civil War. However fearful and inflamed southern opinion became by 1859, especially after John Brown's 'raid', northern opinion remained pacific and hoped, for the most part, that a further compromise would be forthcoming. Republican leaders were prepared to accept a compromise only if the restriction of slavery was conceded; this was never likely. Leading planters explained secession in 1860–61, not in terms of cultural differences but of the defence of slavery. The election of a Republican president, in Alexander H. Stephen's words, put to the test 'the proper status of the Negro in our form of civilization'.[3]

Of course, the immediate origins of the Civil War grew out of the sense of a political crisis in the 1850s. Yet it is they, and not the political crisis itself, which explain why the war came in 1861 and the *way* it came. The prime reason for the coming of war in that year was the southern decision not to accept the choice made by a majority of voters (almost all in the North) who had supported the Republican Party. Where the two-party system had disintegrated secessionist fervour advanced – especially in the Deep South, much less so in the Upper South. It was 1860, and not 1857[4] (the year of Lecompton, Kansas violence, and Dred

2. Peter Kolchin, *American Slavery* (Harmondsworth: Penguin, 1993, 1995), p. 93.

3. Bruce Levine, *Half Slave and Half Free: The Roots of Civil War* (New York: Hill & Wang, 1992), pp. 227–8.

4. As argued by Kenneth M. Stampp, *America in 1857: A Nation on the Brink* (New York: Oxford UP, 1990).

Scott) that was the crucial year of decision. It is the presidential election that triggers off the secession crisis that provides *the* issue between the secessionists and the Federal government.

The manner in which unilateral state secessions were carried out was pregnant with war. Separatism itself does not lead to war; but secession almost always does. And in the case of 1860–61 secession led to anarchy in the United States with no coherent programme of government or plan. This was accompanied by a rapid increase in armaments among the seceded states. It is as well to recall that the Confederacy opened fire on Fort Sumter *before* Virginia, Tennessee, North Carolina and Arkansas had seceded. This was a rash, ill-thought-out act of foolishness, but characteristic of the impetuosity that secession had brought in its train. The role of newspapers in contributing to the overwrought atmosphere, especially in the Deep South, should not be underestimated. The casual attitude of secessionists to the use of force (which so contrasts with the agonizing of both the Buchanan and Lincoln Administrations) and over-reliance on its efficacy, was the product of an attitude of mind that did not envisage war as a thing of armies and organized destruction, but of casual gatherings of romantic adventurers and warriors, who 'whipped' the enemy: and it was modelled on the wholly misleading example of Kansas. This is a supremely important factor that explains the coming of war in 1861. It is often overlooked.

Secession was based ultimately on *force*. It was enforced in the seceded states by local 'vigilance' committees and by state militias or vigilantes; it was secured by opening fire on Fort Sumter; it was extended into Kentucky and elsewhere by Confederate armies. Force and secession worked hand in hand in managing a highly aggressive *coup d'état*. On 1 October 1862, in the only state where secession had been confirmed by the popular vote, Texas state militia arrested more than 200 unionists; some 44 were executed, and many others lynched. Frontier violence and secession are clearly related; this does not mean that the South enjoyed a coherent military tradition. On the contrary, its casual and ill-informed attitude to violence led it to precipitate a suicidal civil war.[5]

There can be no doubting either, despite so much southern special pleading to the contrary, that the South was the aggressive

5.   Richard B. McCaslin, *Tainted Breeze: The Great Hanging at Gainesville, Texas, 1862* (Baton Rouge: Louisiana State UP, 1994).

party. One interesting feature that the American Civil War shares with other wars of the nineteenth century, is that the actual conflict was ignited by the side that was standing on the *defensive*.[6] Lacking great armed forces to deter the war, the Lincoln Administration called upon the states to provide the manpower to restore the Union. The issue of Lincoln's Proclamation of 15 April 1861 revealed that those who called for compromise on a pro-slavery basis reminiscent of 1850 – especially in Virginia, Tennessee and North Carolina – in the last resort, were prepared to side with the secessionists. Their loyalty was indeed conditional and points up the moral that, even if the Sumter crisis had been resolved by federal concessions, the problem would not have gone away. On the contrary, it would have boosted secessionist confidence and swagger, depressed the North and perhaps fatally damaged Lincoln's prestige. Secessionists would have believed even more fervently that the North lacked resolve and that it could be intimidated further. Sumter was a symptom of this delusion; it was not *the* problem. It was southern conduct during the Sumter crisis that persuaded northern opinion that 'standing up to the South' was necessary even if this should lead to war. In a democracy the climate of public opinion was crucial in strengthening the resolve of statesmen.

Northern resolve to crush the Confederacy was also underestimated by outside powers, who failed to understand the complexity of the conflict. Two polities waging war in North America threatened to restore some semblance of the balance of power in this continent. If Great Britain and France had intervened on the side of the Confederacy, then the war would have been transformed into a general war that might have spread to Europe. Russia, still resentful of her defeat by Britain and France in the Crimea (1854–56), consistently pursued a pro-Union policy. But Britain and France did not intervene because they had no overwhelming reason to do so, and one would not act without the other.[7] Only foreign intervention on behalf of the Confederacy would have restored a balance of power and counter-weighed the balance of forces and resources that favoured the Union.

It took time for these forces to be mobilized, distributed and

6.   See European examples in A. J. P. Taylor, *From Napoleon to the Second International*, ed. C. Wrigley (London: Hamish Hamilton, 1993), p. 336.

7.   Howard Jones, *Union in Peril* (Chapel Hill, NC: University of North Carolina Press, 1992), pp. 4, 8, 43, 89, 96, 152, 229–30.

organized. This was an act of *policy*, not the pursuit of a legal case or democratic ideals, important as these were in justifying the policy. Warfare was not, as so many assumed, a casual, dramatic and rapid affair, but a highly intricate business. The deadly error of supposing that war would be short was committed by both sides. Sometimes such an assumption is justified (as in the Franco-Prussian War of 1870–71) but it is not justified when no military preparations have been undertaken by either side. It is this underestimation of what even a *limited* war – a police action – required that so impresses the twentieth-century reader. This profound miscalculation resulted in a terrible war of attrition unimagined in 1861 for all the soaring rhetoric. Many who suffered in the subsequent four years would utter words more prosaic than those of President Lincoln in his second inaugural address of March 1865, while sharing his heart-felt sentiments. 'Fondly do we hope, fervently do we pray, that this mighty scourge of war may speedily pass away'.

Bibliography

BOOKS

* Paperback edition available. For university presses (UP), the place of publication is the university city unless otherwise indicated.

ADAMS, CHARLES FRANCIS, Jr, *An Autobiography, 1835-1915* (New York: Chelsea House, 1983).*

ADAMS, EPHRAIM D., *Great Britain and the American Civil War*, 2 vols (London: Longman, 1925).

ADAMS, HENRY, *Democracy: An American Novel* (New York: New American Library, 1961).

ADAMS, MICHAEL C. C., *Our Masters the Rebels* (Cambridge, MA: Harvard UP, 1978; Bison, 1992).*

ALLMENDIGER, DAVID F., *Ruffin: Family and Reform in the Old South* (New York: Oxford UP, 1990).

ANGLE, PAUL M. (ED.), *The Lincoln Reader* (New Brunswick, NJ: Rutgers UP, 1947).

ARON, RAYMOND, *The Imperial Republic* (London: Weidenfeld & Nicolson, 1973).

ASHWORTH, JOHN, *'Agrarians and Aristocrats': Political Ideology in the United States 1837–1846* (London: Royal Historical Society, 1983).

BAILYN, BERNARD, *Voyages to the West: Emigration from Britain on the eve of the Revolution* (London: I. B. Tauris, 1987).

BARINGER, W. E., *A House Dividing: Lincoln as President Elect* (Springfield, IL: Abraham Lincoln Association, 1945).

BARNEY, WILLIAM L., *The Secessionist Impulse in Alabama and Mississippi in 1860* (Princeton UP, 1974).

BATES, EDWARD, *The Diary of Edward Bates*, ed. Howard K. Beale (Washington DC: Government Printing Office, 1933).

BAXTER, MAURICE G., *One and Inseparable: Daniel Webster and the Union* (Cambridge, MA: Belknapp, 1984).

BERINGER, RICHARD E., HATTAWAY, HERMAN, JONES, ARCHER, and STILL, WILLIAM N., Jr, *Why the South Lost the Civil War* (Athens, GA: University of Georgia Press, 1988).*

BIRD, EDGEWORTH, *The Granite Farm Letters*, ed. John Rozier (Athens, GA: University of Georgia Press, 1988).

BLAINE, JAMES G., *Twenty Years of Congress*, 2 vols (Norwich, CT: Henry Bill, 1884).

BLAINEY, GEOFFREY, *The Causes of War*, 3rd edn (London: Macmillan, 1988).

BLUE, FREDERICK J., *Salmon P. Chase: A Life in Politics* (Kent, OH: Kent State UP, 1987).

BOGUE, ALLAN G., *The Congressmen's Civil War* (Cambridge UP, 1989).*

BOLTON, CHARLES C., *Poor Whites of the Antebellum South: Tenants and Labourers in Central North Carolina and North East Mississippi* (Durham, NC: Duke UP, 1994).*

BOORSTIN, DANIEL J. *The Genius of American Politics* (Chicago UP, 1953).

BOOTH, KEN, and WRIGHT, MOORHEAD, *American Thinking about Peace and War* (Brighton: Harvester, 1978).

BORDEN, MORTON, *Parties and Politics in the Early Republic, 1789–1815* (London: Routledge, 1968).

BRADEN, WALDO W., *Abraham Lincoln, Public Speaker* (Baton Rouge: Louisiana State UP, 1988).*

BROCK, WILLIAM R., *The Character of American History*, 2nd edn (London: Macmillan, 1965).*
Conflict and Transformation: The United States, 1844–1877 (Harmondsworth: Penguin, 1973).*
Parties and Political Conscience: American Dilemmas, 1840–1850 (New York: KTO, 1979).

BRODIE, FAWN M., *Thomas Jefferson: An Intimate History* (London: Eyre Methuen, 1974).

BROGAN, DENNIS W., *American Aspects* (London: Hamish Hamilton, 1963).

BROGAN, HUGH, *Tocqueville* (London: Fontana, 1973).
Longman History of the United States of America (London: Longman, 1985).

BROWNING, ORVILLE HICKMAN, *Diary*, 2 vols, eds Theodore C.

Pease and James G. Randall (Springfield, IL: Illinois State Historical Library, 1925).

BUCHANAN, ALLEN, *Secession: The Morality of Political Divorce from Fort Sumter to Lithuania and Quebec* (Boulder, CO: Westview, 1991).

BUTLER, BENJAMIN F., *Butler's Book* (Boston, MA: Thayer, 1892). *Private and Official Correspondence of Benjamin F. Butler*, 5 vols (privately issued, Norwood, 1917).

CARWARDINE, RICHARD, *Transatlantic Revivalism: Popular Evangelicalism in Britain and America, 1790–1865* (Westport, CT: Greenwood, 1978). *Evangelicals and Politics in Antebellum America* (New Haven, CT: Yale UP, 1994).

CASE, LLYN M. and SPENCER, WARREN F., *The United States and France: Civil War Diplomacy* (Philadelphia, PA: University of Pennsylvania Press, 1970).

CASH, W. J., *The Mind of the South* (Harmondsworth: Penguin, 1971).*

CEADEL, MARTIN, *Thinking about Peace and War* (Oxford UP, 1987).

CHANNING, STEPHEN A., *Crisis of Fear: Secession and South Carolina* (New York: Simon & Schuster, 1970).

CHASE, SALMON P., *Inside Lincoln's Cabinet*, ed. David Donald (New York: Alfred A. Knopf, 1954).

CHESNUT, MARY, *Mary Chesnut's Civil War* ed. C. Vann Woodward (New Haven, CT: Yale UP, 1981).*

COMMAGER, HENRY S., CUNLIFFE, MARCUS and JONES, MALDWYN A., *Illustrated History of the American Civil War* (London: Orbis, 1976).

COLLINS, BRUCE, *The Origins of America's Civil War* (London: Edward Arnold, 1981).* *White Society in the Antebellum South* (London: Longman, 1985).*

CONNELL-SMITH, G., *The United States and Latin America* (London: Heinemann, 1974).

CONNELLY, THOMAS L., *Army of the Heartland* (Baton Rouge: Louisiana State UP, 1967, 1986).

COOPER, WILLIAM J., *Liberty and Slavery: Southern Politics to 1860* (New York: Alfred A. Knopf, 1983).

COOPER, WILLIAM J, Jr., HOLT, MICHAEL F. and McCARDELL, JOHN (EDS) *A Master's Due: Essays in Honour of David H. Donald* (Baton Rouge: Louisiana State UP, 1986).

COULTER, E. MERTON, *The Confederate States of America* (Baton Rouge: Louisiana State UP, 1950).

CRAVEN, AVERY O., *The Coming of the Civil War*, 2nd rev. edn (Chicago UP, 1942, 1957).*

Civil War in the Making, 1815–1860 (Baton Rouge: Louisiana State UP, 1959, 1980).*

CROOK, D. P., *The North, the South and the Powers* (New York: Wiley, 1974).

CUNLIFFE, MARCUS, *The Nation Takes Shape, 1789–1837* (Chicago UP, 1959).*

Soldiers and Civilians: The Martial Spirit in America, 1775–1865, 3rd edn (London: Eyre & Spottiswoode, 1969; Gregg Revivals, 1993, with a new preface by Brian Holden Reid).

Chattel Slavery and Wage Slavery: The Anglo-American Context, 1830–1860 (Athens, GA: University of Georgia Press, 1979).

In Search of America: Transatlantic Essays, 1951–1990 (New York: Greenwood, 1991).

CURRENT, RICHARD N., *Lincoln and the First Shot* (New York: Lippincott, 1963).*

CURRY, LEONARD P., *The Free Black in Urban America, 1800–1850* (Chicago UP, 1981).*

DANGERFIELD, GEORGE, *The Awakening of American Nationalism, 1815–1828* (New York: Harper & Row, 1965).*

DAVIS, JEFFERSON, *Private Letters, 1823–1889*, ed. Hudson Strode (New York: Harcourt Brace, 1966).

The Rise and Fall of the Confederate Government, 2 vols (London: Longmans Green, 1881).

DAVIS, MICHAEL, *The Image of Lincoln in the South* (Knoxville University of Tennessee Press, 1973).

DAVIS, WILLIAM C., *Breckinridge: Statesman, Soldier, Symbol* (Baton Rouge: Louisiana State UP, 1974).

Battle at Bull Run (Baton Rouge: Louisiana State UP, 1977).*

Jefferson Davis: The Man and his Hour (New York: HarperCollins, 1991).

DAWSON III, JOSEPH G. (ED.) *Commander in Chief: Presidential Leadership in Modern Wars* (Lawrence, KS: University Press of Kansas, 1993).*

DENNETT, TYLER, *Lincoln and the Civil War in the Diaries and Letters of John Hay* (New York, 1939; Da Capo, 1988).*

DILLON, MERTON L., *The Abolitionists: The Growth of a Dissenting Minority* (New York: Norton, 1974, 1975).*

DONALD, DAVID, *Lincoln's Herndon: A Biography* (New York: Alfred A. Knopf, 1948).
Charles Sumner and the Coming of the Civil War (New York: Alfred A. Knopf, 1960).
Charles Sumner and the Rights of Man (New York: Alfred A. Knopf, 1970).
Lincoln Reconsidered, 3rd edn (New York: Vintage, 1989).*
DOUGLASS, FREDERICK, *Narrative of the Life of Frederick Douglass: An American Slave by Himself* (New York: Anchor, 1973).*
DUMOND, DWIGHT L., *The Secession Movement, 1860–1861* (New York: Macmillan, 1931).

EATON, CLEMENT, *The Freedom-of-Thought Struggle in the Old South*, rev. and enlarged edn (New York: Harper, 1940, 1964).*
The Growth of Southern Civilization, 1790-1860 (New York: Harper, 1963).*
The Waning of the Old South Civilization (New York: Pegasus, 1968).*
ELKINS, STANLEY M., *Slavery: A Problem in American Institutional and Intellectual Life*, 3rd rev. edn, (Chicago UP, 1959, 1976).
ESCOTT, PAUL D., *After Secession: Jefferson Davis and the Failure of Confederate Nationalism* (Baton Rouge: Louisiana State UP, 1978).

FALK, RICHARD A. (ED.) *The International Law of Civil War* (Baltimore, MD: Johns Hopkins UP, 1971).
FALLS, CYRIL, *The Place of War in History* (Oxford: Clarendon, 1947).
FAUST, DREW GILPIN, *A Sacred Circle: The Dilemma of the Intellectual in the Old South, 1840–1860* (Baltimore, MD: Johns Hopkins UP, 1977).
FEHRENBACHER, DON E., *Prelude to Greatness: Lincoln in the 1850s* (Stanford UP, 1962).
The Dred Scott Case: Its Significance in American Law and Politics (New York: Oxford UP, 1978).
The South and Three Sectional Crises (Baton Rouge: Louisiana State UP, 1980).
Lincoln in Text and Context: Collected Essays (Stanford UP, 1987).
FIELDS, BARBARA JEANNE, *Slavery and Freedom in the Middle Ground: Maryland during the Nineteenth Century* (New Haven, CT: Yale UP, 1985).

FOGEL, ROBERT W. *Without Consent or Contract: The Rise and Fall of American Slavery* (New York: Norton, 1989).

FOGEL, ROBERT W. and ENGERMAN, STANLEY L., *Time on the Cross: The Economics of American Negro Slavery*, 2 vols (Boston, MA: Little, Brown, 1974).

FONER, ERIC, *Free Soil, Free Labor, Free Men: The Ideology of the Republican Party before the Civil War* (New York: Oxford UP, 1970).*

Politics and Ideology of the Age of the Civil War (New York: Oxford UP, 1980).*

Reconstruction: America's Unfinished Revolution, 1863–1877 (New York: Harper, 1988).

FORD, LACY K., *Origins of Southern Radicalism: The South Carolina Upcountry, 1800–1860* (New York: Oxford UP, 1988).

FRANKLIN, JOHN HOPE, *The Militant South, 1800–1861* (Cambridge, MA: Belknapp Press, 1956).

The Emancipation Proclamation (Edinburgh UP, 1963).

FREDRICKSON, GEORGE M., *The Black Image in the American Mind* (New York: Harper & Row, 1971).

FREEHLING, WILLIAM W., *Prelude to Civil War: The Nullification Crisis in South Carolina, 1816–1836* (New York: Oxford UP, 1992).*

The Road to Disunion: Secessionists at Bay, 1776–1854 (New York: Oxford UP, 1990).*

The Reintegration of American History (New York: Oxford UP, 1994).

GARA, LARRY, *The Presidency of Franklin Pierce* (Lawrence, KS: University of Kansas, 1991).

GENOVESE, EUGENE D., *Roll, Jordan, Roll: The World the Slaves Made* (London: André Deutsch, 1975).

GOLDIN, CLAUDIA D., *Urban Slavery in the American South, 1820–1860* (Chicago UP, 1976).

GRAEBNER, NORMAN A., *Empire on the Pacific*, 2nd edn (Santa Barbara, CA: ABC Clio, 1983).

GUNDERSON, ROBERT G., *The Old Gentlemen's Convention: The Washington Peace Conference of 1861* (Madison, WI: University of Wisconsin Press, 1961).

HAFFNER, RICHARD D., *A Documentary History of the United States* (New York: New American Library, 1965).*

HAMILTON, HOLMAN, *Prologue to Conflict: The Crisis and Compromise of 1850* (University Press of Kentucky, 1964).

HAMILTON, MICHAEL P. (ED.) *American Character and Foreign Policy* (Grand Rapids, MI: Eerdmans, 1986).*

HAMMOND, JAMES H., *Secret and Sacred: The Diaries of James H. Hammond*, ed. Carol Bleser (New York: Oxford UP, 1988).

HEALE, M. J., *The Making of American Politics* (London: Longman, 1977).

HIETALA, THOMAS R., *Manifest Design: Anxious Aggrandizement in Late Jacksonian America* (Ithaca, NY: Cornell UP, 1985).

HIGHAM, JOHN (ED.) *The Reconstruction of American History* (London: Hutchinson, 1962).

HITCHCOCK, E. A., *Fifty Years in Camp and Field*, ed, W. A. Croffut (New York: G. P. Putnam, 1909).

HOFSTADTER, RICHARD, *The American Political Tradition* (London: Jonathan Cape, 1962).

The Progressive Historians (London: Jonathan Cape, 1969).

America at 1750: A Social Portrait (London: Jonathan Cape, 1972).

HOLIEN, KIM B., *Battle at Ball's Bluff* (Alexandria, VA: Rapidan, 1985).

HOLT, MICHAEL F., *Forging a Majority: The Formation of the Republican Party in Pittsburgh, 1848–1860* (New Haven, CT: Yale UP, 1969).

The Political Crisis of the 1850's (New York: Norton, 1983).

HOPLEY, CATHERINE C., *Life in the South*, 2 vols (New York: Augustus M. Kelley, 1971).

HOWARD, MICHAEL, *Clausewitz* (Oxford UP, 1983).*

HUBBELL, JOHN T. (ED.) *Battles Lost and Won* (Westport, CT: Greenwood, 1975).

HUFF, ARCHIE V., *Langdon Cheves of South Carolina* (Columbia, SC: University of South Carolina Press, 1977; Tricentennial Studies, no. 11).

JELLISON, CHARLES A., *Fessenden of Maire* (New York: Syracuse UP, 1962).

JENKINS, BRIAN, *Britain and the War for the Union*, 2 vols (London: McGill and Queen's UP, 1974).

JOHANNSEN, ROBERT W., *Stephen A. Douglas* (New York: Oxford UP, 1973).

To the Halls of the Montezumas: The Mexican War in the American Imagination (New York: Oxford UP, 1985).

JOHNSON, MICHAEL P., *Toward a Patriarchal Republic: The Secession of Georgia* (Baton Rouge: Louisiana State UP, 1977).

JOHNSON, MICHAEL P. and ROARK, JAMES L., *Black Masters: A Free Family of Colour in the Old South* (New York: Norton, 1984).

—— (ED.) *No Chariot Let Down* (Chapel Hill, NC: University of North Carolina Press, 1984).

JOLL, JAMES, *1914: The Unspoken Assumptions* (London: Weidenfeld & Nicolson, 1968).

JORDAN, WINTHROP D., *White Over Black: American Attitudes to the Negro, 1550–1812* (Baltimore, MD: Pelican, 1969).

—— *Tumult and Silence at Second Creek: An Inquiry into a Civil War Conspiracy* (Baton Rouge: Louisiana State UP, 1993).

JULIAN, G. W., *Political Recollections, 1840–1872* (Chicago: Jansen, McClurg, 1884).

JONES, HOWARD, *Union in Peril* (Chapel Hill, NC: University of North Carolina Press, 1992).

KAMMEN, MICHAEL, *People of Paradox* (New York: Vintage, 1972, 1973).

KATZ, IRVING, *August Belmont: A Political Biography* (New York: Columbia UP, 1968).

KEMBLE, FRANCES ANNE, *Journal of a Residence on a Georgia Plantation in 1838–1839*, ed. John A. Scott (London: Jonathan Cape, 1961).

KING, WILLARD L., *Lincoln's Manager: David Davis* (Cambridge, MA: Harvard UP, 1961).

KOHN, RICHARD H. (ED.) *The United States Military under the Constitution of the United States, 1789–1989* (New York UP, 1991).

KOLCHIN, PETER, *American Slavery* (Harmondsworth: Penguin, 1993, 1995).

LEVINE, BRUCE, *Half Slave and Half Free: The Roots of Civil War* (New York: Hill & Wang, 1992).

LEWIS, LLOYD, *Sherman: Fighting Prophet* (New York: Harcourt Brace, 1929).

LINCOLN, ABRAHAM, *Collected Works of Abraham Lincoln*, 9 vols (New Brunswick, NJ: Rutgers UP, 1953–55).

LIPSET, SEYMOUR MARTIN, and RAAB, EARL, *The Politics of Unreason: Right-Wing Extremism in America, 1790–1970* (London: Heinemann, 1971).

LONGSTREET, JAMES, *From Manassas to Appomattox* (New York, 1896; Da Capo, 1992).*

LUARD, EVAN, *War in International Society* (London: I. B. Tauris, 1986).

MAIZLISH, STEPHEN E. (ED.) *Essays on American Antebellum Politics, 1840–1860* (College Station: Texas A&M UP, 1982).

MALONE, DUMAS, *Jefferson the President: Second Term, 1805–1809* (Boston, MA: Little, Brown, 1974).

MASON, PHILIP, *The English Gentleman* (London: André Deutsch, 1982).

MATHEW, COLIN and GARRETT, JANE (ED.), *Revival and Renewal since 1700: Essays Presented to John Walsh* (London: Hambledon Press, 1993).

MATHEWS, DONALD G., *Religion in the Old South* (Chicago UP, 1977).

MCCASH, WILLIAM B., *Thomas R.R. Cobb: The Making of a Southern Nationalist* (Macon, GA: Mercer UP, 1983).

MCCASLIN, RICHARD B., *Tainted Breeze: The Great Hanging at Gainesville, Texas, 1862* (Baton Rouge: Louisiana State UP, 1994).

MCFEELY, WILLIAM S., *Grant: A Biography* (New York: Norton, 1980).*
Frederick Douglass (New York: Norton, 1991).

MCPHERSON, JAMES M., *Battle Cry of Freedom: The Civil War Era* (New York: Oxford UP, 1988).*
Abraham Lincoln and the Second American Revolution (New York: Oxford UP, 1990).

MCWHINEY, GRADY, *Cracker Culture: Celtic Ways in the Old South* (Tuscaloosa: University of Alabama Press, 1988, 1989).*

MILLER, MERLE, *Plain Speaking: Conversations with Harry S. Truman* (London: Gollancz, 1974).

MOHR, CLARENCE L., *On the Threshold of Freedom: Masters and Slaves in Civil War Georgia* (Athens, GA: University of Georgia Press, 1986).

NEELY, MARK E., Jr, *The Fate of Liberty: Abraham Lincoln and Civil Liberties* (New York: Oxford UP, 1991).

NEVINS, ALLAN, *The Ordeal of the Union*, 2 vols (New York: Scribner's, 1947).
The Emergence of Lincoln, 2 vols (New York: Scribner's, 1950).

NICHOLS, ROY F., *The Disruption of American Democracy* (New York: Macmillan, 1948).
The Stakes of Power, 1845–1877 (London: Macmillan, 1965).

NIVEN, JOHN, *Martin Van Buren* (New York: Oxford UP, 1983).

NORTON, ANNE, *Alternative Americas: A Reading of Antebellum Political Culture* (Chicago UP, 1986).

OATES, STEPHEN B., *With Malice Toward None: The Life of Abraham Lincoln* (London: Allen & Unwin, 1977).*
To Purge This Land with Blood: A Biography of John Brown, 2nd edn (Amherst, MA: University of Massachusetts Press, 1970, 1984).
OWSLEY, FRANK L., *King Cotton Diplomacy* 2nd edn, (Chicago UP, 1959).

PALUDAN, PHILLIP S., *The Presidency of Abraham Lincoln* (Lawrence, KS: University Press of Kansas, 1994).
PARISH, PETER J., *The American Civil War* (London: Eyre & Spottiswoode, 1975).
Slavery: History and Historians (New York: HarperCollins, 1989).*
(ed.) *Abraham Lincoln: Speeches and Letters* (London: Dent, 1993).*
PARKS, JOSEPH H., *Joseph E. Brown of Georgia* (Baton Rouge: Louisiana State UP, 1977).
PEASE, WILLIAM H. and PEASE, JANE H., *The Web of Progress: Private Values and Public Styles in Boston and Charleston* (New York: Oxford UP, 1985).
PENDLE, GEORGE, *A History of Latin America*, 2nd edn (Harmondsworth: Penguin, 1971).
PERKINS, DEXTER, *A History of the Monroe Doctrine* (Boston, MA: Little, Brown, 1950).
POTTER, DAVID M., *The Impending Crisis, 1848–1861*, completed and ed. by Don E. Fehrenbacher (New York: Harper, 1976).*
Lincoln and his Party in the Secession Crisis (1942, 1962; New York: AMS Press, 1979).
PRESSLY, THOMAS J., *Americans Interpret their Civil War* (Princeton UP, 1954).

RABOTEAU, ALBERT J., *Slave Religion* (New York: Oxford UP, 1978).*
RANDALL, JAMES G., *Lincoln the President: From Springfield to Gettysburg*, 2 vols (London: Eyre & Spottiswoode, 1947).
RANDALL, JAMES G. and DONALD, DAVID, *The Civil War and Reconstruction*, 2nd edn (Boston, MA: D. C. Heath, 1969).
RANSOM, ROGER L., *Conflict and Compromise: The Political Economy of Slavery, Emancipation and the American Civil War* (Cambridge UP, 1989).
RAWLEY, JAMES P., *Race and Politics: 'Bleeding Kansas' and the Coming*

of the Civil War (Lincoln: University of Nebraska Press, 1969, 1979).

REID, BRIAN HOLDEN, and WHITE, JOHN (EDS) *American Studies: Essays in Honour of Marcus Cunliffe* (London: Macmillan, 1991).

REMINI, ROBERT V., *Andrew Jackson and the Course of American Freedom, 1822–32* (New York: Harper & Row, 1981).

The Life of Andrew Jackson (New York: Harper & Row, 1988).

REYNOLDS, DONALD E., *Editors Make War: Southern Newspapers in the Secession Crisis* (Nashville, TN: Vanderbilt UP, 1966, 1970).

RHOADES, JEFFREY L., *Scapegoat General* (New York: Archon, 1985).

ROSE, ANNE C., *Victorian America and the Civil War* (New York: Cambridge UP, 1992).

ROYLE, EDWARD, *Radical Politics, 1790–1900* (London: Longman, 1971).*

RUSSELL, WILLIAM HOWARD, *My Diary North and South*, ed. Eugene H. Berwanger (New York: Alfred A. Knopf, 1988).*

SCHOFIELD, JOHN M., *Forty-Six Years in the Army* (New York: Century, 1897).

SEARS, STEPHEN W., *George B. McClellan: The Young Napoleon* (Boston, MA: Ticknor & Fields, 1988).

SELLERS, CHARLES G., *The Market Revolution: Jacksonian America, 1815–1846* (New York: Oxford UP, 1991).

SEWELL, RICHARD H., *Ballots for Freedom: Anti-Slavery Politics in the United States, 1837–1860* (New York: Norton, 1980).*

SHANKS, HENRY T., *The Secession Movement in Virginia, 1847–1861* (New York: AMS Press, 1934, 1971).

SILBEY, JOEL H., *The Partisan Imperative: The Dynamics of American Politics Before the Civil War* (New York: Oxford UP, 1985).

SIMKINS, F. B., *A History of the South* (New York: Alfred A. Knopf, 1961).

SINGLETARY, OTIS, *The Mexican War* (Chicago UP, 1960).

SLAUGHTER, THOMAS B., *The Whiskey Rebellion* (New York: Oxford UP, 1986).

SMITH, ELBERT B., *The Death of Slavery: The United States, 1831–65* (Chicago UP, 1967).

The Presidency of James Buchanan (Lawrence, KS: University of Kansas Press, 1975).

The Presidencies of Zachary Taylor and Millard Fillmore (Lawrence, KS: University of Kansas Press, 1988).

SOMKIN, FRED, *Unquiet Eagle: Memory and Desire in the Idea of American Freedom, 1815–1860* (Ithaca, NY: Cornell UP, 1967).

STAGG, J. C. A., *Mr Madison's War* (Princeton UP, 1983).

STAMPP, KENNETH M., *Indiana Politics during the Civil War* (Bloomington: Indiana UP, 1949, 1978).

And the War Came (Louisiana State UP, 1950).

The Peculiar Institution: Negro Slavery in the American South (London: Eyre & Spottiswoode, 1964).

The Imperiled Union: Essays on the Background of the Civil War (New York: Oxford UP, 1980).

America in 1857 (New York: Oxford UP, 1990).

(ed.) *The Causes of the Civil War*, 4th edn (New York: Simon & Schuster, 1991).

STEWART, JAMES B., *Wendell Phillips: Liberty's Hero* (Baton Rouge: Louisiana State UP, 1986).

STRONG, G. T., *The Diary of George Templeton Strong* ed. Allan Nevins and Milton H. Thomas, 5 vols (New York, 1952; University of Washington Press 1987).

STROZIER, CHARLES B., *Lincoln's Quest for Union* (Chicago: University of Illinois Press, 1982, 1987).*

SUMMERS, MARK W., *The Plundering Generation: Corruption and the Crisis of the Union, 1849–1861* (New York: Oxford UP, 1987).

SWANBERG, W. A., *First Blood: The Story of Fort Sumter* (New York: Scribner's, 1957).

TAYLOR, A. J. P., *From Napoleon to the Second International*, ed. C. Wrigley (London: Hamish Hamilton, 1993).

TAYLOR, WILLIAM R., *Cavalier and Yankee: The Old South and American National Character* (London: W. H. Allen, 1963).

TEMPERLEY, HOWARD, *British Anti-Slavery, 1833–1870* (Columbia, SC: University of South Carolina Press, 1972).

THOMAS, BENJAMIN P., *Abraham Lincoln* (London: Eyre & Spottiswoode, 1953).

THOMAS, BENJAMIN P. and HYMAN, HAROLD H. *Stanton: The Life and Times of Lincoln's Secretary of War* (New York: Alfred A. Knopf, 1962).

THOMAS, EMORY M., *The Confederacy as a Revolutionary Experience* (Englewood Cliffs, NJ: Prentice-Hall, 1971).*

Bold Dragoon: The Life of J. E. B. Stuart (New York: Harper & Row, 1986).

THOMAS, JOHN L., *Abraham Lincoln and the American Political Tradition* (Amherst, MA: University of Massachusetts Press, 1986).

TISE, LARRY E., *Proslavery: A History of the Defense of Slavery, 1701–1860* (Athens, GA: University of Georgia Press, 1988).

TOCQUEVILLE, ALEXIS de, *Democracy in America*, ed. Phillips Bradley, 2 vols (New York: Vintage, 1954).

TREFOUSSE, HANS L., *Benjamin Franklin Wade: Radical Republican from Ohio* (New York: Twayne, 1963).

Andrew Johnson: A Biography (New York: Norton, 1989).

TREVELYAN, GEORGE M., *An Autobiography and Other Essays* (London: Longman, 1949).

TROLLOPE, FRANCES, *Domestic Manners of the Americans* (London: Folio Society, 1974).

VAN BUREN, MARTIN, *Political Parties in the United States* (New York: Hurd & Houghton, 1867; Augustus M. Kelley, 1967).

VAN DEUSEN, GLYNDON G., *William Henry Seward* (New York: Oxford UP, 1969).

WALZER, MICHAEL, *Just and Unjust Wars* (Harmondsworth: Penguin, 1978).*

WARD, JOHN WILLIAM, *Andrew Jackson: Symbol for an Age* (New York: Oxford UP, 1962).*

WEIGLEY, RUSSELL F., *Quartermaster General of the Union Army: A Biography of M. C. Meigs* (New York: Columbia UP, 1959).

WELLES, GIDEON, *The Diary of Gideon Welles*, ed. Howard K. Beale, 3 vols (New York: Norton, 1960).

WELLS, DAMON, *Stephen Douglas: The Last Years, 1857–1861* (Austin: University of Texas Press, 1971).*

WELTER, RUSH, *The Mind of America, 1820-1860* (New York: Columbia UP, 1975).

WEST, RICHARD, Jr, *Lincoln's Scapegoat General* (Boston, MA: Houghton-Mifflin, 1965).

WHITE, JOHN, *Reconstruction After the American Civil War* (London: Longman, 1977).*

Black Leadership in America: From Booker T. Washington to Jesse Jackson, 2nd edn (London: Longman, 1990).*

WHITE, JOHN and WILLETT, RALPH, *Slavery in the American South* (London: Longman, 1970).*

WILLIAMS, T. HARRY, *Lincoln and the Radicals* (Madison, WI: University of Wisconsin Press, 1965).*

P. G. T. Beauregard: Napoleon in Gray (Baton Rouge: Louisiana State UP, 1955, 1989).

WILLS, GARRY, *Inventing America: Jefferson's Declaration of Independence* (London: Athlone, 1980).
Cincinnatus: George Washington and the Enlightenment (London: Robert Hale, 1984).
WILSON, EDMUND, *Patriotic Gore: Studies in the Literature of the American Civil War* (New York: Oxford UP, 1962).
WILSON, MAJOR L., *Space, Time and Freedom: The Quest for Nationality and the Irrepressible Conflict* (Westport, CT: Greenwood, 1974).
WILTSE, CHARLES M., *The New Nation, 1800–1845* (London: Macmillan, 1965).
WOODWARD, C. VANN, *The Strange Career of Jim Crow* 2nd rev. edn (New York: Oxford UP, 1966).
WOOSTER, RALPH A., *The Secession Conventions of the South* (Princeton UP, 1962).
WYATT-BROWN, BERTRAM, *Southern Honor: Ethics and Behavior in the Old South,* (New York: Oxford UP, 1982).

ZAREFSKY, DAVID, *Lincoln, Douglas and Slavery* (Chicago UP, 1990).

Articles

ALEXANDER, THOMAS B., 'The Civil War as Institutional Fulfilment', *Journal of Southern History* 47 (1981).
ASTIER, HENRY, 'Americans and Conspiracy Theories', *Contemporary Review* 261 (Oct. 1992).

BELOFF, MAX, 'Great Britain and the American Civil War, *History* 37 (1952).
BERWANGER, EUGENE H., 'The Case of Stirrup and Edwards, 1861–1879', *Georgia Historical Quarterly* LXXVI (Spring 1992).
BLUMENTHAL, HENRY, 'Confederate Diplomacy: Popular Notions and International Realities', *Journal of Southern History* XXXII (1966).
'British Sympathies in the American Civil War', *Journal of Southern History* XXXIII (1967).

CARWARDINE, RICHARD, 'Evangelicals, Whigs and the Election of William Henry Harrison, *Journal of American Studies* 17 (Apr. 1983).

CLARK, MICHAEL D., 'More English than the English: Cavalier and Democrat in Virginia Historical Writing', *Journal of American Studies*, 27 (1993).

COLE, ARTHUR C. and de ROULHAC HAMILTON, J. G., 'Lincoln's Election an Immediate Menace to Slavery in the States?', in Sidney Fine and Gerald S. Brown (eds) *The American Past: Conflicting Interpretations of the Great Issues*, vol. 1 (New York: Macmillan, 1961).

CRAWFORD, MARTIN, 'Politicians in Crisis: The Washington Letters of William S. Thayer, December 1860–March 1861', *Civil War History*, XXVII (Sept. 1981).

CUNLIFFE, MARCUS, 'New World, Old World: The Historical Antithesis', in Richard Rose (ed.) *Lessons from America* (London: Macmillan, 1974).

DEGLER, CARL, 'The Two Cultures and the Civil War', in Stanley Coben and Lorman Ratner (eds) *The Development of an American Culture* (Englewood Cliffs, NJ: Prentice- Hall, 1970).

GIENAPP, WILLIAM E., 'The Crime Against Sumner: The Caning of Charles Sumner and the Rise of the Republican Party', *Civil War History* XXV (1979).
'Nativism and the Creation of a Republican Majority in the North before the Civil War', *Journal of American History* 72 (Dec. 1985).

HORSMAN, REGINALD, 'American Indian Policy in the Old Northwest, 1783–1812', *William and Mary Quarterly* XVIII (1961).

JOHNSON, LUDWELL H., 'Fort Sumter and Confederate Diplomacy', *Journal of Southern History* 26 (1960).

JONES, W. D., 'British Conservatives and the American Civil War', *American Historical Review* LVIII (1953).

KRUMAN, MARC W., 'The Second American Party System and the Transformation of Revolutionary Republicanism', *Journal of the Early Republic* 12 (winter 1992).

LATNER, RICHARD B., 'The Nullification Crisis and Republican Subversion', *Journal of Southern History* 43 (1977).

MEERSE, DAVID E., 'Buchanan, Corruption and the Election of 1860', *Civil War History* 12 (1966).

MORTON, W. L., 'British North America and a Continent in Dissolution', *History* XLVII (June 1962).

O'BRIEN, MICHAEL, 'The Lineaments of Antebellum Southern Romanticism', *Journal of American Studies* 20 (Aug. 1986).

PARISH, PETER J., 'The Instruments of Providence', in W. J. Sheils (ed.) *The Church and War* (Oxford: Basil Blackwell, 1984).
'American Nationalism and the Nineteenth-Century Constitution', in Joseph Smith (ed.), *The American Constitution* (University of Exeter Press, 1988).
'A Talent for Survival: Federalism in the Era of the Civil War', *Historical Research* 62 (June 1989).

PELZER, JOHN D., 'Liverpool and the American Civil War', *History Today* 40 (March 1950).

PIERSON, WILLIAM W., 'The Committee on the Conduct of the Civil War', *American Historical Review* XXI (1917–18).

RAMSDELL, CHARLES W., 'Lincoln and Fort Sumter', *Journal of Southern History* III (1937).

RATCLIFFE, DONALD, 'The *Das Kapital* of American Negro Slavery? *Time on the Cross* After Two Years', *Durham University Journal* 100 (Dec. 1976).

REID, BRIAN HOLDEN, 'A Survey of the Militia in 18th Century America', *Army Quarterly* CX (Jan. 1980).
'The Crisis at Fort Sumter in 1861 Reconsidered', *History* 77 (Feb. 1992).
'First Blood to the South: Bull Run, 1861, *History Today* (March 1992).
'Historians and the Joint Committee on the Conduct of the War', *Civil War History* 38 (Dec. 1992).
'The Grip of the Anaconda Plan, 1861', *The British-American* 5 (winter 1993).
'Rationality and Irrationality in Union Strategy, April 1861–March 1862', *War in History* I (March 1994).

STAGMAIER, MARK J., 'Zachary Taylor versus the South', *Civil War History* 33 (1987).

TREFOUSSE, HANS L., 'The Joint Committee on the Conduct of the War: A Reassessment', *Civil War History* X (1964).

WHITE, JOHN, 'Whatever Happened to the Slave Family in the Old South?', *Journal of American Studies* 8 (1974).
'Novelist as Historian: William Styron and American Negro Slavery', in David H. Burton (ed.) *American History – British Historians* (Chicago: Nelson Hall, 1978).

WYATT-BROWN, BERTRAM, 'Modernizing Southern Slavery: The Proslavery Argument Reinterpreted', in J. M. Kousser and J. M. McPherson (eds) *Region, Race and Reconstruction: Essays in Honour of C. Vann Woodward* (New York: Oxford UP, 1982).

Maps

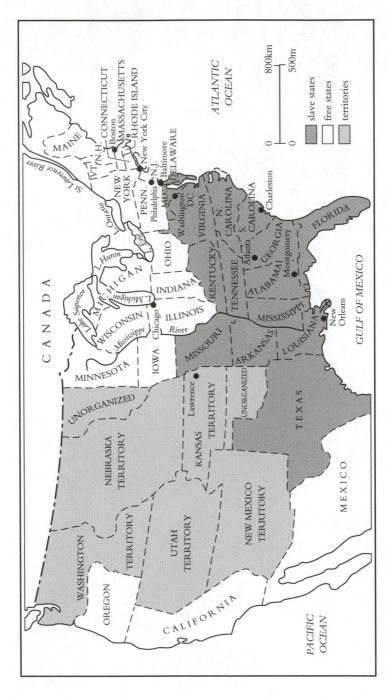

Map 1 The United States in 1860: slave states and free states

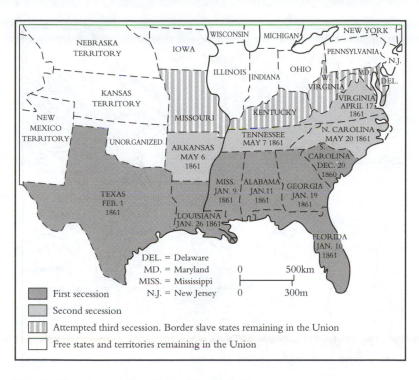

Map 2   The phases of southern Secession

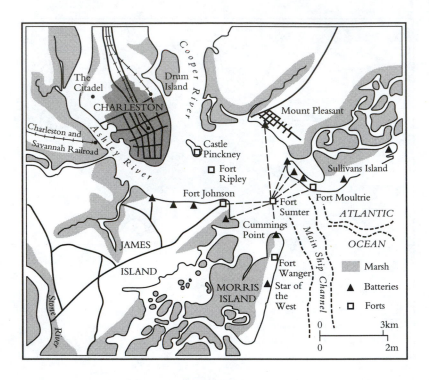

Map 3   Charleston Harbour and Fort Sumter

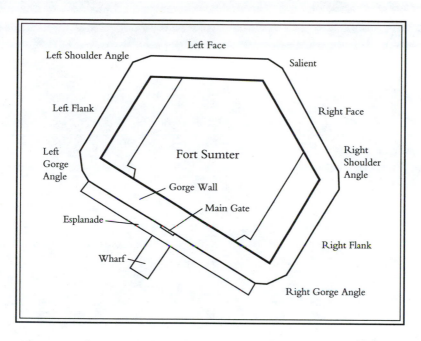

Map 4 The layout of Fort Sumter

Index

425